The Trainer's Professional Development Handbook

Ray Bard
Chip R. Bell
Leslie Stephen
Linda Webster

with
Sheila C. Henderson
Barbara Peek Loftin
Anne Durrum Robinson
Linda M. Standke

The Trainer's Professional Development Handbook

 Jossey-Bass Publishers

San Francisco • London • 1987

THE TRAINER'S PROFESSIONAL DEVELOPMENT HANDBOOK
by Ray Bard, Chip R. Bell, Leslie Stephen, and Linda Webster

Copyright © 1987 by: Jossey-Bass Inc., Publishers
                       433 California Street
                       San Francisco, California 94104
                       &
                       Jossey-Bass Limited
                       28 Banner Street
                       London EC 1Y 8QE

Library of Congress Cataloging-in-Publication Data

The Trainer's professional development handbook.

   (Jossey-Bass management series)
   Bibliography: p.
   Includes index.
   1. Employees, Training of.   I. Bard, Ray.   II. Series.
HF5549.5.T76633   1987   658.3'124   87-45507
ISBN 1-55542-067-2

The Jossey-Bass Management Series
Consulting Editors: Leonard and Zeace Nadler
College Park, Maryland

Manufactured in the United States of America

The paper in this book meets the guidelines for
permanence and durability of the Committee on
Production Guidelines for Book Longevity of the
Council of Library Resources.

A BARD PRODUCTIONS BOOK

Editing: Alison Tartt
Jacket Design: Suzanne Pustejovsky
Test Design: Mary Ann Noretto/Suzanne Pustejovsky
Text Illustrations: Mike Krone
Typesetting: Pamela Winsier, The Composing Stick
Production: Mary Ann Noretto, The Composing Stick

First Edition

Code 8723

Contents

 Introduces the field with a brief historical profile (1800s to present) of trends and events that established human resource development as a profession. Assesses contemporary and future implications for the field with profiles of trainers in various organizational settings and discusses trends that will impact the field (demographics, work forms and expectations, and technology). Reading list for continued professional development.

 Examines the state of the field in HRD (salaries, industries, background, and career opportunities), presents HRD roles and competencies, and suggests career development strategies (job enrichment, lateral mobility, special assignments, changing organizations, management, professional activities, and training and education). Reading list for continued professional development.

 Provides a five-step process for developing an individual learning plan: assessing learning needs, setting learning objectives, creating a plan, implementing the plan, and monitoring and evaluating progress. A thirty-seven point assessment scale can be used alone or with supervisor and others. Case example illustrates how to use this process along with other chapters in the book to create a professional development plan. Four-point organizational analysis helps assess the amount of organizational support for the plan. Reading list for continued professional development.

continuing education; and future studies. Includes directory of publishers.

Describes services, membership, cost, and publications of forty organizations and associations providing information and services for the profession. Organized as follows: human resource development; special-interest trainers and meeting planners; instructional design and technology; organization development and consulting; management; behavioral sciences; adult and continuing education; and future studies.

Describes forty-seven conferences, independent workshops, and academic programs. Organized into the following sections: noncredit conferences, seminars, and workshops; campus-based non-credit programs; and academic degree programs and certificate programs. Also included is a listing and description of noncredit and credit course directories and books on going back to school.

Describes twenty-five print sources of training exercises and ideas for group experiences for employee training and training other trainers. Organized into two sections: (1) training exercises and other resources and (2) lists and directories of instructional materials and training resources. Includes directory of publishers.

Describes nonprint media dealing with HRD or topics of professional interest. Can be used for one's own learning, training other trainers, or with participants in training programs. A wide variety of learning resources are described: eighteen sources of audiotapes, fifty-two key films and videotapes, sixteen directories and reference books of media and equipment, and sixteen film and video producers of supervisory and management development. Includes directory of producers and publishers.

Figures and Tables

Preface

Historically speaking, human resource development is a relatively new organizational activity. Although work skills have for generations been transferred from one person to another through informal means, only in the last few decades have large numbers of people become involved in teaching other adults employment-related knowledge and skills. As more people entered the field, the trappings of a profession began to take shape: the creation of a national association, the formulation of conceptual models and philosophies specific to the area, and the development of academic programs for preparing people for the field.

We are still a profession in process. Although the number of undergraduate and graduate programs in human resource development continues to increase and the American Society for Training and Development has grown to an impressive size, most people enter the field today with little or no understanding about its roots, mission, significant concepts and theories, important contributors, and the availability of resources for them to begin and continue the development of their professional competencies. And many who have been in the field for a number of years have a limited perspective of the scope and availability of resources for their development.

We visualized this book as a "Whole Earth Catalogue" for trainers—a collection of resources and strategies to help people in HRD learn more about and become more competent in the field. All of us have been involved with the field for a number of years. Several years ago, we realized that there was no handbook for helping trainers organize strategies and resources for their own professional learning. There were many excellent books on the theory and practice of delivery of training programs, but none really focused on the learning of the trainer. So we set out to organize, research, and write a comprehensive learning guide and handbook for trainers to use in their individual professional development—an all-inclusive reference for professional learning.

The Trainer's Professional Development Handbook is intended to be a useful addition to any trainer's library. It was developed to serve as a core reference work for trainers in any organizational setting—private or public, large or small—and its learning strategies and resources can be used in almost all organizations. The book deals with a process of personal professional development that is applicable to any industry, governmental agency, or nonprofit organization. It can be adapted and used by the newcomer to the field, the experienced professional, the part-timer, and the student.

The book will be most valuable for those just entering the field. One who is hired or transferred into a training department for the first time often has the overwhelmed feeling of "where do I begin?" Part One, which contains a learning plan and strategies, offers a systematic approach to learning that will yield greater competence in a shorter period of time. Part Two, a catalogue of resources, offers a collection of learning aids that could take years to discover on one's own. Part Three, an encyclopedia of human resource development and organization development, provides a quick summary of the key concepts, theories, and contributors for the field.

For experienced trainers the book will be a unique personal resource. The book's broad perspective and coverage offers a way to fill in information gaps and locate new sources of continuing professional development. The book's encyclopedia of HRD and OD and its comprehensive coverage of individual learning resources will be especially valuable for those with experience in the field.

There are many people in organizations who have more than one important responsibility. In small companies human resource development is often one of those responsibilities given to someone who already has other things to do. Because the book quickly identifies resources and provides other important information, it will be a valuable, time-saving guide for those who work in the field part time.

Students in academic programs for human resource development and adult education can use the book's wide variety of learning resources in their studies. The encyclopedia can serve as an introduction to the critical concepts, theories, and individuals in the field. The book can serve as a bridge to the real world of human resource development.

Really three books in one, *The Trainer's Professional Development Handbook* is organized as three parts: Part One, "A Guide to Planning Your Professional Development" (Chapters 1–9); Part Two, "A Catalogue of Learning Resources" (Chapters 10–17); and Part Three, "An Encyclopedia of HRD and OD: Key Concepts and Contributors." The introduction provides suggestions on how to use the various parts of the book. Chapter 1 gives a historical perspective of human resource development and a look at contemporary and future issues in the field. Chapter 2 covers the roles of the training and development specialist and examines career possibilities in the field. Chapter 3 gives you a systematic process for identifying your learning needs, working with your manager to select priorities, and using the resources available to develop a learning plan. Chapter 4 examines learning styles and how they influence individual approaches to learning. The remainder of Part One contains chapters that explore specific learning strategies for use in one's professional development. These strategies include classes, seminars, and workshops (Chapter 5); learning networks (Chapter 6); role models and mentors (Chapter 7); study skills (Chapter 8); and learning from yourself (Chapter 9). The eight chapters of Part Two include a wealth of resources for professional development: the best books (Chapter 10); journals and periodicals (Chapter 11); organizations and associations (Chapter 12); conferences, workshops, and academic programs (Chapter 13); training exercises and group experiences (Chapter 14); audiotapes, films, and videos (Chapter 15); computer data bases (Chapter 16); and microcomputer software (Chapter 17). Each of the chapters in the catalogue contains a directory of publishers and producers of the relevant resources. Part Three is an encyclopedia of human resource development and organization development covering the key concepts and contributions in the field. A comprehensive index makes the book easy to use as a tool in constructing a professional development plan or as a handy reference.

It is impossible to write a book like this without the support of one's family, friends, and colleagues. At the book's very beginning stages Sondra Ayers, Geoffrey Bellman, Peter Block, Martha Brown, Richard Casper, Carol Cassell, Nora Comstock, Dean Holt, J. Stephen Kirkpatrick, Margaret Ladd, Anne Markley, Anthony L. Renzi, Tom Roberts, Stephen Sauer, Kay Scott, Linda Shewmaker, Deborah Stedman, Karen Stelzner, and Marilyn Tedesco reviewed our outline and proposal for the book and encouraged us to carry on with the project. Larry N. Davis's comments and assistance were especially helpful in the early phase of the book's development. Malcolm Knowles read parts of the manuscript and gave us his usual cogent comments. Dugan Laird gave us priceless advice on how to make the book more illuminating to HRD practitioners.

Leonard and Zeace Nadler, consulting editors at Jossey-Bass, read the manuscript at various stages and made many valuable suggestions that helped make this a much better book.

The talents and energies of our contributors—Sheila C. Henderson, Barbara Peek Loftin, Anne Durrum Robinson, and Linda N. Standke—brought special perspectives to the book and helped make it richer.

As part of this project we surveyed everyone who had held an office in the American Society for Training and Development in the last five years. These professionals generously shared their time and their unique perspective by identifying significant contributors to HRD and OD theory and practice. We are grateful to John W. Aldrich, Terry K. Broomfield, Barbara L. Carpenter, Neal Chalofsky, Virgil E. Collins, Judith Estrin, R. W. Free, Charles G. Hahne, Robert H. Hess, Peggy G. Hutcheson, John S. Jenness, Maurice C. Lungren, Lynda McDermott, Stephen K. Merman, Kenneth O. Michel, Vincent A. Miller, John Newstrom, Kevin O'Sullivan, Carlene Reinhart, Edward E. Scannell, Walt Thompson, and several others who participated in our survey but wished to remain anonymous.

Many others assisted in the editing and production process. Sheila Henderson helped us by rethinking, reorganizing, and rewriting some of the most troublesome parts of our early drafts. Sherry Sprague helped with the word processing. Alison Tartt made the whole manuscript ready for publication; she challenged our faulty thinking, smoothed the rough edges of our phraseology, and flawlessly performed the usually thankless task of copyediting. Mary Ann Noretto of The Composing Stick coordinated the production of the camera-ready manuscript, and Pamela Winsier provided timely and competent typesetting services. Suzanne Pustejovsky transformed our rough ideas into the attractive and functional jacket design.

Our families pitched in, too. Gloria and John Stephen did library research. George Stephen provided computer and software. Anthony L. Renzi gave us his half of the Stephen-Renzi study, made photocopies, compiled surveys, and cooked a lot of meals. Nancy Bell provided pragmatic review and suggestions to portions that failed the "snicker test" early in the process.

To all of you, thanks.

Austin, Texas
July 1987

Ray Bard
Chip R. Bell
Leslie Stephen
Linda Webster

Authors and Contributors

Ray Bard is an independent book producer and training consultant in Austin, Texas, with fifteen years' experience in his dual careers. He received his B.A. degree in business from the University of Oklahoma (1966) and has undertaken postgraduate studies in the behavioral sciences at the University of Oklahoma and New Mexico State University (1966–68). As a book producer specializing in business, training, and high-tech books, he has worked with such major houses as Simon & Schuster, McGraw-Hill, Henry Holt, and Scott, Foresman.

Among the ten business and training titles to his credit are *Breaking In: A Guide to America's Top Corporate Training Programs* (2nd ed., with Susan Elliott, forthcoming), *Own Your Own Franchise: Everything You Need to Know About the 160 Best Opportunities in America* (with Sheila Henderson, 1987), and *Winning Ways: A Management Performance Game* (with Larry N. Davis, 1979).

In 1972, he founded an educational publishing company, Learning Concepts, and directed it to the million-dollar sales level before selling to a New York Times subsidiary in 1978. In the late 1960s he was executive director of a large private nonprofit foundation. Bard has been a speaker at several publishing and writing conferences and has conducted management and training workshops from coast to coast and internationally.

Chip R. Bell is an independent consultant in Charlotte, North Carolina. He holds graduate degrees in organizational psychology and human resource development from Vanderbilt University (1971) and George Washington University (1977). His consulting practice focuses on leadership training, team building, and service management consulting. He was formerly a partner with LEAD Associates, Inc., a training and consulting firm. Prior to that he was vice-president and director of Management and Organization Development for NCNB Corporation, a large financial holding company.

Bell is the author of *Influencing: Marketing the Ideas That Matter* (1982) and the co-author of *Instructing for Results* (with Fredric Margolis, 1986), *Clients and Consultants* (with Leonard Nadler, 1985), and *Managing the Learning Process: Effective Techniques for the Adult Classroom* (with Fredric Margolis, 1984). His articles have appeared in numerous professional journals, including *Advanced Management Journal, Management Review, Journal of Management Consulting, Personnel Journal, Training and Development Journal, Personnel Administrator, Data Training, Training, Educational Technology, Journal of European Training,* and others.

He has consulted with many Fortune 500 companies and has addressed numerous major national conferences, including the American Society for Training and Development, American Society for Personnel Administration, *Training* magazine's national conferences, National Society for Sales Training Executives, Top Management Conference of Southeast Executives, and Data Training National Conference.

Sheila C. Henderson is the owner and operator of The Writing Consultant, a training and consulting firm based in Austin, Texas, that specializes in business and professional writing. Henderson received her B.A. degree in English from Southwest Texas State University (1973) and her M.A. degree in organizational communication from the University of Texas at Austin (1982). She has ten years of professional writing experience, extending from freelance journalism to corporate communications, as well as six years of experience presenting courses and workshops on management and communication topics. She has consulted on communication issues for both private and public organizations.

Barbara Peek Loftin is a freelance technical writer currently associated with Organization and Human Resources Development Associates in Austin, Texas. She received her B.A. degree in English literature from Middlebury College (1940) and continued her education with graduate study in journalism at Syracuse University.

Loftin was employed at the University of Texas at Austin as a business and industrial education writer until her retirement in 1986. She has also served as a technical writer for Scientific Methods, Inc., in Austin, Exxon, and J. Walter Thompson Company in New York. Her work has appeared in numerous trade journals.

Anne Durrum Robinson is a human resource development consultant in Austin, Texas. She received her B.S. degree from Texas Women's University (1936) and her M.A. degree in journalism from the University of Texas at Austin (1957). She has been a researcher, teacher, and trainer in the brain/mind field since 1971 and a featured speaker at regional, national, and international workshops and conferences. She has written for newspapers, radio, television, film, and stage. Among her recent publications are articles that have appeared in *Training, Training and Development Journal,* and *Adult and Continuing Education Today.*

Linda M. Standke is an associate with McLagan International, Inc., an HRD consulting firm based in Saint Paul, Minnesota. She received her B.A. degree in advertising and communications from the University of Minnesota (1971) and has undertaken postgraduate study in industrial relations. Formerly she was the program director for the conferences sponsored by *Training* magazine. While at *Training*, she was also a senior editor on the magazine staff and co-editor of four books. She has also held several professional positions in the training and development department at Target stores, a retail store division of the Dayton Hudson Corporation.

Leslie Stephen is the U.S. marketing manager for Butterworth Legal Publishers, a worldwide publisher of books, periodicals, and on-line data bases in law, tax, accounting, and related professions. She is an honor graduate of the University of Texas at Austin, where she completed her B.A. degree in Latin American studies (1968) and graduate work in community and regional planning (1970–72). She began working in HRD in the early 1970s, writing materials and conducting small-group training sessions for VISTA volunteers going into service in the southwestern states. The former manager of supervisory training for the City of Austin, she was editor in chief of Learning Concepts, Inc., and a managing editor for University Associates, Inc., two leading publishing houses in the HRD field. She has also worked as a freelance editor for publishers of professional, educational, and trade books.

Linda Webster is the owner and operator of an editorial and indexing service. She received her B.A. degree in English from Louisiana State University (1967) and her M.A. degree in library science from the University of Texas at Austin (1972), and has undertaken postgraduate study in adult and continuing education and instructional design at the University of Texas at Austin (1972–73). Her previous work experience includes being a book editor at Louisiana State University Press and Learning Concepts; continuing education program coordinator at Southwest Texas State University; manager of continuing education at the Texas State Library; and faculty member at the School of Library Science, Emporia State University.

Webster's publications include *Censorship: A Guide for Successful Workshop Planning* (1984), *Continuing Education Needs Assessment Manual* (1981), and *Workshops for Jail Library Service: A Planning Manual* (1981). As a conference and workshop planner, she has conducted and participated in numerous national and regional conferences dealing with continuing education, women's issues, and library services.

Introduction: Mastering Your Role in HRD

Ray Bard

We don't exist in a static world. Our workplaces are ever changing. New technologies, more information, evolving employee attitudes and needs, and changing organizational strategies, structures, and goals are fluid forces in our professional lives. Human resource development is assuming a larger, more important role in contemporary organizations. And with this change comes greater visibility and more accountability for our contributions. As the needs of our organizations and their employees change, we must change.

Human resource development in the last several years has become identified as a separate field and recognized as a profession. The 1983 ASTD training and development competency study, *Models for Excellence*, classified training and development as one of nine areas of human resource practice. It defined training and development as "identifying, assessing, and—through planned learning—helping develop the key competencies which enable individuals to perform current or future jobs" (American Society for Training and Development, 1983, p. 25). Leonard Nadler introduced the term *human resource development* in 1969 and shortly thereafter provided his definition of the term as "a series of organized activities, conducted within a specified period of time and designed to produce behavioral change" (Nadler, 1970, p. 3). He has polished his definition over the years, but it remains essentially the same. It was also Nadler who distinguished among the concepts of *training, education,* and *development*. Training has as its function the improvement of performance on the job. Education is geared to moving the employee on to a different position in the organization. Employee development is concerned with preparing the employee to move with the organization as it develops (Nadler, 1970). Our references to the profession and the field throughout this book are congruent with Nadler's conceptual architecture. However, we have chosen to use the term *trainer* in the title and throughout most of the book because the alternative *human resource development specialist* seems unwieldy.

1

Most of us will go through several major job changes during our lifetimes. Sometimes the changes will be dramatic; other times, incremental. Taking charge of one's professional development is a way to anticipate inevitable change. Chalofsky and Lincoln (1983) have defined professional development as "a process of keeping current in the state of the art, keeping competent in the state of the practice, and keeping open to new theories, techniques and values" (p. 21). Moreover, they have stated that professional development is "related to present and near-future positions and usually based on work objectives" (p. 21). Professional development implies a planned, thoughtful approach to becoming more competent and effective. It suggests an acceptance of the environment in which we work and the value of a positive, expectant attitude. It assumes the capacity for individual change and the possibilities for human growth and self-renewal. Challenge, exploration, and achievement are inherent in its process. The benefits that come from the effort include the commitment required of work and the joy of learning. A striving for mastery is a driving force—mastery in the sense of being in control of your job and the direction of your professional growth. It implies reaching for excellence— becoming the best you can be in your profession. Professional development bears with it the hope and expectation of better performance and success. The rewards it offers are a sense of achievement, more confidence, earned recognition, and often greater financial compensation.

Whether you are new to the field and trying to grasp the basics or have been on the board for years, there are always areas for personal improvement. As Malcolm Knowles (1983) has commented, "Trainers—even the most experienced and best trained—must keep learning or become obsolete" (p. v). This learning may involve new content, new technologies, or greater competence with a learning process. Sometimes our immediate job responsibilities provide us with new learning opportunities. But we must be aware of the overall direction we want our careers to take and consciously chart our professional development rather than let the ebb and flow of our daily work carry us into the future.

Professional development is a process of becoming. Carl Rogers (1969) has said that "the only man who is educated is the man who has learned how to learn . . . how to adapt and change; the man who has realized that only the process of seeking knowledge gives a basis for security" (p. 104). In *Learning How to Learn* Robert Smith (1982, p. 16) characterizes the adult who has learned how to learn as one who knows:

How to take control of his or her own learning.
How to develop a personal learning plan.
How to diagnose strengths and weaknesses as a learner.
How to chart a learning style.
How to overcome personal blocks to learning.
The criteria of sound learning objectives.
The conditions under which adults learn best.
How to learn from life and everday experience.

How to negotiate the educational bureaucracy.
How to learn from television, radio, and computers.
How to lead and participate in discussion of problem-solving groups.
How to get the most from a conference or workshop.
How to learn from a mentor.
How to use intuition and dreams for learning.
How to help others learn more effectively.

Almost all of the points on Smith's list are covered in this book – and we have added a few more in order to make this book a complete guide and reference for your professional development.

Throughout the book, the focus is on individual learning – your learning – as opposed to helping others learn. However, at the end of the chapters on learning styles and strategies you will find short postscripts that offer suggestions for using the information presented in those chapters when you are designing and delivering training programs. This information is included because we have found that both new and experienced trainers tend to apply these concepts not only to their personal situation but also to their professional role in designing training for others. We have also included with these chapters a list of resources that can be used for one's own learning. In a few cases, because of the natural inclination of trainers to focus on materials for helping others learn, we list resources that are primarily for participant use.

The book is divided into three parts. Part One provides an overview of the past, present, and future of human resource development; a discussion of career considerations and options; and a guide for creating your professional development plan. Part Two is a catalogue of a wide variety of learning resources for implementing your plan. Part Three is an encyclopedia of concepts and contributors in the fields of human resource development and organization development.

The book can be used in two ways: with a formal plan and without. If you choose to systematically develop a learning plan, the chapters in Part One will carry you through the creation and implementation of your plan. The collection of resources in Part Two is a storehouse of information to help you find the means to achieve your learning objectives. The encyclopedia in Part Three offers a quick and easy way to become familiar with the field. If you don't want to develop a formal plan, the chapters in Part One as well as the resources and encyclopedia in Part Two and Part Three will collectively serve as a useful reference work for the field, to be sampled and used to expand your knowledge as needed.

We encourage you to develop a written professional development plan. As practitioners of HRD, we assist others in becoming better self-directed learners. We know the value that comes from developing a learning plan, particularly when we have structured our own plan. Even if you don't have time to fully complete the process, it is worthwhile to develop a rough outline. By going through the process you create your vision of how you want to develop professionally and then work toward its fulfillment. You achieve a certain power by putting your plans in writing; they become more focused and tangible—and with timetables and required resources they come closer to reality. A written plan becomes a road map that provides a greater sense of purpose and direction.

If you are new to HRD and plan to make it your career, you will probably want to systematically use the planning process to ensure the development of your expertise in the areas important to your immediate success in your present job. If you plan to spend only a few years in an HRD position before moving up the organizational career ladder, this book can give you almost instant benefits if you use it as a quick-study guide to the field. With the systematic use of the planning process you can maximize your development while in HRD. If you have been in the field for several years, you may choose to use the planning process as an opportunity to assess your current status and to plan for renewal and redirection. Or you may want to use the book as a reference and a refresher when designing programs or assisting others entering the field. And if you are one of the many busy people whose responsibilities include more than training, the book can serve as a one-stop guide to finding resources and answering your questions about HRD.

PART I

A GUIDE TO PLANNING YOUR PROFESSIONAL DEVELOPMENT

Part One of this book has nine chapters covering background information about the field, career options in HRD, a step-by-step process for creating a learning plan, a discussion about learning styles, and a variety of learning strategies to use in carrying out a learning plan. Chapter 1 ("HRD: Past, Present, and Future") provides a historical profile of HRD and assesses trends in the field. Chapter 2 ("Charting Your HRD Career") profiles the field, examines the roles and competencies of a trainer, and offers strategies for career development. Chapter 3 ("Developing Your Learning Plan") offers a five-step process that enables you to assess your learning needs, set priorities, and create a plan. Chapter 4 ("Assessing Your Learning Style") explores several approaches to learning and considers the implications of these models for developing your learning plan. Chapter 5 ("Selecting and Learning Through Classes, Seminars, and Workshops") discusses the advantages of using these various learning formats and provides suggestions for choosing and making the most of them. Chapter 6 ("Building a Learning Network") discusses networking as a learning strategy and offers resources and tips for using networking as part of your learning plan. Chapter 7 ("Learning from Role Models and Mentors") focuses on the mentor's role, the benefits of a mentoring relationship, ways of finding and working with a mentor, and the process of disengaging from the relationship. Chapter 8 ("Developing Effective Study Skills") covers ways to improve individual learning: space and time management, concentration, memory, study skills, and the use of libraries and computer data bases. Chapter 9 ("Tapping Your Inner Resources and Learning from Yourself") presents techniques for getting the most learning from your experience and making better use of your inner resources.

You may use this part of the book in an organized, formal way to approach your professional development or you may choose to read those chapters of immediate interest and use the remaining chapters for reference. If you choose the more organized approach, reading the chapters in the order of their presentation will probably work best. They have been organized in a sequence that will facilitate the development of your learning plan. As part of the process of creating your learning plan in Chapter 3, you will use Chapter 4, which deals with learning styles, and Chapters 5 through 9, which offer various learning strategies. You will also use the resources in Part Two. We encourage you to put your plan in writing and to work with your manager to gain the commitment and best use of your organization's resources. A clear vision of your professional development opportunities and outcomes greatly enhances their potential for success. Part One can help you create your professional development vision and turn it into a reality.

HRD: Past, Present, and Future

Chip R. Bell

We all come into this world as trainers. No person in the Stone Age ever hired a trainer or attended a train-the-trainer seminar. Yet, without some facility at training, humans would not have progressed from spear makers to space walkers. The history of HRD, no doubt, starts with the dawn of civilization, that point at which knowledge acquisition was not a function of genes, DNA, instinct, or imprinting; when efficiency of growth depended on another person.

Why look at history? What difference does it make whence we have come? There is more to history gazing than Thucydides' warning of repeating what was not understood. A sense of professional roots provides greater depth, more grounding, and a stronger foundation. By knowing where we have been, we can look at where we are and where we're going with more wisdom and maturity. History has more to do with mission than tactics; it strengthens the whys behind the whats and hows.

Archimedes, the discoverer of the principle of leverage, once said, "Give me a staff with length enough and a place whereupon to stand and I will move the world." This book begins by providing "a place whereupon to stand"—a foundation from which to view this fast-moving, rapidly changing field. While our tale of the past, present, and future is by no means complete, it will perhaps highlight some major events and issues. As a chapter of perspectives, it aims to foster more wisdom than skill.

A History of HRD

We know little of organized training prior to the industrial revolution in the mid to late 1700s. Skilled craftsmen and artisans paid homage to a closely supervised "demonstration-practice-feedback-practice-again" method. More knowledge-based apprenticeships occurred in lecture halls with experts espousing philosophy, theology, law, and medicine. There were, no doubt, some who employed the Socratic method, involving the learner through carefully chosen questions. We do know people got trained—armies were organized, pyramids were built, and high priests learned the "laws of God."

The industrial revolution was the start of a giant knowledge explosion. Between 1750 and 1900, human knowledge doubled. It doubled again by 1950, and again by 1965. Concomitant with this rapid expansion of knowledge was the requirement to transfer it in more efficient ways to adults in the world of work. The time line between skill acquisition and skill obsolescence began to shorten, further fueling the need for updating skills.

The early 1800s witnessed the birth of schools for mechanical arts, an outgrowth of a burgeoning patent rate—from 77 per year prior to 1810 to over 4,500 per year by 1860. The lion's share of patents impacting industry were in the mechanical arts. The Mechanic's Apprentice Library was formed in Boston in 1824; the Ohio Mechanics Institute in Cincinnati in 1818. The Morrill Land Grant Act of 1862 added to postsecondary development by starting agricultural and mechanical colleges.

Cloyd Steinmetz (1976) credits Hoe and Company of New York as having established in 1872 the earliest factory school aimed at training machinists for printing presses. Westinghouse Company established a factory school in 1888 and, by 1898, provided training for engineers. General Electric started a factory school in 1901 designed to prepare new workers for the world of work. By this time in the history of HRD, little was done in the formal classroom to improve or upgrade skills of workers. Most of this training would be referred to today as OJT— on-the-job training.

The history of HRD really begins after the turn of the century. A history of any aspects of an era has meaning only when displayed against a backdrop of culture. Each decade outlined below will be spiced with a smorgasbord of other events happening during the same period. The items in the backdrop provide a deeper understanding of happenings in the HRD field.

Correspondence schools that started in the late 1800s brought training to many workers of the 1900s. The concept was fully developed in England by the turn of the century. Ivan Harper, after visiting England, brought the idea to America and developed it further when he went to the University of Chicago in 1892. The other major impetus in correspondence schools was the work of Foster in the newspaper the *Mining Herald*, and in 1891 this activity spun off into what was to become the International Correspondence Schools.

Dean Scheider of the University of Cincinnati introduced the first plan in 1906 for cooperative education. Students learned part time in a school and worked part time in a factory. The banking industry formed the American Institute of Banking in 1901 to provide continuing education for banking employees. The U.S. government started the National Bureau of Standards Graduate School in 1908 as the first agency training center for federal employees.

The 1900s saw the continued transition of a society from farm to factory. It was a time of inventiveness—Henry Ford, Marie Curie, the Wright brothers—and a time of bootstrap pioneerism—Teddy Roosevelt, Jack London, and Robert Peary. Learning was most valued as an extension of work. The success of correspondence and cooperative education was linked to a reliance on self-discipline and learner initiative that characterized the period.

In the next few years HRD became the business of associations. Brought together by war (and later the issues of Prohibition and women's suffrage), associations became a useful vehicle for change. The National Society for the Promotion of Industrial Education (NSPIE) was formed in 1906 at Cooper Union in New York City to provide a vehicle for ideas and standards. The National Association of Corporation Schools (forerunner of the American Management Association) was formed in 1913. That same year, the National Vocational Guidance Association was founded. In 1918 NSPIE became the National Society for Vocational Education. Late in the decade, major corporations formed their own educational bodies. Among the first was General Motors Institute, established in 1919 to provide part-time training programs for employees in Flint's growing complex of auto plants.

A major drive for association-sponsored training lay in part with the reaction of a nation drawn together by war. Sergeant York, Irving Berlin, and Charlie Chaplin pulled at the heartstrings of Americans who feared the aloneness caused both by war and industrial mechanization. The Keystone Kops, Theda Bara, and Zane Grey offered temporary escape. But in the final analysis people needed people to help them learn.

Little change happened in the world of HRD during the 1920s. The Smith-Hughes Act of 1917 made government funds available to provide vocational education in public schools. The effort was amplified in 1929 by the George-Reed Act, which expanded vocational education to include agriculture and home economics. The Agricultural Extension effort would ultimately become a major resource of training. The American Management Association, an outgrowth of the National Association of Corporation Training, was formed in 1923.

It is not surprising that the 1920s represented a standstill for training. A euphoric country, feeling the relief of world calm and the sense of prosperity as the United States grew in world stature, turned to the trivia of flagpole-sitting, dance marathons, and such diverse heroes as Al Capone, Jack Dempsey, Rudolph Valentino, and Charles Lindbergh. A time of frivolity, the Roaring Twenties came to a close with the Great Depression.

The depression-ridden country saw the formation of the Civilian Conservation Corps (CCC) and National Youth Administration, both involved in job training of youth and young workers. The Bureau of Apprenticeship and Training was formed in 1934. The Training Officers Conference in Washington was started in 1938 by government training officers. The first training films began to appear as a part of classroom instruction.

HRD in the 1930s reflected the ambivalence of the time. Early training films were often a combination of rigid rules or procedures and simplistic humor. The times had similar mixes — Will Rogers and Sinclair Lewis; Shirley Temple and Franklin Delano Roosevelt. John L. Lewis wanted a labor coalition, Hitler wanted more power, Jack Benny wanted to save a dollar, Amelia Earhart wanted another aviation record, and John Dillinger was wanted, dead or alive!

A previous decade of paucity in training due to the Great Depression made up for lost time in the forties. A technique developed by Charles R. "Skipper" Allen in World War I was resurrected in the forties. The four steps of JIT or job instruction training (tell, show, do, and review) helped supervisors assume responsibility for training their new employees. The HRD field went into full gear as soldiers prepared for combat and nonsoldiers (just about everybody else) trained in support of the Allied forces. The G.I. Bill sent thousands of former soldiers to the college campuses for needed training after the war. The American Society for Training and Development was formed in 1944, and its first conference was held in 1945.

HRD was honored if it made a difference and promoted cohesiveness. It followed a "good guys always win" attitude, symbolized in the 1940s culture of Roy Rogers, Jimmy Stewart, Doris Day, Babe Ruth, and Arthur Godfrey. As desire pent up by the war went public with *Casablanca*, Tennessee Williams, and the Kinsey report, HRD also came out of the closet as an important tool to facilitate worker productivity and efficiency.

In the early fifties, sparked by the rediscovery of Elton Mayo's studies at the Hawthorne Plant of Western Electric, HRD began to focus on intensive supervisory training in human relations. Off-site management and executive development programs grew in popularity. By the mid-fifties, the HRD field had begun to develop an interest in educational technology. Training hardware burgeoned, along with teaching machines and programmed instruction (grounded in the educational theories of B. F. Skinner of Harvard University). They would become hot commodities in the 1960s. Training for government was legitimized by the Government Employees Training Act in 1958.

Again, HRD echoed the era. The human relations movement was as dfiferent from teaching machines as Joe McCarthy was from Sir Edmund Hillary or the young Queen Elizabeth II was from the battle-weathered Dwight Eisenhower. Coupled with such diversity was the soberness of racial strife and the shock of *Sputnik* in the late 1950s.

In the 1960s and 1970s the HRD field responded to a younger work force. The below-34 age group increased from 38 percent of the work force in 1960 to 42 percent by 1970, while the 35–44 age group (the realm of middle managers) dropped from 23 percent to 19 percent. Widespread social programs encompassed training with the Manpower Development and Training Act of 1962 and the Economic Opportunity Act of 1964. The growing allure of television promoted growth in training films and other media-based learning programs. Simulations and social consciousness training had grown in use by the end of the 1960s.

No two professionals had more impact on the HRD field in the 1960s and 1970s than Malcolm Knowles and Leonard Nadler. The predominant learning philosophy of the day had been behaviorism. The scientific, analytical era of the fifties and early sixties found the rational, objective approach to learning appealing. Knowles spoke for a more human approach—learner-centered instead of content-centered; experiential instead of exclusively didactic. His concepts encouraged changing the trainer from controller to facilitator, all occurring in a supportive climate responsive to the learner's needs.

The time was marked by major changes in the HRD field. As new concepts emerged and new roles were developed, there was significant need for structure and order. Leonard Nadler observed that the purview of the profession had grown well beyond the "corporate schoolhouse." Coining the term *human resource development* to apply to the field, he developed HRD concepts that organized the thinking of the field. His prolific writings and teachings minimized ambiguity and fostered communication, thus advancing the HRD field toward the status of a true profession.

Recent Trends in HRD

The 1980s witnessed a continued interest in blending bottom-line pragmatism with heartfelt compassion by workers in leadership roles. Books like *In Search of Excellence* (Peters and Waterman, 1982) and *The One-Minute Manager* (Blanchard and Johnson, 1982) dominated the best-seller lists. Bootstrap vigor (characterized by such popular films as *Rocky, Flashdance, The Natural,* and *Gandhi*) was played out in the HRD world with program emphasis on assertiveness, quality, and excellence.

The 1980s marked a major shift in HRD from largely a dispenser of occupational competences to a catalyst for change. HRD experienced greater credibility and power as more organizational leaders used HRD practitioners and practices in strategic planning. The change was caused by two thrusts: a recognition by organizations that effective development of people is central to success and a maturity of the HRD field, marked by a recognition that responsiveness *and* responsibleness are central to quality service in organizations.

Few things reveal priority more than the allocation of financial resources. As the 1980s moved to a close, the amount of dollars spent on training exceeded $200 billion a year. According to a study conducted by the Research Institute of America (1986), over $30 billion was spent in 1986 on formal employee training and around $180 billion more was spent on informal training, including on-the-job programs run by managers.

Training magazine's 1986 annual survey indicated that over 36 million employees annually received training representing over 1.3 billion person-hours. In the first half of the 1980s there was a 38 percent increase in the number of people assigned to corporate training responsibilities on a full-time basis ("Training Magazine's Industry Report, 1986," 1986). A survey of senior HRD managers of Fortune 500 companies reported in the *Training and Development Journal* echoed much the same theme—HRD "stock" was high as organizations discovered rich rewards for their investment in the growth of their human resources. Eighty-nine percent of the country's largest companies designated a chief human resources executive at the corporate level (Ralphs and Stephen, 1986).

The Future of HRD

The 1990s should see a continuation of the same active role presently enjoyed by HRD in most organizations. No longer simply the repository of training films and manuals, HRD will continue to be seen as a vital part of strategic planning and complex change management. Corporations have been shifting away from reactive training toward proactive, anticipatory learning. To compete, enlightened organizations are more regularly calling on training to minimize the crushing effects of obsolescence.

Almost overnight the United States has become a service society that performs more than it produces. In 1986, 73 percent of all jobs and 65 percent of the GNP came from the service sector. Marvin Cetron and Thomas O'Toole, authors of *Encounters with the Future*, have predicted that, by the end of the 1990s, 92 percent of all jobs and 85 percent of the GNP will come from those who serve rather than simply supply (Albrecht and Zemke, 1985). Such a shift will focus more training toward the interpersonal skills vital to high-quality service delivery.

The trainer who is successful in the 1990s will be the one who not only possesses a keen knowledge of the business and the strategic direction of the organization but also demonstrates that knowledge by providing HRD services which both respond to present needs and anticipate future requirements. HRD will draw its justification and value from its capacity to effectively create something important, to change something, or to foster the mission and vision of the organization it serves.

Figures and statistics are useful in portraying the future scope of the field. They do little to capture the tone. What follows are a series of vignettes showing a slice-of-life view of a complex and diverse field. While fictitious, their inclusion will serve as a metaphoric peephole into the world of HRD in the 1990s. The vignettes may lend color to the macro picture of the exciting years ahead.

Christopher Lay is a tax accountant for Steele-Spurlin, a medium-sized accounting firm. Since he joined the firm as a new accountant, he has devoted three weeks each year to teaching new tax regulations to other accountants in the firm. At the age of thirty-six he looks forward to continuing the practice even after becoming a partner in the firm.

Rachel Rainey has enjoyed her two-year tour of duty in computer-based training at Walnut Ridge Technologies. As a curriculum builder she has been able to combine her years as a field engineer as well as her three years in computer sales. Her next assignment should be overseas in a totally different part of the company. She should soon see the payoff of the training she has been designing.

Larry Hollar was one of the lucky ones. After five years as a professor of adult education and part-time HRD consultant, he got a position with Night's Inn as an internal consultant. He was quickly promoted to senior learning specialist at Night's Inn University, where he has been applying his research on learning styles to creative learning experiences for multilingual motel managers. He is rumored to be the next director of HRD for Night's Inn Europe.

Sarah Adam was pleased when the company president asked her to become education director for the Georgia Association of Bow Hunters. As a learning specialist, she had created a new career-development artificial intelligence device that the president used to select her for the directorship. Now she would oversee all systems and programs aimed at preparing association employees for future positions. She might even turn some of her systems into tools for members to use in local GABH chapters.

This was the most unique assignment Ron Underwood had gotten at Perdue Labs. As an in-house organization development consultant, he had been asked to spend one day a week for the next six months working with a task force to design an interactive video-based training program for chemical engineers all over the world. He was finally going to put to use his ten years as a cultural anthropologist with the Reagon Foundation.

Preparation for the future is best accomplished through careful examination of the projections and predictions of the next ten or fifteen years. The following issues either will have a direct impact on HRD or will alter the context in which HRD is practiced, thus indirectly affecting the field.

Demographics

The shape of the work force is more projection than prediction. Barring a major famine, war, or other catastrophe, there is little guesswork in population shifts of the next decade. The work force of the 1990s is already born!

The average age of workers in the 1990s will exceed 40 as the postwar baby boomers occupy most work slots. (The average age of workers in 1978 was 28.) A significant challenge for the field is providing updated skills for an increasingly older work force. As their numbers grow, the number of slots for middle-aged workers may decrease. There is concrete evidence that skill obsolescence becomes more severe after age 35. Gene Dalton and Paul Thompson (1986) found in their research that professionals who reached the age of 35 without regular promotions received steadily lower performance reviews.

The work force of the 1990s will experience a paucity of entry-age (18–22) workers. Additionally, while there will be from 18 to 20 million new jobs created, 75 percent of those filling them will be women and minorities. By the end of the century women will make up 40 percent of the blue-collar workers and will hold over half of the professional jobs—both major firsts in U.S. history. The change in the diversity of the work force will result in new worker values, requiring major assistance from HRD.

Work Forms and Expectations

The era of eight-to-five work, done in the office or factory under the watchful eye of one boss, is fast coming to a close. In the 1990s nearly half of the U.S. work force will be permanent part-time workers, and 30 percent of the work force will work under a flex-time scheduling arrangement (compared with 15 percent in 1985). Thirty-five percent of all paid work will be done in homes; Alvin Toffler's concept of the electronic cottage will finally come of age.

The 1990s will witness a metamorphosis in worker values. The average worker will have formed his or her values during the 1960s era of rejection of authority and the yearning for individuality. Gregory Curtis, editor of *Texas Monthly*, commented on the 1990s work force by saying, ". . . they are not working in order to earn a place in heaven nor are they working to pay off the mortgage and put the kids through college, the way people did in the '50s . . . . the new worker is a maverick, working for himself and answerable only to himself" (Zemke, 1987, p. 40).

The 1980s worker prefers teamwork and participative management. The 1990s worker will seek more autonomy and the minimal amount of supervision possible. Instead of viewing work as an opportunity for a meaningful growth experience, he or she will view work as a means to more leisure time. As the most educated work force in history (75 percent with high school diplomas; 33 percent with college degrees), workers of the 1990s will expect more and demand more. The present advent of entrepreneurship and intrapreneurship appears to be a glimpse of what is around the corner.

New Technologies

One major technology affecting the field is the growth of robotics. Some have indicated that the robotics field in the late 1980s is where the automobile industry was in 1910. Office automation of varying types will dictate how training will occur. According to some estimates, $300 to $500 billion will be spent in the 1990s on automation. Electronic mail will be as common as the telephone is today. Over 2.5 million laser technicians will be needed. Five of the ten fastest-growing jobs of the 1990s will be computer-related. Production workers will become "automation technicians" requiring complex cross-training and skills in trouble-shooting (Zemke, 1987).

The most provocative change in the field may be spawned by the present revolution in the computer and information technology world. There is little need to belabor the impact of the advent of microcomputers on the work world. According to projections, 25 million microcomputers will be in place by 1992. The more colorful crystal-ball watchers claim that if the auto industry had made the advances that the computer industry has in the past twenty years, today you could buy a Rolls Royce for ten dollars that would get a million miles to the gallon!

But even the most sophisticated and exciting computer hardware is nothing more than an expensive piece of hi-tech office decoration without equally sophisticated software. In research labs all over the country, new and powerful methods are being developed and tested to represent knowledge in computer-usable form. This makes it possible to "capture" (and, therefore, make available by a computer) expert knowledge about how things work and how to get things done, opening the door for the most far-reaching technology—artificial intelligence.

Artificial intelligence (or AI, as it is now universally known) has gained enough momentum that it has been hailed in some quarters as "the second computer revolution." Recent advances in artificial intelligence make possible computer programs that have expert, reliable knowledge about important topics and that are capable of interacting with human beings in a flexible and responsive way. Interacting with these new AI programs closely simulates interacting with another human being; in short, metaphorically speaking, they are artificial persons who live in a computer. With this historic convergence of microcomputers, advanced computer languages for knowledge representation, and artificial intelligence, we will see the emergence of a new and potentially transforming tool of HRD: the AIDE (Artificial Intelligence DEvice), the artificial person in a microcomputer who exists solely to support humans in accomplishing work.

What would an AIDE look like and what would it do? Most popular accounts of AI emphasize "expert systems" and dwell on the "intelligence" contained in them. But, as any trainer can attest, intelligence per se does not get many jobs done. What is needed is intelligence finely focused on the programmatic concerns of specific tasks. We do not need someone who can prove esoteric theorems; we need someone who can keep an eye on accounts receivable and let the right people know when some accounts show trouble signs. In general there is a need for people—artificial or otherwise—who know how to support us in our enterprises by accomplishing important, complex, but often pretty mundane jobs. To grasp the scope of the AIDE and its impact on the future of HRD, it may be useful to look at a few broad categories of artificial persons. Each category is "expert" in the sense of knowing substantially and in detail about some area of endeavor.

The role of guide is one obvious use of the AIDE. Since it is in the microcomputer on the desk, talking to it is easier than calling up a human guide on the phone—with the additional advantage that, with an AIDE, the line is never busy, the guide is never out to lunch or in another meeting, and it does not matter how naive or repetitious your question. Whether the question is one a new worker might ask ("What is expected of someone in my position?") or the question of a seasoned worker ("What am I supposed to do with my copy of Form P88M?"), the guide is always there to assist.

The AIDE can function as an excellent coach. Such a role could cover a variety of situations: talking a person through the steps involved in a procedure, digging into detail on a particularly tricky part, stopping to give "the big picture," and helping to troubleshoot when a mistake has been made. Artificial coaches in the areas of people management, marketing, and performance review have been built by Tony Putman and his associates in recent years.

The AIDE can also be an assistant—looking things up, keeping track of things, doing the picky little calculations, making sure all the forms are filled out, and remembering to notify everybody about the meeting or reminding a worker of an important check or infrequent work operation.

What does all this mean for the future of HRD? AIDEs may cause trainers to profoundly rethink and alter their approach to accomplishing their objectives. Consider the objective of providing a particular worker with the knowledge needed to accomplish a given job—for example, the job of supervisor. The major (if not the only) components of such a training program typically are some form of supervisory training, supplemented with policy and procedural manuals. While training can make a difference and manuals are important, certain irreducible difficulties remain:

1. Since we can never take supervisors off the job long enough to train them in everything they need to know, it is necessary to make some more or less arbitrary decisions about what portions of the whole we will cover.
2. Even with the best design and presentation skills, not everyone will grasp all of the material during the session.
3. Of the material actually grasped, unfortunately a very large amount fades with the passage of a disconcertingly short amount of time after the session.
4. It is often difficult for the learner to see how to apply the general principles or concepts learned in his or her own specific on-the-job situations.

By contrast, consider a situation using a supervisory AIDE. Since we do not have to take supervisors off the job to use the AIDE—on the contrary, they use it on the job—there is no need to give them an incomplete set of knowledge and skills. They engage with the material precisely at the time and under the circumstances that make for quality learning: when they need to know the material in order to accomplish a task at hand. And if they forget or are uncertain about a particular area, they can go over it again and again, quickly and easily. In a nutshell, having an AIDE is equivalent to having the supervisory skills instructor chained to your desk, available for instructing at all times (Putman, Bell, and Van Zwieten, forthcoming).

If artificial intelligence devices revolutionize training, however, there are certain logical consequences that seem likely. In order to develop an effective AIDE, for example, the tools and techniques of performance analysis will need to be developed and emphasized. Trainers will have to be able to specify exactly what knowledge, skills, and judgments are required in order to do the job in question as it is actually—not theoretically or in principle—done. Performance observation and description in technically useful detail might become crucial competencies.

The "knowledge engineer," a new professional within training who interviews experts and observes them in action in order to "capture" their knowledge and translate it into computer-usable form, will be central to the development of artificial intelligence devices. In the very near future, we will all need to become very familiar and comfortable with computers; a training professional who is not may be like a surgeon lacking in scalpel literacy.

Thus, a major part of being an effective trainer is to function as an ally of change. Whether the trainer is training employees to improve performance on their present jobs, educating them for a future job, or developing them to grow with the organization as it evolves, change is the common commodity. Pursuing such a vital responsibility cannot occur effectively without one foot in the future. We are charged by the role to be serious purveyors of the future, not simply a mild curiosity.

As Ron Zemke (1987) has said, "The future is what we make out of the complexity of the here and now, as well as the thousand and one surprises that invariably lie beyond the next hill" (p. 53). The more we are keenly aware of our history and tradition as well as future projections and predictions, the better we are able to prepare ourselves and those we serve to function successfully over time. This chapter is our welcome to the field. Our rich and illustrative past gives us roots and tradition. Our challenging and demanding present offers us meaning and value. And our exciting and provocative future provides us inspiration and hope.

For Your Continuing Professional Development

Bell, C. R. "Future Encounters of the HRD Kind." *Training and Development Journal*, 1981, *35* (8), 54–57.

Cetron, M., and O'Toole, T. *Encounters with the Future*. New York: McGraw-Hill, 1982.

Putman, A. O., and Bell, C. R. "The Future of HRD." In L. Nadler (ed.), *The Handbook of Human Resource Development*. New York: Wiley, 1984.

Toffler, A. *The Adaptive Corporation*. New York: McGraw-Hill, 1985.

2

Charting Your HRD Career

Linda Webster and Sheila C. Henderson

The field of human resource development is diverse in organizational job settings and roles—reflecting the many uses of training and development as well as the ever-changing nature of both work and the work force that performs it. Likewise, career paths in HRD are as diverse and individualized as the backgrounds of HRD practitioners and as constantly changing as the opportunities in the field. You are unique in your educational background, professional experience, personal temperament, special aptitudes, and vision of the future. You must be realistic in assessing your strengths, flexible in evaluating your job possibilities, and creative in planning your career options. This chapter is designed to fill you in on the state of the HRD field, the roles HRD practitioners perform on the job and the competencies they need in those roles, and strategies for career development in HRD. If you want more information about career and life planning in general, there are a number of good books listed in Chapter 10.

State of the HRD Field

Each year *Training* magazine surveys its readers on a number of diverse career-related subjects—educational and professional background, long-term career objective, salaries, industries, career opportunities—and publishes the results in the October issue. While statistical details will change from year to year, overall trends that became evident during the first half of the 1980s will most likely continue into the second half of the decade and beyond. Below are highlights of some of these trends.

Salaries

Overall, in the 1980s average trainers' salaries have risen from the low thirties to the high thirties. Unfortunately, women typically earn about 25 percent less than men in the same positions, which results in gaps ranging from $7,000 to $11,000 per year in the average salaries of men and women. Of course, number of years of experience also makes a difference; those with three years of experience or less earn about 15 percent less than the average. The Northeast and the Pacific Coast regions tend to offer the highest salaries, with the Southeast and West Central regions offering the lowest. However, salaries vary more by type of industry than by geographical region. The best-paying industries are manufacturing, transportation, communications, and public utilities. The worst-paying industries are health services, finance, insurance, and banking. By position, training managers and specialists in management and in career and organization development tend to earn the highest salaries, while classroom instructors and instructional designers earn the lowest salaries ("U.S. Training Census and Trends Reports," 1982–1986).

Industries

During the early part of this decade, trainers tended to agree that communications, banking and finance, and health services were the industries offering the best career opportunities in the training field. Mining and oil, construction, government (local, state, federal), and retail trade were considered the worst industries for trainers seeking career growth. Opinions were mixed about training career opportunities in manufacturing and education (meaning the training of employees in educational institutions, not the educating of students). However, the majority of the respondents to the *Training* surveys have tended to be in manufacturing, finance, insurance, banking, and business services.

Background

Approximately 60 percent of those in the training field have undergraduate or graduate degrees in either education, business or management, or social science (psychology in particular). Most HRD specialists were formerly professionals in other occupations, technical specialists of some sort, schoolteachers, line managers, or staff supervisors. Most HRD managers were formerly technical specialists, schoolteachers, line managers, or personnel specialists.

Career Opportunities

Most trainers responding to *Training*'s surveys believed that the best career opportunity for the remainder of the decade is in designing and developing computer-based instructional programs. Following that, they ranked management development specialist and organization development specialist as very promising career goals. Less attractive but still very promising were instructional program designer/developer (traditional rather than computer-based), career development specialist, and classroom instructor.

Roles and Competencies in HRD

In 1983 the American Society for Training and Development completed an extensive study of the training and development field, focusing in particular on the various job functions or roles these practitioners must perform as well as the attributes, knowledge, and skills necessary for performing them well. In the study, called *Models for Excellence* (American Society for Training and Development, 1983, p. 29), fifteen key HRD roles and thirty-one areas of competency within the field were identified. Any particular job or position in HRD may consist of only one function or role—or it may conceivably include them all—and each role requires its own special array of knowledge and skill competencies. These fifteen key roles are as follows:

Evaluator. Identifies the extent of impact of a program, service, or product.

Group Facilitator. Manages group discussions and group processes so that individuals learn and group members feel the experience is positive.

Individual Development Counselor. Helps an individual assess personal competencies, values, and goals and identify and plan development and career actions.

Instructional Writer. Prepares written learning and instructional materials.

Instructor. Presents information and directs structured learning experiences so that individuals learn.

Manager of Training and Development. Plans, organizes, staffs, and controls training and development operations or projects and links training and development operations with other organizational units.

Marketer. Sells training and development viewpoints, learning packages, programs, and services to target audiences outside one's own work unit.

Media Specialist. Produces software and uses audiovisual, computer, and other hardware-based technologies for training and development.

Needs Analyst. Defines gaps between ideal and actual performance and specifies the cause of the gaps.

Program Administrator. Ensures that the facilities, equipment, materials, participants, and other components of a learning event are present and that program logistics run smoothly.

Program Designer. Prepares objectives, defines content, and selects and sequences activities for a specific program.

Strategist. Develops long-range plans for what the training and development structure, organization, direction, policies, programs, services, and practices will be in order to accomplish the training and development mission.

Task Analyst. Identifies activities, tasks, subtasks, and human resource and support requirements necessary to accomplish specific results in a job or organization.

Theoretician. Develops and tests theories of learning, training, and development.

Transfer Agent. Helps individuals apply learning after the learning experience.

In analyzing the data, the ASTD task force recognized that the key functions fall into groupings or clusters according to the number of important knowledge or skill competencies they share. The roles of group facilitator, instructor, marketer, and transfer agent form a grouping called the interface cluster. The research cluster is composed of the evaluator, needs analyst, and task analyst roles. The concept development cluster includes the roles of instructional writer, program designer, and theoretician. The two roles of manager and strategist form the leadership cluster. Three roles, however, did not overlap significantly with others and were not included in any groupings: media specialist, individual development counselor, and program administrator.

So what does all of this mean to you? As you study the brief role descriptions in this list, you can identify those which interest you as well as those which either are included in your present job functions or are a logical addition or next step. We recommend that you read *Models for Excellence* for complete information about the study and its findings.

Strategies for Career Development

When you have decided which roles you would like to perform as an HRD practitioner and the type of industry or content specialty you would like to concentrate on, then it's time to focus on strategies for achieving your goals. You'll need to assess your current situation — within your community as well as your organization — for the possibilities it offers and select the most promising options. Some strategies you will be able to exercise immediately, but others will require that you watch for opportunities, wait patiently, and influence others to cooperate with your plan. And, of course, you'll need to be flexible, recognizing when your original plan is no longer workable or has been preempted by an unanticipated opportunity or interest. Here are some career development strategies that you can employ to reach your career goals.

Job Enrichment

Find ways to increase your responsibility and independence by enlarging the scope of your job. You can expand into a new content area – presenting programs on sales training as well as on supervisory skills training – or you can increase your role functions. If you are currently teaching computer literacy, for example, you might become involved in revising the existing training program and designing new training modules. Or you could perform needs assessments and then evaluate the training based on employee performance. Assume responsibility for an entire task or project. Increase the significance and impact of what you do.

Lateral Mobility

You may decide to make a lateral move with no change in pay or status to broaden your skills or to use your skills within a different specialization. Maybe you are currently a technical skills trainer but want to move into management development, so you decide to switch to supervisory training to prepare yourself for the transition. Or you might decide to take a beginning management position to get the managerial experience you will need to move into managerial training or even into an HRD management position.

Special Assignments

Volunteer for task forces or research projects. Special assignments provide not only good learning opportunities but also ways of generating job possibilities. Use the opportunity to learn more about topics or issues that interest you while increasing your visibility in the company. You can broaden your perspective on organization goals, long-range planning and budgeting, corporate politics, and interdepartmental relations. Working with other departments will also keep you informed about possibilities for lateral or vertical mobility.

Changing Organizations

Expand your skills and your professional perspective by shifting locations in your company, moving to a larger company, or changing industries. If you're working in a field office to provide training, you could transfer to headquarters and get involved in designing, coordinating, and contracting for training. If you're looking for expanded responsibilities – a larger training program or function within a wider range of training programs – you may want to move to a larger organization or one with a different focus, from public to private sector, for example, or from a manufacturing to a service-oriented company.

Management

It's a good idea to build management experience into your career path, whether your goal is an HRD management position or one in a related human resource area like personnel selection, employee assistance, or organization and job design. Management experience can also be a valuable professional asset if you are interested in moving into organization development or HRD consulting. You may need to move to another organization if no promotion opportunities exist in your company. However, if you want to stay with your present organization, you can improve your management skills while waiting for the right position to open up by taking courses in your company's management development program, volunteering for some management-related responsibilities in your department, and working on company task forces.

Professional Activities

Increase your skills, gain visibility and credibility, and get support from others in the field by involving yourself in professional activities outside of your job. One of the best ways is to participate in professional associations, like ASTD or the OD Network. Attend conferences, but don't stop there. Arrange to present papers and workshops. Publish articles in professional journals and industry magazines. Contribute chapters to books, or write one of your own. Perhaps you might want to teach part time at a local college or university. You can also arrange to supervise interns from a local or area HRD program within your training department. Finally, volunteer your services as a trainer or organization development practitioner to agencies or nonprofit organizations in your community.

Training and Education

Attend seminars, programs, and workshops that focus on the knowledge and skill competencies you want to develop. You can also apprentice yourself to specialists from whom you want to learn — volunteer to assist them free of charge during a training session or on a consulting assignment. Another training option is to contract for a program or consultant service that you want to learn how to conduct and then arrange to observe or even directly assist the trainer or consultant. If you want structured and systematic learning experiences — or your career development plan calls for an advanced degree — then enroll in a university.

Career Growth Through Education

There are hundreds of academic programs geared toward human resource development, available through departments of business administration, education, communication, psychology, human services, instructional technology, organization development, and public administration. These programs offer bachelor's, master's, and doctoral degrees as well as certificates in adult education, instructional design, industrial education, communication, and organization development. In addition to traditional academic programs, there are a number of nontraditional external graduate degree programs, some of which require only minimal residency— like those of University Associates and the NTL Institute. See Chapter 13 for listings of academic programs in HRD.

The career development of HRD practitioners is a combination of work experiences, training, and academic course work. Many experienced practitioners suggest that, after you earn your undergraduate degree, you accrue some practical work experience before seeking an advanced degree. A master's degree built on practical experience will broaden both your understanding and capabilities in whatever HRD or management skills you will need to meet your career objectives. Corporate employers seek out HRD practitioners who understand the bottom-line business perspective, and many feel that candidates with an M.B.A. have more credibility than those with an M.A. or M.S. An M.B.A. can help you take advantage of a broader range of opportunities within an organization if you decide to expand your skills outside the training field or enter management. An M.P.A. (master's in public administration) offers similar benefits for those interested in the public sector. Some academic programs provide for HRD specialization within M.B.A. or M.P.A. degree plans, but most HRD programs are in education, communication, and the behavioral sciences.

If you want to pursue an academic career or be a high-level consultant, then you'll want to go on for a doctoral degree. A word of warning, however: while nontraditional external doctoral degrees are becoming accepted by employers in general, they are still not accepted by universities in hiring their teaching and research faculties. The Ph.D. is becoming attractive in high-tech fields, but it can be a liability in the corporate world, creating an impression of "ivory tower" impracticality. Practical experience and knowledge of business realities are essential if you choose to work in the corporate sector. An advanced degree may get you in the door, but what counts after you cross the threshhold is your performance.

What are some of the advantages of an advanced degree in addition to the knowledge and skills you will gain? While you are in school, you will have access to professors who are experts in the field and to a large network of students who may become professional contacts in the future. Furthermore, if you want practical experience in skill or content areas that are new to you, an academic program can provide access to internships. Universities also provide job placement services.

More employers are looking for trainers with advanced degrees, especially in the high-tech fields, and will pay them starting salaries that are $1,500 to $5,000 higher per year than those earned by trainers with a bachelor's degree only. In the competitive HRD job market, in which one-third to one-half of the practitioners have advanced degrees, a master's or doctorate combined with appropriate experience can get you hired more easily and promoted more quickly. An advanced degree may provide you with increased access to publishing and speaking opportunities, which will further contribute to your development and advancement.

A Special Word for Job Changers

If your career development plan necessitates moving to a new position in a new organization, there are several resources you can tap to find the job that's right for you. HRD openings are listed in the business section of the *New York Times* and the Tuesday edition of the *Wall Street Journal. Training* magazine, *Training and Development Journal,* and the other professional journals listed in Chapter 11 also carry some job listings; newsletters from local ASTD chapters list job openings as well. ASTD has a job placement service for its members, as do other professional associations (see Chapter 12), and you can find out about jobs at state and national association conferences. You might want to register with a search firm, such as Abbott Smith Associates, a New York–based recruiting firm that specializes in HRD personnel. Keep in mind, however, that many corporate employers will interview on the basis of personal recommendations from their colleagues or staff, so stay involved in professional activities and develop the personal contacts that can open doors.

For Your Continuing Professional Development

American Society for Training and Development. *Models for Excellence: The Conclusions and Recommendations of the ASTD Training and Development Competency Study.* Baltimore: ASTD Press, 1983.
Bridges, W. *Transitions: Making Sense of Life's Changes.* Reading, Mass.: Addison-Wesley, 1980.
Burack, E. H. "The Sphinx's Riddle: Life and Career Cycles." *Training and Development Journal,* 1984, *38* (4), 52–61.
Chalofsky, N., and Lincoln, C. I. *Up the HRD Ladder: A Guide to Professional Growth.* Reading, Mass.: Addison-Wesley, 1983.
Collins, N. W. *Professional Women and Their Mentors: A Practical Guide to Mentoring for the Women Who Wants to Get Ahead.* Englewood Cliffs, N.J.: Prentice Hall, 1983.
Geddie, C., and Strickland, B. "From Plateaus to Progress: A Model for Career Development." *Training,* 1984, *21* (6), 56–61.
Hagberg, J., and Leider, R. J. *The Inventurers: Excursions in Life and Career Renewal.* (2nd ed.) Reading, Mass.: Addison-Wesley, 1982.
Potter, B. A. *The Way of the Ronin: A Guide to Career Strategy.* New York: AMACOM, 1984.
Rosenthal, S. M. *How to Enter the Field of Human Resource and Organization Development.* (Pt. 1) Portland, Ore.: OD Network, 1981.
"U.S. Training Census and Trends Reports." *Training,* October issue, annual.

3

Developing Your Learning Plan

Ray Bard and Leslie Stephen

This chapter assists you in developing a one-year professional development plan. Many benefits can result from creating an individual learning plan. You obtain insights into your professional learning needs, clarify your (and your manager's) expectations about the direction of your development, solicit and acquire management and colleague support, and outline a road map to guide your learning during the year. Most important, the process of putting your plan in writing brings your needs out of the wish or dream stage into reality. The act of making your plan concrete, with target dates and budget requirements, demands a seriousness and commitment that leads to the successful achievement of your learning objectives.

If you plan to work in HRD for a few years as part of your career path, the development of a learning plan can help you focus your professional growth while in the field. You will also find that the expertise acquired in learning how to direct your development will be valuable when you move to other departments in the organization. If you have chosen HRD as your profession, the continued acquisition of new skills and knowledge is one of the essentials of becoming – and remaining – a competent professional. The use of a yearly planning process provides an opportunity to regularly review the progress of your career and respond to new technology, information, or trends in the field. Whether HRD is only a stop along your career ladder or your professional calling, your time can be spent more productively if you are aware of what skills and knowledge you need to competently perform your job duties.

You, like most trainers, have probably come to HRD with other academic backgrounds and work experience. You may have a technical speciality such as computer science, engineering, or medicine, or your experience and academic preparation may be in education or the behavioral sciences. This assessment and planning process is designed to start where you are, irrespective of your previous formal preparation and work experience. By working through the process, you should be able to determine and plan for increased effectiveness in the HRD functions that are important to your development now.

This is not meant to be an exhaustive process but rather an operational means for you to chart a course and monitor your progress. The assessment scale presented in this chapter includes eight major functional areas and thirty-seven performance statements. If you are interested in reviewing or using a more detailed assessment model, we suggest that you obtain the ASTD study *Models for Excellence* (American Society for Training and Development, 1983). Its model includes thirty-one competencies in fifteen training and development roles. You may also want to adapt the model in this book. Tailor the process to work for you as long as it facilitates the planning of your professional development.

The recommended process involves you and your manager working together to identify the knowledge and skills most important for you and the organization. The best way to involve your manager is to discuss the planning process, explain what you hope to achieve, and request his or her participation. You may choose to work the process alone, but if organizational resources and commitment are required for the accomplishment of your plan, you will probably be more successful if your manager is involved throughout the process. You may also want to include others in the assessment phase. Co-workers in the same department, others who are familiar with your duties and performance, and subordinates are good sources of feedback about your learning needs. You may choose to approach the process in a formal, structured way and spend a substantial amount of time. Or you may choose a shorthand, less formal approach that requires less time and effort. The important thing is to take the time to create a vision of what you want to learn and the level of competence you wish to achieve.

Here are the basic steps in the process: (1) assessing your learning needs; (2) setting your learning objectives; (3) developing your learning plan; (4) implementing and monitoring your plan; and (5) evaluating your results.

Step One: Assessing Your Learning Needs

The assessment scale in Figure 1 generates two kinds of data: your most important job functions and your present competency level for thirty-seven areas within eight functions. When completing the scale, choose a number from 1 to 5 to rate each; 1 is the lowest rating, 5 the highest.

For the priority rating use the following guide:

0 you do not perform that function.
1 you occasionally perform the function, but it is not critical to the organization now or in the near future.
2 you regularly perform the function, but it is not critical and is unlikely to become so in the near future.

3 you regularly perform the function, and it is necessary and may become more important in the near future.
4 you perform the function occasionally now but may perform it more frequently in the future, and it is critical to your job.
5 you perform the function frequently, and it is critical to your job.

For the competency rating use the following guide:

0 you are not able to perform the function.
1 you can perform the function partially or with difficulty and lack most of the skills and knowledge you require.
2 you can perform the function, but there are significant skills and knowledge you need to acquire.
3 you are competent in performing the function but still need to acquire more knowledge or experience to feel fully confident.
4 you are at mastery level but can still increase your performance by increasing your skills and knowledge.
5 that you can perform at a level of excellence and don't need any additional skills or knowledge at this time.

As in any rating scale, the scoring is somewhat arbitrary. What is being recorded is your and your manager's perceptions about your learning needs. But it is those same perceptions that enter into your working relationship and job assignments. You may decide to use the form as a master list to choose the areas you need to work on without rating each. Remember the purpose of this step in the process is for you to determine what you want and need to learn to perform your job better. Choose the method that works best for you.

After you complete the assessment scale, list your five most important learning needs. You may use the function as stated on the assessment scale, or you may reword it to more accurately reflect your job or needs.

At the time you complete the assessment step, provide your manager a copy of the assessment form. Ask him or her to complete the priority and rating columns and to list your five most important learning needs. Set a time for you and your manager to meet and compare information. If you choose to obtain feedback from others, it should be done before the meeting with your manager so that information can be included. If the department's management style and working relationships permit, you may want to include others in the meeting with your manager. The development of a learning plan is a positive activity, and working with others may help create a more supportive environment for the achievement of your plans. Or you may feel that it is a personal activity that is best pursued by you and your manager.

When you meet with your manager, begin by comparing ratings and then agree on the areas for you to work on. After this meeting you can begin to write down some learning objectives and develop your plan.

Learning Needs Assessment Scale

	Ratings (0–5 scale)			
	Priority		Competency	
Functions and Performance Statements	Mine	Manager's	Mine	Manager's
1. Learning Needs Assessment				
Use competency-based models, performance analysis, and other needs assessment techniques.				
Design and use various instruments, surveys, questionnaires, and other data-collection methods.				
Analyze data and translate into program needs.				
2. Develop Learning Strategies and Designs				
Select best strategies to meet learning needs.				
Use adult learning theory and principles.				
Develop learning objectives and designs.				
Use diverse learning methods.				
3. Provide Learning Materials				
Research and collect information from print and nonprint sources.				
Develop multimedia materials.				
Write and produce case studies, exercises, manuals, and other print materials.				
Evaluate film, software, packaged programs, and other vendor materials for rental and purchase.				
4. Facilitate Group Learning Activities				
Use effective presentation methods.				
Use group interaction methods.				
Use full range of learning methods.				
Use audiovisual equipment and materials.				
Use computer-based instruction.				
5. Evaluate Learning Results				
Design and use methods and instruments to collect learning-related data.				
Formulate recommendations for program redesign.				

Figure 1. Learning Needs Assessment Scale.

Source: *The Trainer's Professional Development Handbook* by Ray Bard, Chip R. Bell, Leslie Stephen, and Linda Webster. San Francisco: Jossey-Bass. Copyright © 1987 Jossey-Bass. Permission to reproduce granted.

| | Ratings (0–5 scale) | | | |
| | Priority | | Competency | |
Functions and Performance Statements	Mine	Manager's	Mine	Manager's
6. Internal Consulting				
Conduct data collection and problem analysis.				
Formulate strategies and develop plans to solve learning-related problems.				
Contract with in-house clients regarding problem analysis as well as strategies and resources required to solve learning problems.				
Prepare organizational climate for change.				
Work with a wide variety of personalities and styles to implement plans.				
Evaluate effectiveness of strategies and plans.				
7. Individual Counseling				
Assist individuals to assess learning needs and develop learning plans.				
Provide learning-related information and resources.				
8. Management				
Develop and maintain a positive working relationship with line and upper management.				
Communicate the importance of human resource development to line management and upper management.				
Develop yearly and multiyear training and development plans.				
Develop yearly and multiyear budgets.				
Select competent staff.				
Develop positive work environment for staff.				
Effectively supervise and motivate staff.				
Contract with, manage, and evaluate consultants.				
Schedule and coordinate staff, facilities, materials, and equipment to meet program goals.				
Develop and maintain an information system providing performance data to staff, management, and other departments.				
Evaluate individual staff and program performance.				

Figure 1.   Learning Needs Assessment Scale (continued).

Source: *The Trainer's Professional Development Handbook* by Ray Bard, Chip R. Bell, Leslie Stephen, and Linda Webster. San Francisco: Jossey-Bass. Copyright © 1987 Jossey-Bass. Permission to reproduce granted.

As an example, let's take the case of Bob Anderson, who is relatively new to HRD. He has a technical background and has primarily used lectures as an instructional method for his classroom teaching. He and his manager agree that he needs to learn a wider range of teaching methods, especially more participatory techniques. Since Bob is scheduled to teach several courses over the next year, it is an important area for the organization and one in which he would like to increase his competency. Bob and his manager both included this area of need in their list of his top five learning needs. The worksheet in Figure 2 shows how Bob developed his learning plan.

> LEARNING NEEDS
>
> Bob Anderson   August 4, 1987
>
> 1. Wider range of classroom teaching methods
>
> 2. More learning needs assessment models and techniques.
>
> 3. Wider range of methods in learning design
>
> 4. Better understanding of adult learning theory and principles
>
> 5. Methods for evaluating training programs

Figure 2. Learning Needs Worksheet.

Bob and his manager agreed that Bob should concentrate on his top three learning needs. They assumed that developing and using a wider range of learning methods would include reading about adult learning theory and principles, so the fourth item on the list was also targeted. Then Bob's manager made a suggestion that became Bob's fifth learning need. Other departments in the organization were beginning to use desktop publishing composition software to design and develop camera-ready copy for the printer. The manager thought that more professionally designed training materials could be developed for less cost, but first someone needed to learn to use the software. Since Bob was the computer training specialist on the staff and used the department computers more than anyone else, he was a natural choice. Bob enthusiastically agreed and added this to his list of learning needs.

Step Two: Setting Learning Objectives

In this step of the process you convert your learning needs into learning objectives. The standard form of a learning objective is to begin with an action verb and list what knowledge, skill, or attitude you wish to acquire or change within a specified time. Each objective should be stated specifically enough to be measurable, identifying the result the learner hopes to achieve. Writing specific learning objectives will help focus your efforts and provide a means to monitor your progress and evaluate the final result.

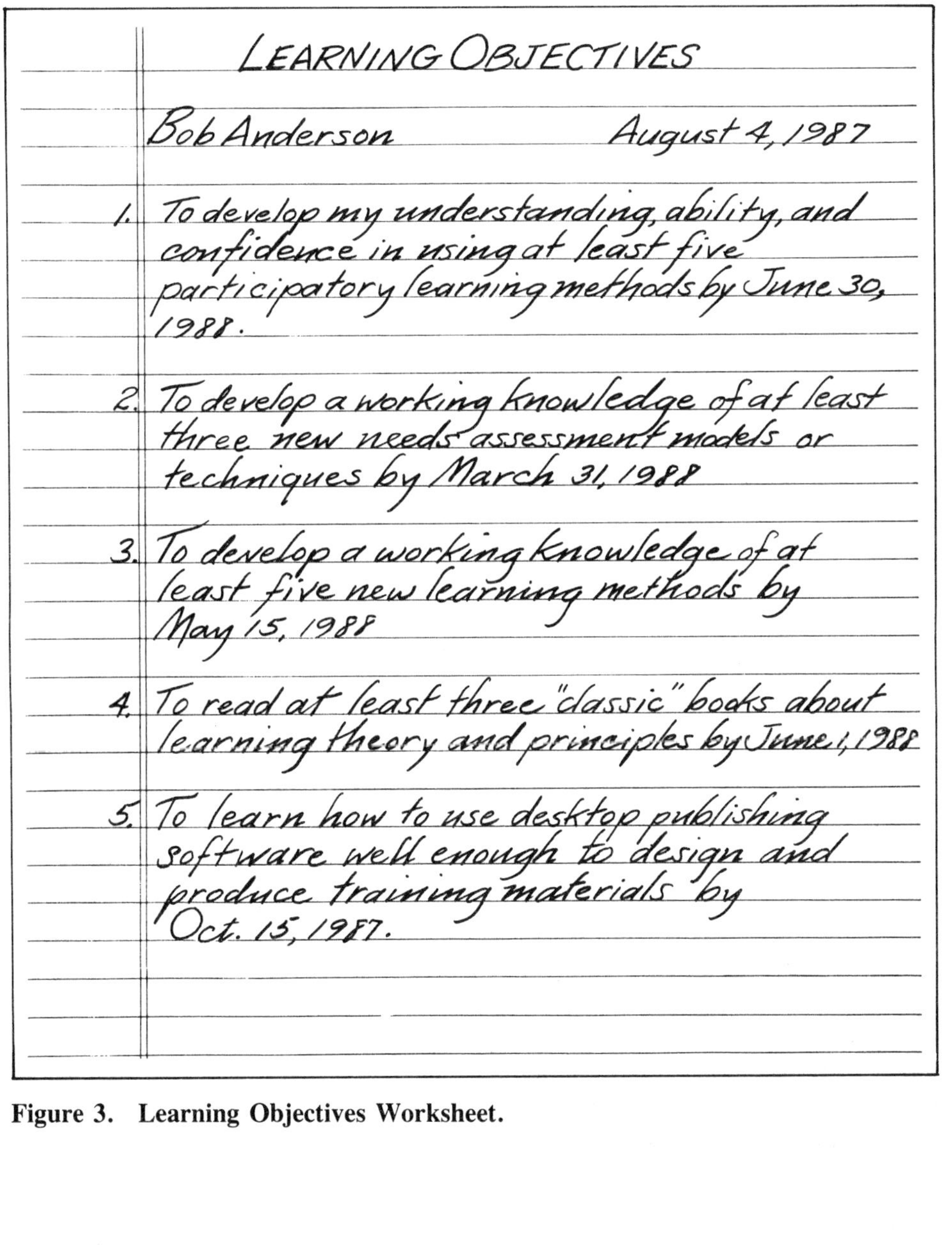

LEARNING OBJECTIVES

Bob Anderson   *August 4, 1987*

1. *To develop my understanding, ability, and confidence in using at least five participatory learning methods by June 30, 1988.*

2. *To develop a working knowledge of at least three new needs assessment models or techniques by March 31, 1988*

3. *To develop a working knowledge of at least five new learning methods by May 15, 1988*

4. *To read at least three "classic" books about learning theory and principles by June 1, 1988*

5. *To learn how to use desktop publishing software well enough to design and produce training materials by Oct. 15, 1987.*

Figure 3.   Learning Objectives Worksheet.

Let's look at Bob's learning objectives (Figure 3). On his first learning objective, for example, Bob has begun with the action verb *to develop*. He has specified the date on which he hopes to achieve the objective and the number of methods he wants to learn. The target date and the number of learning methods provide a good guide and help make the objective measurable. But a purist could ask, "How is Bob's understanding, ability, and confidence going to be measured?" There could be a pre- and post-test of Bob's understanding of the methods, an experienced trainer could observe Bob using the methods before and after the learning process (or he could be videotaped before and after), and Bob could use a pre- and post-attitude scale that would quantify the increase in his confidence. These are operational learning objectives. They are for you and your manager to use to guide your professional development. To that end they need to state clearly enough what you hope to achieve so that you and your manager can have the same understanding at the beginning of the process (planning), during the process (monitoring), and at the end (evaluation). If your objectives meet that test, they are probably sound and well-phrased.

Step Three: Developing Your Learning Plan

As a preliminary activity, it is helpful to brainstorm some ways to accomplish each objective by thinking in terms of appropriate strategies, potential outcomes, and possible resources. Figure 4 shows some possible strategies for Bob. When you begin to consider learning strategies and resources for your plan, consult Chapters 5 through 9, which deal with learning strategies and can serve as good references.

Your selection of learning strategies has a lot to do with your personal learning style. Research has shown that there are differences in the way people take in and process information. Some people want to grasp the "big picture" before focusing on the details while others prefer to absorb concrete facts and examples before drawing conclusions about underlying principles. Some learn best by reflection, others by becoming immediately involved in a hands-on way. Some rely primarily on person-to-person contact to acquire new information. Others prefer to work alone using printed material and other resources. Individual learning style also influences other facets of how a person goes about learning. To develop your personal learning plan, you need to know your strengths and weaknesses as a learner so that you can mix and match your learning strategies and resources to best accomplish your learning objectives. Chapter 4 should give you some insights about your learning style.

The resource chapters in Part Two cover the best books, periodicals, professional organizations and associations, professional development programs, and materials like audiotapes, videotapes, data bases, and software for individual professional development. When you begin to look for resources, Chapters 10 through 17 provide a good place to start.

OBJECTIVE No. 1

STRATEGIES/OUTCOMES/RESOURCES

Bob Anderson   August 4, 1987

APPROPRIATE STRATEGIES	POTENTIAL OUTCOMES	POSSIBLE RESOURCES
Collaboration with experienced colleague	Co-design Co-train	Manager Other dept. trainers Local ASTD chapter Other contacts
Networking	Methods that work best	Local ASTD chapter Training contacts in other companies
Outside workshop	New ideas Modeling New contacts	Private and university 1-week courses, conferences (ASTD, TRAINING, etc.)
Reading materials	New ideas Adult learning theory & principles	Dept. library Various publishers

Figure 4. Learning Strategies Worksheet.

Bob's learning plan for one of his objectives is shown in Figure 5.

OBJECTIVE NO. 1

LEARNING PLAN

Bob Anderson   August 4, 1987

OBJECTIVE: To develop my understanding ability and confidence in using at least 5 participatory learning methods by June 30, 1988.

Activities	Target Dates	Resources
Make arrangements with in-house staff for co-design and co-training	Oct. 1	In-house staff
Check dept. library for books on design and adult learning theory—begin reading	Oct. 1	Dept. library
Order catalogs from training and development publishers	Oct. 10	——
Attend or join local ASTD chapter to make new contacts	Oct. 15	Local trainers

Figure 5.   Learning Plan Worksheet.

Activities	Target Dates	Resources
Send for latest training offerings from ASTD, TRAINING, University Associates, NTL, etc.	Oct. 15	—
Co-design a program with an inside or outside trainer	Dec. 15	budget commitment for materials
Schedule one outside program for 1st quarter on next year	Dec. 1	budget commitment
Deliver co-designed program with co-trainer in 1st quarter	Mar. 31	$150-$200
Attend outside program	Mar. 31	$1,200 for fee, travel, & lodging
Review new ideas from program with in-house trainers & incorporate into learning designs	April 5	—
Use new methods as much as possible in 2nd quarter	June 30	—

Figure 5. Learning Plan Worksheet (continued).

After you draft your plan, it's time to meet again with your manager to review this step of the process and obtain the support and commitment you need. The two most obvious review points deal with your time and any budgetary allocations.

Organizational support is often a critical element in your professional development. Granted, you can do a lot on your own, but for certain kinds of development your manager must at least give permission for you to spend the time engaging in the activity, and at times financial resources may be required. The following scale provides a way for you to evaluate the support you are getting or will get for your learning plans.

Organizational Analysis

Resources	Favorable ————————	Unfavorable
Manager's approval	Favorable ————————	Unfavorable
Support and encouragement	Favorable ————————	Unfavorable
Payoffs	Favorable ————————	Unfavorable

Resources may consist of money, equipment, and time. Approval from your manager is critical for many plans. Support and encouragement may come from your manager, your co-workers, others in the organization, or the participants in your training programs. Payoffs may be opportunities to learn, a salary increase, a new title, opportunity to travel, or recognition of your achievements.

If you find that your development is being retarded by lack of support on many of the above points, it may be time to consider changing organizations. If you decide to stay with your present organization while looking for a new position, modify your learning plans to include activities that you can do on your own. Don't let the organization stop you from continuing your development. And when you're looking for a new organization, make support for your continued learning one of your criteria for your new employer.

Step Four: Implementing Your Plan and Monitoring Your Progress

As you begin to implement your plan, it is usually a good idea to check schedules and confirm the availability of any resources needed. If you are counting on others to help with your plan, call to make sure the specifics in your plan fit their expectations.

As you implement your plans, periodically check them to see how you are progressing. This monitoring or pulse-taking gives you a sense of accomplishment and lets you know whether the plan is off schedule or over budget. An individual monthly review and a quarterly review with your manager provides a good opportunity for monitoring your progress. If mid-stream corrections are necessary, this periodic monitoring provides time to make adjustments early rather than waiting until the projected end of the plan.

Step Five: Evaluating Your Results

When you have completed a plan or reach the target date in your learning objective, it's time to review your plan and meet with your manager. You can report your results and evaluate the complete plan as well as check how realistic the target dates and budget allocations were and how well the learning objective facilitated the desired outcome or result. You may have found that you tried to work on too many plans during the period or that the financial resources were inadequate or that you didn't get the support you needed from others in the organization. Or you may find that all went well and you achieved the desired results. The purpose of an evaluation at the end is to ascertain what worked and why (so you can replicate it) and what didn't work and why (so you can make corrections next time). Often this analysis phase of the evaluation focuses only on what needs to be corrected, not the reasons for success. It's just as important to learn from our successes. And it's also a time to pause and celebrate your accomplishments.

The process covered here encompasses one year. Some of you may want to work on two- or three- or even five-year plans. The additional years in your plan are sketched in less detail but provide an outline of your longer-term vision. The advantage of having a multiyear plan is that it enables you to place your more detailed one-year plan in the context of a much longer perspective.

The keeping of a notebook or file for your plans over a period of years provides a record of your professional development over time. You'll get a sense of achievement from reviewing your learning record, and it can remind you of strategies and approaches that worked well as well as some that didn't. Your evaluation notes from other years can also be helpful as you being to plan for a new year.

For Your Continuing Professional Development

American Society for Training and Development. *Models for Excellence: The Conclusions and Recommendations of the ASTD Training and Development Competency Study.* Baltimore: ASTD Press, 1983.

Chalofsky, N., and Lincoln, C. I. *Up the HRD Ladder: A Guide to Professional Growth.* Reading, Mass.: Addison-Wesley, 1983.

Hagberg, J. and Leider, R. J. *The Inventurers: Excursions in Life and Career Renewal.* (2nd ed.) Reading, Mass.: Addison-Wesley, 1982.

Knowles, M. *Self-Directed Learning: A Guide for Learners and Teachers.* New York: Cambridge Book Company, 1975.

Miller, D. B. *Personal Vitality and Personal Vitality Workbook: A Personal Inventory and Planning Guide.* Reading, Mass.: Addison-Wesley, 1977.

4

Assessing Your Learning Style

Leslie Stephen

As you design and execute your professional development plan, you will need to know your strengths and weaknesses as a learner so that you can mix and match learning strategies and resources to best accomplish the goals you have set.

This chapter introduces several different ways of describing and assessing learning style—that is, the typical ways a person behaves, feels, and processes information in learning situations. It begins by describing the research and theories of several prominent authorities on adult learning—Kenneth and Rita Dunn, David Kolb, W. E. (Ned) Herrmann, Dudley Lynch, and Karl Albrecht—and directing you to the assessment instruments based on their work. The chapter also includes a brief survey of other instruments and informal methods for diagnosing your learning style. Finally, at the end of the chapter, a "postscript" suggests ways to adapt the information here to HRD programs you create and conduct for other learners.

Dunn and Dunn: The Five Elements of Learning Style

Rita and Kenneth Dunn (Dunn, 1981; Dunn and Dunn, 1978) suggest that your learning style is based on your response to five categories of "elements"—environmental, emotional, sociological, physical, and psychological (Table 1). Your needs or preferences in each category add up to your learning style.

Take the first element in the environment category, for example, and think about how you respond to sound. When you are concentrating, do you require absolute silence? Are you able to block out distracting noises? Or are you one of those people who cannot concentrate in a quiet setting because the "white," background noise intrudes on your thinking?

Table 1. The Dunn Learning Style Model

Environmental	Emotional	"Elements" of Learning Style Sociological	Physical	Psychological
sound	motivation	self	perceptual	analytic/global
light	persistence	pair	intake	cerebral dominance
temperature	responsibility	peers	time	impulsive/reflective
design	structure	team	mobility	
		authority		

Source: Based on Dunn (1981).

The Dunns' model is a complex, comprehensive picture of the needs and preferences that influence how—or whether—we learn something. It acknowledges that learners differ in their reliance on auditory, visual, tactile, and kinesthetic perception processes; in their orientation to self, peers, and authorities; in the power of their motivation to learn; and in the strength of their sense of responsibility for the results of the process.

It admits that individuals differ in their needs for mobility; in their daytime and nighttime energy levels; in their "intake" needs—do you need to smoke, chew gum, or drink something when you are concentrating? The Dunns' model is unique among the models discussed here in its coverage of various environmental and physical elements of learning style and its recognition that people respond differently to their surroundings in learning situations, especially if what they are learning is complex or difficult.

Based in large part on the Dunns' model of learning style, the Productivity Environmental Preference Survey, or PEPS (Price, Dunn, and Dunn, 1982), is designed to identify and analyze the conditions that encourage your best performance in such things as solving problems, making decisions, and learning. It is concerned with *how* you prefer to learn, not why, and reveals the pattern of needs and preferences that is your learning style.

Your responses to 100 items on a Likert-type scale produce a profile clustered around twenty-one different elements. Sample items from the inventory include "I can block out noise or sound when I work," "The things I remember best are the things that I see or read," "If I can go through each step of a task, I usually remember what I learned," and "When I concentrate, I like to sit on a soft chair or couch."

It takes twenty to thirty minutes to complete the PEPS; you'll have to send in your answer sheet to be computer-scored by the publisher for a small fee. You can order a specimen set from Price Systems, Inc. (Box 3067, Lawrence, Kansas 66044), which includes a manual, inventory booklet, and answer sheet.

Kolb: The Cycle of Learning

David Kolb's (1978, 1984) view is that effective learners need four different kinds of learning abilities—concrete experience, reflective observation, abstract conceptualization, and active experimentation abilities. In his four-stage experiential learning cycle (Figure 6), learning begins with a concrete experience, which is the basis for observation and reflection. Observation and reflection lead to the development or reinforcement of a "theory" that suggests certain actions or behaviors, thereby creating a concrete experience—and so on.

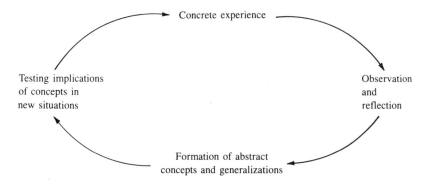

Figure 6. Kolb's Experiental Learning Model.
Source: Kolb (1978, p. 2). Reprinted by permission.

Progression through the experiential learning process demands abilities that are polar opposites, so people develop a characteristic way of resolving the tensions between the concrete/abstract and active/reflective aspects of Kolb's cycle. The extent to which you rely on some learning abilities over others is what Kolb terms "learning style," which he classifies into four types: assimilator, accommodator, converger, and diverger (Table 2).

Table 2. Characteristics of Kolb's Learning Style Types

	Assimilator	Accommodator	Converger	Diverger
Dominant Learning Abilities	Abstract conceptualization and reflective observation	Concrete experience and active experimentation	Abstract conceptualization and active experimentation	Concrete experience and reflective observation
Greatest Strength	Ability to create theoretical models	Doing things and involving self in new experiences	Practical application of ideas	Imaginative ability
Excels at or Prefers	Inductive reasoning and fitting diverse observations into integrated explanation	Adaptation to immediate circumstances	Single correct answer to question or problem	Viewing concrete situations from many perspectives
Stereotypical Occupations	Research, planning	Marketing, sales	Engineering	Counseling, personnel, organization development

Source: Based on Kolb (1976).

Convergent thinkers, for example, rely most heavily on their abstract conceptualization and active experimentation abilities. Convergers prefer to tackle technical tasks rather than social or interpersonal issues; their greatest strengths are in problem solving, decision making, and the practical application of ideas. Divergers have the opposite learning strengths. Their fortes are the ability to imagine and their awareness of meaning and values. In contrast to convergers, they are able to look at specific situations from many different angles, come up with alternatives, and grasp the various implications of an action.

Kolb's model appeals to many adult learners because it explains how people learn not only in "educational" situations but also in the broader sense of adaptation to life. Understanding his model allows you to see learning as a "central life task," one that can expand the scope of your personal and professional development planning process.

Kolb's Learning Style Inventory or LSI (1976) is a straightforward, self-descriptive assessment of an individual's strengths and weaknesses as a learner. It involves rank-ordering nine sets of four words each—for example, *feeling, watching, thinking,* and *doing*—according to which words best and least describe the way you learn.

Your LSI score indicates your relative emphasis on the four learning abilities embodied in Kolb's model of learning style: concrete experience, reflective observation, abstract conceptualization, and active experimentation. Your four scores can be plotted on a graphic profile for comparison with norms collected from a sample of almost 2,000 men and women, ranging in age from 18 to 60, from a variety of occupations. Two additional composite scores are used to plot your learning-style type—that is, whether as a learner you are dominantly a converger, diverger, assimilator, or accommodator.

An LSI sample packet containing one copy of the self-scoring test and interpretation data plus the technical manual detailing Kolb's conceptual model as well as reliability, validity, and normative data is available from McBer and Company (137 Newbury Street, Boston, Massachusetts 02116) at a reasonable cost.

Herrmann: Whole Brain Teaching and Learning

Ned Herrmann (1981, forthcoming) has developed a teaching and learning design model based on new understanding of how the brain works, not only in terms of specialization of the two cerebral hemispheres but also the two lobes of the limbic system. His research shows brain specialization to fall into four distinct quadrants: the cerebral left, which is the domain of logical and technical specialization; the limbic left, which is organizational and administrative; the cerebral right, the integrative and imaginative; and the limbic right, which is emotional and people-oriented (Figure 7).

Almost everyone can be characterized in terms of a dominant quadrant. That is, there is a predictable array of mental processes that we feel most com-

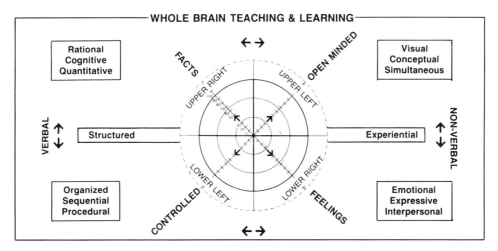

Figure 7. Herrmann's Whole Brain Teaching and Learning Model.
Source: Herrmann (forthcoming). Reprinted by permission.

fortable using most of the time. An equally important finding from Herrmann's research is that we have the ability to learn to use the nondominant quadrants more effectively and thus take advantage of the whole brain.

If your dominant brain function is limbic left—orderly and results-oriented— you will probably feel comfortable and have no problem assimilating new information by working through a self-paced computer program; you would probably learn less efficiently and effectively in an open, small-group brainstorming session. If your limbic right functions are dominant, you are probably a master at using a network of friends and colleagues to collect information about a new project, but would dread digging through stacks of books or doing a data-base search at the library.

If you are after the most efficient, effective way to absorb new information or master a new skill, you will tend to use learning strategies that complement the way your brain processes information best. If you have little choice about the structure of your learning experience, as in many outside workshops, look at it as an opportunity to exercise the other quadrants of your brain. You can also deliberately choose learning strategies that do not match your brain dominance whenever you want to stretch your capacity for learning.

The Herrmann Brain Dominance Profile (BDP) is a diagram that displays your unique thinking preferences in terms of Herrmann's model. The profile is based on the information you provide by completing the Herrmann Participant Survey Form (1984). The survey form is a 120-item self-report questionnaire used to date by more than 75,000 people worldwide and validated with various populations as to its ability to identify and measure an individual's brain dominance characteristics (Herrmann, forthcoming; Schkade and Potvin, 1981).

The survey form includes preference ratings for adjectives or phrases describing yourself and your approach to work and leisure activities. In one part of the instrument, for example, you choose the word or phrase that better describes your-self from such adjective pairs as "problem-solver/planner," "detailed/holistic," "originate ideas/test and prove ideas," "controlled/emotional." The instrument also elicits self-reports on your tendency toward introversion or extroversion, your daytime or nighttime energy levels, and other characteristics.

Write The Whole Brain Corporation (Harvard Square, P. O. Box 1301, Cambridge, Massachusetts 02238) for information on its current fees and services for scoring the instrument, producing the graphic Brain Dominance Profile, and providing an individual interpretation and other information for your professional development plan.

Lynch: Biologically Based BrainFrames™

Dudley Lynch, the editor of *Brain & Strategy* and author of numerous works on brain function research (Lynch 1981, 1984), has developed a "biologically based" instrument that uses the structure of the brain as its basis for describing how humans think. Called The BrainMap™ (Lynch, 1985), the instrument is a whole-brained approach to describing thinking style in terms of the main charac-teristics of the posterior, the anterior, the right, and the left areas of the brain.

The posterior includes the back and lower parts of the brain, the main characteristics of which are the moment-by-moment, automatic handling of real-life situations. The anterior brain, particularly the frontal lobes, houses the ability to plan, to visualize new possibilities, to develop new goals, and to handle com-plexity. The left brain is characterized as verbal and sequential, able to process parts or details in an orderly fashion. The modus operandi of the right brain is metaphorical, analogic thought; it excels at recognizing spatial patterns and nonse-quential information.

The BrainMap™ consists of sixty-three items and takes about thirty minutes to self-administer. The instrument requires you to assign preference ratings to adjectives or phrases to best describe your self-image and your problem-solving, information-processing, and other thought/behavior characteristics as well as your work and leisure activities. The instrument quickly yields four scores, which are plotted on a grid for interpretation (see Figure 8).

The BrainMap™, complete with scoring and interpretation instructions, can be obtained from Brain Technologies Corporation (414 Buckeye Street, Fort Collins, Colorado 80524). A supporting workbook with optional slides, overhead transparencies, and a video tape are also available for group use.

Albrecht: Earth-and-Sky Thinking

Management consultant and author of the popular *Brain Power* (1980), Karl Albrecht has also proposed an appealing scheme, an "earth-and-sky" model of think-

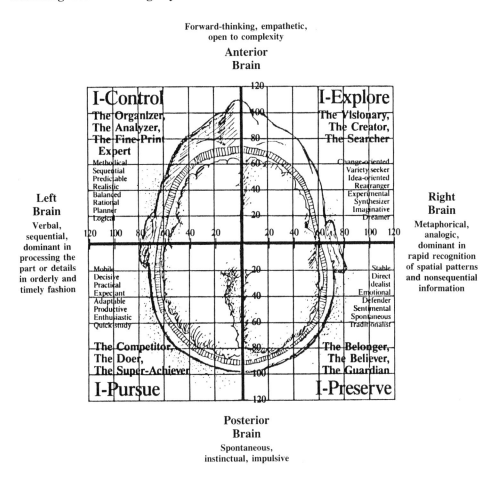

Figure 8. Lynch's Brain Map™.
Source: Lynch (1985, n.p.). Reprinted by permission.

ing style (1983a). Based on our current understanding of brain lateralization, his scheme uses the dimensions of abstract concepts/concrete experience preferences and left-brained/right-brained tendencies to form a two-by-two matrix, making four possible combinations of thinking style. To make these styles easy to understand and remember, Albrecht uses the metaphors "red" and "blue" in combination with "earth" and "sky" to name the cells (see Figure 9).

For example, left-brained thinking is dubbed "blue," since we tend to see analytical people as somewhat "cool," while right-brained thinking is "red" because we tend to think intuitive people have "warm" personalities. Similarly, thinking that is concrete, immediate, and results-oriented is "earth" thinking, while "sky" thinking is imaginary, visual, and conceptual. A blue earth thinker is pragmatic and detail-oriented, likely to focus on here-and-now issues. A red sky thinker has a visionary, global perspective, achieving understanding through synthesis rather than analysis.

Albrecht's self-scoring self-assessment instrument, Mindex (Albrecht, 1983a), is designed to help you understand your characteristic way of organizing and processing ideas. Your responses to 100 self-descriptive statements, rated on a Likert-type scale, produce a numerical profile of twenty different components of thinking style, with each component normalized to a scale of 1 to 100. It takes twenty to thirty minutes to answer the questions and score the instrument. The Mindex booklet also contains a brief discussion of the theory of thinking styles and an explanation of the twenty scales on the profile. The *Mindex Leader's Guide* is a resource kit for doing workshops using the instrument. Both are published by Shamrock Press (1277 Garnet Street, San Diego, California 92109).

Abstract Concepts	Blue Sky	Red Sky
Concrete Experience	Blue Earth	Red Earth
	Left-Brained	**Right-Brained**

Figure 9. Albrecht's Earth–Sky Thinking Styles.
Source: Albrecht (1983b, p. 13). Reprinted by permission.

Other Models, Other Instruments

There are numerous other models and instruments for getting a handle on your learning style. We selected those described below to represent the many others that are equally useful for your personal assessment (see, for example, Smith, 1984, and Zemke, 1984a).

Janet Hagberg and Richard Leider's Learning Style Inventory, published in their book *The Inventurers* (1982), surveys learning abilities from a conceptual framework similar to Kolb's but uses the labels "imaginative," "logical," "pragmatic," and "enthusiastic" for its types of learning styles. The inventory has two sets of fourteen pairs of words or phrases that are rated to describe how you learn best and how you tend to behave in learning situations. Examples: "I learn best by changing as I go," "I learn best by mapping out in advance," "In learning situations, I am prone to analyze by myself," "In learning situations, I am eager to discuss with others." You plot your scores along the feeling/thinking and doing/watching dimensions of a four-cell matrix to arrive at your "most enjoyed learning style."

While Hagberg and Leider's inventory lacks the rigorous research underpinning of Kolb's instrument, it is less abstract and complex—which makes it popular with trainers who just want a simple snapshot of their own or others' needs and preferences. It is quick to take and easy to score, and it produces intuitively valid profiles of certain aspects of learning style. The book also includes a great many useful examples of the way people put knowledge of their learning styles to work in everyday learning situations.

Lane D. Ward (1983) also offers a handy, intuitively valid model by breaking typical adult learning styles into four profiles—the idealistic, the pragmatic, the realistic, and the existentialist (Table 3).

Table 3. Ward's Adult Learning Style Profiles

Type	Credo	Favorite Methods
Idealistic	"You may know what it is, but don't tell me how."	Discovery learning. Inquiry. Brainstorming. Parables. Most self-paced methods.
Pragmatic	"I'm not sure that the laws, rules, and information you give me will really be applicable."	OJT. Coaching. Mentorship programs. Custom-designed simulation, role play, and games.
Realistic	"Let's get on with it. Just tell me what needs to be done and let's do it."	Behavior modeling. CAI. Most programmed instruction.
Existentialist	"There's no one right way. Let me prove myself."	Interpersonal games. Team building. Participant presentations. Most individualized instruction.

Source: Based on Ward (1983, pp. 31–33).

The idealistic learner is an independent reasoner who is usually put off by learning environments or strategies that are highly controlled or structured, preferring exploration and experimentation instead as learning strategies. The pragmatic learner, on the other hand, prefers heavy doses of hands-on experience, believing that learning is relevant only when it takes place in a situation where it is to be applied. "I'll believe it when I see it work" is the credo of this learning style. The realistic learner responds best to efficient, get-to-the-point learning strategies. Typically, he or she is turned off by the intellectualization that idealists thrive on as well as by the group process work that appeals to existentialist learners. The existentialist's learning style is based on the belief that no single way is the right one, that there are many paths to the same goal.

All the writers on the subject of thinking and learning style are careful to stress that nobody fits perfectly into any single classification. People use different styles at different times, and some shift quite easily from one style to another. The best use of these instruments is to identify which style or styles seem to characterize your particular way of processing information and responding to your environment most of the time, so that you can make informed decisions about what strategies to use in your professional development plan.

Postscripts for Helping Others Learn

How can you accommodate individual differences in learning styles and preferences among the participants in training programs you present? There are three areas in which you can have an impact on your participants' learning experiences: designing the program, structuring the learning environment, and managing the participation and interaction of the learners.

Designing the Program

• If you have the opportunity, "pretest" your participants' learning styles before you put your training program together. Often trainers pretest to discover exactly what sorts of information or skills the participants are lacking in the targeted subject, so having them fill out a learning styles inventory at the same time would not be too difficult. If you simply don't have the luxury of this sort of advance pretesting, then you might be able to slip a simple instrument into the first few minutes of your program. You'll have a better idea of the needs of your participants and can adapt your program as you go along.

• Combine the techniques or methods you use to facilitate learning. Depending upon the subject you are covering, you might want to mix short lectures with group discussions, role playing or simulations, paired activities, and solo activities, like completing worksheets, writing out ideas or planning steps, or even just reading and thinking about a handout. If your pretest shows that most of your participants have "realistic" learning-style profiles (from Ward's four-type scheme), then you'll want to include behavior modeling activities and more step-by-step structured learning experiences. However, if your group consists of primarily "idealistic" and "existentialist" learners, you'll need to design the program to include lots of group activities that are more loosely structured and exploratory. Create opportunities for your participants to passively absorb information, by listening to lectures or watching others role play, as well as to actively participate in learning activities.

• Combine various forms of content in your presentation. Again, depending upon your subject and the learning needs of your participants, you'll want to mix abstract theory with concrete facts, details, and examples. Some of your material can be structured so that the participants will have to think inductively, taking specifics and drawing general conclusions from them (the learning style of an "assimilator" in Kolb's model). At other times, you can give the participants the opportunity to reason deductively, looking at an abstract concept and applying it to practical, everyday situations (like Kolb's "converger" and "diverger"). By combining types of information so that your participants are required to both analyze and synthesize, to think in both the abstract and the concrete, you will maximize each individual's learning experience.

Structuring the Learning Environment

• Obviously, you can't provide that favorite easy chair and rock-and-roll music that some people find best for learning, but you can try to ensure that chairs are comfortable, that seating arrangements are roomy, that everyone can see and hear what's going on, and that distracting noises or window views are kept to a minimum. While you're never going to have unanimous agreement on the most comfortable room temperature (someone is always either freezing or burning up), you can still try to keep the thermostat at a moderate setting.

• Some learners need an hour or two of uninterrupted time to feel they've really grasped a subject, while others can focus for only twenty or thirty minutes before they need a change of pace to reflect or refresh their attention. In the structure of a formal training format, like a workshop or seminar, the general rule of thumb is to never go longer than a couple of hours without having a break so people can stretch, move around, visit the restroom, have a snack or a drink, or even just pause and reflect on what they are learning. Provide coffee, juice, soft drinks, and other refreshments if you can—you'll find that overall your group will be much more alert and responsive.

• Because your participants will have different perceptual patterns—some will need to see information in order to understand and remember it, others will need to hear it, and others will need to write it down—be sure to cover all the bases. Have a chalkboard, flipchart, or overhead projector handy to write key ideas and information on. Some trainers tear off flipchart sheets as they are filled and tape them to the walls, so the information is always visible. Also rely on a mix of prepared handouts and notetaking so that both visual and motoric learners have the opportunity to apply the learning skills they use best.

Managing Participation and Interaction

• In any group of participants, you are likely to find big differences among individuals in their desire and willingness to learn what you are there to teach them. In the Dunns' model of learning style, these factors fall within the catetory of "emotional" elements—motivation, persistence, responsibility, and structure. A different sort of pretest that you can give asks about each participant's reason for attending your program—was she "sent" to improve a professional weakness or is your program a reward for good performance, a stepping stone for professional advancement? Is your program "required" by his development plan or is he truly curious about this subject? While you may not be able to increase someone's motivation to learn your subject or his or her sense of responsibility about attending your program, you can accommodate differences by allowing whatever level of involvement an individual feels comfortable with. You can also group and pair various participants for learning activities so that "low-investment" individuals are encouraged to contribute and "high-investment" individuals get the stimulation and quality of learning experience they want and deserve.

• Depending upon the combination of thinking and learning styles among the participants in a training group, from time to time you will need to deal with individual participants who are out of sync with the rest of the group. Perhaps there is one participant who has a more authoritarian cognitive style—a "converger," according to Kolb, or a "realistic" learner, according to Ward. This person may try to dominate discussion or demand that you provide a single "right" answer to a complex question. On the other hand, maybe what you are facing is two or three "blue sky" thinkers (or "assimilators" in Kolb's model) who can't seem to stop analyzing the implications of a concept you have introduced, wasting the class's time by probing farther and farther away from the subject at hand. By recognizing the natural frustrations and temptations that are a part of each person's learning style, you will be able to respond to everyone's needs without shortchanging the group as a whole. For example, you might be able to provide the troublesome "converger" with extra materials—case studies or situational guidelines, for instance—during a class break. Give the group of "assimilators" an extended reading list and arrange to meet with them sometime after the session for more in-depth discussion. In these cases, as well as when participants express frustration during activities that run counter to their natural preferences, you can make everyone's learning experience more meaningful by pointing out these natural differences in learning style and explaining how your program is designed to handle them.

For Your Continuing Professional Development

Albrecht, K. "Earth and Sky: A Meeting of Minds—Getting Through to People with Mind-to-Mind Communication." *Training and Development Journal,* 1983, *37* (10), 70–75.

Dunn, R., and Dunn, K. *Teaching Students Through Their Individual Learning Styles: A Practical Approach.* Reston, Va.: Reston Publishing Division, Prentice-Hall, 1978.

Gorowitz, E. S. "The Creative Brain II: A Revisit with Ned Herrmann." *Training and Development Journal,* 1982, *36* (12), 74–88.

Herrmann, N. "The Creative Brain." *Training and Development Journal,* 1981, *35* (10), 11–16.

Kolb, D. A. *Experiential Learning: Experience as the Source of Learning and Development.* Englewood Cliffs, N.J.: Prentice-Hall, 1984.

Lynch, D. *Your High-Performance Business Brain: An Operator's Manual.* Englewood Cliffs, N.J.: Prentice-Hall, 1984.

O'Brien, R. T. "Blood and Black Bile: Four-Style Behavior Models in Training." *Training,* 1983, *20* (1), 54–61.

"Training Today: Two Brains, Four Styles." *Training,* 1983, *20* (11), 10–17.

Ward, L. D. "Warm Fuzzies vs. Hard Facts: Four Styles of Adult Learning." *Training,* 1983, *20,* (11), 31–33.

Zemke, R. "Cognitive Style: Thinking About the Way People Think." *Training,* 1984, *21* (1), 74–76.

5

Selecting and Learning Through Classes, Seminars, and Workshops

Linda M. Standke

Seminar. Session. Class. Workshop. Program. Course. Institute. By whatever name they are called, these learning experiences offer advantages not gained by using any other kind of learning medium. Although Webster's makes some differentiation among these terms, there is no consistency of use in the HRD field. A seminar may be a piece of a larger event like a convention or conference where an exhibition and planned social events are attended by hundreds of people. Week-long institutes may be offered by a vendor or an academic institution. A consultant may put on a one-day workshop for your entire training staff. Regardless of who makes the offering, your attendance at such sessions can help you more quickly develop the skills needed for future assignments. The words will be used interchangeably throughout the chapter.

Before looking at some of the reasons to build workshops and the like into your learning plan, let's discuss the terms used for the person who will conduct the session. *Instructor, seminar leader, facilitator, teacher, consultant, process consultant, trainer,* and *faculty* are all words used to describe the person leading a seminar. *Vendor* is a term used to identify the company offering the workshop. *Outside resource* or *supplier* are also used to describe a vendor. Words like *facilitator* and *process consultant* tend to imply that the session is very participative. *Teacher* and *instructor* tend to imply that the program relies heavily on a lecture-type method, but these definitions are not conclusive. The terms will be used interchangeably to have variety, not to imply a process style.

Advantages of Classroom Learning

What makes a workshop or seminar so special? Attendance at one certainly costs more than a book, takes more time than listening to a cassette, and requires more work than using a network or mentor. And knowledge gained in the classroom doesn't guarantee that it will be applied automatically or appropriately back on the job. Yet classes are a powerful learning strategy for you to consider as you design ways to meet your learning goals. No other method is as interactive or offers as safe an opportunity to practice in a learning environment. Books can't give you feedback on your ideas and cassettes can't answer your questions. Networking can provide you with information, but you probably can't find someone in your network who will spend an entire day with you while you practice a skill.

Each learning strategy has its own advantages and disadvantages. No one approach is best in all situations. The following listing of advantages should help you determine whether a class or workshop is the best way to fulfill your learning goals. If so, you could also use these reasons to convince your boss that you should attend that two-day workshop instead of reading a book on the subject!

• *You will learn from an expert.* Here's your chance to question, challenge, voice your concerns – the obvious benefits of working with someone rather than on your own. Of course, you could read one of Martin Broadwell's books and learn something valuable about supervisory training. But if you took his course, you could get your questions answered. He would be able to give you advice on what to do within your own organization and other feedback on issues of importance to you. You could listen to his words of wisdom and then put theory into practice in role plays that he observes. And you'd get honest comments about your behavior during class and perhaps in a later follow-up session.

• *You will work with peers.* Exposure to others will help broaden your horizons as a trainer. You'll gain the benefit of new ideas and alternate ways of looking at situations. You will participate in helping others solve their problems before you encounter those problems within your own organization. While you work with this group, remember that you are building a network for the future! Classmates can become valued colleagues with whom to share learning and the applications of ideas.

• *You'll be in a learning environment.* An often overlooked advantage of a seminar is the learning atmosphere away from the office. No meetings, phone calls, drop-in visitors, and other potentially disruptive office routines. You can devote your total attention to the learning process. Whether the session is held in your company's training room or a hotel room or a remotely located conference center, you'll be sitting in a classroom and not at your desk. The room will be arranged to encourage interaction and small-group discussion. Audiovisual aids will most likely be used to illustrate concepts. Materials will be available to use as reference or practice tools. (I'm assuming the session is away from your office. Yet the principles are the same whether the session is in your company training room or 2,000 miles away.) Most seminar organizers even take care of incidental planning such as organizing your lunch and assisting with travel needs so that you needn't spend time or energy on anything but the learning process.

- *You will have time to practice and make mistakes.* Practicing a skill or applying knowledge in an exercise at a workshop is a low-risk way to gain experience before you implement a new skill or behavior back at the office. You'll most likely be able to use a trial-and-error approach on many different methods and procedures to see what works best or feels most comfortable for you.

- *You will have an opportunity to watch the process as well as learn content.* Workshops are a good opportunity to see a trainer in action. He or she can model ways of giving instructions, processing group feedback, handling objections, and presenting technical information. What is said is important for your immediate learning. How it is said is a model for you to watch for future application.

- *You will get a certificate of completion.* Granted, those certificates don't really measure anything more than attendance, and in most cases they aren't meant to. Yet the fact that you did attend is something to tout. Be sure it gets noted in your personnel record. Keep track of the important data for your resume. Attending a seminar isn't proof of learning, but it does indicate that you had exposure to the knowledge if nothing else. It's up to you to demonstrate that knowledge back on the job.

Disadvantages of Classroom Learning

The disadvantages of classes as a learning strategy are mainly those of risk. Even if you complete your background research prior to attending (more on that later), you could still end up in a session that just doesn't suit your immediate needs. Accept the fact that workshops and seminars are designed for the mass market, not you as an individual. Therefore, you won't have any significant control on the content or design of the class.

Going to a workshop is not as easy as taking home a book to read or a cassette to listen to when the mood or time suits you. Sessions may not be available at a convenient time or place. And obviously cost is a consideration. Travel, meals, hotel costs, and other expenses must all be added to the cost of the seminar itself. Another very practical consideration is lost work time. Even if you are able to budget a number of professional development days into your timetable each year, work will still be waiting when you get back. However, the return on your learning investment should be worth the extra hours needed to catch up on your backlog of work.

The Great Seminar Search

Once you've declared your intentions to become a trainer, you'll find your mail multiplying like paper bags behind your refrigerator. The direct mail industry in the HRD field is a booming one—vendors will find you. Join an association or subscribe to a magazine and you'll get on at least a dozen mailing lists. Some trainers object to this glut of direct mail; others regard it as an information source. A comparison of vendor literature will give you an overview (admittedly biased) of courses available, depth of content, focus, price range, and other items. Some trainers have the time and energy (and space) to keep a comprehensive filing system of brochures for future use. Others quickly peruse each item when it arrives and file only those of interest, to be read more carefully when the need arises.

Associations provide another good resource for educational experiences. Consider joining one or more of the organizations and associations listed in Chapter 12. These organizations sponsor national, regional, and chapter events ranging from dinner speeches to week-long conferences. Usually a product directory is published annually and available for purchase without membership fees. Association magazines and newsletters contain advertisements and editorial features describing products and services. Use your network to help you locate and evaluate seminars. Call your colleagues and ask for their advice on the best program to meet your needs. Find out what they have found helpful in their own learning processes. Don't forget to determine what sessions are *not* good. When you are asking for an opinion, find out why a workshop was good or bad, helpful or useless.

An excellent low-risk way to assess a workshop is to attend a preview session, often offered by large companies. This preview is usually a condensed, two- or three-hour version of a longer workshop, costing very little or nothing and presented in major metropolitan cities. Conference sessions presented by consultants are another low-risk source of information, although they will cost more. A conference often employs the best people in the field to make presentations. If you have the time and money, this is a good shopping experience.

Consider subscribing to one or more of the journals and magazines listed in Chapter 11. They rely on advertisers to help keep them in business, so they are a sure source of listings. In addition to paid advertising, regular columns listing seminars and workshops give information on topics, dates, prices, and locations. Product directories or special supplements can usually be purchased separately through the reader services department.

Don't pass up the opportunity to attend a local or national exhibition. An exhibit hall is a gold mine of information for both the new and the experienced trainer. Here's your chance to do some one-stop shopping. You can talk to vendor representatives, see samples of program handouts and media, and compare and contrast products in order to evaluate content. Program designers and leaders may be available to answer your questions and explain their approaches to learning. Plan to bring home a bag or briefcase full of literature and samples.

Your Research Is Just Beginning

When your learning plan has been written and some brochures listing possible course offerings are neatly piled on your desk, it's time to begin the first round of the process of elimination. First, toss or refile any literature describing sessions that don't fit into your budget or time frame. Then read the remaining pieces carefully. Do they appear to match your learning needs? Look for behavioral objectives or learning outcomes that are similar to the objectives in your learning plan. Then toss or refile anything that isn't a good fit at this point in your career. You should now have at least two or three remaining possibilities.

Now for the second round of elimination. No brochure or direct mail piece can accurately cover all the information you'll want to know about a seminar. So where do you get the facts and figures you need? Call the program organizers and ask to speak with either the instructor or the designer or both. A receptionist or registrar may be pleasant and helpful but not able to answer all your questions. Don't be too concerned if someone can't talk to you immediately. But do expect a call back within at least two days from someone who can give you honest and complete answers. If you don't get the information you need, cross that company off your list. An organization unwilling or unable to help a potential client isn't going to do a good job with the real one. Reputable vendors will not see your call as an intrusion and will welcome the chance to do some informal marketing.

Start the conversation by explaining your learning plan. Tell the listener something about youself, your background, your company, and your objectives in attending this course. With this kind of introduction you can expect more suitable and accurate information. And remember that there are no right or wrong answers to your questions.

The following questions are ones that many of us have found useful over the years. They are not arranged in any order of importance. Put them in your own words and add or delete items to fit your needs.

- Are there any recommended readings that would provide helpful background information? (Try to find out whether the instructor has published any articles or books that cover the seminar topic.)
- What theories, models, or practices form the basis of the program? (This can be a tricky question if you have no knowledge or understanding of the answer. Take notes anyway and discuss the data with someone who does know.)
- What is the design format? What is the proportion of small-group work to lecture? How much time will be allocated to discussion, question and answer, practice, feedback? (Ask for a brief overview of the agenda.)
- How many people will probably be in the class? Is there an attendance limit?
- What is the profile of a typical participant? (Will you feel comfortable with this group?)
- What are the program objectives? (Are they obtainable for you?)
- How much information will be covered? (With this question you are trying to determine whether the time allotted to the course is suited to its content. Is a half-day session stretched into a two-day program? Is the information too complex to be adequately discussed in one day?)

- At what level will the information be presented? How is "beginner," "intermediate," and "advanced" defined?
- Is the instructor willing to modify the design/content somewhat in order to meet the group's needs? Is the program totally canned or will adaptation be made on site based on group needs or speed of learning?
- What are the instructor's credentials?
- What is the background and qualifications of the company?
- Is there any preview that I can attend free or at a low cost?
- How will the instructor know I've learned the material? Is there a pre-test? A post-test?
- What kind of feedback on my behavior will I receive during the session?
- What follow-up will be conducted?
- Will someone in the organization (preferably the instructor) be available for help after I'm back on the job?
- What has been incorporated into the design of the session to ensure transfer of training from the classroom to my workplace?
- Is satisfaction with the program guaranteed? If not, why not? If so, how does it work?
- Are there any "hidden" costs for testing or materials?
- Who can I contact for references? (Count on getting favorable responses. They'll be biased, but you can use these sources as another opportunity to get an opinion on the match between your goals and the seminar objectives. You can also ask how past participants applied the knowledge and skills gained.)
- Will I receive sample materials, handouts, or other pertinent information?
- Remember to ask the necessary questions about meals (which meals are included, type of food offered), transportation, lodging, directions, appropriate dress, and availability of recreational facilities.
- Add your own questions to this list.

It's a good idea to take notes of your conversation and review them with your supervisor or someone who can help you make a decision about attending. He or she can advise you if this is a good risk or if you need to continue shopping.

Now you're at round three of the elimination. If the phone interview doesn't generate the answers you need, toss or refile the information for future use. Making a decision among the remaining choices needs to be based on a careful comparison of the seminar objectives and your personal learning plan. Price, timing, and availability may also be deciding factors. Here's a good opportunity to get your supervisor or manager involved. He or she can help you clarify your goals, so you'll get the added advantage of reinforcing your plan with a commitment to your growth.

When you've made your final decision, it's time to mail in the registration form and check and to start thinking about your role as a participant.

Defining Your Goals as a Participant

Your actions in the classroom can maximize your learning experience as well as help contribute to the success of the class. Can you imagine sitting through a program in which no one asked questions or volunteered information? What if one or two people monopolized the conversation and dominated your small-group work?

The instructor has the responsibility to provide you with information and assist in helping you learn. You have an obligation to participate appropriately. Your classmates and the trainer expect it.

Consider making a contract with yourself defining your desired behavior in a seminar. You could make this an informal addendum to your learning plan. The specific kinds of behaviors to list would be dependent upon the session content and format. Here are some ideas:

1. *Give information.* Unless it's considered proprietary, be prepared to give information about your job, your company, and the problems and opportunities in your organization. Knowing your background will help the instructor tailor the class in whatever way is necessary and will give your classmates a chance to learn from you and your experience.
2. *Share your goals and expectations.* Be prepared to discuss your goals and expectations with the trainer and your classmates. Consider bringing extra copies of your learning plan along with you to discuss with others as appropriate. Use your classmates to help you determine how realistic your expectations are and how they compare with those of others.
3. *Participate with an open mind.* You may feel uncomfortable playing a role or taking part in a small-group exercise. These feelings are natural, particularly if you have never taken part in these kinds of activities. This discomfort should cease as you become familiar with the group and see the value of the exercise. Be ready to express your discomfort. Many times this sharing of feelings is an appropriate part of the debriefing period.
4. *Listen objectively.* Reserve your judgment until the instructor has had a chance to make the point. Options, perceptions, and assumptions new to you may be addressed. Allow the material to be completely presented before you decide that it isn't right for you or won't work in your company.
5. *Be willing to make mistakes.* The classroom is the place to practice. You're a learner, remember, not the expert. Your session leader won't expect you to be perfect. After all, if you were, why take the class?
6. *Openly give and get feedback.* State your views if you feel that they are warranted. Be prepared to respond when you are asked to comment on something. Welcome feedback from the instructor and your classmates about your ideas, statements, and behavior.
7. *Take notes, use worksheets, and complete materials.* You probably won't flunk the course if you don't complete the assignments, but you will decrease your

chances of adequately learning the topic. Pat McLagan, a noted authority in the field of adult learning, has written a book that should be mandatory reading for anyone planning to attend a workshop. It gives concrete advice for handling program materials and information and gives suggestions for action planning and note taking. It's called *Getting Results Through Learning: Tips for Participants in Workshops and Conferences.*

8. *Be on time.*   Nothing is more frustrating than waiting for latecomers when you were on time. Why punish people who played by the rules by making them wait? And why go through two sets of introductions or instructions?

We've reviewed items that focus primarily on you and your individual learning. Remember, though, that you are only one piece of the total learning experience. Others in the class will also be looking for feedback, voicing opinions, and making mistakes while they learn. Be courteous and respectful of their needs. Assuming that your instructor is well trained in group facilitation, reticent, obnoxious, and overly eager participants will all be handled in a way that fosters appropriate learning for all. How people are encouraged to participate is a good process to watch. You may find helpful models for your future role as an instructor.

From Trainee to Trainer

Conducting a training session for trainers is a bit like Johnny Carson performing for Jack Benny and Joan Rivers. Both will laugh at his jokes while critiquing his delivery. Every session you attend will present you with models for the delivery—as well as the content—of the seminars you conduct. While you can't expect to become the Johnny Carson of training in just one seminar, you could learn many secrets of his timing and gestures in delivering a joke.

You might find it helpful to take notes on what you thought was effective and not effective about a seminar and how it was presented. It is easiest to do this at the end of a session or during a break if the program lasts more than one day. Then your attention won't be divided between content and process. This simple trick will teach you, for example, phrases to use when dealing with problem participants, questions to ask in order to get good group feedback, tips for using flipcharts, and models for structuring small-group exercises.

Lest you think this is sanction to steal the shop, a few words of caution are in order here. Modeling someone's behavior or style is a sincere form of flattery. Stealing their materials is against the law. Copyright infringement is punishable by fine—and invites ridicule or ostracism by the training community. Save yourself some legal hassle and professional embarrassment. Before you take or adapt anyone's materials for your own or your company's use, check with the author or designer to determine proprietary rights.

As you gain experience in the field, you'll find that your approach to learning in a seminar will be influenced by how you intend to use the material. When you are first getting started, you'll take courses to build your knowledge and skill base—adult learning theory, instructional design, and classroom techniques. As you get more sophisticated, you'll sign up for sessions that teach you how to teach. The first part of the workshop, for example, would focus on performance appraisal theory, proper completion of the forms, and the elements of a good review. The second part would train you to train supervisors on how to give performance appraisals to subordinates.

Seminars can continue to be an important source of learning throughout your career. Keeping up with new developments, meeting with your peers in the field, and acquiring new skills are all good reasons to utilize this learning strategy. And as you become more expert, you'll be lucky enough to conduct training sessions for trainers. An invitation to speak at a national conference or public workshop, aside from being a tribute to your expertise, can give you a whole new learning experience as you face a class of trainers. If that happens, suggest they read this chapter before coming to class!

Tips to Help You Get the Most from Your Learning Experiences

Spending time at an out-of-town seminar, away from family and friends, can be a stressful experience—especially if it's your first trip. Absence of your personal creature comforts—your own bed and pillow, those patched jeans, a cat on your lap while you read the paper—can put you on edge, cause you discomfort, and give you insomnia. Bringing your family along with you or holding the session in your living room are not practical ideas, but here are things that will help make you feel as comfortable as possible. The following tips have become part of my own survival kit over the past fifteen years of coordinating and attending seminars. As you become a more experienced seminar participant, you'll want to add your own items to this list:

1. Dress comfortably. Business attire is usually not mandatory unless you plan to visit a theater or restaurant that has a formal dress code. Check with the program coordinator to find out what is considered appropriate attire for the session, the site, and the season.
2. Wear a jacket or sweater you can don or doff depending on the vagaries of the site's heating and cooling system.
3. Pack your play clothes. You'll feel better if you get some exercise. Take along your jogging shoes and sweats, a swimsuit, a tennis racket. If the program materials don't mention sports facilities, call the site and ask what is available. Use the hotel and/or your program facilitator to help you line up partners. When introductions are being made at the session opener, announce that you are looking for someone to run with, play a game with, or exercise with.
4. Wear and/or bring along comfortable walking shoes—especially if you intend to spend time in the exhibit hall. Most halls have concrete floors that are brutal

to your arches and back. When your feet hurt, you can't think. If you can't think, you can't learn. If you can't learn, you've wasted your time and money. So take good care of your feet. Incidentially, I've seen both men and women in business attire wearing jogging shoes at numerous conferences. No one seemed to find it strange, and many commented that they wished they had thought to do the same thing.

5. Eat sensibly. A sweet roll or doughnut for morning break will taste good but put you on a sugar high that quickly turns into a reverse reaction. Before noon you'll want to put your head down on the desk. The same advice holds true for lunch. A light meal will help keep you more alert throughout the afternoon than the steak, mashed potato, and apple pie special will. Many seminars offer alternatives to caffeine, heavy meals, and refined sugar. If they don't, ask whether these alternatives can be provided. Fruit juices, decaffeinated coffee, whole-grain muffins, fresh fruit, soups, and salads are all desirable options. You may even find it helpful to pack your own lunch on occasion. A can of juice, a piece of fruit, and a granola bar can easily fit into your briefcase.

6. Take advantage of your break time to flex, bend, touch your toes, twist, turn. Get the blood moving a bit. Ease the cramp out of your muscles, and you'll feel invigorated enough to sit until the next break.

7. Smoking is always an issue at seminars, so be prepared to deal with it. If you smoke, be considerate. If you don't smoke, ask to be seated with other nonsmokers. A word of caution: hotels will inevitably place ashtrays on every table in the room. It may be necessary for you to arrange with the program instructor for a designated no-smoking area.

8. Bring along a book, craft, hobby, or whatever works to help you relax enough to sleep well. Napping in class will do nothing to boost your learning speed or promote your professional image!

9. Exercise caution when drinking, dining, and dancing until the wee hours. Late-night excursions can be fun, but be prepared to pay your dues the next day.

10. Resist the temptation to call the office. After all, what can you really accomplish long-distance? Let your staff know you'll respond only in an emergency. Rushing to the phone, trying to do office work during the session, or thinking about your messages instead of the topic will only distract you from the learning process.

11. Pack plenty of your business cards. If your company doesn't supply them, consider having them made yourself. A quick-print shop can usually accommodate you with 500 cards for less than twenty dollars. Remember to take along a special envelope or business-card holder for the cards you collect. Keep this envelope in your purse or pocket and it will always be handy. If you keep cards in one place, you're also less likely to lose them or find them *after* you've done the laundry.

12. Buy a small notebook and pencil to keep in your pocket or purse. When you socialize with other participants, you'll end up talking shop much of the time. Notebooks work much better than cocktail napkins for jotting down information you want to keep.

Postscripts for Helping Others Learn

As a trainer there are several things you can do to help participants get the most from their classroom learning:

• When announcing the program offering (whether public or in-house) provide the class learning objectives in your brochure so that potential participants can check their learning needs against your learning objectives. Stating the instructional methods you will use also gives potential participants an opportunity to match your teaching style with their learning style.

• At the beginning of the class discuss the agenda, learning objectives, and methods so that the course design is clear. Allow time for participants to ask questions and provide input into the course design. If your plan is not going to meet their needs, let them know. This procedure at the beginning of a session ensures that you and the participants have the same expectations.

• At the beginning of the session take a few minutes for participants to write down their individual objectives for the class and their plans to achieve those objectives. They can use the list strictly as a personal guide for their behavior in the session. Or they can share in small groups or with the entire class and thus use the list as a means at the end to evaluate the class and their participation.

• Encourage participants to take full advantage of the learning opportunity. Let them know that you expect them to take the responsibility for their learning by asking questions and requesting information that meets their learning needs.

• Encourage participants to build their networks. Participants likely have similar interests and learning needs. Make them aware that this is an opportunity to make some good contacts for information sharing after the class. Use learning methods that provide an opportunity for participants to share information and get to know each other.

• Build in time at the end of the class for participants to plan how they will use the knowledge or skills they have acquired. Five or ten minutes provide participants time to develop a rough action plan with target dates. Encourage them to meet with their supervisors when they return to work and discuss their plans for using their new skills and knowledge.

For Your Continuing Professional Development

McLagan, P. A. *Getting Results Through Learning: Tips for Participants in Workshops and Conferences.* St. Paul: McLagan and Associates Products, 1983.
Training Marketplace Directory. Minneapolis: Lakewood Publications, annual.

6

Building a Learning Network

Ray Bard and Barbara Peek Loftin

Networking became a social phenomenon in the 1980s. Jerry Rubin was organizing his "networking salons" at Studio 54 in New York. A high-tech CEO network was operating in Los Angeles. Networking was happening all across the country from corporate meetings to backyard barbecues. John Naisbitt (1982) characterized it as a departure from traditional hierarchies and included networking in his ten megatrends.

Although we have become much more aware of networking in the last few years, networking is a human activity that is as old as human history. Anthropologist Virginia Hine has called networking "perhaps our oldest social invention" (McInnis, 1984, p. 9). Only recently has the process taken on a label and made its way into our popular vocabulary. Social scientists are studying networks. Women have been creating networks to counter the "good ole boy" networks. There are special-interest networks for health, ecology, personal growth, education, politics, and economics. And Marilyn Ferguson in her book *The Aquarian Conspiracy* (1980) contends that a worldwide network is transforming society, raising it to a higher level of consciousness. Many networks are now becoming electronic. With personal computers now commonplace, computer networking is growing by leaps and bounds. And almost all of us regularly reach for our Rolodex to send someone to a contact of ours that will help provide the requested information. It's part of our social existence—and an important way we learn, acquire knowledge, and meet people from whom we learn new skills and attitudes. By learning some of the tricks of the trade, you can use networking strategies to help advance toward your learning goals.

Networking for Learning

A network can be described as a system of people connections. Max Gunther (1977) in his book *The Luck Factor* calls networking "the spiderweb structure." Networks are like spiderwebs: a person is at the center with the web going out in all directions. All of us have networks. Some have simple webs with only a few outgoing connections. Others build and maintain complex structures that they rely on for information and support.

There are different networking styles. Some people make a conscious effort to meet the "right" people. They develop a master plan that includes many ways to make contacts. They keep records of telephone numbers, personal interests, and even children's names and birthdays. Their networks are structured according to a plan; nothing is left to guesswork. Others go about it very casually, with no apparent scheme. They just naturally seem to meet people, enjoy exchanging ideas about their personal and professional lives, and remember the right person to call at the right time. There appears to be no system. It just all seems to happen. They know hundreds of people all over the country and can call on them often for information, advice, or a sympathic ear.

These examples represent the two extremes, but lessons can be learned from each. The "natural" networkers enjoy meeting people. They have a genuine interest in learning about the person seated next to them on the airplane or a person attending the same workshop. They use the old standbys of asking questions and active listening. Learning to enjoy people and being interested in their stories is a key element in successful networking. Honing communication skills and using them is part of developing a network. And some record-keeping system is probably needed if a broad-based network is to be developed and maintained.

Starting to develop a more extensive network can begin by becoming more aware that people are learning resources and enjoying the learning opportunities that come into your life, planned or unplanned. Introducing yourself to someone at a meeting or on the phone should become an easy, comfortable act. After all, what is the worst thing that can happen? Someone can seem uninterested, be too busy, or not prove a good contact. Most people welcome the opportunity to meet new people and share information. They are interested in networking, too. Even the apparent bold move of calling someone whom you have not met, introducing yourself, and asking for information or assistance works remarkably well most of the time. Most people like to be thought of as a helpful resource. Some senior professional people have consciously chosen that as one of their roles.

Good candidates for the core of your network are the people with whom you frequently interact—your peers and colleagues, management, subordinates, participants in your training programs, and sales people and vendors. Peers and colleagues are invaluable as both technical and general learning sources. They may provide friendly advice on strategies for implementing a new program in your department or critique a presentation you plan to make. Subordinates often enjoy sharing information about areas in which you have limited knowledge. They may also supply you with invaluable feedback about your actions and behavior. And they can help you learn information about the organization—often advance information—derived from sources that you are not privy to. Contacts with management can yield different approaches and strategies as well as helpful information gained from their experience and position. Participants in training programs can be a source of information about the organization and the specialized functions of their work. Sales people, whether you buy their products or not, can teach you about many areas. You need only to ask questions and listen. They can also be a source for printed material not only about their products but about industry information and trends. There are many types of networking opportunities within our organizations. We have only to be aware of our needs.

There are many ways to develop a more extensive network with other trainers. Joining the American Society for Training and Development (ASTD) is probably the easiest. Many contacts can be made at regional and national ASTD conferences. Local chapters provide an opportunity for meeting others who have similar interest and needs, and the national office offers members several networking-related services.

The national ASTD structure has a council of networks that includes over fifty special networks in such wide-ranging areas of interest as computer-based learning, hospitals and health, brain trainers, retailing, neurolinguistics, and state/local government. By joining a special-interest network you can meet with the group at the national conference and share information with colleagues in the same area. If you can't make it to the national conference or would like to keep in touch with members of the group during the year, the chairperson of the group typically keeps a list of names and addresses for the group and could refer you to some key people. There are also several divisions that you can join for an additional yearly fee. Some of those include Sales and Marketing, Organization Development, and Technical Skills. Check the ASTD listing in Chapter 12 for details about all the divisions and special-interest networks.

The national ASTD office also offers a networking service. The Member Information Exchange Service includes approximately 4,000 members who have joined the exchange and who list five areas of personal expertise. If you would like to talk with someone in a specific area or industry, you may call the national office, which will provide you with three names. Only members can use the service, and each member is allowed two requests a month. Each member of the exchange is limited to one referral per month so that no one gets overloaded.

If there is no ASTD chapter in your city, you can start your own local network with ASTD members from nearby cities or other local trainers. By making a few telephone calls to trainers employed by major area businesses, you could organize a meeting at lunch or after work. Calling a few companies to learn the name of their training officer and inviting that person to a lunch meeting can't be very risky or time-consuming. The worst thing they can say is that they're not interested. And that beginning organizing effort may result in a local network of fellow trainers. The same applies to using the telephone to make new contacts in other cities. Using the ASTD membership directory or just making a few cold calls to trainers in organizations like yours can provide an opportunity to obtain needed information or solve a problem. For example, suppose you are a bank trainer and you call a trainer in another bank in a distant city. If you introduce yourself and ask how a particular situation is handled in that bank, you will probably get a favorable response and at the same time establish a contact with whom you can share information in the future. Sometimes all it takes is knowing what information you need and taking the small risk of asking someone for help.

Networking Etiquette

There is an unwritten protocol, an etiquette, of networking that you should keep in mind. The primary rule is that of reciprocity. Networking is the trading of information. There must be a balance in the information sharing, so you must keep putting information back into your network. If you keep drawing on your network and don't replenish it with information, it will dry up. After a time people will become reluctant to keep giving information if they are not getting something in return. Of course, you may not feel that you have much to offer. That's a normal feeling, particularily when contacting a highly respected person. Just remember that we all have information that is of value. Inventory your areas of expertise and information strengths. Become more aware of your networking assets. When you are talking with someone, become more sensitive to information that might be helpful to the other person and offer to share your information.

Another aspect of networking etiquette is the selective referring of others to members in your network. Sending a person to someone else with your blessing should not be taken for granted. Don't overload a person with others looking for information. After so many calls with the introduction "So-and-so told me to call you," your network buddy may be less of a buddy. A good network is built on trust. Don't violate that trust by sharing privileged information or indiscriminately giving others access to your network.

Record-Keeping

Record-keeping for your network is a matter of personal preference. The most important thing is having the information available when you need to contact someone. It can be arranged in an address book, a card file, or whatever system works for you, but essential information such as name, address, and telephone number is almost a necessity unless a person has a phenomenal memory. Some network experts suggest developing a list of key persons in your profession and making a plan for contacting each person on the list. You may separate potential contacts into subnetworks or areas of expertise. Another suggestion is to code them by immediacy of use: now, soon, or future.

Networking Tips

Here are some tips that summarize the key points about networking:

1. Don't be afraid to take the first step. Become comfortable introducing yourself and taking the lead.
2. After you make an important contact, follow up with a call, a letter, or an invitation to lunch.
3. Maintain your network. People connections need ongoing attention. Remain available for others in the network. Don't be active only when you need help.
4. Join the local chapter of the American Society for Training and Development and other professional organizations that provide opportunities to meet others with similar interests and needs.
5. Make your networking base as broad as possible. Don't rely on only a few contacts.
6. Periodically evaluate your network. You can't keep in touch will everyone you meet. But are you keeping in touch with the key contacts?
7. Remember that networking is like a barter system: you are trading information. Keep up your end of the deal; continue to put new and valuable information into your network.
8. A strong network is built on trust and at times confidentiality. Respect and honor those expectations.
9. Share information in a positive, constructive way. Gossiping and backbiting do not develop a strong network.
10. Don't send hordes of people running through your network. Use discretion when sending someone to a friend for assistance. Don't overload members of your network.
11. Review your present system of keeping track of people in your network. Is the information required to make contact with all the people complete and easily accessible? If not, work on developing a better system, which need not be complex. In fact, the simpler, the better.
12. Have fun. Enjoy each person. The joy of networking is learning new things from all kinds of people.

Postscripts for Helping Others Learn

Here are some suggestions for helping others take advantage of networking:

• Become more aware of each participant in your training programs as a learning resource. Each participant has experience and information that are valuable and can be helpful to other participants and you.

• When you develop a training program learning design, build in networking opportunities. At the beginning of the program encourage participants to add to their network by getting to know others in the class; give participants time to introduce themselves and to make contacts. Don't forget the value of breaks and lunchtime for networking.

• Use learning methods such as case studies, role plays, buzz groups, brainstorming, and other methods that enable participants to work together and discover common interests.

• Encourage people to change groups during the session. Help them make new contacts by forming new groups several times during the session.

• Develop a training module that helps participants develop networking skills.

• Examine the overall structure of your training offerings. Are they primarily short sessions that allow little or no time for networking? Can longer sessions be developed to afford more networking opportunities?

• Make a list of participant names, addresses, and telephone numbers available to all participants at the end of training sessions.

Encourage and provide support for the group to meet after the session to continue as an informal, problem-solving group.

• Add books about networking and networking resources to your training library.

• Establish networking groups outside the formal training program. Your organizational needs assessment may identify needs that can best be met by having people share expertise and information through informal networking groups within the organization.

For Your Continuing Professional Development

Barrett, J. *Joys of Computer Networking*. New York: McGraw-Hill, 1984.

Glossbrenner, A. *The Complete Handbook of Personal Computer Communications: Everything You Need to Go Online with the World*. New York: St. Martin's Press, 1983.

Lipnack, J., and Stamps, J. *Networking: People Connecting with People, Linking Ideas and Resources*. New York: Doubleday, 1982.

Smith, L., and Wagner, P. *The Networking Game*. Denver: Network Resources, 1980.

Welch, M. S. *Networking: The Great New Way For Women To Get Ahead*. New York: Warner Books, 1980.

7

Learning from Role Models and Mentors

Barbara Peek Loftin

As a novice trainer, you may find that learning from a knowledgeable and seasoned pro is a rewarding strategy in your professional development plan. Your learning style may be "pragmatic" or "realistic" by Ward's (1983) four-style scheme. That is, you may prefer concrete experience before theory, working in pairs rather than alone or in groups, behavior modeling, and immediate feedback. This learning style provides an efficient and practical way to learn approaches to training. It includes both learning theories and techniques for program design and facilitation. You can also broaden your understanding of the ins and outs of the training profession. And you will develop relationships that will prove personally and professionally rewarding long after you have "graduated" from protégé to master trainer.

This chapter takes a look at two basic forms of learning "one on one"—from role models and from mentors. Throughout our lives we find people who are outstanding in some way and make them our role models, learning through imitation. As a strategy for professional development, you can take this natural process one step further by consciously identifying respected figures in the HRD field and patterning your style or approach after theirs. A strategy that is more personal and that has more potential for boosting your career is to find a mentor, someone who has reached a stage of profesional maturity and can serve as your adviser, ally, and friend. Your relationship with a mentor can be informal, growing out of a common interest and affinity between the two of you, or it can be part of a formal, institutionalized program in your company. However it develops, this form of apprenticeship can grow with you, continuing to provide you with valuable learning opportunities for many years.

Role Models

One way to think of role models is as "silent" mentors. Like silent partners, they provide the means for your success without getting involved in the day-to-day nitty-gritty of achieving that success. Since childhood, you have unconsciously and consciously imitated people whom you admire—parents, friends, athletes, teachers, club leaders, employers. As a professional, you may look up to one or more managers or executives who exemplify leadership and success in your organization. Or there may be several outstanding members whom you admire in your local ASTD chapter or another professional association.

Think of people who fit the image of what you would like to be, those who represent standards you would like to adopt. As you are considering possible role models, here are some benchmarks to help you evaluate and select those who might serve you best:

- Look for a role model who seems to have power or clout.
- Notice the person who is able to turn problems into opportunities.
- Identify someone who can spot opportunities early.
- Study those who are willing to take risks.
- Find people who have insight plus the ability to plan meticulously rather than act precipitously.

To expand the role-model method of career development, you can look outside your particular organization and community to discover on a national scale those thinkers and doers who are recognized standard-bearers in the field of HRD. As you become more familiar with the big names in HRD—both the "granddaddies" of the field and the "comers" in the following generations—you'll begin to find some who interest you in a special way. Perhaps you are fascinated by the subject in which they are experts. Or perhaps you find a special elegance in the theories they have developed or the solutions they have proposed. Or perhaps you have seen them in action—at a podium or in a classroom—and were exhilarated by their energy or style or responsiveness. Whatever draws you to such a role model, trust your instincts; you intuitively know who has the most to give you at your current stage of development.

Once you have identified a role model for yourself, you need to put that individual to work for you. For a role model in your organization or community, it may mean getting to know him better by observing his behavior and listening to what others have to say about him. You will need to be clear on what characteristics you want to emulate. Is it his career trajectory? His subject expertise or training speciality? His personal style in the classroom or the boardroom? Define what he has that you seek for yourself, then do your best to follow in his footsteps. This may mean seeking positions and industry experience similar to his, or pursuing the same type of education, or even imagining and mentally imitating his way of judging situations and responding to people.

If your role model is a national figure, you can begin putting him to work for you by reading everything he has written. And read what others have written about his work and ideas. See what you can discover about his career history by inquiring among more experienced trainers or reading *Who's Who*. Find out whether he has produced any audiotapes, videotapes, or films—if so, try to get your hands on them. And, of course, if he is still actively making presentations at conferences or seminars, do your best to attend them. By becoming an expert on the work of your role model, you are making that person's success a solid building block in your own career development.

Nevertheless, it is important to remember the limitations of the role-model relationship as a learning strategy. Role models are not mentors; your relationships with them are not typically personal, although you may be personally acquainted with them. Rather, your relationship is with their ideas, talents, wisdom, and work. The role models we select reflect our values as well as our interests, our talents as well as our goals. As you expand as a professional and continue to develop your career, you will find that your vision of yourself changes and, with it, your choices of role models. Typically, you won't sever your relationship with a previous role model; it's more likely that you'll simply direct your focus elsewhere.

Mentors

The term *mentor* comes from the name of a character in Greek mythology and originally meant "wise one" or "adviser." Through the years the word has taken on a generic meaning—someone who excels in a particular subject or skill and takes an interest in guiding and instructing a less experienced, usually younger person. Only in recent years has mentoring been redefined from the point of view of those concerned with management development as a label for a specific type of business relationship. From this point of view, mentors are counselors, confidants, protectors, allies, and sponsors. Some call them godfathers (or godmothers). Edgar Schein (1985) describes a mentor as a developer of talent and an opener of doors. The term connotes adopting the stance of a kindly parent interested in the long-term well-being of the protégé or "mentee" (a term recently coined and popularized in the business literature). In business, it particularly suggests giving advice, sharing contacts, and using influence to oversee the career development of a promising young friend.

The variety of labels for mentors reflects the diverse nature of their activities. Good mentors are, first of all, godfathers. They give their protégés advice on goals and how to achieve them. They give them technical instruction. They develop their social-management skills and organizational skills. They provide inside knowledge about tricks of management. In short, mentors teach their protégés. But that is only the beginning. In addition, mentors counsel their protégés on their problems. They supply feedback on tactics for handling people and on solutions to problems. They give support and help build self-confidence by encouraging their protégés with pep talks. Mentors also run interference for their protégés. They watch for opportunities that will contribute to a protégé's progress, and they advise their protégés on how to make the most of such opportunities. Finally, good mentors often put their own heads on the block for their protégés. They recommend them for more responsibility, for promotion, for the paths to higher-level careers. They provide visibility, risking their reputations in the process. Herein lies the key responsibility of a protégé—performing in such a way that it reflects positively upon the judgment of the mentor.

Finding a Mentor

You probably have never given much thought to choosing a mentor, but you have probably had at least one in different situations throughout your academic and professional life. Try to identify past or present mentors in your life. Think of actions they have taken (or failed to take) on your behalf. Unless you currently have a "working" mentor—and a satisfactory one, at that—you may want to begin looking for one.

Remember that a mentor is both a transient in your multifaceted career and a potential lifelong friend. Find someone you believe will fulfill your expectations as a listener; someone you respect who will help you solve your problems, discover your skills, and develop and influence (but not determine) your plans and goals; someone who trusts you and has faith in your judgment and abilities; someone who respects your autonomy and individuality and won't try to remodel you into a carbon copy of himself or herself; and, finally, someone who will serve both as a resource for information and contacts and as a public promoter of your career. This is a tall order. However, with effort and patience you can find and cultivate a mentor who will not only meet your needs but also benefit from the relationship personally and professionally. You may find your mentor within your company or your community, in professional organizations, at meetings or conferences, at your local college or university, or even among family and friends.

Women often have special problems in finding and cultivating mentors. Typically, they must seek out male mentors, since appropriate female mentors are scarce. However, cross-gender mentoring presents dilemmas for both the male mentor and the female protégé. Each must be clear about the nature of their developing relationships, and both need to be prepared to deal with the sometimes suspicious attitudes and overactive imaginations of those not involved in the mentoring effort. Read *The Mentor Connection* (Zey, 1984) for an especially insightful view regarding the mentoring of women who are building professional careers.

What You Can—and Can't—Learn from a Mentor

What you can learn from a mentor depends upon your situation: What is your position in your company—newcomer or old hand? What is your mentor's position—is she in the same company? If so, is she in the same department? How many levels above yours? If she is in another department, how closely do the two departments work together? If she is in another company, what is her role there? Her status? Does her company have dealings with yours? If so, how close? Is she acquainted with your supervisor or others higher up? Does your mentor have direct experience in training and development or responsibilities in a broad range of human resource areas? Or is this person directly involved with neither and employed as a line or staff manager in another area? And then, of course, there are questions regarding your career goals and the developmental paths you have identified for yourself, subjects discussed in Chapters 2 and 3.

While it's hard to specify exactly what you can learn from your mentor, here are some general guidelines about what to expect:

- Stories about what has worked and not worked for your mentor and for your mentor's colleagues in the past.
- Tips about what to watch for—and watch out for—in planning, selling, implementing, and evaluating training and development programs.
- Suggestions about sources of more information on a subject.
- Informed opinions about new theories or techniques.
- An overview of how your work fits into the department and how the department fits into the company (the implementation of mission and goals).
- Tips on handling difficult situations—with your supervisor, with colleagues, and with program participants.
- Alternative solutions to a problem you are facing.
- Guidance on how to round out your professional competence and how to solve personal development problems.
- Affirmation of your particular strengths and special abilities.
- Inside information about what's happening in the company and who's making it happen.
- Inside information about what's happening in the HRD field and who's making it happen.
- Tips on what to say or do to improve your professional standing in your department or company.
- Rules of business etiquette.
- Introductions to important or useful business associates.
- Warnings about people or situations that could threaten your progress.
- Advice about what steps to take next in developing your career.

Despite the broad scope of knowledge that you can expect to acquire from a mentor, there are some things that are simply not within the mentor role. Foremost among these is specific, in-depth knowledge about an HRD subject or technique; your mentor is not meant to be used as a tutor but rather as an adviser or guide. Likewise, your mentor is not a coach; don't expect her to observe you in action, give immediate, detailed feedback, and then model the appropriate performance behavior for you. The most valuable things that your mentor has to offer will most often be general and intangible, such as support, insight, and hunches. Treasure them for what they are—you aren't likely to find them with much consistency elsewhere.

What Your Mentor Can—and Can't—Expect from You

As with any important relationship, there must be reciprocity between you and your mentor. By the nature of the mentoring process, the principal benefits will be yours; however, you have responsibilities toward your mentor, benefits that you must be conscientious about providing. First among these is your loyalty. Just as your mentor serves as your ally, you must serve as his. Show solidarity— do not criticize him but rather defend him against the criticism of others and find opportunities to talk about his accomplishments and successes. Another of your obvious responsibilities is discretion. During the course of your discussion and conferences, your mentor will probably reveal sensitive or confidential information about people, projects, and politics in your organization and other organizations. Because your mentor has entrusted you with this knowledge, guard it carefully. Never give him cause to regret confiding in you. Likewise, you also have the responsibility of being completely open and aboveboard in confiding in your mentor. Keep him informed about what's going on in your area and what you have heard through the grapevine. Don't keep secrets; don't hide your true thoughts and feelings; and don't say or do things that you don't sincerely mean in order to manipulate a situation. If you do not feel you can trust your mentor, then you have the wrong mentor and should begin searching for another. Finally, remember that your performance reflects upon your mentor. If he has recommended you for a special assignment or introduced you to an influential contact, make extra efforts to perform well, even (or perhaps especially) if you aren't sure how your career will benefit.

While your mentor can reasonably expect a great deal from you in return for guidance and support, there are some things that are not part of your role as protégé. For example, he should not ask you to do anything that would compromise your loyalty to your supervisor or manager, nor should he ask you to perform work that ought to be carried out by his subordinates. Likewise, if you notice that your mentor often requests that you do his dirty work—such as spying on his political adversaries or feeding certain information into the company grapevine—then you should seriously question the relationship. Finally, your mentor should not impose his career ambitions upon you or expect you to follow in his footsteps or fulfill his unfulfilled dreams. If your mentor does not encourage your individuality and work with you to help you achieve your own fulfillment, then again you should begin to seek out someone truly interested in your success and well-being.

Formalized Mentoring

So far we have been considering informal mentoring, the somewhat spontaneous development of a special helping relationship. However, a number of companies have institutionalized mentoring programs. Linda Phillips-Jones, author of *Mentors and Protégés* (1982), describes these programs as "arranged relationships." They are mainly for the purpose of indoctrination: to enhance a newly hired or promoted employee's understanding of the organization. They also help the organization spot good candidates for advancement as well as identify those managers and executives who are good "spotters." As a side effect, these programs also aim to raise the level of company loyalty and reduce turnover.

These formal programs are found among numerous companies and in the government sector as well. Companies with outstanding formalized mentoring programs include Bell Labs, Hughes Aircraft, Leo Burnett, Bank of the West, Federal Express, and Merrill Lynch. Their programs are set up so that sponsors and trainees are given prescribed amounts of time to pursue each phase of the mentoring process or discontinue their relationship. Specified goals are to be accomplished, and set activities are to be followed. Often several mentors are lined up in advance for the entering candidate, each with responsibility for guiding him or her through a particular stage of development. The Internal Revenue Service and the U.S. Department of Agriculture have outstanding formalized mentoring programs, although they go by other names. The IRS refers to mentors as "coaches" or "sponsors," while the Department of Agriculture calls them "senior advisers." In these programs protégés are called "trainees," "interns," or "candidates."

Companies like Jewel Tea Company have adopted the mentoring concept formally, yet have made a special effort to retain the spontaneous nature of informal mentoring relationships. At Jewel all senior executives are encouraged to have protégés, but rather than being assigned a candidate, they select their protégés themselves. Most companies that have a mentor system put much time and effort into matching mentor and protégé. They take steps to ensure that participation on both sides is voluntary and that both the protégé and the mentor are satisfied with being paired.

Nevertheless, there is no question that formalization of mentoring reduces the intimacy shared by mentor and protégé, an element that has worked well to support many informal relationships. George Odiorne (1985), who is recognized for his management-by-objectives work, views mentoring's rapid growth in the 1980s as a result of EEO actions and other efforts to accelerate groups left behind — women and racial and ethnic minorities. Used in this way, mentoring has departed from the essential meaning of the word, since it eliminates what some call the "infatuation" stage and is no longer expected only to serve the mentor's and protégé's natural goals. Rather, it has become a tool for accomplishing a preconceived set of organizational purposes. James G. Clawson (1985) describes these programs as "compartmentalized mentoring" and suggests substituting different programs that would center on the workplace rather than trying to emulate the mentor philosophy. He sees the concept of "coaching" by supervisors as more useful. Perhaps what is expected of the mentor determines what is intended by the use of the term "mentoring."

If you are joining an organization, find out whether it has a mentor program and make sure that you will be included in it. Explore the program's features. Ask questions of those who interview and hire you and of any other members of the organization with whom you interact. Discover how much latitude you have to select your own mentor. Also be sure to seek explicit answers to questions about the organization's expectations regarding what your mentor will provide and whether the program has "phases." If you would have more than one mentor, find out how long you would be mentored by each. Delve into the purposes of the program—is it strictly for career development, or is there a hidden agenda for resolving a problem situation in the organization (with EEO, for example)? Find out all you can before accepting the job.

When you have become a protégé within a formalized mentoring program, take full advantage of the opportunity. Learn all that you can from your mentor or mentors, but also notice what each seems less able to teach you or do for you. Observe the negative results of your mentoring relationships as well as the positive. If you should feel that the experience is not proving productive for your career, you have three choices: resign your job, seek out another mentor, or turn the situation itself into a learning experience that you can pass on to protégés of your own someday.

Drawbacks and Pitfalls of Mentoring

A mentor relationship, whether informal or formalized, can go awry in any number of ways. Here are only a few of the negative effects you should watch out for:

- An unsatisfactory mentor can cause what Zey (1984) calls the "black halo effect." That is, the ineffectiveness or unpopularity of the mentor can rub off on the protégé, hindering rather than helping his or her career.
- An unsuccessful protégé's reputation can reflect on the mentor and give a bad name to the mentoring program or the mentoring concept in general.
- Mentor-supervisor competition, conflict, or jealousy can reduce the benefits to the protégé. The mentoring program may undermine supervisory authority.
- Political situations within the organization can have negative effects on both the mentor and the protégé.
- Peer resentment can cause discomfort for protégés.
- "Crown princes" among protégés—those selected as outstanding—may develop attitudes of superiority and increase peer resentment.
- Overdependence of protégés on mentors can actually inhibit their growth and development.

- Lost contact with mentors following promotions or other career moves can change relationships and render the mentoring process less useful, thus lowering protégé morale.
- Mismatching, a big risk under formalized programs, will probably produce negative results.
- Feelings of being trapped may eventually overcome either protégé or mentor. That is, when one of the two perceives the relationship as having outlived its usefulness, it may be very difficult for that party to dissociate from the other. This can be particularly devastating in a cross-gender mentor relationship.
- Mentoring can be limiting. According to Kathy Kran (1984), sometimes those not identified for inclusion in formalized mentoring programs are simply not developed within the company.

Making the (Inevitable) Transition

Just as you can psychologically and professionally outgrow a role model, you can—and will—outgrow your mentor. The estrangement can be slow and subtle, or it can happen relatively quickly when major changes happen in one or both of your lives. The most natural shift is from protégé to peer: as you develop greater expertise in your specialty and more interpersonal and organizational competence, you will tend to turn to your mentor less frequently. Another possibility is that you may discover that your professional interests and goals are moving away from those of your mentor, causing the two of you to drift apart. Transfers and job changes, particularly if they involve moving to another city, also put an inevitable strain on the mentor-protégé bond (and remember, it can as easily be your mentor's career change as yours). And, awkward as it may seem, sometimes a change in your relationship can result from finding another mentor, one who seems better suited to your interests, needs, and goals.

Parting ways with your mentor typically involves little more than shifting the balance of your involvement toward the friendship underlying your relationship and away from the advisorship/sponsorship. You may continue to meet for coffee, but rather than asking your mentor for suggestions about how to handle a problem, you spend your time together discussing your accomplishments of the past week or your plans for the weekend. If one of you is changing departments, companies, or even cities, the change in your relationship may be more marked. No longer part of the same environment or operating within the same system, time and distance will cause the bond to atrophy gradually; you may have friendly feelings toward each other but simply not the time or opportunity to stay closely in touch.

Unfortunately, sometimes the change in your relationship with your mentor may involve some breach of trust or betrayal, real or perceived, on either side. If your parting is marked by anger or bitterness, you need to strive to behave with dignity and fairness. Remember the many benefits that the relationship has brought to you in the past. Refrain from criticizing your former mentor to others, and do your best to maintain civil, if not friendly, interaction. Most importantly, look at the situation as one more valuable learning experience gleaned from the mentoring process.

Postscripts for Helping Others Learn

Here are some things you can do to help others benefit from the mentoring concept:

• Purchase books on mentoring for the training library and make them available to company employees. If the company has a newsletter or other means of communicating with its employees, include an article about mentoring and highlight relevant books and magazine or journal articles.

• Add a module about mentoring to your training program offerings. A class that would introduce mentoring as a learning strategy could be built around the structure of this chapter.

• Establish a mentoring program in your company. Read the books and articles about mentoring and research other company programs (start with the names provided in this chapter). Build a model that you think would be successful in your company. Prepare a proposal for management to review and approve. Start small and expand with your success.

For Your Continuing Professional Development

Collins, N. W. *Professional Women and Their Mentors: A Practical Guide to Mentoring for the Woman Who Wants to Get Ahead.* Englewood Cliffs, N.J.: Prentice-Hall, 1983.

Kran, K. E. *Mentoring at Work: Developmental Relationships in Organizational Life.* Glenview, Ill.: Scott, Foresman, 1984.

Levinson, D. J. *The Seasons of a Man's Life.* New York: Knopf, 1978.

Phillips-Jones, L. *Mentors and Protégés.* New York: Arbor House, 1982.

Zey, M. *The Mentor Connection.* Homewood, Ill.: Dow Jones–Irwin, 1984.

8

Developing Effective Study Skills

Linda Webster and Anne Durrum Robinson

In his landmark book *The Adult's Learning Projects* (1979), Allen Tough reported that adults take on an average of eight different learning projects a year, for an annual total of 700 hours. Self-directed study and research—following your own curriculum at your own pace—may very well be the core of your professional development plan.

What you study, of course, depends upon your interests or your job. How you study, on the other hand, depends upon a combination of your learning style, your educational resources, and your pocketbook. If you seem able to absorb what you hear more easily than what you read, then you may seek out audiotaped materials rather than books. If verbal explanations leave you in the dark—you need to see an idea in action to really comprehend it—then you'll make the best use of visual media (video, film, slides) rather than either tapes or books. If a structured sequence of learning steps with lots of feedback on your progress appeals to you, then maybe computer-assisted instruction (CAI) will be the most productive strategy for you to follow.

Whichever approach seems appropriate for your learning style, you're faced with the challenge of finding the information you need in the medium you want—which the library and computer data-base research sections in this chapter and the resources listed in Part Two are designed to help you do.

However you prefer to tackle your self-directed learning projects, you're going to need to organize yourself, sharpen your mind, and hone your study and research skills in order to get the best return on your time and energy investment, whether you put in 700 hours or only 70.

Getting Organized

Space Management

We all learn best in settings that fit our individual personalities – those that reflect our particular learning styles and preferences.

As a learner, you should create the type of learning climate and space most suited to you. You are seeking a nurturing, encouraging setting. If comfort is your goal, design your study space as a comfort zone. If cleanliness and beauty motivate you, do a bit of housecleaning first; set a vase of flowers and a bowl of fruit nearby; situate yourself by a special painting or near a window with an inspiring view. If you learn better when things are not too structured and orderly, don't plant yourself rigidly at an immaculate desk. If you find untidiness distracting, don't flop into the nearest upholstered chair, staring at a sinkful of unwashed dishes.

If you are planning a regular program of home study, you may discover that you need to have a special work area, a space devoted to study. Your study space doesn't have to be a separate room, nor does it need to be particularly large, but it should be comfortable (according to your personal standards of comfort); it should be roomy enough to hold your study materials and supplies; and it should allow you the privacy and freedom from distraction that you'll need to concentrate.

What are the advantages of having a study space? You don't waste time gathering together your study materials every time you need them. Also, you're less likely to be forced to contend with people walking through to get to the refrigerator or sitting down next to you to watch television – you have designated your study "turf," declaring that space off-limits to others while you are working. You're also likely to discover that your concentration improves when you condition yourself to associate productive learning activities with one particular place. Finally, you convey a subtle (or perhaps not so subtle) message to yourself – and to your family, friends, and co-workers – that your professional development is important to you and that you take your learning program seriously.

Time Management

Once you have made space in your life to study, you'll have to face the issue of making time. Whether you are comfortable with very little structure and organization or have found that careful planning and scheduling are absolutely vital for your self-directed learning, you will need to establish some sort of objective to reach within some sort of time line. Whether it's as loose as "I want to finish this book within the next two months" or as tight as "I will read twenty-five pages every day," this mental organization will enable you to schedule your learning project in a way that is productive for you.

Managing your time begins with assessing your personal "clock." Are you a day person or a night person? Do you wake up with a clear mind and lots of energy, or are you sharpest after dinner and the news? Schedule your study time to take advantage of your natural peaks of energy and attention. The same holds for deciding upon the length of your study periods. If you usually need half an hour just to get into your material, then using your lunch hour to study won't be very productive—you'll need to schedule two- or three-hour blocks of study time to really get the most out of your development plan. On the other hand, if you are the type who can focus and concentrate quickly, then you can be more flexible in mapping out your study schedule.

If you are adding a study project to your weekly schedule, be sure to take into account other priorities and necessities in your life—family commitments, work, adequate sleep, time with friends, leisure time—and make adjustments so that you don't neglect what is important to you. If you do, you will either resent the time you spend on your learning project—which may affect your concentration or even your capacity to absorb and understand information—or neglect your project for your real priorities.

Getting the Most from Yourself

Concentration

You've had a hard day at work. Or you're worried about your teenager. Or maybe you're not really that interested in what you're studying. How do you cope with the constant and competing demands for your time, energy, and attention?

Before you begin your study session, there are a number of things you can do to improve your concentration. First, decide how long you will study and what you will accomplish. Then remind yourself how this work fits into your overall personal and professional development goals and visualize yourself accomplishing these goals. Then visualize yourself in your study space, accomplishing your objective for this session within the time frame you have given yourself. At the same time, use a self-coaching statement about your ability to concentrate, something like "My attention is focused and I am completely absorbed in the material I am reading (or hearing)." Finally, do some basic organizing to reduce potential distractions as much as possible: put the cassette player and all the tapes you plan to listen to within easy reach, make sure your highlighter pen hasn't dried up, and turn on your telephone answering machine.

After you get started, you can improve your concentration by being an active learner. Active learning techniques will be covered more fully in the sections on memory, reading and listening, and notetaking; however, the basic principles are important enough to repeat here:

- Think about what you are studying—preview the material beforehand and then mentally review it periodically.
- Repeat key facts or ideas to yourself.
- Generate mental pictures to graphically illustrate the information to yourself.
- Question and analyze any evidence or logical arguments presented.

Our minds often wander because we are reading or listening too slowly, so try pushing your eyes more rapidly down the page (or computer screen) or increase the speed of the audiotape (cassette players are available with adjustable controls). Also, use your book or workbook while you read or listen—highlight or underline material, write comments in the margin, take notes.

If the material is particularly difficult or challenging for you, take more frequent breaks and give yourself rewards for accomplishing smaller tasks. Whether the material is hard or easy for you, if you find your attention wandering, remind yourself of your intent to concentrate: "Never mind the noise. I've got thirty more minutes to study." "I'm ready to stop daydreaming about my vacation and get back to studying for fifteen more minutes." "Come on, now. I'll study a little faster, and my mind will stop wandering." Don't reward yourself for daydreaming by taking a break when your mind wanders; work rapidly for a short time, then take a break to reward yourself for regaining your concentration.

What you do during your breaks also affects your concentration. Staying too long in one position saps both your physical and mental energy. Your body becomes stiff; your brain becomes dulled. Without sufficient stimulation, your attention wanders, your concentration fades, your memory weakens. So don't let yourself go longer than about one hour or one and a half hours without moving around. Stretch, do some aerobic exercises, go for a walk. At the same time, give yourself a change of scenery—go outdoors if you can, or at least go into another room. You may want to change your mental scenery, too, particularly if you're in the middle of a large block of study time—read a magazine article or the newspaper, call a friend for a short chat, even indulge yourself in that daydream about your vacation. After these physical and mental excursions, repeat the visualizations and self-coaching statements that you used to start the session. Then begin studying again.

Keep in mind that, no matter how much you practice maintaining concentration, you will always have days when it will be hard for you to concentrate, when distractions in your environment or your head keep your mind unfocused.

Memory

Short-term memory is a low-capacity, short-term holding tank for new information—it can hold about seven items (like a telephone number) for only fifteen to twenty seconds. Unless you intentionally move the information into long-term memory, you'll forget it quickly. Here are some useful strategies for making that transfer, no matter what your thinking and learning styles are:

- Employ "chunking." Seek out any possible patterns in the material and cluster pieces of information together according to those natural logical or verbal similarities. Create patterns if none are obvious. For example, let's say you have just finished reading a description of performance appraisal that you need to remember. Here is the original, taken from

Effective Motivation Through Performance Appraisal (Lefton and others, 1980): "Performance appraisal differs from ordinary feedback and coaching and counseling in five ways: (a) More preparation goes into performance appraisal. (b) Appraisal covers more ground; it focuses on all of a subordinate's performance for a period of several months, whereas ordinary feedback and coaching and counseling zero in on one performance (or a few at most) or on part of a performance. (c) Appraisal usually takes longer, because it covers more ground. (d) Appraisal usually take place wherever the superior and subordinate happen to be. (e) Appraisal is the most structured of the three methods; it follows a carefully organized format" (pp. 9–10). You could use chunking to remember these five characteristics of performance appraisal by reducing their meaning to single words or phrases that have similar grammatical structures—more preparation, more ground, more time, more office (or more formal), more structure.

- Repeat the fact or idea to yourself—or write it down—immediately after learning it. This is not rereading a page or replaying a tape but saying the information to yourself without cues. In the case of the information about performance appraisal, you might cover the page and see how many of the concepts you can explain.
- Turn the new piece of information around, making it into a question, then answer that question by restating the information. You might ask yourself, "How is performance appraisal different from ordinary feedback and coaching and counseling in regard to time?" Your response would then be, "It differs in two ways. First, the time frame of the employee's performance—months instead of weeks or days. Second, the time frame of the appraisal interview—because more performance is being considered, it takes longer to discuss."
- Ask yourself how this information fits in with what you already know. How is it like or unlike other concepts; how does it support or contradict other facts? Anchor the new information by linking it to old information. If you have studied feedback, for example, you might note to yourself that while good feedback is given at the earliest opportunity after observing performance, performance appraisal cannot meet that criterion, since it addresses many actions over several months' time.
- Sleep on it. Review your notes before going to bed and then again when you wake up. Your unconscious and conscious minds will work together to implant the new information in your long-term memory. This is particularly useful when you are studying for an exam or preparing for a presentation—like your first training program on performance appraisal for supervisors.
- Use mnemonic devices as memory aids to hook the new information into your long-term memory. Mnemonic devices elaborate upon information

and dress it up in some way that makes it more memorable. Typical mnemonic devices include catchwords or catch phrases, acronyms, rhymes, tunes, rhythms, and visual images. For example, you might help yourself remember the five aspects of performance appraisal by (1) turning your "chunks" into an acronym—PGTOS—and then using the phrase "More Pig Toes" to trigger your memory; (2) using your "chunks" to create a saying, like "If I don't prepare the ground in time, my office won't have any structure"; (3) creating an image in your mind that includes the five pieces of information expressed visually—such as a supervisor sitting in her office, with a clock and a calendar on the wall behind her, along with a plaque saying "Be Prepared," while she is building a Tinkertoy structure on her desk (maybe the letters P and A). Mnemonic devices can be as silly and absurd as you like—whatever helps you to remember.

- Finally, try to use the information in your regular day-to-day activities, at work or at home. When you tell your son he did a good job mowing the lawn, recall to yourself that you are giving him ordinary feedback and that a performance appraisal would involve sitting down in the living room after dinner and discussing, in addition to yard work, room cleaning and garbage takeout over the past three months.

Study Skills

Reading Skills

Reading is our main avenue for learning. Even if your thinking and learning styles predispose you to listening (to lectures or audiotapes) or viewing (slides or videotapes) as the best way to comprehend new information, you'll probably have to spend more than 50 percent of your self-directed learning time with books and journals. Improving your ability to read for comprehension and retention will help you get more from your study sessions. One technique that is particularly helpful is known as SQ4R—a mnemonic device that stands for Survey, Question, Read, Record, Recite, and Reflect.

First, *survey* the material before reading. Take about fifteen minutes to read the book jacket (if there is one), the title page, the introduction and preface, the table of contents, chapter headings and section headings, boldface and italicized words in the text, any illustrations and graphic material, the chapter summaries or conclusions, any review questions at the end of each chapter, and any lists of references or suggested readings. Surveying is a mental warm-up that helps build a structure or framework into which the new information will fit (which will make it easier to remember).

Next, ask *questions* to focus your attention and generate interest. Why are you reading this journal article or book chapter? Consider what you want to find out, what you want to learn from this material. Turn chapter titles or headings into questions to be answered as you read.

Once you are familiar with the structure and scope of the book or article and have clarified your purpose, *read* with attention and concentration. In addition to using the concentration techniques explained earlier, you can enhance your concentration by not stopping when you come across especially difficult material or unfamiliar words. Keep your momentum going — simply mark these words or sections and keep reading. Information presented further on may clear up your question, but if not, you can take advantage of a natural stopping place or a break to pull out the dictionary, translate poorly written passages into "English," or analyze the complex concepts that had you baffled.

As you are reading, *record* important facts and ideas that you want to remember. If the book or journal isn't yours, you can use one of the various forms of note taking explained later in this chapter. Otherwise, add your own personal markings to the printed page — underline, highlight, or number key points; draw brackets, vertical lines, arrows, and asterisks; write questions, comments, and summaries in the margin. But don't overdo it. Be selective in marking only the most important terms and phrases. This is the most common mistake people make, forgetting that, at review time, they won't be able to distinguish key information from that which is simply helpful or interesting.

Stop reading whenever you reach a saturation point and *recite* the most important points to yourself. This may be after only two or three paragraphs of difficult material or after two or three pages of easier reading. As explained in the memory section earlier, transferring information from short-term to long-term memory involves making an active effort to remember. Think about what you've learned and paraphrase the key points out loud or in writing.

Finally, take the time to *reflect* or elaborate on what you've read by thinking of examples, possible applications, and your personal experience. Consider how the new information relates to your own ideas and other material you have learned. Use mnemonic devices or note-taking techniques to anchor the information in your memory. You can even draw diagrams or flowcharts, storing the information in both right and left sides of the brain, one verbal and one pictorial.

Obviously, you won't read every book or article you pick up with such intensity. In fact, an important reading skill to practice is reading for different purposes and at different speeds. Rapid reading is efficient and effective for easy material, for times when you don't need high recall, and for skimming more difficult material to find specific information or to review. Typically we read about 250 to 350 words per minute for light reading, about 200 to 250 words per minute for medium to difficult reading, and 100 to 150 words per minute for very difficult reading. If you are interested in testing your reading speed and comprehension, contact your local community college, college, or university — its counseling center, student services office, or continuing education office can direct you to the testing services available. You may decide to take a speed reading course, or you can use the following suggestions on your own to increase your reading rate (and, not incidentally, improve your concentration):

- Try not to vocalize words as you read them. Often without realizing it we move our lips and throats as we read, as if we were speaking, or we "say" the words silently in our minds. This is an unfortunate by-product of the way we learned to read in the first place—by following along as our parents and teachers read aloud to us and by reading aloud in class.
- Move your eyes continually forward, taking in more than one word at a time. Keep pushing, pushing, pushing. At first you may miss something, but you will soon discover that your comprehension can keep up with the more rapid pace you have set for yourself.
- Try to focus on "chunks"—phrases, lines, sentences—rather than each "bit" of information—words. Use your peripheral vision to take in the information surrounding the spot where your eyes are actually focused. Use the more global, space-perceiving skills of your right brain to enhance the sequential, linear operating mode of your left brain.
- Keep pushing forward. Don't allow your eyes and attention to circle back to earlier words or lines. If you realize you don't comprehend something you've just read, then it is likely that you were reading too slowly (and were, therefore, bored and distracted) rather than too quickly. Maintain a forward-moving pace that demands your full attention.

Listening Skills

Just as we become distracted if reading too slowly, our attention also starts to wander if we must listen too slowly. Our minds can process the spoken word at rates of from 400 to over 800 words per minute, but people speak at only about 120 to 180 words per minute. If you are using audiotapes as your learning tool, the simplest solution to this dilemma is to rent or purchase a speech compressor or rate-controlled recorder. These machines can slow down or speed up an audiotape while controlling for pitch distortion (so that you won't get a "chipmunk" effect at higher speeds). However, if you are learning from a videotape or film or attending a live presentation, you need other strategies.

Many of the concentration, memory, and reading-comprehension techniques explained previously apply to effective listening as well. Essentially, what you must do to get the most benefit out of listening as a learning strategy is to use your spare mental processing time to actively think about what you are hearing. Here are some suggestions for effective listening:

- Preview the material—by going over any descriptions, outlines, or supplementary readings or exercises—before you begin listening to the tape. Then, as you listen, anticipate each new point or conclusion. Prepare yourself to hear what you are listening for.
- As you are listening, do more than take notes—ask questions about the material. These questions can range from a simple "What does the speaker mean by *intervention*?" to broader inquiries like "How does this team-

building intervention technique fit in with what I learned about job enrichment last week?" or "How can I integrate behavior modeling into team-building activities in order to meet the learning style needs of Ward's 'realistic' learners?"

- Actively weigh any evidence presented, testing it against your own common sense as well as other knowledge you have acquired. Consider not only whether the facts are accurate or true, but also whether they have been interpreted without glaring bias and whether conclusions drawn are reasonable.
- Take the next step and think of ways the ideas and information can be applied.
- Visualize what you are hearing. Imagine yourself conducting a team-building workshop, see the initial resistance of some participants, and then see yourself using the techniques you are hearing about to process their resistance.
- Finally, as with reading, review the material regularly, repeating key items aloud, rereading your notes, and perhaps even typing them.

Note Taking

The sort of note-taking system you use depends on two things: your preferred thinking style and the purpose of your study. What are you reading or listening for? Concepts, facts, themes, new ideas, or evidence to support or refute an argument? The traditional outline form of note taking uses indentation and letters, numbers, or dashes to indicate major and subsidiary ideas. However, there are three other techniques that you could find useful for recording and organizing information so that it is easy to understand and remember: fact-principle notation, the Cornell note-taking system, and whole-brained note taking.

To use the fact-principle notation system, draw a line down the middle of your notepaper, then label one column "Facts" and the other "Principles." As you read or listen, write generalities, laws, rules, or doctrines in the "Principles" column; write statistics, actions, events, findings, or observations — any piece of information that is verifiable — in the "Facts" column. For clarity, you can number the principles with roman numerals and the facts with arabic numerals. You can also draw lines between facts and principles to show relationships or write the arabic numbers of pertinent facts in parentheses under the principle they support. The "Principles" column is a handy place to write comments and questions as well.

The Cornell note-taking system was developed by Walter Pauk, director of the Reading-Study Center at Cornell University. It is based on what he calls the "Five R's" of note taking: record, reduce, recite, reflect, review. The latter three "R's" were discussed in the previous sections on memory and reading/listening skills. Recording and reducing information is a useful way to make note taking a form of learning. As in fact-principle notation, you divide the page into two columns; however, in this case, the right-hand column is about twice as wide as the left. The right-hand column, "Record," is for taking down information as you read or hear it. The left-hand column, "Reduce," is for summarizing and generalizing the blocks of information taken as notes. With the recall step, you boost your learning in several ways—simply by considering the information again, you reinforce it in your long-term memory; by summarizing or generalizing the information, you transform it to a more abstract form of knowledge, linking it into patterns or systems of thought (which also embeds it more solidly in your memory); and by writing your summaries on a separate area of the page, you simplify the process of locating and reviewing information in the future. You can scan the left-hand column to find the material you are looking for; you can use the generalization to trigger recall of the specifics that support it; or you can focus on either the general or the specific, depending upon what your purpose is.

You can use this note-taking system to compensate for weaknesses in your thinking style. If you typically focus primarily on facts, then generalizing facts—putting them in a large intellectual context—will help you discover themes and relationships between ideas that otherwise might not have occurred to you. On the other hand, if you naturally think in terms of principles and generalities, then your mastery of a subject will be enhanced by continually reminding yourself of the connections between those broader concepts and the specific evidence on which they are founded.

The basic idea of whole-brained note taking is to capture thoughts, ideas, and impressions as they occur to you—with your individual thinking style, fund of knowledge, and memories—in a form that is organic rather than "unnatural," like outlining or the other verbal-linear note-taking methods included in this section. The whole-brained technique goes by many different names—mind mapping, clustering, thought trails—but the principle is simple and straightforward. Draw a box or circle in the middle of the page and inside it write your subject or central theme—like "Program Design" or "Coaching." Then, from this central axis draw lines and branches outward as you record connected chains of information and ideas. Use words, brief phrases, and symbols/images rather than sentences to convey meaning. You can color-code related items by using colored pens or pencils and make connections by drawing arrows between items or bubbles around groups of items.

Whole-brained note taking is a global rather than a linear approach to organizing information. No "first-second-third" order is forced on your mind when you go back over your notes; instead, your attention can move "horizontally" or "circularly." And because you record information graphically as well as verbally, you engage your right brain as well as your left brain in learning and remembering. This technique can also be used for reflecting and problem solving—using a process of free association—as well as recording notes. Because whole-brained note taking is very individual and obviously very different from other note-taking systems that we have been trained in, you may find it confusing in the beginning. But the more you work with whole-brained note taking, the more facile you will become and the more readily you can adapt the system to your own uses.

Using the Library

Whether you're searching for the classic text on andragogy to expand your understanding of how adults learn or seeking out a recent issue of *Training* for the latest techniques in program design, using libraries successfully is no less than essential to your professional self-development program. But using libraries well is more than just knowing how to use a card catalogue, reference books, or abstracting services—it involves developing a search strategy.

Before you even set foot in a library, take time to plan your search strategy— you'll locate more useful information, in less time, with much less frustration. Begin by answering these questions:

- Specifically, what information do I need? (You might want to write a brief description of your topic to help you focus your thoughts.)
- How soon do I need the information?
- Where am I most likely to find this information? (For example, would it be in recent journals, books, newspapers, reference materials?)
- Do I want nonprint materials like microfiche, audiotapes, photographs? If so, what type?
- What library in my community is likely to have this information?
- Do I know a librarian who has expertise in this area?
- Would a computer search be effective for this topic?

Your chances of finding "just the thing" are increased when a logical search plan is combined with intuition and serendipity.

If you need to review basic library research skills and general reference books, you may want to look over either Bell and Swidan's *Reference Books* or Todd's *Finding Facts Fast*. In addition, there are several specialized guides to library research in training-related fields that you might find valuable: Lavin's *Business Information*; McInnis's *Research Guide for Psychology;* and Woodbury's *A Guide to Sources of Educational Information*. Finally, Barzun and Graff's *The Modern Researcher* is an excellent in-depth manual on doing research and writing up the results. These resources and others are listed at the end of the chapter.

And don't forget to take full advantage of the services offered by the library staff. Librarians are trained to find information and materials quickly. Their job is to help you clarify your research needs and consult with you on the most effective research methods. They are more familiar with what's in the library than anyone else, and they probably know about other libraries and other librarians who can assist you. They can often refer you to knowledgeable faculty and staff at the nearest college or university or experts in the community who share some of your interests. In addition, they generally keep track of community organizations, services, and activities.

How do you find a librarian to work with? Usually you will want to contact a librarian in the reference department or information services department of the main library—not a branch library, unless it is a specialized branch of a university library. If you want to consult with a reference librarian regarding a research project or for guidance the first time you use the library, arrange a personal meeting when he or she is not scheduled for reference desk duty. This will give you time to discuss your research thoroughly and to get better acquainted. You will probably find at least one or two librarians in your community who share some of your interests and who have specialized skills in unearthing the information and materials that you need. Librarians enjoy networking, too, and take pride in being able to make your work easier for you.

Using Computer Data Bases

On-line data bases can provide an avalanche of information—to your local library as well as your home or office. With computer access, you can find the information you are seeking much more quickly and thoroughly than with tradition research methods. In fact, sometimes the information you need is available only through data-base searching. Most data-base searches produce a bibliography of references on the subject of your choice—books, journal articles, and research reports. Some data bases provide statistics, and a few have the full text of the item you want to read. Especially in complicated searches with a number of key subject terms, the computer can screen literally millions of items and select only those that match your request.

Many of these on-line data bases are available at an academic library, a community college library, or possibly a large public library near you. A reference librarian will interview you about your information needs and then conduct the search for you. You pay for the amount of time the data base was used (based on a fee charged by that specific data base, from $25 per hour to $125 per hour), telecommunication costs, and the costs of printing the information or references you want ($.10 to $1.00 each). Generally, a search takes about fifteen minutes.

The Basics of Data Bases

A data base is a computerized catalogue of information—perhaps comprehensive in scope but often covering only a narrow range of topics. Data are stored in a large mainframe computer, probably hundreds of miles away. You access the data from a terminal or microcomputer connected to the mainframe computer by telephone lines. In addition to your computer terminal, the only equipment you will need to conduct a data-base search is a modem to connect it to the mainframe computer and a printer. Your expenses will also include a data-base subscription fee, an hourly charge based on the amount of time you use the data base, and sometimes communication charges for use of the telephone lines.

Most data bases are supplied by distributors that provide a variety of data bases. Two of the major distributors are Bibliographic Retrieval Services (BRS) and DIALOG Information Services. You can request catalogues from these distributors for more information on the large number of available data bases (addresses and phone numbers are included in Chapter 16). The encyclopedic data bases available from BRS and DIALOG have been designed for professional searchers, so to use them effectively you'll need to spend time learning and practicing the special search language and search strategy required. Since they are much more expensive to use than the more general information utilities—as much as $100 an hour—you probably won't have the luxury of leisurely browsing for information.

Data-base suppliers can help you become a more effective searcher. All major suppliers put on workshops and training sessions at various locations and offer user manuals for purchase. They provide free connect time or only nominal charges for their practice files—subsets of regular data bases that you can access to improve your search techniques. Many provide free access to new data bases for the first two to four weeks. And they have a toll-free telephone number for answering questions.

Both BRS and DIALOG have data-base services geared to the home market. BRS/After Dark and Knowledge Index are available at reduced rates during evenings and weekend hours. BRS/After Dark is easier to search than BRS because it uses a special software interface to prompt users and help the search go quickly. Knowledge Index includes twenty-three of DIALOG's more popular data bases. New information utilities—The Source, CompuServe, and Delphi—are designed primarily for home use. In addition to international and national news, shopping catalogues, travel and entertainment information, and business and financial data, they provide full texts of encyclopedias and references to magazine and journal articles in selected fields. Delphi provides access to DIALOG's 200 data bases. It also has a service called "Dear Oracle," which allows users to ask questions to be answered by other subscribers.

Another service you may be interested in is SDI (selective dissemination of information). SDI is a monthly updating service available from libraries with computer searching or directly from data-base distributors. You indicate what topic(s) you want updated, then the computer prints out references to all articles matching your subject profile that have been added to the data base during the previous month. You pay for each printout, but the number of items will usually not be large and the price should be less than for a regular search.

If your primary interest is newspaper articles, you can use Dow Jones News/Retrieval for business, financial, and investment data from *Barron's,* the *Wall Street Journal*, and the Dow Jones News Service. The New York Times Information Bank provides both the full text and summaries of the *New York Times* as well as summaries of nine other major newspapers, business magazines, international news sources, and science and news magazines. For the latest information from specialized newsletters, NewsNet includes newsletters from technical fields, different industries, business and finance, high technology (video and computers), legislative developments, and funding sources. You can get summaries of information on your topic, or you can read the full text of the newsletter.

Designing and Implementing Your Search

Computerized searching is called for when your topic combines two or three key terms, when your topic would be difficult or time-consuming to search in regular indexes, or when you need a comprehensive review of the literature. For example, the computer can list all materials about training women managers for executive positions. It can further list only those articles published since 1980 in the English language. However, a list of all materials ever published on executive development would run to hundreds, perhaps thousands, of items—obviously much too broad a topic for computer searching. Likewise, if you want only a few articles published on executive development in the last year or so, simply check the *Business Periodicals Index* rather than launch a computer search. A librarian who does computer searching in an academic library or a large public library can advise you on what to expect from a computer search on your topic.

To prepare for your computer search, answer these questions:

- What information do I need?
- How much information do I need—about how many articles?
- What are the key words, including synonyms, related terms, and alternative spellings? Are there terms that I want to exclude?
- Are there important authors who have written on this topic?
- Do I want to limit the search to English-language works?
- What years do I want to search?
- Do I want to print titles only or abstracts as well?
- Do I want to print the references on-line (more expensive but immediate) or request an off-line printout to be mailed to me within one week?
- Do I have a maximum cost for the search?

Probably the most important step in preparing for a search is identifying the key words to use. To help you select key words, many data bases have a thesaurus of subject headings. To assure that you are using the major data-base headings, select your terms from this list. Most data bases allow you the flexibility to extend your search beyond the subjects found in the thesaurus—including words that might appear in the titles of articles (called free-text searching). The advantage of free-text searching is that it allows you to locate new terms (like "interactive video" or "mentoring") that are commonly used in the field but may not be in the thesaurus (which often uses older terminology).

When you have answered all the search design questions, you are ready to begin. Here is the procedure for the actual search:

- After logging on to the service, select the data base that fits your subject area. Be sure your printer is turned on so that you can have a record of the results of your search.
- Enter the key words and tell the computer how you want them combined.
- Limit the search by date or language, if desired.

- The computer will give you the number of references that match your request. Tell it to print out the references it has found.
- Request a printout of abstracts or summaries of the references that look interesting—or you can request an off-line printout of results of the search and have it mailed to you.
- Request photocopies of the entire article or publication, which will be mailed to you at an additional charge. Or you can borrow these items from a nearby library or request them on interlibrary loan.

You can expand your search by running it on a number of different data bases using the technique for cross-data-base searching available from the major distributors. When you get your results, save the printouts in case you want to do a similar search later on.

A Special Note About Electronic Classes

On-line classes are becoming more and more available. The National Education Corporation (315 Post Road, Westport, Connecticut 06880) and the Electronic University of Telelearning Systems, Inc. (505 Beach Street, San Francisco, California 94133), are two of the primary electronic classrooms. Through its EdNet System, the National Education Corporation offers more than forty independent-study courses, including courses on computer literacy, management principles, and accounting. The Electronic University serves all age groups with both nonacademic and academic courses, ranging from the liberal arts to the social and physical sciences.

Postscripts for Helping Others Learn

As you design and present training programs, you can integrate many of the techniques presented in this chapter into both the content of your program and the instructional methods you employ. Sometimes all or part of a training program will be devoted to one of these skill areas. For example, communication training often covers listening skills; memory improvement is a popular workshop subject; and the whole-brained method of note taking is frequently included in programs on creativity and problem solving. You may even find occasion to present workshops on reading skills and library/data-base research techniques.

Most often, however, you will probably incorporate your knowledge of study skills into training programs on other subjects, either directly through instruction or indirectly through program design. Here are suggestions for helping program participants improve their study and research skills:

- Provide mini-lectures on concentration, memory, reading, listening, or note taking, following up with practice or warm-up exercises to prepare workshop participants for a challenging session—one in which the material is particularly "meaty" or difficult.

    • Unless you are purposely aiming for inductive, experiental learning, always preview each segment of the program by telling participants what topics are going to be covered and what methods (lecture, film, role play) will be used. Then regularly review both the material you have presented and that which you presented earlier, linking each segment to the others in a clear and logical plan.

    • With audiovisual presentations, be even more specific in previewing the material, telling participants what to watch and listen for. If possible, select audiovisual materials that are designed with breaks for discussion and problem solving.

    • Provide handouts that also serve as study worksheets—giving topic headings, key terms, and perhaps important definitions or explanations, but also requiring participants to write in definitions, summaries, supporting facts, and other information. This is another way of previewing the material you will cover and letting participants know what information will be stressed.

    • Boost participants' retention of the material you are presenting by actively employing the memory-strengthening techniques you know. Use "chunking" to phrase important concepts; use mnemonic devices—like absurb visual images, silly rhymes, or acronyms—to hook into participants' imaginations; link new facts or concepts to other related material that participants might be familiar with; ask questions about the implications of a fact or the application of a theory; give examples—and ask participants to give examples—of how ideas or information you are presenting may be applied back on the job.

    • Use the different notation systems to write information on the flipchart or blackboard as you make presentations or lead discussions. If your subject requires clear distinctions between broad or abstract ideas and the narrower or more concrete pieces of information that either support or arise from those ideas, then fact-principle notation might clarify those relationships for participants. On the other hand, the whole-brained method of note taking might work well for a brainstorming/problem-solving activity or perhaps as a technique for presenting complex, nonhierarchical information.

    The following materials will provide you with more ideas and exercises for teaching learning skills: Devine's *Teaching Study Skills;* Diekhoff's "How to Teach How to Learn"; and Smith's *Learning How to Learn*, which are listed below along with other resources.

For Your Continuing Professional Development

Adler, J., and Van Doren, C. *How to Read a Book.* (rev. ed.) New York: Simon & Schuster, 1972.

Apps, J. *Study Skills for Adults Returning to School.* (2nd ed.) New York: McGraw-Hill, 1982.

Barzun, J., and Graff, H. F. *The Modern Researcher.* (4th ed.) New York: Harcourt Brace Jovanovich, 1985.

Bell, M. V., and Swidan, E. A. *Reference Books: A Brief Guide.* (8th ed.) Baltimore: Enoch Pratt Free Library, 1978.

Buzan, T. *Use Both Sides of Your Brain.* (rev. ed.) New York: Dutton, 1983.

Devine, T. G. *Teaching Study Skills: A Guide For Teachers.* Newton, Mass.: Allyn & Bacon, 1981.

Diekhoff, G. M. "How to Teach How To Learn." *Training,* 1982, *19* (9), 36–40.

Edelhart, M., and Davies, O. (eds.). *OMNI Online Database Directory.* New York: Macmillan, 1985.

Glossbrenner, A. *The Complete Handbook of Personal Computer Communications: Everything You Need to Go Online with the World.* New York: St. Martin's Press, 1983.

Lavin, M. R. *Business Information: How to Find It, How to Use It.* Phoenix: Oryx, 1987.

Lefton, R. E., and others. *Effective Motivation Through Performance Appraisal.* Cambridge, Mass.: Ballinger, 1980.

McInnis, R. G. *Research Guide for Psychology.* Westport, Conn.: Greenwood Press, 1982.

Rico, G. L. *Writing the Natural Way: Using Right-Brain Techniques to Increase Your Expressive Powers.* Los Angeles: J. P. Tarcher, 1983.

Rubin, C. "Touring the On-Line Data Bases." *Personal Computing,* 1984, *8* (1), 82–95, 196.

Smith, R. M. *Learning How to Learn: Applied Theory for Adults.* Philadelphia: Taylor and Francis, 1984.

Todd, A. *Finding Facts Fast: How to Find Out What You Want to Know Immediately.* Berkeley, Calif.: Ten Speed Press, 1979.

Wolf, F. I., and others. *Perceptive Listening.* New York: Holt, Rinehart & Winston, 1983.

Wolvin, A. D., and Coakley, C. G. *Listening.* Dubuque, Ia.: William C. Brown, 1982.

Woodbury, M. *A Guide to Sources of Educational Information.* (2nd ed.) Arlington, Va.: Information Resources Press, 1982.

9

Tapping Your Inner Resources and Learning from Yourself

Anne Durrum Robinson

Living organisms continually use feedback as an inherent part of their survival systems, but this mechanism is at times forgotten by the highest living form. Most of us simply don't take full advantage of the learning that can come from our experience. We stay so busy with our daily affairs that we don't stop to examine what is happening to us so that we can benefit and make adjustments in similar future situations. Nor do we routinely tap our full complement of inner resources for learning.

This chapter surveys several ideas and techniques for getting the most learning from your experience and for making better use of your innate wisdom and creativity to spark changes in your knowledge, attitude, and behavior. From simple reflection at the end of the day to mind-calming and visualization techniques that require practice in order to achieve mastery, the tips in this chapter may be of particular interest if you tend to be self-reliant and reflective in your learning style or if your learning goals lie in the realm of values, attitudes, or insights.

Reflection

In experiential learning theory, reflection on one's experience is what really starts to move the cycle of learning forward. It is not difficult to build this simple but effective strategy into your learning plan.

Reflection can be as simple as an impromptu pause at the end of a workshop session when you look back on the day to identify new platform skills that the workshop leader used. Many people who have learned the value of reflection supplement such impromptu episodes with regular feedback sessions with themselves, using the calendar or major events in their lives to schedule their reflection time.

You can schedule a pause for reflection daily, monthly, quarterly, yearly, or whatever. Some people have built a daily pause into their lives, almost a ritual; they take some time alone at the end of each day to review the day or at the beginning of each day to plan for the day ahead. Birthdays and New Year's provide a traditional time for review. In our organizational life there is the annual performance review and the periodic revision of our professional learning plan.

The other opportunities to review our experience and learn from it turn on events in our lives. If you get a new assignment or promotion, review the events leading up to it and analyze them for learnings. If you are conducting your first class for management or are using a new training method, plan some time at the end of the event to collect all the data you can to review what happened. This time of evaluation should focus not only on the things that did not go as planned but also on the things that did. It is important that we learn how to replicate our success as well as how to correct our mistakes.

Keeping a Journal

An invaluable ally in learning from yourself is a journal. Journals have four important uses in the learning process: to save information and ideas obtained from others; to express emotions and reactions; to stimulate creativity and ideas; and to develop insights.

In order to enrich your self-teaching as much as possible when filling the pages of your journal, keep in mind the following suggestions:

- Select surroundings (light, temperature, formal or informal settings) that suit you best.
- Write at times best suited to your schedule and temperament—whether you are a "day" or "night" person.
- Emphasize your reactions to auditory, visual, kinesthetic, or tactile stimuli.
- Explore your own motivations.
- Record your reactions to self, peers, authorities.
- Report on concrete experiences.
- Reflect on your observations.
- Describe changes in your thinking.
- Chart actions that you intend to experiment with.

Naturally you won't use your personal journal to record all the information you're covering, nor will you try to capture all your observations from a particular learning experience. But do record gems of thought, impressive quotations, needed formulas, and conclusions you have formed. In your private writing, unlike the classroom, you may feel much freer to compare and speculate, to postulate theories, and to question authorities (even to poke a little fun at some of the more pompous ones). A journal also frees you to acknowledge that something you've learned has moved you deeply or produced great exhilaration. In the confidential pages of your own book you can be open and honest about any of your thoughts, emotions, or reactions. If you want to encourage your insights, jot down any intuitive flashes that may come to you. Get down key words to help you recall them. Date them; and then check later to see what the outcomes were.

A journal can also be a consistent prod to your own creativity. Keep a set of colored pencils handy and record in words and/or pictures your ideas (even half-formed ones), fantasies, dreams, peak learning experiences, and mental wanderings . . . or wonderings, too, for that matter. To help your right-brain resource, make your journal as visual as possible; you needn't be a budding Michelangelo to add colorful illustrations or symbols to your words.

If you want more guidance on unleashing the full power of journal keeping for your personal learning plan, consult the work of Ira Progoff, who designed what he calls the Intensive Journal, which is described in his book *At a Journal Workshop*. Two other volumes that can be helpful to the first-time journal keeper are Rainer's *The New Diary* and Baldwin's *One to One*. These books, along with other resources, are listed at the end of the chapter.

Mind Calming and Body Relaxing

Our brains are composed basically of cells called neurons that fire little bursts of energy at varying frequencies, called brainwave frequencies. Throughout most of our active day, our brainwave frequencies usually lie in the range of fourteen to twenty-eight cycles per second, or the beta frequency. This is an essential frequency but a wearing one inasmuch as it is the range of apprehension, anxiety, and competitiveness. Beta is the frequency in which we are bombarded with sensory input. Obviously this is not the best learning frequency because too many outside factors are fighting for our active attention.

Alpha, the second highest major brainwave frequency, occurs at approximately seven to thirteen cycles per second, with a strong amplitude around ten. Alpha is a more tranquil frequency than beta but at alpha we are still capable of being quite aware. We can choose to be diffusely aware or have a more narrow focus. Alpha is a strongly concentrative frequency, much more conducive to learning than the more frenetic beta.

You can learn faster and more easily from your inner resources if you lower your brainwave frequency to alpha. How can you do this? Sit quietly, breathe deeply, and take yourself through the relaxation exercises described below. They will put you in a calm, energized, and focused alpha state.

At first the described procedure may seem too long. However, once you are familiar with the routine you will be able to complete it in a very short time — five minutes at most. When you are relaxed, receptive, and concentrating, you will recall information more easily and remember it longer.

In his book *The Knack of Using Your Subconscious Mind* (1971), John K. Williams described a deliberate intuitive process that you can set in motion at any time. When you use this process, you don't wait for some intuitive lightning to strike. Simply sit down, breathe deeply, lower your brainwave frequency to alpha, and open an imaginary "awareness window" between your conscious and your subconscious minds. Then confide to the *subconscious* all the relevant information that the *conscious* mind knows about a subject, assignment, problem, or project. Make a specific assignment to the subconscious: "This is the kind of help I need and this is when I need it." Then direct the conscious mind to something else.

Meanwhile the subconscious mind is freed to pursue its "incubation" process. Later, at a time when your conscious mind is receptive, when the "awareness window" is open, you will experience an "Aha!" moment—your time of insight. You may be in a warm shower, you may be listening to music, or you may be simply daydreaming when the subconscious proudly presents to your conscious mind the sum of its findings to that moment. Your journal is a great place to record those "Aha!" realizations and to comment on them, even to speculate on the routes your subconscious mind followed to produce them. Thus you risk no exposure of your private illuminations, no possibility of derisive laughter from other students over your unusual ideas.

Some relaxation approaches take the tension from the body, but the mind still capers about (as they say in India) "like a drunken monkey." Other techniques send the mind into a calm, euphoric state, but the body retains its various itches and twitches. Georgi Lozanov (1978), originator of internationally recognized techniques for accelerated learning, has found a simple way to relax both mind and body: listening to baroque music while sitting or lying with the eyes closed. Lozanov's experiments indicate that the music of the eighteenth century (the impersonal, repetitive compositions of Bach, Telemann, Vivaldi, and their contemporaries) relaxes mind and body simultaneously. You may achieve the same effect with New Age musical sounds, like Steve Halpern's *Spectrum Suite, Zodiac Suite, Starborn Suite,* or *Comfort Zone*, or Don Campbell's *Crystal Meditations.*

Some people find that they relax best when listening to soothing environmental sounds, like waves lapping on the shore, soft breezes blowing through trees, or the soft brush of rain against a windowpane. The best approach for your personal use is to keep sampling until you find the sounds or music most effective for you.

Mind Calming and Body Relaxing Exercises

Getting in Position

You may sit on the floor or in a chair. If you are on the floor, you may arrange yourself in the lotus position of meditation with your legs crossed and hands resting lightly on your thighs, preferably palms up. If you are sitting in a chair, you should have your feet flat on the floor, with arms at your sides and hands resting lightly in your lap. In either case, your spine should be as straight as you can manage while still remaining comfortable. Your energy centers (or *chakras*) are located close to the spine. If you crumple down in an accordion-pleated way, you close off those centers and interfere with your inner flow of energy.

Deep Breathing

To breath deeply, you should imagine that your lungs are big bellows that expand and contract as you inhale and exhale. Imagine, too, that you have a long column going from the back of your throat down into your body. As you inhale, mentally see yourself filling that column with clean, fresh air. As you exhale, envision yourself completely emptying that column. If you wish to test your lung action, place your hands over your rib cage, with the tips of your middle fingers barely touching. As you inhale, feel your lungs expanding and note that your middle fingertips part slightly. As you exhale, emptying the air column, note that the middle fingertips come back together. The quality of your breathing is closely linked to the amount of tension in your body. When you are rigid and tense, you cannot learn as readily as when you are relaxed and receptive. Therefore, you should work with your deep breathing until the breath pattern is rhythmic and flowing.

Head and Neck Relaxation

Sit comfortably straight, close your eyes, and start your deep rhythmic breathing. Gently drop your head forward as far as it will comfortably go, then gently drop it backward as far as is comfortable. Repeat this exercise three times, synchronizing it with your breathing. For example, as you drop your head back, inhale. As you drop your head forward, exhale. At the end of the three repetitions, stop and reestablish your breathing pattern.

Next, gently drop your head toward your right shoulder as far as it will comfortably go, then toward your left shoulder. Repeat this exercise three times, synchronizing it with your breathing. Stop and reestablish your breathing pattern.

Now, turn your head to the right as far as is comfortable, then to the left, each time looking back over your shoulder. Repeat this exercise three times, synchronizing it with your breathing. Stop and reestablish your breathing pattern.

Facing forward as much as possible, rotate your head in a complete circle very slowly. Inhale as your head passes over your right shoulder and exhale as it passes over your left shoulder. Remember to roll your head very slowly. When you have gone three times around to the right, reverse the direction and repeat the procedure going around to the left. When you have finished, hold your head straight up and reestablish your deep breathing.

Comparative Progressive Relaxation

Close your eyes and imagine that you are full of grey-green water, which represents everything you want to rid yourself of: anger, frustration, fatigue, anxiety, boredom, resistance to learning—anything negative.

Keeping your eyes closed, imagine this smog-green water filling you all the way up to your hairline. Inhale; tense your forehead and scalp; exhale; relax; and picture the water level dropping to your eyelids.

Take a deep breath; tense your eyelids and the muscles around your eyes; exhale; relax; and mentally see that water level drop to your jaw muscles.

Inhale again; tense your jaw muscles; exhale; relax your lower face; and see the water level dropping to your neck, chest, shoulders, and arms.

Take another deep breath; tense your neck, shoulders, and upper chest; exhale; relax that entire area; and mentally picture the water dropping to your rib cage and abdomen.

Follow this same procedure all the way down to your hips and thighs, your knees and calves, your ankles and feet. When you reach your feet, as you relax them, mentally picture yourself pulling a plug out of the bottom of each foot and see the remainder of the grey-green water run out on the floor. Then sit for a moment, savoring the feeling of being completely relaxed and drained of all negativity.

Finally, imagine that a light (any kind, any color), representing new energy and positive direction, is coming in through the openings in the bottoms of your feet. Feel the light progressing up your body, filling your legs, your abdomen, your chest, your arms and shoulders, your neck, and finally all the way up to the top of your head. Imagine the light showering in a glorious burst of energy out the top of your head and running into every crevice of your body, so that you feel yourself glowing and vibrant, ready for learning. Before you take one last deep breath and open your eyes, mentally plug those holes in your feet so you can keep all that new-found energy inside.

Mental Imagery

When the discovery of the potency of using "the mind's eye" was first touted, the process was called "visualization." We were instructed to picture what we wanted in terms of accomplishment, healing, reward, prestige, or other personal or professional goals. More recently the term "visualization" has been supplanted by "mental imagery," which connotes all of the imagination's five senses: hearing, tasting, touching, smelling, as well as seeing.

In teaching yourself, you can derive enormous advantages by using the power of imagery in a number of ways. You can devise your own images. You can use a completely structured image or you can consciously plan your image up to a point and then let your imagination have free rein. Another possibility is to repeat for yourself the facts that you have learned about a given topic; then you can lie back, close your eyes, and see what your fertile imagination brings to your "mental classroom."

As you know, your subconscious mind often communicates with your conscious mind by means of pictures: unbidden images, dreams, memories, visions. Conversely the conscious mind can often make a better connection with the subconscious by "showing" instead of merely "telling." For example, say you are computer-phobic. You can train yourself to cast off your fears by using mental images of yourself mastering a difficult spreadsheet program or doing a dazzling job of conducting a class on computer simulations.

Mental imagery is the perfect way to conduct risk-free experiments. Many great inventors, for example, not only hatched their ideas in their mental laboratories; they even went so far as to build imaginary prototypes and to subject them to imaginary testing before ever exposing them to the outside world.

You will come up with many ideas for using your powers of mind in this way. The next time you design a workshop, for example, do an imaginary dry run and bid your unconscious, creative mind to improve the learning design you have developed by troubleshooting potential problems or embellishing a sketchy exercise.

As with much of your inner learning, the best time to employ mental imagery is when you're relaxed and in the tranquil but aware alpha frequency. Lie or sit back, close your eyes, and open your "mind's eye"—imaging as vividly as possible and including sounds, tastes, fragrances, and textures along with the sights.

Don't be concerned if you can't actually "see" as you think you should. You may not be projecting pictures on a screen or on the backs of your eyelids or whatever other imagers do. Each person images in his or her own way. If you were instructed to "imagine" or "think of" your living room, then your bedroom, then your kitchen, you'd have your own way of differentiating. So don't fret over an inability to match the technicolor displays of a strong right-brainer. Be happy and comfortable in doing your own thing in your own inimitable and imaginative way.

Self-Talk

We all talk to ourselves—silently or aloud—probably more than we realize. We tell ourselves how we are doing, judge ourselves against others, and criticize, congratulate, blame, or terrorize ourselves. By this primarily inner conversation we turn our daily lives into a series of crises, catastrophes, collaborations, or celebrations. Self-talk includes all the thoughts we have as well as the messages we give ourselves. And such "closet comments" affect not only the way we feel about ourselves but how well and how easily we learn.

Unfortunately much of our self-talk is damagingly negative. Consider these examples:

- "I'm so slow. Everyone else has finished with the case study, but I'm only halfway through. Why can't I ever do anything on schedule?"

- "I've never been good at math. How am I ever going to learn this new budgeting system well enough to train all the department managers to use it?"
- "I'm so stupid! I learned about interactive video techniques at the workshop just this afternoon, and already I've forgotten them."

If you're using negative self-talk, you're blocking optimal learning in a number of ways. When you remind yourself of past failures and criticize yourself for once again not meeting some self-imposed standard, you increase the probability that you will continue to fail. You're establishing a self-fulfilling prophecy. Furthermore, your negative self-talk becomes a distraction; it interferes with your concentration and keeps your attention away from your learning goal. You can't focus clearly on what you're doing when you're chastising yourself for how badly you're doing it! Finally, self-talk that is full of self-doubt and fear of failure can raise your anxiety level during tests or interviews, thereby preventing you from being as competent and knowledgeable as you really are.

On the other hand, positive self-talk facilitates learning. It builds self-confidence and keeps you on course. When you focus on success rather than failure, you automatically increase the probability that you will succeed.

Positive statements are always beneficial, but you can multiply that benefit many times by repeating them to yourself when you are in a relaxed alpha state. At such a time you have improved the communication between your conscious and subconscious minds. Your subconscious mind, therefore, more readily absorbs the image your conscious mind is holding. When you synchronize both planes of your mind, when you focus on your learning goals and your ability to achieve them, you turn yourself into a powerhouse of positive results.

To make your self-talk pay off handsomely in improved self-image and learning ability, go through the mind-calming and body-relaxing exercises described earlier. Then say affirmations like these to yourself (either mentally or aloud):

- I am intelligent, curious, articulate, and nurturing.
- I learn important facts and ideas easily.
- I find learning exciting and fun.
- I feel calm, relaxed, and confident while learning and while practicing what I have learned.
- I am an effective teacher for myself.
- I can easily recall the knowledge I already have.
- I can find sources for the knowledge I need to add.
- I am patient with myself when I do not immediately understand.
- I have confidence in my ability to learn.
- I applaud myself for all my learning successes.
- I am reaching my learning goals every day.

Think of other affirmations or conditioning statements that suit your particular situation. After all, you know best what kind of encouragement you need to give yourself. In fact, you may find that from time to time you want to alter your statements to fit changing circumstances.

There are a few simple reminders. Affirmations are always worded as if the goal has already been attained. Not "I plan to learn important facts and ideas easily" but "I learn important facts and ideas easily." Statements are always couched in the present tense. Not "I will become an effective teacher for myself" but "I am an effective teacher for myself." And they are always stated in positive terms. Not "I don't get distracted" but "I concentrate well."

You may simply write down your affirmations and read them to yourself while you listen to your mind-calming music or sounds, or you can record them on audiotapes and play them to yourself (in your own voice) while you are relaxed and receptive.

Remember that affirmations are not incantations. They are not magic. They are a tool for reprogramming your self-concepts and altering your negative self-talk. If you have spent years implanting negative images about study and learning, you will need to allow yourself some reprogramming time for maximum results. The idea is to keep repeating your positive statements; your attitudes will slowly shift to what you want them to be.

Postscripts for Helping Others Learn

Keeping a Journal

Suggest that each participant invest in a notebook (preferably a three-ring binder with plain paper) and keep a "learning journal." Go over with participants the four reasons for keeping such a journal. Emphasize the privacy of the writing and the necessity for making the journal both verbal and visual. Emphasize, also, the importance of tailoring the approach to journal keeping to each individual's preferred learning style. If possible, show some examples of portions of learning journals (after, of course, having secured the permission of the writers).

Mind Calming and Body Relaxing

If you are teaching or training others, explain the brainwave frequencies (perhaps using charts or transparencies) and their effects on learning. Show the connection between brainwave frequencies and mind calming and body relaxation. Demonstrate and let your learners practice deep breathing. Lead them through a sample relaxation exercise, making clear that there are many equally effective ones. Demonstrate different kinds of baroque and New Age music and musical sounds as well as several environmental ones. Help learners understand the importance of preparing both mind and body for peak learning.

Mental Imagery

When teaching others about mental imagery, stress the fact that each person images in his or her own way. Start with simple examples. Use the words "imagine

. . ." or "think of . . ." rather than "image." Also emphasize the fact that imaging includes all the same senses involved in normal perception: seeing, hearing, tasting, touching, and smelling, where appropriate. Using appropriate music, take students through a completely guided image, then a semiguided image. Then let them experience spontaneous imaging.

Self-Talk

If you are assisting others with affirmations, make clear to them what affirmations are and why they work. Outline the simple rules for affirmations: worded as if the goal has already been attained; always couched in the present tense; and always stated in positive terms. Suggest some sample affirmations. Then allow time for learners to write their own. Check samples (voluntary ones) to see that learners understand the guidelines. Explain how and when affirmations are most effectively used. At the beginning of each class allow some time for mind-calming and relaxation, using music. Then allow additional time for each participant to repeat silently his or her learning affirmations while the music is still playing.

An excellent exercise is Win Wenger's "image streaming," in which partners sit with eyes closed and take turns describing their images (either around a central topic or free-flowing). One partner talks for a few sentences; then the other describes his or her images. Wenger is president of Psychegenics (P. O. Box 332, Gaithersburg, Maryland 20760) and has much good material on the use of imaging. Susan Claire (Claire Communications, 2-1645 East Cliff Drive, Santa Cruz, California 95062) has described "visioning," in which a table group follows much the same procedure as the partners follow in "image streaming." Both processes can continue for a given time. Then the instructor can lead group discussions about the experiences.

For Your Continuing Professional Development

Albrecht, K. *Brain Power: Learn to Improve Your Thinking Skills.* Englewood Cliffs, N.J.: Prentice-Hall, 1980.

Baldwin, C. *One to One: Self-Understanding Through Journal Writing.* New York: M. Evans, 1977.

Benson, H. *The Relaxation Response.* New York: William Morrow, 1975.

Bry, A., with Bair, M. *Visualization: Directing the Movies of Your Mind.* New York: Barnes & Noble, 1978.

Edwards, B. *Drawing on the Artist Within: A Guide to Innovation, Invention, Imagination, and Creativity.* New York: Simon & Schuster, 1986.

Geba, B. *Breathe Away Your Tension: A Five-Week Program of Body Relaxation.* New York: Random House, 1977.

Goldberg, P. *The Intuitive Edge: Understanding and Develping Intuition.* Los Angeles: J. P. Tarcher, 1938.

Houston, J. *The Possible Human: A Course in Enhancing Your Physical, Mental, and Creative Abilities.* Los Angeles: J. P. Tarcher, 1982.

Khatena, J. *Imagery and Creative Imagination.* Buffalo, N.Y.: Creative Education Foundation, 1984.

Lynch, D. *Your High-Performance Business Brain: An Operator's Manual.* Englewood Cliffs, N. J.: Prentice-Hall, 1984.

Parnes, S. *The Magic of Your Mind.* Buffalo, N.Y.: Creative Education Foundation, 1981.

Progoff, P. *At a Journal Workshop: The Basic Text and Guide for Using the Intensive Journal.* New York: Dialogue House Library, 1977.

Rainer, T. *The New Diary: How to Use a Journal for Self-Guidance and Expanded Creativity.* Los Angeles: J. P. Tarcher, 1978.

Rico, G. L. *Writing the Natural Way: Using Right-Brain Techniques to Release Your Expressive Powers.* Los Angeles: J. P. Tarcher, 1983.

Singer, J. L., and Switzer, E. *Mind-Play: The Creative Uses of Fantasy.* Englewood Cliffs, N.J.: Prentice-Hall, 1980.

Vaughn, F. E. *Awakening Intuition.* Garden City, N.Y.: Doubleday, 1979.

von Oech, R. *A Whack on the Side of the Head.* New York: Warner Books, 1983.

Williams, J. K. *The Knack of Using Your Subconscious Mind.* Englewood Cliffs, N.J.: Prentice-Hall, 1971.

Wonder, J., and Donovan, P. *Whole Brain Thinking.* New York: William Morrow, 1984.

PART II

A CATALOGUE OF LEARNING RESOURCES

Part Two is a catalogue and directory of resources for using in your learning plan. These chapters list and describe resources that will make it easier for you to foster your own personal and professional development as an HRD practitioner, OD specialist, and consultant. We have provided you access to a number of learning formats to suit your learning style and personal preferences. You can learn from books, keep up with the latest trends with periodicals, join professional associations, attend noncredit workshops or credit courses, use print and nonprint instructional materials (group exercises, audiocassettes, or films), search on-line data bases for a wealth of information, and participate in computer-assisted instruction. This part of the book tells you what these resources are and how to find them. You'll find references to materials on some topics in different learning formats. So if you're interested in computer-assisted instruction or the latest ideas for small-group instruction, for example, you'll have to check each chapter to see what's available. We usually provide cross-references when closely related material is found in more than one chapter.

You will also find information on periodicals and newsletters, review sources, and periodical indexes—all items that will help you keep up with new materials that come out after the publication of this handbook.

The resources in these chapters are primarily for you. Materials for general employee development have been kept to a minimum unless HRD practitioners would be interested in them for their own learning as well. However, at the end of most chapters, you will find directories and bibliographies that will give you access to instructional materials for employee training and supervisory/management development.

Each chapter has an introduction to what's in the chapter, how it's organized, and how to update the information in the chapter. At the end of many of the chapters, you will find bibliographies and directories for updating and locating additional instructional resources.

Most of the items listed in the resource chapters are available for purchase from the source listed in the entry. Addresses and phone numbers of the order departments of publishers and producers are listed within the text or at the ends of the chapters. Cost information changes rapidly, so view all prices as approximate. Addresses and phone numbers also change.

Many of these books, periodicals, directories, and indexes can be found in your local public or university library. In addition, on-line computer data-base searches may also be available. And libraries can help you track down current cost information and addresses that may have changed. If you have a corporate library, your librarian can be a great help in locating any of these resources.

10

The Best Books

Linda Webster

These "best books" have been chosen from the fields of adult learning, human resource development, adult and continuing education, consulting, management, organization development, and career development. Some are classics with continuing significance for today's practitioners. Some represent the best of the newest books. Many are personal favorites. Beginning trainers should note the starred books in each category—recommendations for essential reading. More experienced trainers will use this list to broaden their reading and study.

This chapter is arranged in the following sections:

Adult Learning Theory and Practice
Human Resource Development
  Basic Principles and Practices
  Determining Needs
  Design
  Delivery
  Evaluation
Managing HRD Programs
Computer-Based Training
Media Selection, Management, and Production
Conferences, Meetings, and Workshops
International HRD Practice
Group Theory and Practice
Organization Development
Consulting
Career Development
Self-Directed and Lifelong Learning Methods
Keeping Up to Date
Directory of Book Publishers and Distributors

Almost all of the books in this chapter are still in print. Publishers' addresses for mail orders are listed at the end of this chapter. Get on the mailing list for the publishers' catalogues that interest you. Many of these books can also be purchased through specialized book distributors, which are also listed at the end of this chapter. In addition, the American Society for Training and Development provides a discount book-ordering service for its members.

Prices change frequently. Some publishers make yearly changes, so view price information as approximate. Addresses and phone numbers also change.

Adult Learning Theory and Practice

Houle, Cyril O. *Continuing Learning in the Professions.* San Francisco: Jossey-Bass, 1980. $24.95.

Houle examines the needs, patterns, methods, and programs of continuing learning in seventeen professions, including the process of becoming a professional, changing learning needs and habits at successive stages in a professional career, and motivations for continuing education. Houle makes recommendations for designing and evaluating effective programs and improving the impact of continuing education on professionals' competence and performance.

Houle, Cyril O. *Patterns of Learning: New Perspectives on Life-Span Education.* San Francisco: Jossey-Bass, 1984. $22.95.

Houle analyzes the learning and teaching techniques of seven eminent personalities, including Thoreau, Montaigne, and Billy Graham, who exemplify innovative, multifaceted approaches to education. Houle advocates using a wide array of instructional methods for each life stage to give breadth and depth to the learning process.

*Knowles, Malcolm. *The Adult Learner: A Neglected Species.* (3rd ed.) Houston: Gulf, 1984. $19.95.

Incisive and thought-provoking, this book reveals what is wrong with commonly accepted methods of teaching adults. Knowles presents concepts for developing meaningful adult learning programs, with a discussion of their application to the HRD field and to the role of training in organization development. Appendixes include behaviorism, a memorandum to the personal computer industry, lifelong learning communities, the teacher as a facilitator of learning, Westinghouse Corporation's andragogical executive forum, releasing the energy of others, reactive versus proactive learning, guidelines for learning contracts, becoming a tutor, and andragogy in developing countries.

Knowles, Malcolm, and Associates. *Andragogy in Action: Applying Modern Principles of Adult Learning.* San Francisco: Jossey-Bass, 1984. $26.95.

Thirty-six case studies from business and industry, continuing professional education, and various school settings illustrate andragogy in practice. Practitioners detail how different organizations and institutions have adapted andragogy to meet their specific needs, revealing what worked, what did not, and why.

Each case study is introduced by Knowles, who also wrote the beginning and concluding chapters, which describe the basic principles of andragogy and the effectiveness of andragogy in various settings.

*Knowles, Malcolm. *The Modern Practice of Adult Education: From Pedagogy to Andragogy.* (Rev. ed.) New York: Cambridge Book Company, 1980. $25.95.

This book is still considered the bible of developing, implementing, evaluating, and administering an adult education program. Knowles distinguishes between practices and techniques of pedagogy (the teaching of children) and andragogy (the teaching of adults), a learner-centered approach to adult learning.

Knowles, Malcolm. *Using Learning Contracts: Practical Approaches to Individualizing and Structuring Learning.* San Francisco: Jossey-Bass, 1986. $23.95.

Knowles provides examples (with his comments) of learning contracts and descriptions of how they were developed. These contracts come from a variety of settings, including independent study, graduate education, continuing professional education, management development, and total academic degree programs. In addition, the book includes a theoretical rationale for contract learning and case descriptions of three institutions that introduced contract learning into their programs.

Knox, Alan B. *Adult Development and Learning: A Handbook on Individual Growth and Competence in the Adult Years for Education and the Helping Professions.* San Francisco: Jossey-Bass, 1977. $34.95.

Knox presents a comprehensive review of research on adult development and learning from the biological, social, and behavioral sciences: the effects of family situation, education, work, and community life on adult development; the influence of health and personality on change and stability; and the best conditions for effective adult learning. Knox examines learning abilities that decline or increase with age and adults' adjustments to events that change or disrupt their lives. He also discusses the implications of these findings for education and the helping professions.

Kolb, David A. *Experiential Learning: Experience as the Source of Learning and Development.* Englewood Cliffs, N.J.: Prentice-Hall, 1984. $32.

Kolb describes the process of experiential learning and presents a model based on research in psychology, philosophy, and physiology. Kolb's thesis is that learning from experience is the major process for human development. Also included are a typology of individual learning styles and knowledge structures in academic disciplines, professions, and careers as well as applications of experiential learning to education, work, and adult development.

Smith, Robert M. *Learning How to Learn: Applied Theory for Adults.* Philadelphia: Taylor and Francis, 1984. Out of print.

Smith provides cogent information on the characteristics of adult learners, optimum conditions for learning, and learning styles based on a synthesis of current research. In addition, there are practical techniques and methods for self-directed/lifelong learning.

*Tough, Allen. *The Adult's Learning Projects: A Fresh Approach to Theory and Practice in Adult Learning.* (2nd ed.) Austin, Tex.: Learning Concepts, 1979. Out of print.

Tough presents landmark research on adult self-directed learning. Findings indicate that adults average eight learning projects a year for a total of 700 hours of learning. Most of these learning projects are self-planned or group learning activities. Tough suggests improvements for self-planned learning, learning one-to-one, and learning in a group.

Tough, Allen. *Intentional Changes: A Fresh Approach to Helping People Change.* New York: Cambridge Book Company, 1982. $22.95.

This pioneering book focuses on the array of intentional changes that people achieve on their own. Based on in-depth interviews, the study describes the processes and steps people follow when they choose to change something important — choosing a new job, changing a personal relationship, becoming physically fit. The findings reveal that people are remarkably successful at choosing, planning, and implementing intentional changes. Most often they obtain help from family and friends, not books or professionals. Tough discusses the implications for specific professional groups and suggests how practitioners can support natural learning processes without assuming undue control.

Human Resource Development

Basic Principles and Practices

Baird, Lloyd S., Laird, Dugan, and Schneier, Craig Eric (eds.). *The Training and Development Sourcebook.* Amherst, Mass.: Human Resource Development Press, 1983. $35.

Experts in the HRD field discuss all aspects of training, including gaining management commitment, new approaches to training needs analysis, and practical techniques for transferring training to the job. The sourcebook also includes a comprehensive collection of ready-to-use instruments — checklists, questionnaires, and training materials.

*Laird, Dugan. *Approaches to Training and Development.* (2nd ed.) Reading, Mass.: Addison-Wesley, 1985. $17.95 paper.

In this classic, Laird offers a practical approach to deciding what training to do, if any; what methods and audiovisual materials to use, including video and computer-assisted instruction; and how to implement and evaluate results. He also discusses training budgets, staffing, roles of training and development officers, the training department in relation to the rest of the organization, and what to do when training is not a useful approach.

McLagan, Patricia A. *Helping Others Learn: Designing Programs for Adults*. Reading, Mass.: Addison-Wesley, 1978. $9.95 paper.

McLagan provides practical techniques for improving learning experiences. She focuses on motivation and the "ideal climate" for learning, personal differences in information processing, and learning application and transfer. McLagan identifies four possible kinds of learning outcomes—new knowledge, understanding, or awareness; new skills or behavior patterns; new attitudes, values, or priorities; and creative ideas. Concise and to the point, this self-study manual has built-in exercises within the text so that readers can easily analyze and improve their training sessions and courses.

Mouton, Jane S., and Blake, Robert R. *Synergogy: A New Strategy for Education, Training, and Development*. San Francisco: Jossey-Bass, 1984. $21.95.

Mouton and Blake present a comprehensive guide to synergogy (working together for shared teaching), using small teams of learners to enhance motivation, learning, and retention. Detailed step-by-step instructions and sample learning materials are presented for four distinct learning designs: (1) Team Effectiveness Design, to teach factual knowledge in depth; (2) Team-Member Teaching Design, to teach a great deal of subject matter in a short period of time for broad understanding; (3) Performance Judging Design, to teach skills; (4) Clarifying Attitudes Design, to improve attitudes, values, and interpersonal functioning.

*Nadler, Leonard. *Developing Human Resources*. (3rd ed.) San Francisco: Jossey-Bass, forthcoming.

Earlier editions emphasize the conceptualization of activities associated with HRD—training, education, and development—and the roles of the HRD specialist as learning specialist, administrator, and consultant. A historical view of the field is also included.

*Nadler, Leonard (ed.). *The Handbook of Human Resource Development*. New York: Wiley, 1984. $59.95.

This handbook is the most current and comprehensive reference guide to the HRD field. Its thirty-five contributors offer an unmatched source of ideas, information, firsthand experience, and research on adult learning, training costs, design of learning programs, instructional strategies, computer-based learning, evaluation, and professional growth for HRD staff. Training in different fields is discussed—sales, executive, management, and supervisory training; technical training; and specific programs for government, schools, labor, and nonprofit organizations. Contributors detail international HRD practice, human resource management, organization development, career development, and future projections.

New Directions for Continuing Education. Gordon Darkenwald and Alan B. Knox, editors-in-chief. San Francisco: Jossey-Bass, 1984–. $11.95 each.

This series of paperback sourcebooks is designed for administrators, instructors, training directors, and counselors in all adult and continuing education programs in a variety of settings. Each sourcebook contains about 100 pages of concise theory, research, case examples, and practical advice on a single topic of key concern. Recent topics include designing effective workshops, interorganizational cooperation, evaluation, learning how to learn, financing and budgeting, materials for teaching adults, older adults, counseling, and effective teaching techniques.

Tracey, William R. *Human Resources Management and Development Handbook.* New York: AMACOM, 1985. $85.

This handbook looks at functions in both the human resources management and human resources development fields. The 108 articles written by practitioners and consultants include a historical background of the fields and the managerial functions of planning and forecasting, programming and budgeting, organizing, staffing, directing, and controlling the HRM/D functions. Experts discuss cost reduction and productivity improvement; support services such as media production, management information, and word processing; and human resources management elements, including workforce planning, recruitment, selection, orientation, performance evaluation, labor relations, discipline and grievances, transfer and promotion, compensation and benefits, incentives, and workplace improvements. Employee services are discussed, including career planning, counseling, safety and security, health services, food services, recreation, and retirement planning. Organization and management development programs are discussed, as are all forms of training—both in-house and external training programs. The final sections detail the analysis, design, development, implementation, and quality control of instructional systems and the calculation of HRD costs and benefits.

Determining Needs

*Zemke, Ron, and Kramlinger, Tom. *Figuring Things Out: A Trainer's Guide to Needs and Task Analysis.* Reading, Mass.: Addison-Wesley, 1982. $29.95.

This is a comprehensive guide to analyzing and finding appropriate solutions for human performance problems. Techniques and procedures are divided into four categories: observational approaches; talking to people about work; questioning; and performance information, fault tree analysis, and learning hierarchies. The authors provide guidance on choosing the right needs assessment technique and emphasize the importance of proper reporting to management. Techniques in this book can be used to gather and analyze performance information for writing job descriptions, setting training and performance standards, developing training programs, constructing competency models, and developing nontraining solutions for employee performance problems.

Design

Gagné, Robert M., and Briggs, Leslie J. *Principles of Instructional Design*. (2nd ed.) New York: Holt, Rinehart & Winston, 1979. $37.25.

    Gagné and Briggs provide learning principles that form the basis for instructional design and discuss different conditions of learning that facilitate the acquisition of intellectual skills, information, attitudes, motor skills, and cognitive strategies. They also provide detailed guidance in methods of instructional design—defining learning outcomes, sequencing, developing lesson plans, arranging optimum learning conditions, and assessing learner performance.

*Kearsley, Greg. *Training and Technology: A Handbook for HRD Professionals*. Reading, Mass.: Addison-Wesley, 1984. $25.95.

    This is a highly informative, easy-to-understand guide to the "hard" and "soft" technologies—audiovisuals, film and video, computers, teleconferencing, job aids, behavior modeling, instructional system development, and learning strategies. Eight case studies from the private and public sectors illustrate how to analyze training needs, decide on appropriate technology, evalute the costs and benefits, and identify problems, obstacles, and sociopolitical implications of implementing technological systems.

*Mager, Robert F., and Pipe, Peter. *Analyzing Performance Problems, or You Really Oughta Wanna*. (2nd ed.) Belmont, Calif.: Davis S. Lake, 1984. $10.95 paper.

Mager, Robert F. *Developing Attitudes Toward Learning, or Smats 'n' Smuts*. (2nd ed.) Belmont, Calif.: Davis S. Lake, 1984. $10.95 paper.

Mager, Robert F. *Goal Analysis*. (2nd ed.) Belmont, Calif.: Davis S. Lake, 1984. $10.95 paper.

Mager, Robert F. *Measuring Instructional Results, or Got a Match?* (2nd ed.) Belmont, Calif.: Davis S. Lake, 1984. $10.95 paper.

*Mager, Robert F. *Preparing Instructional Objectives*. (2nd ed.) Belmont, Calif.: Davis L. Lake, 1984. $10.95 paper.

    This five-workbook set is a straightforward self-study approach to the instructional design process—assessing needs, analyzing goals, writing instructional objectives, developing positive attitudes, and evaluating instruction. Each book is written with step-by-step instructions and includes practice materials with numerous illustrations of correct and incorrect responses. Mager's *Preparing Instructional Objectives* is probably the all-time best-selling book on writing objectives.

Martin, Barbara J., and Briggs, Leslie J. *The Affective and Cognitive Domains: Integration for Instruction and Research*. Englewood Cliffs, N.J.: Educational Technology Publications, 1986. $39.95.

Martin and Briggs call for the integration of cognitive and affective learning in the design of instructional objectives. The authors discuss the importance of the often-neglected affective domain in learning—for example, the learner's attitudes, values, morals, ethics, human relationships, and self-esteem. Affective learning can be evaluated through questionnaires, interviews, self-reporting strategies, and behavior observations.

Nadler, Leonard. *Designing Training Programs: The Critical Events Model*. Reading, Mass.: Addison-Wesley, 1982. $19.95.

Nadler provides a model that identifies and describes the various phases of the training process as a series of critical events: identifying organization needs, specifying job performances, analyzing individual learning needs, determining objectives, building a curriculum, selecting instructional strategies, obtaining instructional resources, and conducting training. Significant differences between the critical events model (CEM) and other published models are that the CEM uses the continuous involvement of managers and supervisors in the design process, makes provision for constant evaluation and feedback throughout the process, and stresses the importance of building management and supervisor support for training.

Robinson, James C. *Developing Managers Through Behavior Modeling*. Austin, Tex.: Learning Concepts, 1982. $20.95. (Distributed by University Associates).

This is a highly readable and practical book on using behavior modeling principles to change and shape the behavior of managers. Step-by-step instructions are included on how to define objectives, create a modeling display, develop skill-practice exercises, get the most out of the modeling display, provide skill practice and feedback, reinforce skills, obtain management support, and evaluate.

Delivery

Davies, Ivor. *Instructional Technique*. New York: McGraw-Hill, 1980. $17.95.

Davies provides expert guidance in instruction methods, lesson planning, instructional settings, verbal and nonverbal communication, and question and discussion techniques. He includes practical examples from business, government, and nonprofit organizations.

*Eitington, Julius E. *The Winning Trainer: Winning Ways to Involve People in Learning*. Houston: Gulf, 1984. $34.95 paper.

This is an immensely practical and comprehensive guide to involve learners fully and actively in the learning process. It is an encyclopedia of techniques, exercises, and worksheets for participative learning, including role plays, case studies, games, brainstorming, small-group techniques, puzzles, instruments, problem-solving techniques, team building, film/video, lecturing, fantasy and visualization, and participative evaluation methods. Eitington discusses how and when to use these methods, how to design and construct training activities to fit the situation, and how to promote retention of learning and transfer back to the job situation.

*Laird, Dugan, and House, Ruth. *The Trainer's Classroom Instruction Workshop.* Glenview, Ill.: Scott, Foresman, 1983. $225. (Workbook: *Interactive Classroom Instruction*, $10 paper).

This is a complete, integrated program for training individuals to be effective trainers and classroom instructors, including a facilitator's manual and participant workbook. *Interactive Classroom Instruction* combines classic and cutting-edge instructional methods with a practical approach and a conversational style. The facilitator's manual contains an easy-to-follow workshop outline plus visual aid masters. The participant's workbook includes worksheets and notes that reinforce all workshop activities.

*Margolis, Fredric H., and Bell, Chip R. *Instructing for Results.* (Rev. ed.) San Diego: University Associates, 1986. $19.95 paper.

Margolis and Bell discuss effective delivery skills for the adult classroom. Readers learn the best ways to give instructions, monitor tasks, manage the reporting process, and guide learning activities.

*Smith, Barry J., and Delahaye, Brian L. *How to Be an Effective Trainer: Skills for Managers and New Trainers.* New York: Wiley, 1987. $39.95.

This is a complete self-paced course, ideal for group training or independent study. It includes workable guidelines for teaching theory and skills; practical tips on using audiovisual materials, group discussions, and lectures; techniques for reducing anxiety and polishing presentation skills; and follow-up and evaluation procedures. Each section includes key concepts and learning objectives for the beginning trainer, exercises, and self-tests.

Williams, Linda Verlee. *Teaching for the Two-Sided Mind: A Guide to Right Brain/Left Brain Education.* Englewood Cliffs, N.J.: Prentice-Hall, 1983. $7.95 paper.

Williams presents techniques for whole-brain learning and teaching for all ages, with background theory and research on brain hemispheres, learning styles, and modes of thinking. Teaching techniques for the right hemisphere include the use of metaphor, visual thinking, fantasy, multisensory learning, and direct experiences. Exercises throughout the book encourage readers to assess their own thinking and learning styles and experience the teaching techniques discussed in the book.

Evaluation

Kearsley, Greg. *Costs, Benefits, and Productivity in Training Systems.* Reading, Mass.: Addison-Wesley, 1982. $17.95.

Kearsley provides practical information for planning, conducting, and interpreting a cost-benefit analysis in any training system. He includes different types of cost models and examples of how to apply them, data collection methods, use of results for planning and forecasting, and the cost benefits of computer-based instruction.

Patton, Michael Quinn. *Creative Evaluation*. Newbury Park, Calif.: Sage, 1981. $12.50 paper.

Patton, Michael Quinn. *Practical Evaluation*. Newbury Park, Calif.: Sage, 1982. $12.95 paper.

Patton, Michael Quinn. *Qualitative Evaluation Methods*. Newbury Park, Calif.: Sage, 1980. $26.

Patton, Michael Quinn. *Utilization-Focused Evaluation*. Newbury Park, Calif.: Sage, 1978. $17.95 paper.

These four books represent a holistic approach to evaluation – grounding evaluation in do-ability and applicability. Patton emphasizes practical considerations in data collection, analysis, and interpretation and active involvement of decision makers and information users in evaluation processes. He calls for an awareness of multiple evaluator roles and the importance of the evaluator's individual style. He advises evaluators to help participants think creatively about evaluation options. In *Creative Evaluation*, Patton uses flowcharts, experiential exercises, simulation games, stories, and humor to achieve greater understanding of, commitment to, and use of evaluation results. *Practical Evaluation* has suggestions for working with a task force, developing evaluations with and without goals, using questionnaires and interviews, and managing management information systems. *Qualitative Evaluation Methods* discusses the design of observation strategies and interviewing.

*Phillips, Jack J. *Handbook of Training Evaluation and Measurement Methods*. Houston: Gulf, 1983. $27.

Phillips describes practical methods to evaluate any kind of training program and presents techniques for showing profit contributions from the training function. Specifically he discusses developing programs with an emphasis on getting results, designing measurement and evaluation instruments, selecting evaluation strategies and data-collection methods, calculating the return on investment for an HRD program, evaluating the use of external training programs, and improving management support for the HRD function.

Managing HRD Programs

*Bell, Chip R. *Influencing: Marketing the Ideas That Matter*. Austin, Tex.: Learning Concepts, 1982. $20.95. (Distributed by University Associates).

Bell uses a marketing approach to develop blueprints for persuading decision makers and gaining support for the HRD effort. He presents pragmatic suggestions on structuring the proposal presentation, winning advocates, and presenting the proposal. Bell provides guidance for the realistic introduction and management of organizational change, a pragmatic discussion on power within groups, and a map for the effective avoidance of organization traps. Organized like a workbook, it contains exercises, self-assessment instruments, checklists, and examples throughout.

Bellman, Geoffrey M. *The Quest for Staff Leadership.* Glenview, Ill.: Scott, Foresman, 1986. $18.95.
    Written specifically for managers of staff departments, this book covers both professional and personal aspects of leadership. The book's thirty-four chapters define the staff function and role, examine leadership from a staff perspective, discuss the components of managing for results, provide strategies for leading with confidence and working with management, illustrate the importance of in-house customers, offer suggestions for supervising staff professionals, and review alternatives for managing your career. Written in a personal, easy-to-read style, the book contains many checklists of specific suggestions and recommendations.

Block, Peter. *The Empowered Manager: Positive Political Skills at Work.* San Francisco: Jossey-Bass, 1987. $19.95.
    Block explains how managers can become empowered to make positive changes in their organizations while avoiding the traditional and often destructive political power plays. He outlines how to create a vision of greatness and provides strategies for gaining support of your vision by working with the various organizational players: allies, opponents, adversaries, fence-sitters, and bedfellows. Block also shows how to create methods of handling meetings, restructuring units, and managing communications that garner positive results.

Matkin, Gary W. *Effective Budgeting in Continuing Education.* San Francisco: Jossey-Bass, 1985. $32.95.
    Matkin discusses background and detailed information on budgeting and pricing continuing education courses as well as budgeting and financial planning for continuing education departments.

Nadler, Leonard. *Corporate Human Resource Development.* New York: Van Nostrand Reinhold, 1980. $18.95.
    Written for top managers, this book provides a systematic overview of important topics bearing on the HRD function and enumerates the benefits of HRD to the organization. Nadler thoroughly explores the concerns and responsibilities of managers in regard to HRD: staffing, supplying physical and financial resources, and evaluating HRD. The chapter on organizational support is especially strong.

Nadler, Leonard, and Wiggs, Garland D. *Managing Human Resource Development: A Practical Guide*. San Francisco: Jossey-Bass, 1986. $22.95.

Nadler and Wiggs provide practical advice on all aspects of HRD management, including the organization of the HRD unit, budgeting, staffing, managing equipment and facilities, course scheduling, long- and short-range planning, and maintaining ongoing relations with all departments in the organization. Illustrating the impact of organizational finance on HRD decision making, the authors explain how to prepare and account for the unit's budget. Using case descriptions, the book provides instruction on hiring and supervising staff and on facilitating their career development.

Computer-Based Training

Computer Language Company. *The Computer Glossary: It's Not Just a Glossary!* Englewood Cliffs, N.J.: Prentice-Hall, 1983. $21.95.

This dictionary has clear definitions of terms from the computer field and numerous illustrations for easy undertanding of concepts.

Kearsley, Greg. *Authoring: A Guide to the Design of Instructional Software*. Reading, Mass.: Addison-Wesley, 1986. $11.95.

Kearsley offers clear and nontechnical guidelines for designing interactive software lessons on microcomputers. He discusses the use of graphics, windows, and other attention-getting devices and provides detailed information on designing a functional screen display, establishing effective user control, and formulating interactive exercises. Also included are guidelines for giving directions, asking questions, and providing feedback. An extensive appendix lists sources for further information on programming techniques, authoring software, and instructional design.

*Kearsley, Greg. *Computer-Based Training: A Guide to Selection and Implementation*. Reading, Mass.: Addison-Wesley, 1983. $29.95.

This book is designed to help training professionals understand computer-based training (CBT); determine whether it is right for their organization; and learn how to select, implement, manage, and evaluate a CBT program. Kearsley discusses the risks, benefits, and cost factors of CBT and examines the use of computers in testing, instruction, simulation, and management. He surveys different types of commercial CBT systems and outlines their characteristics. Also included are numerous case studies, illustrations, and checklists for reviewing the steps in the selection and implementation process.

Kearsley, Greg P. *Training for Tomorrow: Distributed Learning Through Computer and Communications Technology*. Reading, Mass.: Addison-Wesley, 1985. $19.95.

Distributed learning means learning that takes place when and where the learner desires and learning that is continuous throughout the learner's lifetime. Communications and computer technologies have made distributed learning possible. Kearsley discusses the pros and cons of introducing distributed learning methods into an organization using computer-based instruction, telecommunications, and audiovisual media. He discusses getting organizational support, designing distributed training materials, and setting up a workable program. Kearsley compares costs of traditional methods versus distributed training.

*Zemke, Ron. *Computer Needs Assessment*. Reading, Mass.: Addison-Wesley, 1984. $24.95.

Zemke guides trainers in how to interview staff and managers to assess their current knowledge about microcomputers; how to determine training needs; and how to design an effective computer literacy program. He also includes a highly useful directory of computer literacy materials, including disk tutorials, classes and seminars, books, videotapes, and audiocassettes.

Media Selection, Management, and Production

*Anderson, Ronald H. *Selecting and Developing Media for Instruction*. (2nd ed.) New York: Van Nostrand Reinhold, 1983. $26.95.

Anderson provides a six-step process with checklists for selecting the right instructional media to meet the objectives. Expanded chapters on computer-assisted instruction and human factors in media planning are of special interest.

Cartwright, Steve R. *Training with Video*. White Plains, N.Y.: Knowledge Industry Publications, 1985. $36.95.

Cartwright explains how to design, produce, and evaluate video training programs. Time and cost requirements are discussed. Profiles of successful video training programs are provided. Featured are new developments in video training, including teleconferencing, interactive video, and videodiscs.

DeBloois, Michael. *Effectiveness of Videodisc Training: A Comprehensive Review*. Arlington, Va.: Future Systems, 1984. $50.

This report summarizes the history and development of interactive videodisc training, including a review of research on the effectiveness of various applications.

*Heinich, Robert, and Molenda, Michael. *Instructional Media and the New Technologies of Instruction*. (2nd ed.) New York: Macmillan, 1985. $24.50.

This handbook is an excellent guide to using media in an instructional setting. Wonderfully laid out and referenced, it has sections on AV presentation skills, making visuals, and equipment troubleshooting.

Kearsley, Greg. *Training and Technology: A Handbook for HRD Professionals*. Reading, Mass.: Addison-Wesley, 1984. $25.95.

Kearsley discusses the selection and use of a variety of media: audiovisuals, film and video, and computers. Eight case studies are included.

Kemp, Jerrold E. *Planning and Producing Audiovisual Materials*. (4th ed.) New York: Harper & Row, 1980. $32.50.

This book includes information on instructional design, selection of media, principles of perception, communication and learning theory, and detailed instructions for the planning and actual production of all types of nonprint media.

Marlow, Eugene. *Managing the Corporate Media Center*. White Plains, N.Y.: Knowledge Industry Publications, 1981. $29.95.

Marlow presents information on how to develop a budget, how the media function should be organized and staffed, how to work with outside consultants and production facilities, how to evaluate programs, and how to sell the department to top management. He also discusses the probable impact of future technological developments.

*Reiser, Robert A., and Gagné, Robert M. *Selecting Media for Instruction*. Englewood Cliffs, N.J.: Educational Technology Publications, 1983. $32.95.

Reiser and Gagné present a clear, concise media selection model for making decisions based on learning objectives, the domain of learning to which each objective belongs, the instructional settings, and the reading competency of learners.

Utz, Peter. *Video User's Handbook*. (2nd ed.) White Plains, N.Y.: Knowledge Industry Publications, 1982. $17.95 paper.

This thorough hands-on manual presents many new and creative ideas for getting professional results with the most basic video setup. Utz provides complete descriptions and instructions in the use of all kinds of studio equipment as well as information on audio, lighting, editing, and graphics. This book is packed with diagrams, photographs, TV screen reproductions, cartoons—all designed to simplify video production.

Van Deusen, Richard E. *Practical AV-Video Budgeting*. White Plains, N.Y.: Knowledge Industry Publications, 1984. $34.95.

This complete guide to audiovisual budgeting is designed for AV managers in corporations, institutions, government, and commercial production. It includes information on budgeting income and expenses, production budgets, adjustments and charge-backs, income control, and monitoring income. Of special interest are sample budget forms and an example of using VisiCalc microcomputer software for budgeting and recordkeeping.

Conferences, Meetings, and Workshops

*Bradford, Leland P. *Making Meetings Work: A Guide for Leaders and Group Members*. San Diego: University Associates, 1976. $18.50 paper.

For everyone who leads groups, conducts meetings, and plans or leads conferences, this book discusses group characteristics and group dysfunction, provides techniques to encourage the active participation of group members, and describes how groups handle task and maintenance functions.

*Davis, Larry N. *Planning, Conducting, and Evaluating Workshops*. Austin, Tex.: Learning Concepts, 1975. $15.95 paper. (Distributed by University Associates).

This best-selling guide to succesful training combines humor, imagination, and solid learning theory to instruct HRD practitioners how to increase the effectiveness of adult learning programs. It offers step-by-step instructions for all phases of the process and practical suggestions for handling all planning details and local arrangements. The section "Tips for Selecting Methods" is a handy reference to ten different instructional methods. The "Staff Packet" has twenty reproducible worksheets to use in carrying out the workshop development process, and the "Manager's Guide to Staff Development" is useful for gaining management support.

Lazer, Ellen A., and others. *The Teleconferencing Handbook: A Guide to Cost-Effective Communication*. White Plains, N.Y.: Knowledge Industry Publications, 1983. $24.95.

This book is designed to help organizations determine whether some form of audio, video, or computer teleconferencing would be practical and useful for their training, marketing, or other communication needs. The authors present needs analysis, costs, logistics, and regulatory and human issues, as well as case studies of successful corporate applications. Included are a technical glossary and a directory of teleconferencing suppliers.

McLagan, Patricia A. *Getting Results Through Learning: Tips for Participants in Workshops and Conferences*. St. Paul: McLagan & Associates Products, 1983. $9.95 paper.

McLagan offers practical tips in a concise and highly readable form for getting the most out of participation at conferences and workshops. Included are what to do before the conference begins, how to concentrate and stay motivated during the program, strategies to increase learning and generate creative ideas, action planning for application back home, note taking, and tips on getting the most from different learning formats—books, journal articles, case studies, computer-aided learning, discussion, lectures, role plays, and nonprint materials.

Nadler, Leonard, and Nadler, Zeace. *The Conference Book*. Houston: Gulf, 1977. $19.

The Nadlers provide a comprehensive look at how to design a successful conference: detailed information on where and when to hold a conference, who should be reponsible for specific duties, and what types of conference activities are most productive. Also included are details involved in registration, exhibits, the conference program book, evaluation, and follow-up.

International HRD Practice

Copeland, Lennie, and Griggs, Lewis. *Going International: How to Make Friends and Deal Effectively in the Global Marketplace*. New York: Random House, 1985. $19.95.

This book provides tips on getting started in another country, marketing to citizens of other countries, negotiation strategies, communication patterns, management, training, business and social etiquette, and managing personal and family life. The book concludes with thirty country summaries that include such information as fundamentals in business, sensitivities, forms of address, courtesies, business dos and don'ts, negotiations, entertainment, language, and religion. (A companion film series titled *Going International* is available from Copeland Griggs Productions, San Francisco.)

*Harris, Philip R., and Moran, Robert T. *Managing Cultural Differences*. (2nd ed.) Houston: Gulf, 1987. $29.95.

Harris and Moran examine how cultural backgrounds influence perceptions and behaviors. Topics include managing effectively in intercultural business relations, culture shock, cross-cultural family preparation, American micro- and macrocultures, methods of cross-cultural training, and specific techniques for working in France, England, Ireland, Japan, Latin America, China, and the Middle East. (A companion video series titled *International Management Productivity Series* is distributed by Masterco.)

Hoopes, David S., and Ventura, Paul (eds.). *Intercultural Sourcebook: Cross-Cultural Training Methodologies*. Yarmouth, Maine: Intercultural Press, 1979. $7.95 paper.

This comprehensive survey includes role plays, simulations, contrast-American techniques, the culture assimilator, self-awareness inventories, workbook approaches, critical incidents, case studies, area-specific training, and small-group exercises applicable for international training.

Kohls, L. Robert. *Developing Intercultural Awareness*. Washington, D.C.: SIETAR International, 1981. $10 paper.

This learning module includes training exercises, a summary of intercultural hypotheses, a list of intercultural bibliographies and area studies resources, and a reading list for trainers.

Miller, Vincent. *The Guidebook for International Trainers in Business and Industry*. Alexandria, Va.: American Society for Training and Development/Van
Nostrand Reinhold, 1979. Out of print.

> Miller provides practical guidelines for international or minority training
> and outlines a complete strategy for starting a training program in a developing
> country, with procedures for setting up administrative arrangements and
> establishing objectives. Thirty-four training techniques are discussed, with appli-
> cations and tips on optimum usage.

*Moran, Robert T., and Harris, Philip R. *Managing Cultural Synergy*. Houston:
Gulf, 1981. $29.95.

> This book examines the dynamics of multicultural cooperative action and
> provides guidelines on how to enhance international management effectiveness.
> In addition, it describes how productive and profitable synergistic behavior can
> be developed in specific national cultures, including Asia, the Middle East,
> Europe, and Central America. (A companion video series titled *International
> Management Productivity Series* is distributed by Masterco.)

Reynolds, Angus (ed.). *Technology Transfer*. Boston: International Human
Resource Development Corporation, 1984. $21.

> The contributing authors are HRD practitioners who discuss the complex-
> ities of international HRD and planning for technology transfer. Also included
> are chapters on management's role in the transfer of technology, the creation
> of culturally appropriate training for supervisors, and the adaptation of course-
> ware for technology transfer.

Taylor, Bernard, and Lippitt, Gordon (eds.). *Management Development and Training Handbook*. (2nd ed.) New York: McGraw-Hill, 1985. $72.50.

> These readings provide an international perspective on management develop-
> ment and training by specialists from different countries. Emphasizing practical
> methods for solving job-related problems, this collection provides an overview
> of management development theories and examples of successful applications.

"Training World." *Training*. July issue. Minneapolis: Lakewood Publications.
Annual.

> Each July issue of *Training* magazine features a section on current develop-
> ments in international HRD practice.

Group Theory and Practice

Bradford, Leland P. (ed.). *Group Development*. (2nd ed.) San Diego: University
Associates, 1978. $17.50 paper.

> This classic collection of readings on group development includes some of
> the best theoretical materials available on topics such as the roles of group

members, diagnosing group problems, improving group decision making, hidden agendas, stereotypes and the growth of groups, trust, small-group behavior, personal goals, and the group's goals for members.

*Bradford, Leland P. *Making Meetings Work: A Guide for Leaders and Group Members*. San Diego: University Associates, 1976. $18.50 paper.

For everyone who leads groups or conducts meetings, this book discusses group characteristics and group dysfunction, provides techniques to encourage the active participation of group members, and describes how groups handle task functions and maintenance functions.

*Guthrie, Eileen, and Miller, Warren Sam. *Process Politics: A Guide for Group Leaders*. San Diego: University Associates, 1981. $12.95 paper. (Also available: *A Trainer's Manual for Process Politics*, $7.95 paper).

This easy-to-understand primer on group dynamics is good for new groups, new group leaders, and beginning trainers or consultants. It explains how the group leader can help the group accomplish its goals, including task concerns and maintenance concerns (activities that have to do with maintaining strong, supportive relationships among group members).

Zander, Alvin. *Making Groups Effective*. San Francisco: Jossey-Bass, 1982. $19.95.

Zander applies research findings on group dynamics to show how all types of groups can solve day-to-day problems and function more effectively. Topics include making group decisions, leading productive group discussions, establishing group standards, identifying external pressures that can affect the group, choosing realistic group goals, handling intergroup conflicts and reconciling individual differences, fostering pride in group achievement, and understanding the role of power in organizations.

Organization Development

Addison-Wesley Series on Organization Development. Reading, Mass.: Addison-Wesley, 1969. $10.50 paper (each).

This classic series on organization development defines organization development, puts it in historical perspective, and describes the types of strategies, tactics, and activities used. Volumes in the original series include:

Beckhard, Richard. *Organization Development: Strategies and Models*.
*Bennis, Warren G. *Organization Development: Its Nature, Origins, and Prospects*.
Blake, Robert R., and Mouton, Jane S. *Building a Dynamic Corporation Through Grid Organization Development*.
Lawrence, Paul R., and Lorsch, Jay W. *Developing Organizations: Diagnosis and Action*.

Schein, Edgar H. *Process Consultation: Its Role in Organization Development.*
Walton, Richard E. *Interpersonal Peacemaking: Confrontation and Third-Party Consultation.*

Argyris, Chris. *Reasoning, Learning, and Action: Individual and Organizational.* San Francisco: Jossey-Bass, 1982. $28.95.

Argyris is concerned with the self-defeating, counterproductive behavior that prevails in organizations, such as conformity, lack of initiative and teamwork, games of deception, and reluctance to accept responsibility. Argyris found that this ineffectiveness stems from faults in the ways people diagnose problems (reasoning), decide how to respond (learning), and implement solutions (action). This book offers proven strategies for improving individual and organizational performance, illustrated with numerous case examples from problem-solving and training sessions.

*Burke, W. Warner. *Organization Development: Principles and Practices.* Boston: Little, Brown, 1982. $30.75 paper.

Written in a clear, easy-to-read style, this book combines academic and practical perspectives. Burke emphasizes diagnosis as the basis of intelligent change, presents a review of change models, discusses a wide range of interventions or possible change actions, and describes the role of the OD consultant.

French, Wendell L., and others. *Organization Development: Theory, Practice, and Research.* (2nd ed.) Plano, Tex.: Business Publications, 1983. $27.95 paper.

This collection of fifty-three articles by experts in the field presents a comprehensive picture of the history, definitions, and descriptions of organization development; the change process; descriptions of a variety of OD interventions; consultant behavior; employee relations; application in the public sector; research issues; criticisms of OD; and values issues. Some of the specific interventions discussed are data gathering and data analysis for diagnosis, team interventions and intergroup activities, survey-guided development, grid organization development, t-groups and group process laboratories, gestalt approaches, transactional analysis, life-career planning, work redesign, management by objectives, collateral organization, and physical settings and OD.

*Lippitt, Gordon L. *Organizational Renewal: A Holistic Approach to Organization Development.* (2nd ed.) Englewood Cliffs, N.J.: Prentice-Hall, 1982. $36.95.

Lippitt addresses the need for organizations to reexamine objectives, review structures, improve relationships, and rediscover responsibilities to members, clients, and employees. Organizational renewal includes the following elements: planning and managing change; information and communication at work; power and leadership issues; managing stress, conflict, and agreement; individual, group, and organization development processes; and renewal as a training and development process.

*Warrick, D. D. (ed.). *Contemporary Organization Development: Current Thinking and Applications*. Glenview, Ill.: Scott, Foresman, 1984. $24.95.

This authoritative collection of thirty-seven articles includes information on affirmative action, team building, participative management, organizational politics, job redesign, quality circles, organizational stress, quality of work life and productivity, and managerial and consultant competence.

*Weisbord, Marvin. *Organizational Diagnosis: A Workbook of Theory and Practice*. Reading, Mass.: Addison-Wesley, 1978. $14.95 paper.

This practical approach to the diagnosis of management problems in organizations is designed as a workbook—with plenty of charts, graphics, and various forms for the reader to complete. Weisbord provides six categories to assist in analyzing an organization: structure, purposes, relationships, rewards, helpful mechanisms, and leadership. Also included are a number of resource readings on diagnosis by different authors.

Consulting

*Bell, Chip R., and Nadler, Leonard. *Clients and Consultants*. (2nd ed.) Houston: Gulf, 1985. $24.95.

This new edition of *The Client-Consultant Handbook* includes twenty-six articles that address the problems of client-consultant compatability, the challenges of working with the entrepreneur owner, and the benefits of writing contracts to clarify goals and prevent misunderstanding. Readers will also learn how to choose, negotiate with, and use a consultant to solve specific problems. The book's structure is based on the steps of the consulting process—entry, diagnosis, response, disengagement, and closure—with a section on ethical issues.

Blake, Robert R., and Mouton, Jane S. *Consultation: A Comprehensive Approach to Individual and Organization Development*. (2nd ed.) Reading, Mass.: Addison-Wesley, 1983. $26.95.

This is the updated, expanded version of the book that has become a classic in consultation. It provides a systematic method of selecting appropriate strategies for resolving organizational problems. Interventions are categorized as acceptant, catalytic, confrontation, prescriptive, and theory and principles. Focal issues initiating change may be based on power/authority, moral/cohension, norms/standards, or goals/objectives. Case studies illuminate the authors' theories and presentations.

*Block, Peter. *Flawless Consulting: A Guide to Getting Your Expertise Used*. Austin, Tex.: Learning Concepts, 1981. $29.95. (Distributed by University Associates).

This practical guidebook describes and demonstrates ways of behaving with clients in many different consulting situations. Block uses illustrative examples, case studies and exercises, sample client-consultant dialogue, and commentary on pitfalls to demonstrate the concepts of consultant integrity and interpersonal dynamics.

Greiner, Larry E., and Metzger, Robert O. *Consulting to Management*. Englewood Cliffs, N.J.: Prentice-Hall, 1983. $32.95.
   Greiner and Metzger describe management consulting, marketing of consultant services, pricing services, ethical issues, and burnout. They provide various models and methods for consulting — strategic planning studies, marketing assignments, financial analyses, organization and systems studies, human resource and compensation studies, and data-gathering methods.

*Lippitt, Gordon, and Lippitt, Ronald. *The Consulting Process in Action*. San Diego: University Associates, 1978. $21.95 paper.
   Gordon Lippitt and Ronald Lippitt describe the six major phases of a consultant-client working relationship and the tasks involved in each phase. They discuss the roles that the consultant plays, decisions that have to be made, ethical dilemmas and guidelines, and action research and evaluation. This is a popular resource full of practical information.

Steele, Fritz. *Consulting for Organizational Change*. Amherst: University of Massachusetts Press, 1981. $9.95 paper.
   These essays explore new perspectives of consultation, including learning from consulting, the client's role, organizational overlearning, using the laboratory method to train consultants and clients, the complete consultant's catalogue (different styles among consultants, including costumes), teamwork in consultation, consultants as detectives, and the impact of the immediate physical setting on the consulting process (the "scene of the crime").

Career Development

*American Society for Training and Development. *Models for Excellence: The Conclusions and Recommendations of the ASTD Training and Development Competency Study*. Baltimore: ASTD Press, 1983. $65.
   This publication presents the results of a three-year study to determine the roles and competencies of training and development managers. Fifteen key training and development roles were identified: evaluator, group facilitator, individual development counselor, instructional writer, instructor, manager of training and development, marketer, media specialist, needs analyst, program administrator, program designer, strategist, task analyst, theoretician, and transfer agent. Also included are thirty-four future forces that are likely to affect training and development practice and 102 "outputs" (products, services, and information) that signify a practitioner's excellence.

*Bolles, Richard N. *What Color Is Your Parachute?* (2nd ed.) Berkeley: Ten Speed Press, 1984. $8.95 paper.

> Probably the most popular guide for job-hunters and career-changers, this book provides up-to-the-minute guidance on planning a career, figuring out how to find the best job, and interviewing effectively. Creative and imaginative approaches are discussed. This book is a gold mine of information.

*Chalofsky, Neal, and Lincoln, Carnie Ives. *Up the HRD Ladder: A Guide to Professional Growth.* Reading, Mass.: Addison-Wesley, 1983. $18.95.

> This career development guide specifically for the HRD profession includes a discussion of roles and competencies of HRD practitioners, a description of professional development activities, and an analysis of career development paths and options within the HRD and the adult/continuing education fields. The authors offer practical advice on designing a self-directed career development program. Self-assessment exercises and checklists are included.

Compensation in Training and Development. (3rd ed.) Baltimore: ASTD Press, 1985. $80 for members, $95 for nonmembers.

> Data are presented in a series of tables that covers trainers at all levels, from entry-level to training executives, those in organization development, and consultants. Information is also available for specific geographic areas. Other variables analyzed include type and size of organization, level of supervisory responsibility, years of education and experience, and primary HRD activity.

Dalton, Gene W., and Thompson, Paul H. *Novations: Strategies for Career Management.* Glenview, Ill.: Scott, Foresman, 1985. $18.95.

> Dalton and Thompson identify four stages in the career development of professionals in organizations: apprentice, independent contributor, mentor, and director. They have found that the concept of novation is critical to successful progression through these career stages. Novation is negotiating and coming to mutual agreement on the new obligations and expectations of the next career development stage. The authors conclude with a discussion of the personal meaning of work, professionals' personal commitments, and organizational implications. A self-assessment guide is included.

Hagberg, Janet, and Leider, Richard J. *The Inventurers: Excursions in Life and Career Renewal.* (Rev. ed.) Reading, Mass.: Addison-Wesley, 1982. $12.45 paper.

> Inventuring is the art of venturing toward discovering one's unique life and career path. This book is a self-directed guide, a workbook with tools to plan, shape, and map life and career options. It provides a chance to reexamine one's current place in the adult life cycle, to assess learning styles, to determine priorities in the balancing act of body-mind-spirit, and to evaluate work styles. The emphasis is on the enjoyment of making improvements and changes in life-style.

Miller, Donald B. *Personal Vitality*. Reading, Mass: Addison-Wesley, 1977. $13.95 paper. (Also available: *Personal Vitality Workbook: A Personal Inventory and Planning Guide*, $4.50).

    Personal vitality is the ability to grow and adapt to new conditions, new information, and new outlooks. Change may occur through personal growth, learning to learn, unlearning, continued learning, job and organization design, career management, and personal assessment. Miller includes suggestions to enhance individual vitality at work (managing change, redesigning the job, physical and mental health, and self-development) and organizational strategies for achieving vitality.

Schein, Edgar H. *Career Dynamics: Matching Individual and Organizational Needs*. Reading, Mass.: Addison-Wesley, 1978. $12.95 paper.

    One of the volumes in the Addison-Wesley Series on Organization Development, this book discusses career dynamics as it relates to individual, organizational, and management concerns. Schein examines the interaction of family, work, and personal development concerns during the adult life cycle. He discusses development of the organizational career, socialization and learning to work, mutual acceptance, development of career anchors, security, autonomy, creativity, and mid-career challenges.

Zey, Michael G. *The Mentor Connection*. Homewood, Ill.: Dow Jones–Irwin, 1984. $19.95.

    Zey examines the politics and personalities involved in mentoring and the relationship between mentoring and career mobility. Guidelines for establishing formal mentoring programs in business are presented, and special attention is given to problems faced by women.

Self-Directed and Lifelong Learning Methods

Gross, Ronald. *The Independent Scholar's Handbook*. Reading, Mass: Addison-Wesley, 1982. $10.50 paper.

    This is an ingenious handbook that maps out a mostly uncharted terrain: the pursuit of knowledge by amateurs. Gross provides ideas and practical information on choosing a field, conducting research, winning credentials as an expert, keeping an intellectual journal, apprenticing oneself to a mentor, obtaining an affiliation or title, getting grants and awards, finding colleagues and networking, and nontraditional avenues of publication. Included are profiles of self-made experts, such as Alvin Toffler, Betty Friedan, Buckminster Fuller, Eric Hoffer, Barbara Tuchman, and economist Hazel Henderson.

Gross, Ronald (ed.). *Invitation to Lifelong Learning*. New York: Cambridge Book Company, 1982. $22.95.

    This wide-ranging collection of readings provides different perspectives on adult learning from Plato's parable of the cave, Benjamin Franklin's study groups and libraries, Margaret Mead's "lateral" learning from peers, Paulo Freire's revolutionary vision based on adult literacy experiences in Third World countries, and Eduard Lindeman's warning in the 1920s about institutionalizing adult education programs. Current authors discuss adult learning as it is viewed today—Cyril Houle, Malcolm Knowles, Allen Tough, Carl Rogers, Patricia Cross, Buckminster Fuller, and Kenneth Boulding.

*Gross, Ronald. *The Lifelong Learner*. New York: Simon & Schuster, 1977. Out of print.

This is an immensely readable handbook for adults who want to pursue learning opportunities in their own community through libraries, learning exchanges, networking, forming a learning group, television, colleges, correspondence study, audiocassettes, educational brokers, and credit for life experience. Gross provides a background of what lifelong learning is, its importance for all individuals, tips on how to learn, and case studies of lifelong learners in action.

*Knowles, Malcolm. *Self-Directed Learning: A Guide for Learners and Teachers*. New York: Cambridge Book Company, 1975. $8.30 paper.

Learners find out what self-directed learning is and its benefits, how to design a learning plan, and how to carry out self-directed learning activities. Teachers learn to define themselves not as content transmitters but as facilitators of learning. The book includes forms, self-assessment instruments, guidelines, and sample materials for climate setting and relationship building, diagnosing learning needs, formulating objectives, using different learning strategies and resources, and evaluating learning activities. This is a powerful and concise book for empowering people to take responsibility for their own learning by providing them with the strategies to effect this change.

Keeping Up to Date

This list is just the beginning! To keep up with new books being published, watch the book review columns in *Training* magazine and *Training and Development Journal*. You can also find book reviews in most of the periodicals listed in Chapter 11. In addition, the following publications list other books and media in a wide variety of HRD-related fields.

American Society for Training and Development, Brain Trainers Network. *1987 Professional Resource Guide*. Alexandria, Va.: American Society for Training and Development, 1987. $12.

An annotated list of articles, books, films, videotapes, music, assessment tools, newsletters, journals, and bibliographies pertaining to brain/mind issues and management.

Contemporary Psychology. Washington, D.C.: American Psychological Association. Monthly. $50.

Critical reviews of books, films, tapes, and other media representing a cross-section of psychological literature are contained in this periodical.

Future Survey. Bethesda, Md.: World Future Society. Monthly. $45.

This periodical features lengthy reviews of books, articles, and reports concerning forecasts, trends, and ideas about the future: world futures, regions and nations, international relations, science and technology, and world environment/resource issues.

HRD Review: A Journal of Professional Opinion. Glen Rock, N.J.: HRD Review. Monthly. $85.

Begun in 1983, this eight-page publication includes six to eight reviews each month by experienced management and training practitioners. Materials reviewed include books, audiocassettes, films, video packages, and computer software.

Human Resources Index. Pasadena, Calif.: Moreland. Annual. $49.95.

This bibliography lists books, newspaper and magazine articles, newsletters, and nonprint materials in the areas of human resource management, training, counseling, and communication skills.

Massarik, Fred. *Bibliography on Human Relations Training and Related Subjects.* (Rev. ed.) San Diego: University Associates, 1985. $14.50.

This bibliography provides references on t-groups and the laboratory method, change process, conflict, consultation, organization development, techniques and training exercises, studies on groups and the individual, gender issues, and the learning process.

Suessmuth, Patrick F., and Cumberland, William H. (eds.). *Weighted Bibliography: Learning Resources for T&D/HRD Practitioners*. Toronto: Ontario Society for Training and Development, 1985. $20.

Listed in this bibliography are some 250 books, journal articles, course kits, and audiotapes arranged according to twelve competencies for HRD practitioners—administration, communications, course design, evaluation, group dynamics/process, instructional techniques, learning theory, manpower planning, person/organization interface, research and development, training equipment and materials, and training needs analysis. Each item is weighted from 1 to 5 to indicate its significance.

Training and Development Alert. Roseville, Calif.: Advanced Personnel Systems. Bimonthly. $75.

Current journal articles and books in the HRD field are summarized and reviewed in this newsletter.

Directory of Book Publishers and Distributors

Those publishers that have a large output of books in the HRD field are marked with an asterisk (*). Book distributors are marked with a bullet (•).

*Addison-Wesley
One Jacob Way
Reading, MA 01867
(617) 944-3700

Advanced Personnel Systems
P. O. Box 1438
Roseville, CA 95661
(916) 781-2900

AMACOM
135 W. 50th St.
New York, NY 10020
(212) 903-8090

American Psychological Association
1200 17th St. NW
Washington, DC 20036
(202) 955-7600

*American Society for Training and
    Development
1630 Duke St., Box 1443
Alexandria, VA 22313
(703) 683-8100

*ASTD Press
P. O. Box 4856, Hampden Station
Baltimore, MD 21211
(301) 338-6949

Brain Technologies Corporation
414 Buckeye St.
Fort Collins, CO 80524
(303) 493-9210

Business Publications
(Subsidiary of Richard D. Irwin)
1700 Alma, Suite 390
Plano, TX 75075
(214) 422-4389

*Cambridge Book Company
888 Seventh Ave.
New York, NY 10106
(212) 957-5300

Davis S. Lake Publishers
19 Davis Dr.
Belmont, CA 94002
(415) 592-7810

•Dean and Director
Division of the Bureau of Business
    & Technology, Inc.
2472 Fox Ave.
Baldwin, NY 11510
(516) 868-5757

Dow Jones–Irwin
1818 Ridge Rd.
Homewood, IL 60430
(312) 798-6000

Educational Technology Publica-
    tions, Inc.
720 Palisade Ave.
Englewood Cliffs, NJ 07632
(201) 871-4007

Future Systems Incorporated
5929 Lee Highway
Arlington, VA 22207
(703) 241-1799

*Gulf Publishing Company
P. O. Box 2608
Houston, TX 77252
(713) 529-4301

Harper & Row
10 E. 53rd St.
New York, NY 10022
(212) 207-7065

Holt, Rinehart & Winston
6277 Sea Harbor Dr.
Orlando, FL 32887
(305) 345-2525

HRD Review
P. O. Box 6
Glen Rock, NJ 07452
(201) 445-2288

Human Resource Development
  Press
22 Amherst Rd.
Amherst, MA 01002
(800) 822-2801

Intercultural Press
P. O. Box 768
Yarmouth, ME 04096
(207) 846-5168

International Human Resource
  Development Corporation
137 Newbury St.
Boston, MA 02116
(617) 536-0202

*Jossey-Bass
350 Sansome St.
San Francisco, CA 94104
(415) 433-1740

Knowledge Industry Publications
701 Westchester Ave.
White Plains, NY 10604
(914) 328-9157

Lakewood Publications
50 S. 9th St.
Minneapolis, MN 55402
(800) 328-4329, (612) 333-0471

*Learning Concepts
c/o University Associates
8517 Production Ave.
San Diego, CA 92121
(619) 578-5900

Little, Brown & Company
34 Beacon St.
Boston, MA 02108
(617) 227-0730

Macmillan Publishing Company
866 Third Ave.
New York, NY 10022
(212) 702-2000

•Masterco
P. O. Box 7382
Ann Arbor, MI 48107
(313) 428-8300

*McGraw-Hill Book Company
Princeton Rd.
Heightstown, NJ 08520
(212) 512-2000

McLagan & Associates Products,
  Inc.
Rosedale Towers, Suite 300
1700 W. Highway 36
St. Paul, MN 55113
(612) 631-2034

Moreland Company
61 S. Lake Ave., Suite 201
Pasadena, CA 91101
(818) 304-1032

Ontario Society for Training and
  Development
111 Queen St. East, Suite 302
Toronto, Ontario, Canada, M5C 1S2
(416) 367-5900

Prentice-Hall, Inc.
200 Old Tappan Rd.
Old Tappan, NJ 07675
(201) 767-5937

•Professional's Library
9 Arch St., P. O. Box 495
Pawling, NY 12564
(914) 855-9545

Random House
201 E. 50th St.
New York, NY 10022
(212) 751-2600

Sage Publications
2111 W. Hillcrest Dr.
Newbury Park, CA 91320
(805) 499-0721

Scott, Foresman & Company
1900 E. Lake Ave.
Glenview, IL 60025
(312) 729-3000

SIETAR International
1505 22nd St. NW, Suite 102
Washington, DC 20037
(202) 296-4710

Simon & Schuster
1230 Avenue of the Americas
New York, NY 10020
(212) 698-7000

Ten Speed Press
P. O. Box 7123
Berkeley, CA 94707
(415) 845-8414

*University Associates
8517 Production Ave.
San Diego, CA 92121
(619) 578-5900

University of Massachusetts Press
P. O. Box 429
Amherst, MA 01004
(413) 545-2217

Van Nostrand Reinhold Company
7625 Empire Dr.
Lawrence, KY 41042
(606) 525-6600

*Wiley & Sons
605 Third Ave.
New York, NY 10158
(212) 850-6403

World Future Society
4916 St. Elmo Ave.
Bethesda, MD 20814
(301) 656-8274

11

Professional Journals and Periodicals

Linda Webster

Periodicals are good for keeping up with the latest developments in the HRD field. In addition to articles by leading practitioners and theorists in the field, periodicals generally include announcements about new learning products and services, book and media reviews, a calendar of upcoming conferences and seminars, and news of interest to the HRD field. Some of these journals are published by professional associations and included in membership dues. Others are available from commercial publishing houses and consulting firms.

In addition to the journals and newsletters in this chapter, check Chapter 12, which covers organizations and associations. Most associations publish journals and newsletters, and these are listed under the description for each organization. Even though you may not choose to join the association, you can usually subscribe to its journal or newsletter.

This chapter consists of the following sections:

Human Resource Development
Instructional Design and Technology
Organization Development and Consulting
Management
Behavioral Sciences and Creativity
Adult Development and Continuing Education
Future Studies
Indexes to Periodical Articles
Directory of Publishers

For finding journals on other topics of interest to you, consult *Ulrich's International Periodicals Directory*, published annually by Bowker. You can find this reference book in most public and academic libraries. Note that there are a number of periodicals and newsletters available on-line in computer data bases. For example, see the descriptions of Executive Information Service, Harvard Business Review, Interactive Video Technology, and NewsNet in Chapter 16.

For keeping up to date on new articles being published in the field, you can subscribe to *Training and Development Alert*, published bimonthly by Advanced Personnel Systems.

Prices change frequently. Some publishers make yearly changes, so view price information as approximate. Addresses and phone numbers also change.

Human Resource Development

ASTD National Report on Human Resources. Alexandria, Va.: American Society for Training and Development. Monthly. $25 for nonmembers (free to ASTD members).
    This newsletter focuses on developments in the federal government, ASTD business, pertinent statistics and survey results, and articles about HRD from a variety of sources.

Bulletin on Training. Washington, D.C.: Bureau of National Affairs. Monthly. $48.
    This newsletter contains up-to-date information on federal legislation impacting training, current HRD issues and trends in the public and private sectors, a conference calendar, and a special section on practical training techniques.

Federal Trainer. Washington, D.C.: U.S. Office of Personnel Management. Quarterly. $9.50. (Order from Government Printing Office).
    This newsletter focuses on training developments in the federal government and announces upcoming training events.

Info-Line: Practical Guidelines for HRD Professionals. Alexandria, Va.: American Society for Training and Development. Monthly. $60 for members, $80 for nonmembers.
    Each issue of *Info-Line* provides a practical focus on one topic, such as preparation and effective use of nonprint media, alternatives to lectures, needs analysis, gaming techniques, use of job aids, evaluation, and surveys. Checklists, techniques, self-assessment instruments, and a copyright-free pull-out tool (such as a job aid, overhead transparency, or handout) is included in each issue.

Journal of European Industrial Training. Bradford, West Yorkshire, England: M C B University Press Ltd. 7 issues per year. $269.95.
    Recent issues have featured employment training, training for influential managers, participative training methods, team training, and the HRD profession.

Training: The Magazine of Human Resources Development. Minneapolis: Lakewood Publications. Monthly. $42.

One of two major U.S. journals devoted exclusively to HRD practitioners and managers, *Training* includes articles by experts to keep readers up to date on all trends affecting training, from robotics to learning preferences to computers. It provides practical tips on training techniques; a calendar of upcoming conferences and workshops; and news on research, opinions, events, and new training products and services. Columns feature profiles of training in business, industry, and organizations. In addition, there are a number of special issues: "U.S. Training Census and Trends Report" (October issue); "Training World" for international trainers (July issue); "Off-Site Meetings" for meeting planners (June issue); and *Training Marketplace Directory* (mailed with the August issue).

Training Aids Digest. Springfield, Va.: Washington Crime News Services. Monthly. $85.

This twelve-page newsletter provides information for law enforcement and criminal justice training directors on current federal legislation and grants, news items, courses, workshops, seminars, conferences, films, and other training products.

Training and Development Journal. Alexandria, Va.: American Society for Training and Development. Monthly. $55 for nonmembers (free to ASTD members).

The official journal of the American Society for Training and Development, this is one of the two major U.S. journals devoted exclusively to HRD practitioners and managers. Articles cover all aspects of HRD, organization development, and consulting. Regular columns focus on news, practical solutions to HRD problems, recent research, book reviews, and new training tools.

Training Directors' Forum Newsletter. Minneapolis: Lakewood Publications. 10 issues per year. $77.

This forum for leaders and managers of training includes articles that interpret the latest trends of importance to training executives and provide information on the developing role of HRD professionals. Columns include "The Problem Column" (questions and answers), "Profile" (featuring successful training executives), "Eye on Training" by Ron Zemke, and "The Director's Notebook" (quick ideas that are immediately applicable). Topics in recent issues have included protecting the training budget, hiring consultants, selecting a CBT authoring program, and evaluating training by using critical incidents.

Training News: A Monthly Newspaper for the Training Professional. (Formerly *Northeast Training News*). Boston: Weingarten Publications. Monthly. $18 (free to those involved in training).

This twenty-six-page newspaper is full of articles on current issues and practical training techniques. It also includes news items, new training products and services, and a calendar of seminars and workshops.

Instructional Design and Technology

Data Training: The Monthly Newspaper for Information Trainers. Boston: Weingarten Publications. Monthly. $30.

This eighty-six-page newspaper contains practical articles on training techniques, computer-based training, management training, and data processing training. It also contains news items, book reviews, listings of new products (including computer software for training) and services, and a calendar of seminars, workshops, and conferences.

Educational Technology: The Magazine for Managers of Change in Education. Englewood Cliffs, N.J.: Educational Technology Publications. Monthly. $89.

Articles provide state-of-the-art information on instructional design, microcomputers in education and training, and videodisc technology as well as practical applications of the new technologies in education and training. Each issue also includes summaries of current research and reviews of print media and educational computer software for all ages.

Interactive Learning International. New York: Wiley. Quarterly. $71.50.

This journal provides an international perspective on current state-of-the-art computer-based instruction, interactive video, and all forms of interactive learning employing computer technology. It includes assessments of new forms of hardware and software and cutting-edge research on artificial intelligence and knowledge-based systems. It also features reviews of books, software, and courseware; user-group news; and a calendar of training events.

Journal of Instructional Development. Washington, D.C.: Association for Educational Communications and Technology. Quarterly. $24.

Theories, techniques, reports, case studies, and critical reviews are presented on the use of video and other media and the instructional design process in adult education and training. Each issue includes book reviews and summaries of current research reports.

Performance & Instruction Journal. Washington, D.C.: National Society for Performance and Instruction. 10 issues per year. $50.

Articles focus on task analysis, training evaluation, government impact on training, employee effectiveness, instructional development, management, and organization development. Each issue includes columns on new technology, research and theory, book reviews, and humor.

Phi Delta Kappan. Bloomington, Ind.: Phi Delta Kappa. 10 issues per year. $20.

Articles survey the entire field of education, including philosophical issues, legislation, teacher education, elementary and secondary education, and academic institutions. Regular features include federal, state, local and international news; court decisions; prototype projects; research summaries; books; and news notes.

Simulation and Games. Newbury Park, Calif.: Sage. Quarterly. $28.

This is the official publication of the Association for Business Simulation and Experiential Learning, the North American Simulation and Gaming Association, and the International Simulation and Gaming Association. Articles feature microcomputer games, business games, and research on gaming and simulation. The journal also includes reviews of games and books about gaming and simulation.

TechTrends: For Leaders in Education and Training. Washington, D.C.: Association for Educational Communications and Technology. 6 issues per year. $24.

Articles focus on new developments and practical applications for media of all types as well as instructional design in education and business. Each issue includes summaries of current research, news items, and information on new materials, equipment, and services.

T.H.E. Journal: Technological Horizons in Education. Irvine, Calif.: Information Synergy. 10 issues per year. $29.

Articles feature computer-based training, interactive video, robotics, and independent study written by leaders in education, business and industry, and state and federal government. It includes applications for training and adult/continuing education as well as the public school system and academic institutions.

Video Manager. White Plains, N.Y.: Knowledge Industry Publications. Monthly. $36.

This news magazine is geared to managers of video networks in business and industry, medicine, government, and education. It includes news stories, in-depth feature material, and the following monthly columns: "Management Matters," "Interactive Video," "Production Techniques," and "Technically Speaking."

Organization Development and Consulting

Consulting Opportunities Journal. Gapland, Md.: Consultants National Resource Center. Bimonthly. $39.

This highly practical, eight-page newsletter includes articles on marketing strategies, descriptions of new publications and services, and announcements of industrial/organizational/technological start-ups and expansions of potential interest to independent consultants.

Group and Organization Studies: An International Journal. Newbury Park, Calif.: Sage. Quarterly. $32.

Articles focus on research in organization development, group dynamics, and training.

Journal of Applied Behavioral Science. Greenwich, Conn.: JAI Press for NTL Institute. Quarterly. $70.

Articles develop theories of planned change, report and evaluate strategies of social intervention or innovation, and analyze the interplay of theory, practice, and values in the area of planned change. Regular features include book reviews and observations on applied behavioral science theory and method. One special issue each year is devoted entirely to a significant topic. In past years these have included small-group research, citizen participation in public policy, bureaucracy in the eighties, leadership and followship, and ethics, values, and human rights.

Organizational Dynamics. New York: American Management Association. Quarterly. $44.

This journal provides the most significant — and controversial — research in organization functioning and behavior. Recent issues have featured articles on alternatives to layoffs, quality circles, participative management and ethics, quality of work life, and downward movement in careers.

Management

Administrative Science Quarterly. Ithaca, N.Y.: Cornell University, Johnson Graduate School of Management. Quarterly. $35.

This journal promotes understanding of administration in all types of organizations — business, government, educational institutions, hospitals, and the military — and in various cultural contexts. It also contains lengthy book reviews.

George Odiorne Letter. St. Petersburg, Fla.: MBO, Inc. Biweekly. $72.

Written by George Odiorne for senior executives, general managers, and HRD professionals in business and nonprofit organizations, this newsletter presents his personal research and unique observations on management by objectives (MBO) and executive effectiveness. It also includes a question-and-answer column.

Harvard Business Review. Boston: Harvard University, Graduate School of Business. Bimonthly. $49.

Articles cover corporate governance, current issues and concerns of managers and executives, and ideas for action in all areas of management. Each issue includes book reviews. This journal is also available on-line (see Chapter 16).

HH Reports. San Jose, Calif.: Hamlin Harkins Ltd. Bimonthly. $72.

This newsletter is designed to keep human resource professionals up to date on the latest research findings in strategic planning, training, productivity, performance evaluation, labor relations, and employee communication.

Management Review. New York: American Management Association. Monthly. $28 (AMA members only).

Well-written articles cover a broad scope of management issues. Monthly features include news items, book reviews, research summaries from the management sciences, and problem-solving management ideas and methods.

Management World. Willow Grove, Penn.: Administrative Management Society. Monthly. $22.

Articles highlight current trends in management, with news briefs, book reviews, information about new equipment, and regular columns on people skills, new systems, and entrepreneurship.

Personnel: The Management of People at Work. New York: American Management Association. Bimonthly. $35.

Articles focus on current issues in the human resources field, such as employee support services, recruiting, employee committees, interdepartmental conflict, management of a racially diverse workplace, and older workers' productivity. Each issue includes book reviews, a calendar of upcoming AMA workshops, and current news items affecting personnel management.

Personnel Administrator. Alexandria, Va.: American Society for Personnel Administration. Monthly. $40.

Each issue has a special focus as well as additional articles on current issues, columns on legal trends, and news items in the field of human resources management. Recent issues have featured compensation, relocation, human resources management, performance appraisals, and the changing workplace.

Personnel Journal: Magazine for Industrial Relations and Personnel Management. Costa Mesa, Calif: A. C. Croft. Monthly. $38.

Articles on human resources management and training have a practical slant. Regular departments include recruitment, labor relations, training, compensation and benefits, a conference calendar, and listings of training materials and new products and services.

Behavioral Sciences and Creativity

Behavioral Sciences Newsletter. Mahwah, N.J.: Roy W. Walter & Associates. Biweekly. $72.

This newsletter provides the latest and most effective new behavioral science applications in business and industry, such as applying techniques for productivity, work effectiveness, organizational change and development, management by leadership, and quality improvement. Also included in the subscription are several special reports providing detailed treatment of the latest developments and information on annual conferences and workshops in human resource training and development.

Brain & Strategy. Fort Collins, Colo.: Brain Technologies Corporation. 10 issues per year. $78.

This newsletter keeps readers up to date with synopses and reviews of the research, authors, and activities that link biology, psychology, biocybernetics, information sciences, general systems, artificial intelligence, neurology, brain chemistry, philosophy, religion, cosmology, management theory, political science, and other aspects of business and organizational development. Each issues also contains book reviews.

Brain/Mind Bulletin. Los Angeles: Interface Press. 17 issues per year. $35.

This four-page newsletter, edited and published by Marilyn Ferguson, is packed with articles about brain science, psychology, education, creativity, and learning research as well as conference and workshop listings and book reviews.

Journal of Creative Behavior. Buffalo, N.Y.: Creative Education Foundation. Quarterly. $16.50.

Articles describe research and practice in creative problem solving, small groups, creativity training, and intellectual development for individuals and groups of all ages.

Journal of Humanistic Psychology. Newbury Park, Calif.: Sage. Quarterly. $28.

This journal publishes experiential reports, theoretical papers, personal essays, and research studies on self-actualization, personal growth, creativity, values, and encountering.

Small Group Behavior. Newbury Park, Calif.: Sage. Quarterly. $28.

Articles provide research findings on therapy, counseling, and training in small groups in work and educational settings.

Adult Development and Continuing Education

Adult Education. Washington, D.C.: American Association for Adult and Continuing Education. Quarterly. $34.

This journal is devoted to research studies on adult education, adult basic education (ABE), and continuing professional education.

Educational Gerontology. Washington, D.C.: Hemisphere Publishing. Bimonthly. $88.50.

Articles discuss such topics as preretirement planning, reentry into the work force, career retraining, learning and aging, and older students in higher education. Each issue also includes book and film reviews.

ERIC Clipboard. Columbus, Ohio: ERIC Clearinghouse of Adult, Career, and Vocational Education. Quarterly. Free on request.

This four-page newsletter provides summaries of current research in the fields of adult education, career education, and vocational education.

Journal of Counseling and Development. (Formerly *Personnel and Guidance Journal*). Alexandria, Va.: American Association for Counseling and Development. 10 issues per year. $40.

Articles focus on counseling services in schools, higher education, community and work settings, career counseling, and adult development.

Lifelong Learning. Washington, D.C.: American Association for Adult and Continuing Education. 10 issues per year. $35.

Articles describe state-of-the-art practices and innovative programs in adult education, adult basic education (ABE), lifelong learning, and training. This journal includes practical techniques in adult education and training and book reviews.

Vocational Education Journal. Alexandria, Va.: American Vocational Association. 9 issues per year. $26.

Articles describe vocational education, the work force, and vocational education in community/junior colleges and the public schools. Each issue includes reviews on significant research, teaching aids, and books. The January issue contains "The VocEd Buyer's Guide," which lists books, teaching aids, audiovisual equipment and materials, computer hardware and software, business education materials, health occupation materials, and items of interest to trade, industrial, and technical education.

Future Studies

Future Survey. Bethesda, Md.: World Future Society. Monthly. $49.

This periodical features lengthy reviews of books, articles, and reports concerning forecasts, trends, and ideas about the future: world futures, regions and nations, international relations, science and technology, and world environment/resource issues.

The Futurist. Bethesda, Md.: World Future Society. Bimonthly. $25.

This journal discusses forecasts, trends, and ideas about the future in a wide variety of areas – business and economics, education, government and international affairs, life-styles and values, natural resources, and science and technology.

John Naisbitt's Trend Letter. Washington, D.C.: John Naisbitt's Trend Letter. Biweekly. $98.

This eight-page newsletter identifies and analyzes new trends in business, communications, education, technology, health care, housing, the global economy, and other areas and explores the implications of those trends on companies and individuals.

Indexes to Periodical Articles

There may be times when you want a list or bibliography of journal articles on a topic of interest. Computer data bases (see Chapter 16) are available for producing such a list of references. In addition, indexes available at public and academic libraries can help you locate pertinent journal articles. The following list will get you started. Those with an asterisk can be searched by computer.

*Business Periodicals Index. New York: Wilson. Monthly.

Articles on the HRD field can be found under the headings Employee Training, Employee Training Department, Employee Training Personnel, and other general business and management terms.

*Current Index to Journals in Education. Phoenix: Oryx. Monthly.

Subjects of interest to HRD professionals include training and training methods, supervisory training, computer-assisted instruction, media, instructional methods, group processes, organization development, evaluation, and adult and continuing education.

*Education Index. New York: Wilson. Monthly.

Subjects of interest include adult and continuing education, instructional techniques, instructional design, media, computer-assisted instruction, and employee training.

Human Resources Index. Pasadena, Calif.: Moreland. Annual.

This bibliography lists books and newspaper and magazine articles in human resource management and training, counseling, and communication skills.

Personnel Literature. Washington, D.C.: Government Printing Office. Monthly.

This index is produced by the U.S. Office of Personnel Management Library. It lists journal articles under such topics as management/supervisory issues, organization change, communication, consultants, creative thinking, executive training programs, motivation, training, training administration, and training methods.

Personnel Management Abstracts. Chelsea, Mich.: Personnel Management Abstracts. Quarterly.

Summaries are provided for journal articles in organizational behavior, behavioral sciences, career strategy, communication, conflict management, consultants, management development, organization development, time management, training, and work automation.

Psychological Abstracts. Washington, D.C.: American Psychological Association. Monthly.
Summaries are provided for the field of psychology. Areas of most interest to HRD practitioners include developmental social processes, group and interpersonal processes, educational psychology, personnel and management, and organizational behavior.

Resources in Education. Washington, D.C.: Educational Resources Information Center. Monthly.
Lengthy summaries are provided for research reports, curriculum materials, conference papers, and other reports and planning documents generated by educational institutions and generally not published elsewhere. The organization and subject areas are the same as those of the *Current Index to Journals in Education*. Most items in *Resources in Education* are available on microfiche in many academic libraries throughout the United States. Paper copies may be ordered from ERIC.

Social Sciences Index. New York: Wilson. Monthly.
This index lists articles in psychology, sociology, public administration, criminology, medical and health sciences, and continuing education for many professional groups.

Work-Related Abstracts. Detroit: Information Coordinators. Monthly.
This is a guide to current literature on labor relations and personnel management. Of interest to HRD practitioners are the following subject categories: Human Behavior at Work, Management Science, and Education and Training.

Directory of Publishers

A. C. Croft
Box 2440
Costa Mesa, CA 92628
(714) 751-1883

Administrative Management Society
2360 Maryland Rd.
Willow Grove, PA 19090
(215) 659-4300

Advanced Personnel Systems
P. O. Box 1438
Roseville, CA 95661
(916) 781-2900

American Association for Adult and
  Continuing Education
1201 16th St. NW, Suite 230
Washington, DC 20036
(202) 822-7866

American Association for Counseling and Development
5999 Stevenson Ave.
Alexandria, VA 22304
(703) 823-9800

American Management Association
135 W. 50th St.
New York, NY 10020
(212) 586-8100

American Psychological Association
1200 17th St. NW
Washington, DC 20036
(202) 955-7600

American Society for Personnel
Administration
606 N. Washington St.
Alexandria, VA 22314
(703) 548-3440

American Society for Training and
Development
1630 Duke St., Box 1443
Alexandria, VA 22313
(703) 683-8100

American Vocational Association
1410 King St.
Alexandria, VA 22314
(703) 683-3111

Association for Educational
Communications and Technology
1126 16th St. NW
Washington, DC 20036
(202) 466-4780

Bowker Company
P. O. Box 762
New York, NY 10011
(212) 337-6934

Brain Technologies Corporation
414 Buckeye St.
Fort Collins, CO 80524
(303) 493-9210

Bureau of National Affairs
1231 25th St. NW
Washington, DC 20037
(202) 452-4200

Consultants National Resource
Center
5000 Kaetzel Rd.
Gapland, MD 21736
(301) 432-4242

Cornell University
Johnson Graduate School of
Management
Malott Hall
Ithaca, NY 14853
(607) 255-5117

Creative Education Foundation
437 Franklin St.
Buffalo, NY 14202
(716) 884-2774

Educational Resources Information
Center (ERIC)
U.S. Department of Education
Office of Educational Research and
Improvement
Washington, DC 20208
(202) 245-3192

Educational Technology Publications
720 Palisade Ave.
Englewood Cliffs, NJ 07632
(201) 871-4007

ERIC Clearinghouse of Adult,
  Career, and Vocational Education
National Center for Research in
  Vocational Education
The Ohio State University
1960 Kenny Rd.
Columbus, OH 43210
(800) 848-4815, (614) 486-3655

Government Printing Office
Superintendent of Documents
Washington, DC 20402
(202) 783-3238

Hamlin Harkins Ltd.
1740 Technology Dr., Suite 290
San Jose, CA 95110
(408) 279-4340

Harvard Business Review
P. O. Box 866
Farmingdale, NY 11737
(617) 495-6182

Hemisphere Publishing Corporation
1010 Vermont Ave. NW
Washington, DC 20005
(202) 783-3958

Information Coordinators, Inc.
1435-37 Randolph St.
Detroit, MI 48226
(313) 962-9720

Information Synergy
P. O. Box 17239
Irvine, CA 92713
(714) 261-0366

Interface Press
4717 N. Figueroa
P. O. Box 42211
Los Angeles, CA 90042
(213) 223-2500

JAI Press
35 Old Post Rd.
P. O. Box 1678
Greenwich, CT 06836
(203) 661-7602

John Naisbitt's Trend Letter
1101 30th St. NW, Suite 301
Washington, DC 20007
(202) 333-3228

Knowledge Industry Publications
701 Westchester Ave.
White Plains, NY 10604
(914) 328-9157

Lakewood Publications
50 S. 9th St.
Minneapolis, MN 55402
(800) 328-4329, (612) 333-0471

MBO, Inc.
P. O. Box 187
Waltwick, NJ 07463
  (fulfillment office)
5531 Ninth St. North
St. Petersburg, FL 33703
  (editorial office)
(813) 525-1360

M C B University Press Ltd.
62 Toller Lane
Bradford
West Yorkshire 3D8 9B4, England

Moreland Company
61 S. Lake Ave., Suite 201
Pasadena, CA 91101
(818) 304-1032

National Society for Performance
  and Instruction
1126 16th St. NW, Suite 102
Washington, DC 20036
(202) 861-0777

Oryx Press
2214 N. Central at Encanto,
   Suite 103
Phoenix, AZ 85004
(602) 254-6156

Personnel Management Abstracts
704 Island Lake Rd.
Chelsea, MI 48118
(313) 475-1979

Phi Delta Kappa
8th and Union
P. O. Box 789
Bloomington, IN 47402
(812) 339-1156

Roy W. Walter & Associates
45 Whitney Rd.
Mahwah, NJ 07430
(201) 891-5757

Sage Publications
2111 W. Hillcrest Dr.
Newbury Park, CA 91320
(805) 499-0721

U.S. Office of Personnel
   Management
Training Information Branch,
   Room 200
P. O. Box 7230
Washington, DC 20044
(202) 653-6132

Washington Crime News Services
7043 Wimsatt Rd.
Springfield, VA 22151
(703) 941-6600

Weingarten Publications
38 Chauncy St.
Boston, MA 02111
(617) 542-0146

Wiley & Sons
605 Third Ave.
New York, NY 10158
(212) 850-6403

Wilson Company
950 University Ave.
New York, NY 10452
(212) 588-8400

World Future Society
4916 St. Elmo Ave.
Bethesda, MD 20814
(301) 656-8274

12

Professional Organizations and Associations

Linda Webster

Membership in professional associations is one of the best ways to keep up to date in the HRD field, whether you are working in business and industry, government, health care, higher education, or other fields. In addition, there are associations for HRD practitioners who work in an international setting, for consultants, and for those in organization development. Also included in this chapter are associations dedicated to management, psychology, personnel/human resource management, instructional design, educational technology, and adult and continuing education. These are all fields that directly impact and contribute to the HRD field. Many of these related associations have an HRD division, committee, or special section.

Most national associations sponsor an annual conference; many have regional, state, and local chapters in which you can participate. Most have journals, newsletters, and other publications available with membership dues or at discount prices for members. In addition, some associations sponsor special seminars and workshops and state or regional conferences. The membership directories of associations you belong to — national, state, local — will provide you with contacts for networking and help you keep in touch with colleagues you meet at conferences.

This chapter provides the following information about each association: name, address, and phone number; dues; membership size; purpose and activities; and publications. The cost of individual membership dues and the size of membership are approximate figures. Dues are for annual individual memberships. They often do not include additional fees for division memberships or affiliations with state and local chapters. Often dues include a subscription to some but not all association journals and newsletters. Many of these associations have institutional membership categories, which have appreciably higher dues than individual memberships.

155

The organizations and associations are listed in the following sections:

Human Resource Development
Special-Interest Trainers and Meeting Planners
Instructional Design and Technology
Organization Development and Consulting
Management
Behavioral Sciences
Adult and Continuing Education
Future Studies

The list that follows is just the beginning. You will be interested in many other professional and personal growth experiences. To locate associations and organizations in every subject, consult the *Encyclopedia of Associations*, an annual published by Gale Research Company. This reference book is available in public and academic libraries.

Prices change frequently, so view this information as approximate. Addresses and phone numbers also change.

Human Resource Development

American Society for Training and Development (ASTD)

1630 Duke St., Box 1443, Alexandria, VA 22313
(703) 683-8100
Dues: $100 plus additional fee for practice area, industry group, and network memberships
Membership: 22,000; chapter-only membership 27,000
Description: ASTD is the largest association for HRD practitioners. It is divided into nine regions with 141 local chapters. It includes six practice areas—Career Development; International; Instructional Technology; Organization Development; Sales and Marketing; Technical and Skills Training—and fifty-one Special Interest Groups representing various businesses and industries, government, brain trainers, computer-based learning, consulting, women, minorities, senior trainers, and students. ASTD operates a Member Information Exchange, a computerized referral service for sharing expertise among ASTD members; provides a specialized training seminar data base, TRAINET; sponsors research of importance to the HRD field; and provides discount book purchasing. The annual conference is in May or June; regional conferences are in the fall.
Publications: *Training and Development Journal* (monthly); *Info-Line* (monthly); *National Report on Human Resources* (monthly); *Impact on Capitol Hill* (monthly); *ASTD Buyer's Guide and Consultant Directory* (annual); books; audiocassettes and videocassettes of national conference sessions.

International Federation of Training and Development Organizations

c/o Derek Wake
Institute of Management Education
7 Westbourn Rd., Southport PR 8 2HZ, England

Dues: Inquire about organizational dues
Membership: 72 organizations
Description: Membership is open only to organizations and associations involved in all areas of development and training worldwide. Existing members include professional associations, educational institutions, government agencies, multinational corporations, and consultant firms. The annual conference is in the summer in different locations worldwide.
Publications: *IFTDO News* (quarterly); *Who's Who in International Human Resource Development* (irregular).

National Association for Industry-Education Cooperation

235 Hendricks Blvd., Buffalo, NY 14226
(716) 834-7047
Dues: $20
Membership: 1,180
Description: Membership includes representatives of business, industry, education, government, labor, and the professions interested in improving the joint efforts of industry and education at all levels. It assists in the development of local Industry-Education Councils for joint planning on the local level and works on curriculum development and staff development projects. National and regional conferences are held throughout the year.
Publications: *Journal on Industry-Education Cooperation* (semiannual); *Newsletter* (bimonthly); handbooks and guides.

National Society for Performance and Instruction

1126 16th St. NW, Suite 102, Washington, DC 20036
(202) 861-0777
Dues: $80
Membership: 2,700
Description: Membership includes practitioners, researchers, and managers involved in increasing productivity in the workplace through the application of performance and instructional technologies. Members come from business, industry, governmental agencies, and universities with job titles of training director, instructional technologist, change agent, organization development consultant, and human resource manager. The association operates a job placement service. There are forty local and regional chapters and an annual international conference in the spring.
Publications: *Performance & Instruction Journal* (10 issues per year).

SIETAR International (Society for Intercultural Education, Training, and Research)

1505 22nd St. NW, Suite 102, Washington, DC 20037
(202) 296-4710

Dues: $60
Membership: 1,500
Description: Membership includes persons involved in and concerned with intercultural interaction and intercultural education, training, and research in public and private agencies and international businesses. The organization sponsors conferences, workshops, annual week-long summer institutes, and an Intercultural Training Certificate Program (three week-long workshops developed by Georgetown University and SIETAR). It maintains a Computerized Professional Data Bank of members' skills for referrals. The annual international conference is usually in May.
Publications: *International Journal of Intercultural Relations* (quarterly); *Communiqué* (quarterly newsletter); books and training manuals.

Special-Interest Trainers and Meeting Planners

American Association of Correctional Training Personnel
1924 Jerome St., Mesa, AZ 85202
(602) 820-1994
Dues: $15
Membership: 800
Description: Affiliated with the American Correctional Association, membership includes professionals involved in training and staff development in the field of corrections. Members work in prisons, jails, community correctional centers, and probation and parole agencies for adults and juveniles. The association cosponsors voluntary certification of correctional trainers with the American Correctional Association. The annual convention is usually in October.
Publications: *Journal of Correctional Training* (quarterly).

American Society for Engineering Education (ASEE)
11 Dupont Circle, Suite 200, Washington, DC 20036
(202) 293-7080
Dues: $40
Membership: 10,550
Description: Members are college and university engineering deans and teachers, practicing engineers, industrial executives, and others interested in engineering education. ASEE sponsors the annual College-Industry Education Conference, cosponsors the Frontiers in Education Conference, and sponsors summer schools, workshops, and effective teaching institutes. The annual conference is in June.
Publications: *Engineering Education News* (11 issues per year); *Engineering Education* (8 issues per year).

American Society for Healthcare Education and Training
840 N. Lake Shore Dr., Chicago, IL 60611
(312) 280-6113

Dues: $75

Membership: 1,800

Description: Affiliated with the American Hospital Association, membership includes those responsible for training and education in health care institutions. Members are instructors, patient educational coordinators, educational managers, human resource developers, staff development specialists, media specialists, and organization development practitioners. The organization conducts national and regional workshops and institutes on a variety of topics and has local chapters. The annual convention is usually in June.

Publications: *Journal of Healthcare Education and Training* (quarterly); *Hospitals* (biweekly); *Healthcare Dateline* (quarterly newsletter).

Continuing Library Education Network and Exchange (CLENE) Roundtable, American Library Association

50 E. Huron St., Chicago, IL 60611

(312) 944-6780

Dues: $30 for ALA membership; $15 for roundtable membership

Membership: 342

Description: For state library and education agencies, library and education associations, library schools, individuals, and institutions, this group has members who are interested in continuing education for library, media, and information science personnel. Its purposes are to disseminate information about current continuing education programs; to identify the continuing education needs of the profession; and to provide a clearinghouse for ideas and information on continuing education. The annual American Library Association conference is in the summer.

Publications: *CLENExchange* (quarterly newsletter); Occasional Paper series.

Council of Hotel and Restaurant Trainers (CHART)

P. O. Box 11988, Lexington, KY 40579

(606) 268-5586

Dues: $50

Membership: 150

Description: Membership includes people responsible for the training and development of employees in the food service and lodging industry. Members meet twice a year at conferences designed for sharing ideas and experience among trainers.

Meeting Planners International

1950 Stemmons Freeway, Dallas, TX 75206

(214) 746-5222

Dues: $175

Membership: 8,000

Description: Membership includes meeting planners, meeting consultants, and suppliers of goods and services to meeting planners. This organization provides workshops and week-long intensive institutes in meeting-planning skills and sponsors two conferences each year, one in June and one in December.
Publications: *Meeting Manager* (monthly); manuals and information booklets.

National Association of County Training and Employment Professionals

440 First St. NW, Washington, DC 20001
(202) 393-6226
Dues: None
Membership: 1,000
Description: Affiliated with the National Association of Counties, members are county employment and training administrators involved in county training programs and employment practices. The annual convention is in the fall.

National Environmental Training Association

8687 Via de Ventura, Suite 214, Scottsdale, AZ 85258
(602) 951-1440
Dues: $30
Membership: 750
Description: Members are environmental trainers who deliver and manage training in the fields of water, wastewater, noise and air pollution control, and solid and hazardous waste management. It provides workshops, publications, and self-evaluation tools to improve instructional and technical skills of trainers. It publishes training standards and criteria for training programs, personnel, and materials and provides high-quality training manuals and courses for employee training. The annual conference is in August; regional conferences are also scheduled.
Publications: *Newsletter* (quarterly); *Regional Training Activities Calendar* (quarterly); directories of members, training sources, and specialized training personnel.

National Society of Sales Training Executives

1040 Woodcock Rd., Suite 201, Orlando, FL 32803
(305) 894-8312
Dues: Inquire about strict membership requirements
Membership: 125
Description: Members include corporate directors and managers of sales and marketing training. Semiannual conferences are scheduled in June and December, and sales trainer clinics are sponsored by the organization.
Publications: *Newsletter* (quarterly).

Society of Company Meeting Planners

2600 Garden Rd. #208, Monterey, CA 93940
(408) 649-6544

Dues: $200
Membership: 200
Description: Membership includes company and corporate meeting planners and hotel convention service managers. This organization operates a Job Opportunity Bank. The annual convention is in November; additional meetings are held in the spring.
Publications: *Newsletter* (quarterly).

Society of Insurance Trainers and Educators (SITE)

c/o Professional Book Distributors
200 Hembree Park Dr., Roswell, GA 30076
(608) 837-3432
Dues: $60
Membership: 500
Description: Membership includes those involved in education and training within the insurance business. The annual convention is in June; regional meetings are scheduled regularly.
Publications: *In-Site Newsletter* (bimonthly); *Training Journal* (biannually).

Instructional Design and Technology

Association for the Development of Computer-Based Instructional Systems

409 Miller Hall, Western Washington University, Bellingham, WA 98225
(206) 676-2860
Dues: $45 for unaffiliated membership
Membership: 825
Description: Members are university, community/junior college, high school, military, and industry users of computer-assisted instruction. Special-Interest Groups pertinent to HRD practitioners are Computer-Based Training; Interactive Instructional System Users; Implementation; and Mini/Micro Users. It sponsors novice mini/micro computer literacy workshops. The annual conference is usually in May or June.
Publications: *Journal of Computer-Based Instruction* (quarterly); *Newsletter* (bimonthly).

Association for Educational Communications and Technology (AECT)

1126 16th St. NW, Washington, DC 20036
(202) 466-4780
Dues: $50
Membership: 5,500
Description: AECT members are audiovisual and instructional materials

specialists, educational technologists, and audiovisual and television production personnel at all levels of education and in the public and private sectors. The organization's purpose is to improve education through the systematic planning, application, and production of communications media for instruction. This is one of the largest national associations devoted exclusively to instructional media, with nine regional groups and forty-six state groups. Divisions of interest to trainers are Educational Media Management; Industrial Training and Education; Information Systems and Computers; Instructional Development; International; Media Design and Production; and Research and Theory. The annual conference is held in February with COMMTEX (Communications Technology International).

Publications: *TechTrends* (8 issues per year); *Educational Communications and Technology Journal* (quarterly); *Journal of Instructional Development* (quarterly); *Membership Directory* (annual).

Council for Adult and Experiential Learning (CAEL) (formerly Council for the Advancement of Experiential Learning)
10840 Little Partuxent Parkway, Suite 203, Columbia, MD 21044
(301) 997-3535
Dues: $50
Membership: 600
Description: CAEL is composed of colleges, universities, service agencies, corporations, and individuals who share a philosophical commitment to adult and experiential learning. It conducts workshops, seminars, consultation, and training services to member institutions, organizations, and business and industry to develop a nationwide network to serve adult learners. Programs include Project LEARN, a network of CAEL members; joint ventures with business and industry; Prior Learning Assessment (PLA); occupational and technical assessment; institutional and professional development; quality assurance and educational auditing; sponsored and nonsponsored experiential learning; and student and employee assessment of potential. The annual assembly is held in November.
Publications: *CAEL News* (6 issues per year); New Directions in Experiential Learning (series published by Jossey-Bass); and other books and handbooks for faculty, administrators, and students in the field of adult and experiential learning.

North American Simulation and Gaming Association
c/o Bob Farzanegan
Department of Political Science
University of North Carolina at Ashville
Ashville, NC 28814
(704) 258-6422
Dues: $35
Membership: 200

Description: Members are teachers, trainers, media specialists, faculty, and researchers in various disciplines who are involved in simulation and gaming. The organization's annual convention is in October.
Publications: *Simulation and Games* (quarterly).

Society for Accelerative Learning and Teaching (SALT)

P. O. Box 1216, Welch Station, Ames, IA 50010
(515) 292-1555
Dues: $40
Membership: 700
Description: Members are interested in accelerative learning and teaching, based on the suggestopedic techniques of Dr. Georgi Lozanov. The essence of this technique is a highly effective combination of physical relaxation exercises, guided imagery, mental concentration, suggestive principles to strengthen a person's ego and expand memory capabilities, relaxing music, and dynamic presentation of material to be learned. The society sponsors teacher-training workshops and an annual conference.
Publications: *SALT Newsletter* (6 issues per year); *SALT Journal* (quarterly).

Organization Development and Consulting

Certified Consultants International (formerly International Association of Applied Social Scientists)

P. O. Box 573, Brentwood, TN 37027
(615) 385-4107
Dues: $100
Membership: 400
Description: Members are practitioners in a variety of helping roles who work with human systems, drawing upon the disciplines of the social and behavioral sciences and the established professions. Individuals may apply for certification in one or all divisions, each having specific criteria for admission: Group Development Consultants; Organization Development Consultants; Personal/ Professional Development Consultants; and Societal Change Consultants. It also includes ten affiliate groups.
Publications: *Newsletter* (quarterly); *Directory* (annual).

Organization Development Institute

11234 Walnut Ridge Rd., Chesterland, OH 44026
(216) 461-4333
Dues: $70
Membership: 432
Description: Members are professionals, students, and individuals interested in organization development. The institute conducts numerous workshops,

seminars, and specialized education programs and maintains a placement service. From worldwide ideas the institute has written an Organization Development Code of Ethics for the OD profession, developed a written OD competency test, and established objective criteria for becoming a Registered Organization Development Consultant. Seventeen committees are working on issues important to the field of OD, including a Committee on the Accreditation of OD/OB Academic Programs. There are thirty-five local groups. The annual Organization Development Information Exchange is in May (in Wisconsin), and the annual international Organization Development World Congress is held outside the United States.

Publications: *Organizations and Change* (monthly newsletter); *Organization and Development Journal* (quarterly); *International Registry of OD Professionals and OD Handbook* (annual).

Organization Development Network (ODN)

P. O. Box 69329, Portland, OR 97201
(503) 246-0148
Dues: $75
Membership: 2,100
Description: Members are practitioners, academics, managers, and students employed or interested in organization development, with international membership. Organized in 1964, ODN conducts a national annual conference in October and cosponsors events with other groups who have similar purposes.
Publications: *Organization Development Practitioner* (quarterly).

Management

Administrative Management Society (AMS)

2360 Maryland Rd., Willow Grove, PA 19090
(215) 659-4300
Dues: $75
Membership: 10,000
Description: Members are managers in administrative services, finance, personnel, information systems, and sales; educators; and management consultants. AMS sponsors professional accreditation for Certified Administrative Manager (C.A.M.). It includes fifteen regions and 130 local chapters. The annual conference is in May; regional conferences are also held.
Publications: *Management World* (8 issues per year); *Managing* (monthly newsletter); *Manager's Careerletter* (bimonthly newsletter); monographs and research reports; salary surveys; videotapes.

American Management Association (AMA)

135 W. 50th St., New York, NY 10020
(212) 586-8100

Dues: $125
Membership: 85,000
Description: This is the largest management association in the United States, with international offices in Europe and South America. AMA conducts conferences, seminars, courses, and workshops and publishes books, periodicals, newsletters, cassette programs, and programmed instruction materials. The Human Resources Division will be of most interest to HRD practitioners. The annual convention is in September; the annual Human Resources Conference is in April.
Publications: *Management Review* (monthly); *Supervisory Management* (monthly); *Personnel* (bimonthly); *International Manager* (quarterly); *Organization Dynamics* (quarterly); additional journals and newsletters, books, cassette programs, and programmed instruction materials. (Request catalogues of books, cassette programs, seminars, and courses.)

American Society for Personnel Administration (ASPA)

606 N. Washington St., Alexandria, VA 22314
(703) 548-3440
Dues: $135
Membership: 35,000
Description: Membership is primarily personnel and industrial relations executives. HRD practitioners will be interested in the Training and Development Committee. There are 400 local chapters and 200 student chapters affiliated with ASPA. The annual convention is in June; regional conferences are also scheduled.
Publications: *Personnel Administrator* (monthly); *Resource* (monthly newspaper); books, reports, and surveys.

Human Resource Planning Society

P. O. Box 2553, Grand Central Station, New York, NY 10163
(212) 490-6387
Dues: $125
Membership: 1,400
Description: Members are human resource planning professionals, including manpower planning and development specialists, staffing analysts, and others concerned with employee recruitment, development, and utilization. The annual conference is in San Francisco in late February or early March, and professional development workshops are sponsored throughout the year.
Publications: *Human Resource Planning Journal* (quarterly); *Newsletter* (bimonthly); *Membership Directory* (annual).

International Association for Personnel Women

5820 Wilshire Blvd., Suite 500, Los Angeles, CA 90036
(213) 937-9000

Dues: $60
Membership: 2,000
Description: Members are women and men in human resource management and industrial relations in business, education, government, and nonprofit organizations as well as others who are also dedicated to the interests of women in human resource management. There are three regions and twenty-four local affiliates in major cities of the United States. An annual conference is sponsored.
Publications: *IAPW Journal* (quarterly); *Connections* (bimonthly newsletter).

National Management Association (NMA)

2210 Arbor Blvd., Dayton, OH 45439
(513) 294-0421
Dues: $16
Membership: 73,000
Description: Members are business and industrial management personnel and supervisors. There are six regions with 255 local groups. NMA conducts over 100 management workshops and conferences annually through local affiliates; offers over 200 management development courses for professional and personal growth on a group-study basis through local chapters; encourages certification of managers through the Institute of Certified Professional Managers; and provides the NMA Certificate in Management Studies, a 200-hour program of study. The annual conference is in September or October.
Publications: *Manage* (quarterly).

Behavioral Sciences

American Association for Counseling and Development (AACD) (formerly American Personnel and Guidance Association)

5999 Stevenson Ave., Alexandria, VA 22304
(703) 823-9800
Dues: $52 plus additional fee for division membership
Membership: 52,000
Description: Members are counselors, counselor educators, and related human development specialists who work at all educational levels in educational institutions, in community agencies, correctional institutions, rehabilitation programs, government, business and industry, and research facilities. AACD includes four regional branches and fifty-six state and international groups. Of interest to HRD professionals are the Women's Issues Committee and the following divisions: National Career Development Association, Association for Humanistic Education and Development, National Employment Counselors Association, Association for Multicultural Counseling and Development, Association for Adult Development and Aging, and Association for Specialists in Group Work. AACD

conducts professional development institutes and maintains a placement service for members. The annual conference is in March or April.

Publications: *Journal of Counseling and Development* (10 issues per year); *Guidepost* (18 issues per year); over 100 books, research studies, pamphlets, films, journals, and newsletters.

American Psychological Association (APA)

1200 17th St. NW, Washington, DC 20036

(202) 955-7600

Dues: $110

Membership: 58,000

Description: This is the major association for psychologists and for educators and students in the field of psychology. APA includes fifty-four state affiliate groups. Of the forty-five special-interest divisions of APA, the following are of most interest to HRD practitioners: Society of Industrial and Organizational Psychology, Adult Development and Aging, Humanistic Psychology, and Psychology of Women. The annual convention is in August.

Publications: *American Psychologist* (monthly); *APA Monitor* (monthly newspaper); *Psychology Today* (monthly); seventeen journals in specialized fields; *Psychological Abstracts* (also available as a computer data base); books.

Association for Humanistic Psychology (AHP)

325 Ninth St., San Francisco, CA 94103

(415) 626-2375

Dues: $55

Membership: 6,500

Description: This is an international network for lay and professional people who are applying humanistic and holistic principles in their lives, their work, and their communities. Members are theorists and practitioners in the human services, including therapists, educators, counselors, artists, social scientists, organization development consultants, administrators, and lay people. AHP includes three regions and twenty-five state and local chapters in the United States and two chapters in Ontario, Canada. It sponsors regional conferences and international events. The annual conference is in August; regional conferences and international events are also held.

Publications: *Journal of Humanistic Psychology* (quarterly); *AHP Newsletter* (monthly).

Adult and Continuing Education

American Association for Adult and Continuing Education

1201 16th St. NW, Suite 230, Washington, DC 20036

(202) 822-7866

Dues: $85
Membership: 3,500
Description: Formed by the merger of the Adult Education Association of the
U.S.A. and the National Association for Public Continuing Adult Education,
this is one of the largest national groups devoted to adult and continuing education and lifelong learning. Of interest to HRD practitioners are its Human
Resource Development Division, Business and Industry Division, Commission
on Continuing Professional Education, and Educational Media and Technology
Unit. Members come from a diversity of settings—public schools, community/
junior colleges and higher education institutions, community education programs,
the field of continuing professional education, and government agencies. As
the private sector works more closely with these groups in designing and conducting employee training programs, HRD practitioners may become involved
in this association. There are eight affiliated regional groups and state adult
education assocations in most states. The annual convention is usually in the
fall with an attendance of over 2,500.
Publications: *Lifelong Learning* (8 issues per year); *Adult Education* (quarterly);
newsletters, books, and research monographs and reports.

American Association of Community and Junior Colleges
National Center for Higher Education
One Dupont Circle, Suite 410, Washington, DC 20036
(202) 293-7050
Dues: Based on enrollment
Membership: 1,000
Description: Institutional and individual members are from two-year colleges.
Community and junior colleges tend to have large noncredit continuing educa-
tion and community education programs and a vocational/technical emphasis;
many work closely with business and industry and local government agencies
to provide contract training for employees. The annual convention is in April.
Publications: *Community and Junior College Journal* (bimonthly); *AACJC
Letter* (weekly).

American Vocational Association (AVA)
1410 King St., Alexandria, VA 22314
(703) 683-3111
Dues: $32 plus state association dues
Membership: 47,000
Description: Members are teachers, supervisors, administrators, and others
interested in vocational, technical, and practical arts education, including industrial cooperative training programs, part-time classes for adults, retraining and
upgrading workers, and supervisory and foreman training. AVA works closely
with a number of federal agencies. Of interest to HRD practitioners is the
Employment and Training Division. In addition to the national association, there

are fifty-seven state groups. The annual convention is in December.
Publications: *Vocational Education Journal* (8 issues per year); *Update* (6 issues per year); and a number of special products (catalogue available).

Association for Continuing Higher Education (ACHE)
c/o Dr. Roger H. Sublett
College of Graduate and Continuing Studies, University of Evansville
1800 Lincoln Ave., Evansville, IN 47722
(812) 479-2472
Dues: $35
Membership: 1,250
Description: Members are colleges and universities and faculty or staff of a university continuing education division. Members are involved in community education, continuing professional education, and cooperative training programs with business and industry. ACHE includes ten regional groups. The annual meeting is in October or November.
Publications: *Journal of Continuing Higher Education* (quarterly); *5 Minutes with ACHE* (9 issues per year); *Proceedings* (annual).

Learning Resources Network (LERN)
P. O. Box 1448, 1554 Hayes Dr., Manhattan, KS 66502
(913) 539-5376
Dues: $125
Membership: 650
Description: Members are free universities, college- and university-affiliated groups, community education organizations, learning networks, and individuals interested in lifelong learning. LERN serves as a national technical assistance network in adult learning and noncredit programming, sponsors workshops, provides speakers, and compiles statistics on continuing education courses. The Annual Conference for Noncredit Programs is in the fall; Issues in Lifelong Learning is the spring retreat.
Publications: *Marketing Classes for Adults* (monthly); *Adult & Continuing Education Today* (biweekly); *Course Trends in Adult Learning* (monthly); publications with a practical slant for both teachers and administrators. (Request current publications catalogue.)

National University Continuing Education Association (NUCEA)
One Dupont Circle, Suite 420, Washington, DC 20036
(202) 659-3130
Dues: $35 (individuals may join only if institution is member)
Membership: 1,550
Description: Members are institutions of higher education with extension and continuing education programs and professional staff who work in these programs. NUCEA includes four councils and twenty-two divisions. Of interest

to HRD practitioners are the Council on Continuing Education Delivery Systems and Formats; the Council for Continuing Education Constituencies; the Division of Career Counseling, Advisement, and Adult Student Services; the Division of Continuing Education for the Professions; and the Division of Programs for Women. The national conference is held each April; each of the association's seven regions holds an annual fall conference.

Publications: *NUCEA News* (monthly); *Continuing Higher Education Review* (triannual journal); *Innovations in Continuing Education: Award-Winning New Programs* (annual); guides, directories, and monographs.

Future Studies

World Future Society
4916 St. Elmo Ave., Bethesda, MD 20814
(301) 656-8274
Dues: $25
Membership: 25,000
Description: Members are interested in how social and technological developments are shaping the future and in the development and improvement of methodologies for the study of the future. Members come from over eighty countries and may be business people, scientists, government leaders, educators, and students. The society sponsors a book service, which includes books, cassette tapes, games, films, and learning kits. It has over eighty local chapters and sponsors Biennial General Assemblies.
Publications: *The Futurist* (bimonthly); *Future Survey* (monthly journal with abstracts of books and articles); *Futures Research Quarterly*.

13

Conferences, Workshops, and Academic Programs

Linda Webster

Y ou can continue your own development as an HRD practitioner by attending national or regional conferences sponsored by professional associations, noncredit courses or seminars conducted through a university continuing education department or business school, and workshops presented by independent seminar organizations. Some noncredit seminars provide CEUs (Continuing Education Units), a nationally recognized method for documenting participation in noncredit structured group learning. One CEU equals ten contact hours of instruction.

You may be interested in an academic degree – a master's or doctoral degree in human resources development, organization development, adult learning, or instructional psychology. This sections lists organizations and associations that provide noncredit programs in human resource development, computer-based learning and mediated instruction, adult learning, and organization development and consulting. Academic degree programs are listed for the HRD field only.

You will find a variety of conferences and independent workshop providers listed. Workshop providers were chosen based on whether their workshops and seminars would be of interest to HRD practitioners and whether they had a variety of training programs available. Inclusion in this section of the book does not necessarily mean recommendation. You will need to contact the sponsoring organizations directly to evaluate the appropriateness and quality of their offerings based on your particular learning needs. Request more detailed information about the conference program or workshop agenda, speakers, and learning outcomes. Talk directly to the instructor to be sure that your learning needs will be addressed and to inquire about the instructional methods used. Check with past attendees from other companies for their evaluation of the seminar.

Your biggest challenge in keeping up to date will be to sort through the vast number of conferences, workshops, and academic programs to identify those that meet your learning needs and the learning needs of other members of the organization (see Chapter 5). Here are some tips on how to keep up to date:

1. *Training* magazine has a monthly "Seminars and Workshops" calendar. Other professional journals and newsletters (see Chapter 11) also list training events.

2. Most professional associations have annual national conferences, and some have regional or state conferences as well. You can attend the conference whether you are a member or not, although conference fees are usually less for members. Check Chapter 12 to identify associations with conferences of interest. Local chapters also sponsor workshops and programs at regular meetings.

3. For noncredit courses offered by universities, contact those nearest you and talk with the continuing education office, the business school, or other departments with courses in your area of interest. Some colleges and universities have all their noncredit courses coordinated through the continuing education office. Some larger universities, however, have a decentralized system in which the business school handles the continuing education programs in business and management.

4. To identify noncredit and credit programs in other fields for yourself and other staff members, consult the listings in this chapter.

5. To identify additional degree programs, consult the *ASTD Directory of Academic Programs in Training and Development/Human Resource Development, 1983-1984*, published in 1983 by ASTD Press ($22).

6. To identify independent seminar organizations and consultants who conduct training sessions on a variety of topics—both in-house and on the open market—check the following annual publications. Consulting firms are listed under a wide variety of content areas in the *ASTD Buyer's Guide and Consultant Directory*, published annually by the American Society for Training and Development, and the *Training Marketplace Directory*, published annually by Lakewood Publications and mailed with the August issue of *Training* magazine.

7. For assistance in locating the right seminar, read "How to Shop for the Right Seminar" in *Training*, June 1986, pp. 17, 77-78, and Mona Piontrowski's "Evaluating the Seminar Marketplace" in *Training and Development Journal*, January 1986, pp. 74-77. Also consult Chapter 5 in this book.

8. For tips on getting the most out of conferences that you attend, read Patricia A. McLagan's *Getting Results Through Learning: Tips for Participants in Workshops and Conferences*, published by McLagan & Associates Products in 1983 ($13.95).

This chapter has the following sections:

Noncredit Conferences, Seminars, and Workshops
Campus-Based Noncredit Programs
Academic Degree Programs
Guides to Noncredit Programs and Credit Courses
Books on Going Back to School
Selected List of Universities with Noncredit Programs
Directory of Publishers

Prices change frequently, so view this information as approximate. Addresses and phone numbers also change.

Noncredit Conferences, Seminars, and Workshops

American Management Association (AMA)
135 W. 50th St., New York, NY 10020
(212) 586-8100

AMA has available over 200 courses in management development, information systems and technology, human resources and employee benefits, finance and accounting, sales and marketing, office administration, manufacturing and technology management, and purchasing and transportation. Seminars of particular interest to HRD practitioners are: Training the Trainer (four and one-half days, 3.4 CEUs); Advanced Training the Trainer (four days, 3.1 CEUs); and Strategic Management of the Human Resources Department (three days, 2.2 CEUs). In addition, AMA sponsors the Annual Human Resources Conference (held in the spring), geared primarily to personnel and human resources management professionals.

American Society for Training and Development (ASTD)
1630 Duke St., Box 1443, Alexandria, VA 22313
(703) 683-8100

ASTD is the major professional association for training practitioners. ASTD sponsors a national conference and exposition in the spring. Each of the nine geographic regions has a conference in the fall. The local chapters (more than 130) often have speakers at their monthly meetings and sponsor training programs, film festivals, and workshops. In 1986 a national satellite teleconference on change strategies was sponsored by the Pittsburgh Chapter of ASTD and sixty additional ASTD chapters throughout the United States.

Applied Creative Services Ltd.
The Whole Brain Corporation
2075 Buffalo Creek Rd., Lake Lure, NC 28746
(704) 625-9153

This organization offers a variety of workshops that translate the latest brain research into practical, highly effective learning programs for companies and individuals. These include Brain Update (one-half to two days), Creative Problem Solving (three days), Creative Communications Workshop (two days), Applied Creative Thinking (five days), and Applied Creative Teaching and Learning (four days).

AT&T Communications
Communications Planning Center
5 Century Dr., First Floor, Parsippany, NJ 07054
(800) 554-6400

AT&T conducts numerous seminars on new communications technology to enhance business and sales/marketing functions. Of interest to HRD practitioners are their seminars on teleconferencing implementation and teletraining design and delivery.

Center for Creative Leadership

5000 Laurinda Dr., P. O. Box P-1, Greensboro, NC 27402
(919) 288-7210

The Center for Creative Leadership conducts research and training programs in leadership development (five and one-half days); organizational action with the Looking Glass Simulation (five days); innovative problem solving and creativity enhancement (five days); negotiating change (five days), as well as other management development and communication workshops. In addition, the Center for Creative Leadership hosts an annual Creativity Week in the fall during which practitioners can discuss the frontiers of applied creativity and experience the latest microcomputer hardware and software to discover applications to innovation.

Computer-Based Training Conference and Exposition

Weingarten Publications
38 Chauncy St., Boston, MA 02111
(617) 542-0146

Data Training, a monthly newspaper for those interested in computer-based training, sponsors an annual week-long conference on computer-based training. The conference features prominent speakers, basic workshops, technical sessions, and exhibits of the newest CBT systems and courseware.

Creative Education Foundation

437 Franklin St., Buffalo, NY 14202
(716) 884-2774

The foundation sponsors annual Creative Problem-Solving Institutes in the winter (West Coast) and the summer (East Coast) as well as an Annual Symposium on Innovation. The Creative Problem-Solving Institutes also have special sessions for participants' children between the ages of nine and fourteen and sessions for those with little or no experience in creative problem solving.

Educational Systems for the Future

5412 Chatterbird Place, Columbia, MD 21045
(301) 997-3860; in Washington, DC, area (301) 982-1577

Seminars include the IDLS—Pro Trainer I (five days) with instruction on how to design, develop, and validate instructional programs; Interactive Teaching Skills (five days); Needs Analysis (five days); and Management of Training (four days), with instruction on how to plan, run, and evaluate a training department. In addition, the company has Learner's Guides and Workbooks ($100–$125 per workshop) and Instructor Guides ($1,200–$2,000 per workshop, including learner's materials and transparencies), which are available for purchase separate from the workshops.

Idea Development Associates
1806 Oxmoor Rd., Birmingham, AL 35209
(205) 870-9559

One- or two-day workshops are available on creative problem solving and decision making, conducted by Anne H. Minton. These workshops enhance creativity and idea power.

Institute for Business & Industry (IBI)
2119 Bristol Pike, Bensalem, PA 19020
(215) 639-4660

IBI provides a wide variety of on-site supervisory and management development training programs, as well as the following workshops for HRD practitioners: Training for Trainers; Advanced Training for Trainers; On-the-Job Training Techniques; Effective Presentations; Conducting a Needs Analysis; Managing the HRD Function; Design, Development, and Installation of Skills Training.

InterCom Workshop in Computer-Based Training
302 E. John St., Champaign, IL 61820
(217) 384-2200

InterCom conducts an annual five-day CBT workshop at its headquarters and several regional workshops and seminars throughout the United States. Content includes steps involved in developing CBT with hands-on experience and information on computer-managed instruction, costs/benefits, authoring systems, and interactive video.

International Communications Industries Association (ICIA) (formerly National Audio-Visual Association)
3150 Spring St., Fairfax, VA 22031
(703) 273-7200

ICIA's national conference is the largest international trade show for the AV communications industry, providing workshops and seminars sponsored by five national associations in addition to ICIA: the Association for Multi-Image International, the International Television Association, the International Association of Business Communicators, the National Association of Local Church Communicators, and the Association of Audio-Visual Technicians. In addition, ICIA and Indiana University cosponsor the annual Audio-Visual Institute for Effective Communications, a five-day hands-on workshop on the design and production of AV materials, interactive video, and computer-assisted instruction.

Mager Associates, Inc.
P. O. Box 1233, Carefree, AZ 85377
(602) 488-2666
    The following are available as either in-house or public workshops:
Classroom Presentation Skills (four days), Instructional Module Development
(ten days), and Criterion-Referenced Instruction (fourteen days).

McLagan International
Rosedale Towers, Suite 300
1700 W. Highway 36, St. Paul, MN 55113
(612) 631-2034
    Workshops available include Communicating about Performance (two days);
Career Strategies (one day); Getting Results Through Learning (one day), which
is about self-directed learning; and Impact Beyond the Classroom (five days),
which teaches trainers instructional models and methods that support learning
transfer and influence forces that inhibit and encourage on-the-job change. Impact
Beyond the Classroom is recommended for experienced instructors.

NTL Institute for Applied Behavioral Science
1501 Wilson Blvd., P. O. Box 9155, Rosslyn Station, Arlington, VA 22209
(703) 527-1500
    NTL (formerly the National Training Laboratories) has been noted for human
relations training and consultation since 1947. In-depth seminars are available
for novice and experienced HRD practitioners in instructional techniques and
group-process skills, consultation skills, and organization development. Other
workshops focus on personal development, management and executive development, change strategies, conflict management, negotiation skills, implementation of innovative ideas, and personal, team, and organizational effectiveness.

Practical Management Incorporated (PMI)
P. O. Box 8789, Calabasas, CA 91302
(800) 423-5099; in California (800) 874-8695 or (818) 348-9101
    PMI offers a variety of workshops for HRD practitioners: How to Make
Training Pay Off in Your Organization (one day, 0.6 CEU); Managing the Training Function (three days, 1.8 CEUs); Effective Classroom Instruction (five days,
3.1 CEUs); Needs Analysis Evaluation and Validation (three days, 1.8 CEUs);
Instructional Design (three days, 1.9 CEUs); Computer-Based Training (three
days, 2.0 CEUs); Teaching Technical Topics (three days, 2.1 CEUs); Fundamentals of One-on-One Instruction (one day, 0.7 CEU).

Scientific Methods, Inc.
P. O. Box 195, Austin, TX 78767
(512) 477-5781
    In addition to Managerial Grid Seminars, Scientific Methods conducts the

Synergogy Seminar (based on the work of Mouton and Blake), which uses team-work to aid learners in any field.

Sony Institute of Applied Video Technology
P. O. Box 29906, Hollywood, CA 90029
(800) 662-SONY

Sony offers eighteen workshops on the use of video as a training medium, including the production of video training tapes and interactive videodiscs.

Training Conferences
50 S. Ninth St., Minneapolis, MN 55402
(800) 328-4329, (612) 333-0471

Training magazine sponsors a number of annual conferences for HRD practitioners: Training Conference, held in New York City (five days in the winter); Cost-Effective Training Conference (four days in San Francisco and Chicago); and Training Directors' Forum (four days in the summer on the East Coast). Training Conference and the Cost-Effective Training Conference both feature a large exhibit area and over 120 seminars and workshops to keep you up to date in the HRD field. The Training Directors' Forum is for training/HRD executives and combines keynote speakers with roundtable discussions, work groups, and a chance for informal networking.

Training House
P. O. Box 3090, Princeton, NJ 08543
(609) 452-1505

This organization provides supervisory and management training, secretarial support systems, sales and sales management training, and the following training programs for HRD practitioners: The Professional Trainer (eight one-day sessions for the novice trainer); Designing the Instructional System (five days); and The Catalytic Instructor (three days), which focuses on highly participative instructional techniques.

University Associates
8517 Production Ave., San Diego, CA 92121
(619) 578-5900

University Associates conducts workshops throughout the United States on organization development, consulting skills, situational leadership, power and conflict management, group dynamics, strategic planning, team building, and the change process. Workshops of particular interest to HRD professionals include Becoming a Professional Trainer (two days); Enhancing Trainer Style (five days); Designing Experiential Training Modules (five days); and Managing the Training Function (two days). University Associates sponsors the annual UA conference to highlight new HRD concepts, issues, trends, and strategies with leading experts in the HRD field and the annual HRD Conference featuring skills-oriented sessions. Both conferences have a number of pre- and post-conference seminars. University Associates also sponsors an annual conference on organization development.

Video Expo
Knowledge Industry Publications
701 Westchester Ave., White Plains, NY 10604
(914) 328-9157
Video Expo is held in the winter in San Francisco and in the fall in New York City. Exhibits feature the latest video equipment. Conference sessions cover video production, uses of video in education, technical information, and management of a video production unit.

Campus-Based Noncredit Programs

Consult colleges and universities in your area to find out what continuing education and professional development courses are available for you and others in your organization. Many universities offer noncredit courses in management and executive development, HRD-related areas, and instructional design. A representative list of universities is included at the end of this chapter to start you thinking about the variety of noncredit programs available.

Academic Degree Programs

There is an increasing number of master's and doctoral programs for HRD practitioners. Degree programs can be housed in a number of different departments or colleges on campus: instructional media, education, adult education, business, vocational education, communications, behavioral sciences, and counseling. The program specialization may be HRD, adult learning and development, instructional technology, human resources management, or organization development.

This section lists some academic HRD programs at the master's and doctoral levels from traditional universities as well as nontraditional programs offered by the American University–NTL (formerly National Training Laboratories), University Associates, and other institutions that are designed for off-campus, self-directed learning. You will find brief information here about the focus of each program and an address and phone number for requesting additional information. You will want to find out about entrance and graduation requirements, the curriculum, and the amount of flexibility you will have in designing a program of study that meets your needs. Check carefully into the accreditation of the program, the faculty, and the number and type of students currently enrolled. Get names of current and former students so that you can find out about the program firsthand.

For additional academic programs that are related to HRD, consult the *ASTD Directory of Academic Programs.*

American University and NTL Institute
American University, Institute for Human Resource Development
215 Ward Circle Bldg., Washington, DC 20016
(202) 885-6206
Degrees: Master of Science in Human Resource Development
Description: The program combines university-based management education with experiential learning in the fields of HRD and organization development. Most of the multidisciplinary courses are held in Washington, D.C., on three-day weekends over a two-year period.

Fielding Institute
Human and Organization Development Program
2112 Santa Barbara St., Santa Barbara, CA 93105
(805) 687-1099
Degrees: Ph.D. in Human and Organizational Systems; Ph.D. in Human Development; Ed.D.; D.H.S. (Doctor of Human Services); and M.A. in Organization Development, Human Development, and Human Service
Description: Participants in the Human and Organization Development Program maintain employment while they complete individually contracted learning plans. Only a brief residence in Santa Barbara is required at the time of admission. Curricular study guides and assessment procedures are available in the following areas: organizational theories, systems theory and practice, social psychology, research, management and leadership, personality theory, human learning and motivation, human services management, change and the future, policy formulation, social ecology, and information and communication systems. Demonstration of competency is required in six of the above areas for the M.A. degree and in eight areas for the doctorate.

George Washington University
Department of Education
2201 G St. NW, Washington, DC 20052
(202) 994-6940, (202) 994-8616
Degrees: Ed.D, Ed.S., and M.A. in Human Resource Development
Description: George Washington University has the oldest academic program in human resource development, begun in 1948. All required work at the graduate level is offered in the evenings and on weekends, with a special weekend program for those coming from a distance. Interdisciplinary work is encouraged.

Norwich University
Vermont College Campus
Montpelier, VT 05602
(802) 223-8750

Degrees: M.A. in various fields in the social sciences and humanities
Description: The Norwich University Graduate Program offers a twelve- to eighteen-month independent master's degree in a variety of fields in the social sciences and humanities. Some of the areas of concentration chosen by students include counseling and psychotherapy, psychology, education, administration and management, human services, and women's studies. Interdisciplinary and cross-disciplinary approaches are encouraged. No campus residence is required.

Nova University
3301 College Ave., Davie, FL 33314
(305) 475-7300
   • Doctor of Arts in Training and Learning Technology is offered by the Center for Computer-Based Learning; Information Sciences. The computer-based program allows students to study at their work site in such areas as software and courseware design, computer science, systems analysis, and strategic management techniques. Also part of the program are practicums and four regional weekend seminars a year. (305) 475-7047.
   • Doctor of Science in Human Resource Managment features regionally located weekend classes, which can be completed in three years. (305) 475-7648.
   • Master of Science in Human Resource Management features corporate-based training and weekend classes, which can be completed in twenty-one months. (305) 475-7647.
   • Certificate in Human Resource Management is designed for those persons who need additional training in HRD beyond the bachelor's degree but who do not require a master's degree. Many students in the certificate program either possess an M.B.A. degree or are pursuing an M.B.A. at Nova while they are working on the four-course certificate program. (305) 475-7647.
   • Ed.D. in Leadership in Higher Education is offered by the Center for Higher Education. This field-based doctoral program consists of formal instruction delivered in seven required seminars, five practicums, independent study, applied research, and week-long summer institutes. (305) 475-7380.

Pepperdine University
School of Business and Management
3415 Sepulveda Blvd., Los Angeles, CA 90034
(213) 306-5598
Degrees: Master of Science in Organization Development
Description: Pepperdine offers an accredited Master of Science in Organization Development. Seven one- or two-week sessions conducted over a twenty-month period provide a convenient format for working professionals.

University Associates
MHRD Programs
8517 Production Ave., San Diego, CA 92121
(619) 578-5900

Degrees: Master's in Human Resource Development
Description: This program includes three required one- or two-week workshops, participation in University Associates seminars conducted at a number of locations throughout the United States, and practicum experience. The program is geared to the needs of working professionals. The content includes human resource development, consulting, small-group facilitation, and organization development. The program is designed to be completed in two or three years.

University of Minnesota
Department of Vocational and Technical Education, College of Education
420 VoTech Bldg., 1954 Buford Ave., St. Paul, MN 55108
(612) 624-4901, (612) 624-9727
Degrees: M.A./M.Ed. with concentration in training and development; Ph.D. in Vocational Education; Ph.D. in Education; Ed.D. in Vocational Education; Ed.D. in Industrial Education
Description: Course work in training and development in industry and business encompasses both employee training and organization development. In addition, strategic planning, needs assessment, and human performance technology are also included in the curriculum as well as course work in economics, education, management, psychology, and sociology.

University of Texas at Austin
Department of Curriculum and Instruction, College of Education
Education Bldg. 406, Austin, TX 78712
(512) 471-4285
Degrees: M.A./M.Ed. in Human Resource Development or Adult and Continuing Education
Description: The master's program in adult and continuing education encompasses lifelong learning systems, adult literacy programs, university extension, professional and in-service continuing education, gerontology, nontraditional study, and continuing education. The Human Resource Development Program provides expertise in a variety of areas: management and supervisory development; design, production, and use of media; management of training departments; career development; and individual, group, and organization development. To serve practitioners in HRD, a graduate emphasis designed for weekend study has been developed with intensive summer and weekend seminars once a month.

Vanderbilt University
Corporate Learning Institute, Peabody College
Box 321, Nashville, TN 37203
(615) 322-8414
Degrees: M.Ed. in Human Resource Development; Ed.D.in Human Resource Development

Description: The master's and doctoral programs include course work, field work, and consultation with practicing HRD professionals. Courses are offered on a full-time basis and on weekends. The graduate programs are closely allied with Vanderbilt University's Corporate Learning Institute, which brings together university and outside human resources professionals who are committed to linking HRD theory and practice. The specific mission of the institute is to produce and disseminate knowledge about how people learn in corporations.

Walden University
1315 Nicolett Mall, Suite 106, Minneapolis, MN 55403
(612) 338-7224; or
3201 Tamiami Trail, Naples, FL 33940
(813) 261-7277
Degrees: Ph.D., Ed.D.
Description: Doctoral programs are available in the fields of business, education, health, or human services from the perspective of social change. Residency options are ten weekends or a four-week summer term, followed by guided distance learning.

Guides to Noncredit Programs and Credit Courses

In addition to the sources below, on-line data bases such as EdVENT, Electronic Registrar, Human Resource Information Network, and TRAINET provide information about noncredit workshops. Gradline is a data base of graduate programs. See these listings in Chapter 16 for more information.

American Council on Education. *Directory of Campus-Business Linkages*. New York: Macmillan, 1983. $14.95.
This directory provides information on 290 training, educational, and outreach programs run by schools and colleges jointly with corporations and government agencies for employed and unemployed workers and community residents. It is also a valuable source of innovative ideas for planning or implementing industry-education cooperative programs.

American Council on Education. *Guide to External Degree Programs in the United States*. (2nd ed.) New York: Macmillan, 1983. $16.95.
This guide describes more than 100 academic programs that are offered off campus and out of the classroom by community colleges, technical schools, and universities. The state-by-state listing provides full information on areas of study and degrees conferred, entrance and other requirements, credit awarded for experiential and nonacademic learning, instructional methods, grading system, and accreditation. Areas of study range from business to health care management, computer science, and a full selection of liberal arts majors. The degrees range from the associate to the doctorate.

American Council on Education. *National Guide to Educational Credit for Training Programs*. Washington, D.C.: American Council on Education, 1986. $37.50.

    This guide includes authoritative college credit recommendations for more than 1,100 courses offered by corporations, unions, and other organizations.

American Society for Training and Development. *ASTD Directory of Academic Programs in Training and Development/Human Resource Development, 1983–1984*. (2nd ed.) Baltimore: ASTD Press, 1983. $15 paper.

    This directory provides detailed information on more than 260 programs from more than 150 colleges and universities. Baccalaureate, master's, and doctoral degree programs are listed as well as certificate and other nondegree programs for HRD professionals. These are usually found in the following academic fields: communication, instructional technology, organization development, business administration, and adult education. Each program description includes type of degree or certificate offered; description of the program; admission stipulations; required courses and program completion requirements; description of the programs' students and graduates, including employment data; contact person; and complete address.

Bear, John. *How to Get the Degree You Want: Bear's Guide to Nontraditional College Degrees*. (8th ed.) Berkeley: Ten Speed Press, 1982. $9.95 paper.

    Bear describes and discusses alternative or nontraditional degree programs through correspondence study, equivalency examination, and credit for life/work experience. Included are 649 innovative schools and programs at colleges and universities that offer fully accredited degrees on a nonresident or short-residency basis.

Bricker's International Directory of University Executive Development Programs. Princeton, N.J.: Peterson's Guides. Annual. $100.

    This directory describes more than 250 general, functional, and special-purpose management programs offered in residence by universities in the United States and Canada, Great Britain, Ireland, Europe, and Australia. Programs last from three to six weeks.

Independent Study Catalog: NUCEA's Guide to Independent Study Through Correspondence Instruction, 1986–1988. Princeton, N.J.: Peterson's Guides, 1986. $8.95 paper.

    Prepared by the National University Continuing Education Association, this guide lists more than 12,000 correspondence courses offered by seventy-two colleges and universities, ranging from elementary through high school, undergraduate, and graduate levels. No descriptions are provided for the courses.

Macmillan Guide to Correspondence Study. (3rd ed.) New York: Macmillan, 1987. $75.

Included are correspondence courses from 174 colleges, universities, and accredited trade, technical, and other proprietary schools. This guide was prepared in cooperation with the National Home Study Council.

SIS Workbook. New York: Seminar Information Service. Annual with monthly updates. $245.

This updating service provides information on over 3,000 business and technical seminars in the following categories: management, organization development, human resource management, training and development, communications, data processing, finance, sales and marketing, personal development, energy and environment, technical/engineering, manufacturing, and purchasing. The description of each seminar includes title and summary of content, audience, sponsor, setting (public or in-house), and dates and locations. Seminars are also listed by sponsor and by date and location. This information is also available on-line through the Human Resource Information Network (see Chapter 16).

Training by Contract: College-Employer Profiles. New York: College Board Publications, 1983. $8.95 paper.

This publication profiles sixty cooperative employee training programs between businesses and colleges and universities and provides practical assistance to organizations developing alternative training arrangements.

Wasserman, Paul (ed.). *Training and Development Organizations Directory.* (3rd ed.) Detroit: Gale Research, 1983. $270. (Supplement: *New Training Organizations*, $105).

This directory describes about 1,455 firms, institutes, seminars, and university programs dealing with management, production, human relations, administration, and supervision.

Books on Going Back to School

Apps, Jerold W. *Study Skills for Adults Returning to School.* (2nd ed.) New York: McGraw-Hill, 1982. $15.95.

Apps has practical advice on learning how to learn, taking notes, improving reading and writing ability, building vocabulary, taking examinations, improving thinking ability, and using resources effectively.

Bear, John. *Bear's Guide to Finding Money for College.* Berkeley: Ten Speed Press, 1984. $5.95 paper.

Bear discusses where to find unconventional, overlooked, and ordinary but not-well-understood sources of financial aid and how to pursue each of these specific sources.

Haponski, William C., and McCabe, Charles E. *New Horizons*. Princeton, N.J.: Peterson's Guides, 1985. $8.95 paper.
   The authors discuss alternatives to college as well as how to apply and be accepted, how to get credit for knowledge and skills you already have, and how to balance college with the demands of job and family.

Hecht, Miriam, and Traub, Lillian. *Dropping Back In: How to Complete Your College Education Quickly and Economically*. New York: Dutton, 1982. $8.95 paper.
   For adults returning to college, Hecht and Traub discuss the choice of a program, financing alternatives, different degrees and their uses, and coping with the unique stresses of college. They explore the benefits of college for adults and recommend that adults be clear about their goals, realistic about what can be accomplished, and confident of their abilities.

Selected List of Universities with Noncredit Programs

American Graduate School of
   International Management
Thunderbird Management Center
59th Ave. and Greenway Rd.
Glendale, AZ 85306
(602) 978-7115

Carnegie Mellon University
Senior Executive Seminar
School of Urban and Public Affairs
Schenley Park
Pittsburgh, PA 15213
(412) 268-2195

Southern California Consortium
5400 Orange Ave., Suite 215
Cypress, CA 90630
(714) 828-5770

University of Akron
Center for Organization
   Development
College of Business Administration
Leigh Hall 109
Akron, OH 44325
(216) 375-7337

University of California–Berkeley
   Extension
Certificate Programs
2223 Fulton St.
Berkeley, CA 94720
(415) 642-4231

University of California–Los
  Angeles Extension
Continuing Education in Business
  and Management
10995 Le Conte Ave., Suite 515
Los Angeles, CA 90024
(213) 825-4801

University of Denver
Center for Management
  Development
2199 S. University Blvd.
Denver, CO 80208
(303) 871-2529

University of Maryland
Center for Management
  Development
College of Business and
  Management
Tydings Hall, Room 3140F
College Park, MD 20742
(301) 454-2403

University of Michigan
School of Business Administration
Executive Education Center
700 E. University, Room E 2540
Ann Arbor, MI 48109
(313) 763-1003

University of Minnesota
Department of Vocational and
  Technical Education
Vocational and Technical Education
  Bldg., Room 210
1954 Buford Ave.
St. Paul, MN 55108
(612) 624-7777

University of Minnesota
Executive Development Center
Hubert Humphrey Center, Room 280,
271 19th Ave. South
Minneapolis, MN 55455
(612) 624-2545

University of Oklahoma
Professional Development
1700 Asp Ave.
Norman, OK 73037
(405) 325-1981

University of Wisconsin–Extension
Management Institute
432 N. Lake St.
Madison, WI 53706
(608) 262-2155

Vanderbilt University
Corporate Learning Institute
Peabody, Box 321
Nashville, TN 37203
(615) 322-8414

Directory of Publishers

American Council on Education
One Dupont Circle, Suite 800
Washington, DC 20036
(202) 939-9300

American Society for Training and
  Development
1630 Duke St., Box 1443
Alexandria, VA 22313
(703) 683-8100

ASTD Press
P. O. Box 4856, Hampden Station
Baltimore, MD 21211
(301) 338-6949

College Board Publications
P. O. Box 886
New York, NY 10101
(212) 713-8000

Dutton
c/o New American Library
120 Woodbine St.
Bergenfield, NJ 07621
(201) 387-0600

Gale Research Company
Book Tower
Detroit, MI 48226
(800) 223-4253, (313) 961-2242

Lakewood Publications
50 S. 9th St.
Minneapolis, MN 55402
(800) 328-4329, (612) 333-0471

Macmillan Publishing Company
866 Third Ave.
New York, NY 10022
(212) 702-2000

McGraw-Hill Book Company
Princeton Rd.
Heightstown, NJ 08520
(212) 512-2000

McLagan & Associates Products,
  Inc.
Rosedale Towers, Suite 300
1700 W. Highway 36
St. Paul, MN 55113
(612) 631-2034

Peterson's Guides, Inc.
P. O. Box 2123
Princeton, NJ 08543
(800) 225-0261, (609) 924-5338

Seminar Information Service
17752 Skypark Circle
Irvine, CA 92714
(714) 261-9104

Ten Speed Press
P. O. Box 7123
Berkeley, CA 94707
(415) 845-8414

14

Training Exercises and Group Experiences

Linda Webster

This chapter lists sources of training exercises and ideas for group experiences in print format, both for employee training and for training other trainers. These resources include games, experiential learning exercises, intervention techniques, and exercises for intercultural awareness and team building. To locate additional print materials to aid HRD practitioners in designing learning experiences, consult the guides to instructional materials and training resources listed in this chapter. In addition, nonprint instructional materials are located in Chapter 15. Computer-assisted instructional materials are listed in Chapter 17.

This chapter has the following sections:

Training Exercises and Other Resources
Guides to Instructional Materials and Training Resources

Prices change frequently. Some publishers make yearly changes, so view price information as approximate. Addresses and phone numbers also change.

Training Exercises and Other Resources

Boshear, Walton C., and Albrecht, Karl G. *Understanding People: Models and Concepts*. San Diego: University Associates, 1977. $11.95 paper.

Sixty behavioral models make for an easier understanding of individual, dyad, group, organization, and problem-solving behaviors.

The BrainMap™. A Guide to How Your Brain Creates Your Personal and Professional Worlds. Fort Collins, Colo.: Brain Technologies Corporation, 1985. $12; multiple-copy discounts available.

The BrainMap™ is a self-scored and self-interpreted learning inventory that provides individuals and groups with a blueprint to the way their minds create their personal and professional worlds. The BrainMap™ has been used in management development training, conflict resolution, group development, individual career and retirement choices, assessment of sales and marketing programs, personal self-awareness and growth goals, and other areas of organizational and personal development.

"CONTACT: The Continuing Education Training and Action Game." In Armand Lauffer. *Doing Continuing Education and Staff Development*. New York: McGraw-Hill, 1978. Out of print.
    Players are from different groups—local administrators of human service agencies, professional association members, state-level trainers, college/university continuing education directors and deans, influential citizens, and potential funders. Participants are interested in continuing education program development, but from different perspectives and with unevenly distributed resources. Players can form coalitions to gain resources, get support for their projects, write proposals to gain funding, and block proposals not in their interests. The game takes about one hour.

Eitington, Julius E. *The Winning Trainer*. Houston: Gulf, 1984. $34.95 paper.
    This book is a gold mine of exercises, games, puzzles, role plays, and group techniques, with ninety-one worksheets ready to photocopy and hand out as well as a discussion of how to use participative techniques in all training situations.

Glaser, Rollin, and Glaser, Christine. *Intervention Guidebook: A Trainer's Quick Reference to Team Development Interventions*. (Rev. ed.) Bryn Mawr, Penn.: Organization Design and Development, 1985. $39.95.
    This reference guide to 142 team-building interventions from fifty readily available sources provides quick access to training interventions that will match issues blocking team effectiveness.

The Instruction Game. San Diego: University Associates, 1971. $59.95.
    Participants work in pairs, taking turns being the instructor and the learner. Each must teach a code of number symbols to the other within a certain time. The learner takes a test to assess the amount learned and provides evaluative feedback to the instructor.

IQ Kit. San Diego: University Associates, 1981. $99.95.
    Practitioners can use these tools and techniques for self-assessment and learning in the field of instructional skills—surveys, assessments, self-inventories, checklists, planning sheets, instruments, case studies, and role plays. Sections include tools for evaluating the effectiveness of instruction, exercises and forms to be used in planning and designing training programs, and self-assessment and training exercises to sharpen skills of instructors.

Kohls, L. Robert. *Developing Intercultural Awareness*. Washington, D.C.: SIETAR International, 1981. $10 paper.

The following exercises are included: Reaching Consensus, Cultural Values, Stereotypes of Americans, the "Majoria-Minoria" simulation, case studies, and the "As If . . ." exercise.

Mill, Cyril R. *Activities for Trainers: 50 Useful Designs*. San Diego: University Associates, 1980. $23.95 paper.

The fifty activities are grouped into eight sections: group dynamics and laboratory training, training trainers, cross-cultural training, stress training, women's issues, supervisory and management training, the training of consultants, and management and organization development. Specific topics addressed by the activities are goal clarification, structural interventions, the whole-brain function, designing training, career planning for women, giving orders, consultants' skills, and team building.

Newstrom, John. *Games Trainers Play*. New York: McGraw-Hill, 1980. $17.95 paper.

This book contains 101 activities and exercises for group training and orientation sessions. Each game can be administered in less than thirty minutes, involves little advanced preparation, and is adaptable to a variety of audiences and purposes. See Scannell and Newstrom's *More Games Trainers Play* for a companion volume.

Pfeiffer, J. William, and Goodstein, Leonard D. *The Annual Series in Developing Human Resources*. San Diego: University Associates, 1972– . $69.95 looseleaf notebook; $29.95 paper.

These annual publications include structured experiences, instruments, and articles on the newest theoretical developments and innovative techniques in HRD, consulting, and organization development. Lecturettes provide brief and to-the-point discussions of key topics and ideas in HRD and OD for use as brief lectures or as participant handouts. The *Reference Guide to Handbooks and Annuals* (University Associates, 1985, $13.95) is an index to the 1972–1985 annuals.

Pfeiffer, J. William, and Jones, John E. (eds.). *A Handbook of Structured Experiences for Human Relations Training*. San Diego: University Associates, 1973–. $14.95 paper (each volume).

This annual collection of group activities deals with interpersonal relations, management development, communication skills, group dynamics, and counseling and can be used in a variety of settings. The description of each activity includes an outline of goals, group size, time and materials needed, suggested variations, and step-by-step instructions. Each activity includes all handouts ready for duplication. The *Reference Guide to Handbooks and Annuals* (University Associates, 1985, $13.95) is an index to volumes 1–10 of the handbooks.

Scannell, Ed, and Newstrom, John. *More Games Trainers Play*. New York:
McGraw-Hill, 1983. $17.95 paper.

This book contains 101 activities and exercises for group training and orientation sessions. Each game lasts no longer than thirty minutes and is adaptable
to a variety of audiences and purposes. See Newstrom's *Games Trainers Play*
for a companion volume.

Session Builders. Harrisburg, Penn.: Training Resource Corporation, 1983.
$119.95.

This packet includes sixty exercises for management or supervisory skills
training on such topics as communication, motivation, leadership, decision
making, and assertiveness. The exercises represent a wide variety of types: case
studies, role plays, simulations, applications, assessments, and discussion starters.
Each exercise comes with detailed instructions and handouts ready for
duplication.

Training Project Planning: A Consensus Task for Trainers. Bryn Mawr, Penn.:
Organization Design and Development, 1982. $4.95 for participants' materials;
$5 for Trainer's Guide.

Individuals and groups of trainers can use this exercise to review and discuss
the elements of training program design. Twenty items are ranked by participants
in terms of their sequential significance to the design process. Results are compared to a modified version of Leonard Nadler's Critical Events Model. The
exercise requires one and one-half to two hours.

Tubesing, Nancy L., and Tubesing, Donald A. *Structured Exercises in Stress
Management*. 3 vols. Duluth, Minn.: Whole Person Press, 1983, 1984, 1986.
$19.95 each volume.

Thirty-six exercises with variations help people assess their personal stress
and coping styles, motivate participants to identify desired changes, build new
coping skills, and plan for a healthier lifestyle. Sections include icebreakers,
stress assessments, management strategies, skill builders, action planning, and
group energizers.

Tubesing, Nancy L., and Tubesing, Donald A. *Structured Exercises in Wellness
Promotion*. 3 vols. Duluth, Minn.: Whole Person Press, 1983, 1984, 1986.
$19.95 each volume.

Thirty-six exercises and numerous adaptations encourage people to adopt
a wellness-oriented attitude and develop more responsible self-care patterns.
Exercises focus on whole-person health—body, mind, spirit, emotions, relationships—in the following categories: ice breakers, wellness exploration, self-
care strategies, action planning, and group energizers.

Weeks, William W., and others (eds.). *A Manual of Structured Experiences for Cross-Cultural Learning*. Washington, D.C.: SIETAR, 1977. $6.95 paper.

Fifty-nine exercises stimulate learning in multicultural groups. Sections include Clarification of Values, Identification of Roles, Recognition of Feelings and Attitudes, and Community Interaction.

Guides to Instructional Materials and Training Resources

ASTD Buyer's Guide and Consultant Directory. Baltimore: ASTD Press. Annual. $35.

This directory lists programs and materials for all types of employee training as well as training of HRD practitioners. Also included is a listing of AV and computer hardware dealers and production services.

Conroy, Barbara. *Learning Packaged to Go: A Directory and Guide to Staff Development and Training Packages*. Phoenix: Oryx Press, 1984. $78.50.

This guide offers concise, practical advice on the selection and use of "off-the-shelf" prepackaged training media. The author discusses the advantages and disadvantages of the various nonprint media for training; demonstrates the cost effectiveness of purchasing prepackaged materials; and provides guidance on locating, selecting, evaluating, and acquiring currently available media programs. Conroy also discusses developing media training packages in-house. Also included is a 160-page listing of employee training media packages in all formats applicable to businesses, public agencies, and nonpublic organizations. Media packages are listed by subject categories and with content descriptions. Subjects include job skills, communication skills, management skills, and social, political, and medical concerns found in organizations.

Horn, Robert E., and Cleaves, Anne. *The Guide to Simulations/Games for Education and Training*. (4th ed.) Newbury Park, Calif.: Sage, 1980. $49.95.

The authors have compiled this comprehensive listing of 1,100 games and simulation experiences for use in education and business training for junior high through adult levels. Descriptions include critical comments on the effectiveness of the game, an evaluation of whether the outcomes are quantitative, and the kinds of activities and interactions the game entails.

Nadler, Leonard, and others (eds.). *The Trainer's Resource 1987: A Comprehensive Guide to Packaged Training Programs*. Amherst, Mass.: Human Resource Development Press, 1987. $59.95 paper.

Detailed information is provided for over 500 packaged training programs in such training areas as career development, computer literacy, negotiation, performance appraisal, productivity improvement, management development, supervisory skills, communication skills, problem solving, employee motivation, sales management and training, time management, trainer training, wellness and health, and technical training. Information for each program includes the intended audience, program description (objectives and topics), delivery system and AV required, instructional strategies, cost, and names of users to contact for comments about the program's effectiveness. Also included is a section entitled "Film Best-Sellers and Classics."

Peters, Douglas. *Directory of Human Resource Development Instrumentation*. San Diego: University Associates, 1985. $105.95.

This directory provides information on nearly 300 instruments divided into six categories: communications, personal growth, career planning, behavioral style, managerial/leadership style, and miscellaneous (including needs assessment and organization climate and culture). Indexes provide access to instruments by forty-nine subjects, forty-four theory bases, title, and vendor. The categories contain profiles of the instruments with the following information: order information, publication date, purpose, intended audience, facilitator training needed, time to complete, number of items, scoring, method of interpretation, validity/reliability, and typical usage.

Training Marketplace Directory. Minneapolis: Lakewood Publications. Annual. (Mailed with August issue of *Training* magazine). $15.

Producers and publishers of training programs, instructional materials, and nonprint media for all types of employee training programs and in a variety of subject categories are listed.

Wasserman, Paul, and others (eds.). *Learning Independently*. (2nd ed.) Detroit: Gale Research, 1987. $210.

This comprehensive directory of self-teaching materials for adults contains 3,500 items arranged under more than 500 subjects. For each subject the directory provides details on available audiocassettes, correspondence courses, films and other audiovisual materials, games and simulations, books, and programmed learning materials.

Directory of Publishers

AMACOM
135 W. 50th St.
New York, NY 10020
(212) 903-8090

ASTD Press
P. O. Box 4856, Hampden Station
Baltimore, MD 21211
(301) 338-6949

Brain Technologies Corporation
414 Buckeye St.
Fort Collins, CO 80524
(303) 493-9210

Gale Research Company
Book Tower
Detroit, MI 48226
(800) 223-4253, (313) 961-2242

Gulf Publishing Company
P. O. Box 2608
Houston, TX 77252
(713) 529-4301

Human Resource Development
    Press
22 Amherst Rd.
Amherst, MA 01002
(800) 822-2801

Lakewood Publications
50 S. 9th St.
Minneapolis, MN 55402
(800) 328-4329, (612) 333-0471

McGraw-Hill Book Company
Princeton Rd.
Heightstown, NJ 08520
(212) 512-2000

Organization Design and
    Development
101 Bryn Mawr Ave., Suite 310
Bryn Mawr, PA 19010
(215) 525-9505

Oryx Press
2214 N. Central at Encanto,
    Suite 103
Phoenix, AZ 85004
(602) 254-6156

Sage Publications
2111 W. Hillcrest Dr.
Newbury Park, CA 91320
(805) 499-0721

SIETAR International
1505 22nd St. NW, Suite 102
Washington, DC 20037
(202) 296-4710

Training Resource Corporation
5 S. Miller Rd.
Harrisburg, PA 17109
(800) 222-9909, ext. 25
(717) 652-6300, ext. 25

University Associates
8517 Production Ave.
San Diego, CA 92121
(619) 578-5900

Whole Person Press
P. O. Box 3151
Duluth, MN 55803
(218) 728-4077

15

Audiotapes, Films, and Videos

Linda Webster

Nonprint media play an important part in both self-study and group instruction. The first section of this chapter lists audiocassettes that may be of interest to HRD professionals in their own continuing learning. The films and videotapes in the second section of this chapter are on topics of interest to HRD practioners and OD consultants in their own continuing development. Audiocassettes, films, and videotapes for employee training and management development programs can be located using the directories at the end of this chapter. Get your name on mailing lists of the film and video producers and distributors that conclude this chapter. These represent producers who have a large number of films available for supervisory training/management development and personal development. In addition, *Training* magazine has reviews of films and videocassettes in each issue.

Nonprint materials can be ordered directly from the producer or distributor in each listing, or you can order some of the titles from specialized HRD media distributors, such as Excellence in Training Corporation, Masterco, and Thompson-Mitchell & Associates. Their addresses are listed at the end of this chapter. Often professional associations, such as the American Society for Training and Development, sell audiocassettes and videocassettes of conference programs. Several of these associations are listed in this chapter. Also check Chapter 12 to find other organizations that might have conference tapes available.

In the case of films, many producers have rates for preview and rental as well as purchase price. Another source for rental films are the fifty university film libraries located throughout the United States. Renting from a university film library generally costs less than renting directly from the film producer or distributor. To identify which film libraries have the film you are interested in, look in *Educational Film Locator* (Bowker, 1986), which is found in most public and academic libraries. You can also write directly to university film libraries to request their catalogues. Universities with large film collections are listed in the directory at the end of this chapter.

The National Narrowcast Service (NNS) of the Public Broadcasting Service provides a daily lineup of training and information programming for business and industry. Every weekday up to five hours of video training programs are distributed directly to the workplace of subscribing businesses, public agencies, and colleges and universities. The programs are produced by over fifty of the best-known video-training producers, including Time-Life Video, McGraw-Hill Training Systems, Training House, and Coronet/MTI Film and Video. Programs are selected using guidelines established by the American Society for Training and Development. In addition, NNS offers subscribers special teleconferences targeted to the specific needs of business and industry. Subscribers can choose from nine tracks or subject areas, each track offering five to ten hours of quality programming each month. Five basic tracks offer programming in management and supervision, sales and marketing, computer literacy, effective communication, and technical skills. Four premium tracks focus on the more specialized information needs of audiences such as accountants, corporate counsels, and computer specialists and feature a track that showcases new training materials. Companies can subscribe to one or more tracks at a charge of from $2,500 to $17,000, depending on the track selected and the number of employees at the training site. The company can then retain any programs on the track for training use for a full year. Because not every public television station is marketing NNS, companies interested in the service should call the NNS office for information about availability at (703) 739-5300.

This chapter is divided into the following sections:

> Sources of Audiocassettes
> Films and Videotapes
> Guides to Media and Equipment
> Directory of Producers, Distributors, and Publishers

Prices change frequently. Some publishers make yearly changes, so view price information as approximate. Addresses and phone numbers also change.

Sources of Audiocassettes

Alessandra & Associates
P. O. Box 2767, La Jolla, CA 92038
(800) 222-4383, (619) 459-4515
Relationship Strategies: How to Deal with the Differences in People (6 cassettes and workbook, $65) presents techniques for recognizing the differences among people; achieving openness, directness, and flexibility; identifying one's own behavioral style; and developing practical approaches in dealing with socializers, thinkers, directors, and relaters. The package also includes a behavioral styles profile questionnaire.

AMACOM
135 W. 50th St., New York, NY 10020
(212) 903-8090
AMACOM's best-selling books are now available on audiocassettes ($15.95 to $19.95 per cassette): Peter Drucker on *The Effective Executive*, *Managing in Turbulent Times*, *Managing for Results*, and *Innovation and Entrepreneurship*; Alec MacKenzie's *How to Save Two Hours a Day*; and Theodore Jackson's *How to Turn Off Stress*.

American Management Association, Extension Institute
135 W. 50th St., New York, NY 10020
(212) 903-8040
Audiocassette/workbook programs for self-study (6 cassettes at $155 each) are available for supervisors, managers, and executive secretaries on the following topics: memory improvement, listening skills, problem solving, time management, public speaking, coaching, and counseling skills. Each program has six one-hour cassettes and a workbook with exercises, case studies, review questions, and a pretest and posttest to measure your skills gain. These are appropriate for an HRD practitioner's own self-development or for use with other staff members. The American Management Association's Extension Institute also has a series of print self-study curriculum guides ($89.95 each) on approximately eighty-five topics of interest to supervisors and managers.

American Society for Healthcare Education and Training
American Hospital Association
840 N. Lake Shore Dr., Chicago, IL 60611
(312) 280-6113
Conference tapes ($12.50 each) are available each year on such topics as instructional diagnoses, aging in America, emerging themes in training, and issues and trends in health care education.

American Society for Training and Development
1630 Duke St., Box 1443, Alexandria, VA 22313
(703) 683-8100
ASTD makes available audiocassettes ($16 each) from its annual conferences. Usually there are over 100 audiocassettes from each conference, featuring the leading HRD and OD professionals and consultants in the field.

Excellence in Training Corporation
8364 Hickman Rd., Des Moines, IA 50322
(515) 276-6569
Cassettes ($65 each) are available for business, management, and personal and professional development by best-selling authors: Ken Blanchard's *Leadership and the One-Minute Manager*, John Naisbitt's *Reinventing the Corporation*, Paul

Hersey's *Situational Leader* and *The Iacocca Tapes*, and Sharon Crain's *Strategies for Career Success for Women on the Move*.

George Odiorne Cassette Library
MBO, Inc.
5531 Ninth St. North, St. Petersburg, FL 33703
(813) 525-1360
    Audiocassette courses on executive skills, supervisory skills, nonprofit organizations, behavioral sciences, personnel administration, training, and selling—all are based on MBO principles. Two courses in particular are of interest to trainers. *The Human Side of Management* (6 cassettes, $65) has cassettes on motivation, communication, small groups, mentoring, and participative management. *Training by Objectives* (6 cassettes, $65) identifies behavior change as the key objective of training and describes the importance of training in economic terms. Subjects include identification of training needs, transfer of training, action training techniques, and evaluation.

Institute for the Study of Human Knowledge (ISHK)
P. O. Box 1062, Cambridge, MA 02238
(617) 497-4124
    Audiocassettes are available on brain/mind, psychology, assertiveness training, wellness, women and health, stress management, pain control, and relaxation training. Of particular interest to trainers is *The Amazing Brain*, a discussion by Robert Ornstein on how the brain evolved, why it is unique, and how the brain functions to control body health. Prices range from $29.95 to $79.95 for an audiocassette series.

Jeffrey Norton Publishers
96 Broad St., Guilford, CT 06437
(203) 453-9794
    Over 3,000 audiocassettes in the Sound Seminar Library present the significant ideas of provocative thinkers from a variety of fields, such as Carlos Castaneda, Margaret Mead, S. I. Hayakawa, Robert Frost, Alan Watts, B. F. Skinner, Buckminster Fuller, Carl Rogers, Erich Fromm, Anna Freud, and many more. Also available is a cassette-of-the-month club with the category Mind-Stretchers.

Jossey-Bass
433 California St., San Francisco, CA 94104
(415) 433-1740
    Understanding and Working with Adult Learners ($21.95) is a two-cassette package that includes half-hour interviews with Malcolm S. Knowles, Raymond J. Wlodkowski, Alan B. Knox, and Leonard Nadler. Stephen D. Brookfield is the interviewer.

Learn Incorporated

Mount Laurel Plaza, 113 Gaither Dr., Mount Laurel, NJ 08054

(609) 234-6100

Audiocassette/workbook courses ($19.95 to $99.95 each) for career and personal goals include speed learning, memory improvement, listening skills, speech power, business writing, and vocabulary improvement.

National Seminars Audiocassette Library

6901 W. 63rd St., P. O. Box 2949, Shawnee Mission, KS 66201

(800) 258-7246, (913) 432-7757

Audiocassettes ($10 each) focus on a variety of management and supervisory topics. HRD practitioners will be interested in tapes on stress management, organizational politics, leadership and supervisory skills for women, and new roles for men and women in the workplace.

Nightingale-Conant Corporation

7300 N. Lehigh Ave., Chicago, IL 60648

(800) 323-5552

There is a wide variety of business, management, sales, personal growth, wellness, parenting, and inspirational topics available. Many tapes are available from best-selling authors. Programs are either two cassettes with a book ($35) or six-cassette sets ($65).

Practical Management Incorporated

P. O. Box 8789, Calabasas, CA 91302

(800) 423-5099; in California (800) 874-8695 or (818) 348-9101

How to Teach Grown-Ups (12 cassettes, 8 workbooks, administrator's guide, $325) is a self-study course for HRD practitioners, instructors, and teachers of adult groups. The eight sessions focus on the following topics: learning versus schooling (principles of adult learning); participative lecture method; discussion methods; using common instructional aids effectively; lesson planning and objectives; experiential methods (role playing, games, simulations, demonstrations, t-groups); one-on-one instruction (demonstrations and coaching); to test or not to test. The tapes and workbooks are highly interactive. Questions, exercises, and self-tests are included frequently on the tape to hold a participant's interest and to check for learning as the tape progresses.

Psychology Today Tapes

Dept. 926, P. O. Box 059061, Brooklyn, NY 11205

(800) 345-8112; in Pennsylvania (800) 662-2444

Self-help and self-improvement cassettes ($10.95 each) from *Psychology Today* include the following topics: mind expansion, interpersonal relations, improving the workplace, parenting, meditation, and therapy by such noted psychologists as Thomas Gordon, Carl Rogers, Albert Ellis, Rollo May, and William Glasser.

R. G. Swartz & Associates
  P. O. Box 7568, Lancaster, PA 17604
  (717) 299-5061
    Self-Accelerated Learning Skills (audiocassette and workbook, $29.20) contains ninety minutes of classical music and relaxation exercises with learning affirmations subliminally embedded within the music. The tape is designed to induce the state of relaxation conducive to increasing learning rate and memory retention. The accompanying workbook includes two physical and mental relaxation exercises, learning affirmations to use while studying, instructions on how to create a learning environment, creativity and imagery exercises, and instructions on how to take and review notes.

Whole Person Press
  P. O. Box 3151, Duluth, MN 55803
  (218) 728-4077
    Training packages for individual and group study are available in the following areas: burnout prevention, stress management, and empathy training and listening skills. Each package includes six cassettes and a workbook ($95).

World Future Society
  4916 St. Elmo Ave., Bethesda, MD 20814
  (301) 656-8274
    The World Future Society makes available over 150 audiotapes ($8 each) of presentations at its national conferences in such diverse areas as brain/mind and human intelligence, communications technology, computers, education, the future, health, information industry and services, management, networking, space, the Third World, values, work, and careers.

Films and Videotapes

Adult Learner. Houston: Gulf Publishing Company Video, 1984. Video. 76 mins.
  $485.
    Malcolm Knowles discusses modern concepts of andragogy: how to understand the adult learner, create effective learning experiences for adults, serve as a resource, and create and use learning contracts.

ASTD Conference Videotapes. Alexandria, Va.: American Society for Training and Development. 1–2 hrs. each. $185–$225 each.
    The American Society for Training and Development makes available videotapes from selected conference sessions. Some of the videotapes that are available for purchase are:

Adult Learning? You've Got to Be Kidding! (Edward E. Scannell)
Assessing Your Organization's Computer Literacy Needs (Ronald Zemke)
Developing, Marketing, and Promoting Seminars, Workshops and Other Training (Robert W. Pike)
Historical and Future Perspectives on Assessment Centers (Cabot L. Jaffee)
Ten Ways to Measure Training's Effectiveness and Return on Investment (Scott B. Parry)
Training 101: Principles, Processes, and People Every Trainer Should Know (Chip R. Bell and Fredric H. Margolis)
Twelve Techniques for Improving Your Skills as an Instructor (Scott B. Parry)

Bits and Bytes. New York: Time-Life Video, 1984. 12 films/videos. 30 mins. each. $5,500.

This twelve-part video course introduces learners to microcomputer basics, including how computers and computer programs work, storage and retrieval of information, communication between computers, computer languages, computer graphics, and the uses of word processing programs and electronic spreadsheets. Of particular interest to HRD practitioners are the segments on computer-assisted instruction, simulations, and games.

Brain Gold. Fort Collins, Colo.: Brain Technologies Corporation, 1987. Video. 27 mins. $495.

This training video portrays brain studies as critical to growth and survival in the next business generation. Written and narrated by Dudley Lynch, president of Brain Technologies Corporation, the video traces how the brain's own "rewiring" both causes and offers the primary solutions to eras of outrageously rapid change. This video can be used alone or in conjunction with The Brain-Map™ self-assessment testing inventory.

Brain Power. Deerfield, Ill.: Coronet/MTI Film & Video, 1980. 16mm film/video. 12 mins. $370.

John Houseman challenges audiences interactively with direct questions and brain-teasers as he shows how to get more out of meetings and learning experiences by understanding three principles of perception: recognition, interpretation, and expectation. Based on the book of the same name by Karl Albrecht (Prentice Hall, 1980).

A Class of Your Own. Rockville, Md.: BNA Communications, 1965. 16mm film/video. 26 mins. $595.

A practical demonstration of effective teaching techniques: preparing the lesson, using the question-and-answer technique, arranging teaching steps in logical sequence, using the chalkboard, making on-the-spot revisions, and using time properly.

Cognitive Learning Styles. Lincoln: Nebraska Educational Television Council for Higher Education, 1978. Video. 30 mins. $225.

This film prompts thought about style-sensitive teaching strategies as it examines Herman Witkin's field-dependent-independent model, Jerome Kagan's reflective-impulsive model, and James McKenney's information-processing model of cognitive learning styles.

Communication and Management: A Conversation with Dr. Carl Rogers. Santa Monica: Salenger Films, 1986. 16mm film/video. 30 mins. $595.

Ron Greenwood interviews Carl Rogers, one of the founders of humanistic psychology. Rogers discusses the importance of open communication and empathic listening.

Going International Series. San Francisco: Copeland Griggs Productions, 1983, 1985, 1987. 7 films/videos. 30 mins. each. $500 each, with discounts available.

These films cover the wide range of issues that the international HRD practitioner confronts in different parts of the world. Titles in the series include *Bridging the Culture Gap* (cultural differences); *Managing the Overseas Assignment* (cultural taboos and accepted standards of business behavior in different countries); *Beyond Culture Shock* (adjustment to living abroad); *Welcome Home, Stranger* (difficulties of reentry); *Going International – Safely* (security issues, including medical and legal emergencies); and two films for citizens from other countries living in the United States, *Working in the USA* and *Living in the USA.*

Hush, Hoggies, Hush: Tom Johnson's Praying Pigs. Memphis: Center for Southern Folklore, 1978. 16mm film/video. 4 mins. $100.

This is a film to reinspire and uplift trainers. The twenty-five years that Tom Johnson spent teaching pigs to say grace before eating is a task trainers can easily identify with. This brief film was a hit at the 1980 Training Conference film festival.

I Walk Softly Through Life. San Diego: University Associates, 1986. Video. 60 mins. $395.

In an interview with Warren Bennis, Carl Rogers covers a wide range of topics, including the potency of groups, racial and governmental relations, world peace, mentoring, the importance of listening and empathy, change, and his personal development and recent work.

International Management Productivity Series. Ann Arbor: Masterco, 1982. 6 videos. 60 mins. each. $2,200.

Philip R. Harris and Robert T. Moran provide information based on their books *Managing Cultural Differences* and *Managing Cultural Synergy.* The following videos make up the series: *The Cosmopolitan Manager, The Transnational Managers as Change Agents, Transnational Managers as Intercultural*

Communicators, Understanding Cultural Differences, Family Relocation Coping Skills, and *Improving the Productivity of International Managers.*

It's All in Your Head. Watertown, Mass.: AMA Film/Video, 1984. 16mm film/ video. 11 mins. $395.

This humorous session starter demonstrates how participants can become more successful once they take responsibility for their own learning. It will sharpen participants' interest in learning by demonstrating the use of such adult learning techniques as taking notes, asking questions, participating in discussions, and applying learning on the job.

Joshua and the Blob. Del Mar, Calif: CRM/McGraw-Hill Films, 1981. 16mm film/video. 7 mins. $250.

Animated, nonnarrated story shows Joshua's initial reaction to the Blob as fearful aggression, but his reaction changes as he becomes acquainted with the Blob. This film suggests the value of an open and positive attitude in response to new ideas, change, and the unknown.

Joshua and the Shadow. Del Mar, Calif.: McGraw-Hill Films, 1981. 16mm film/video. 10 mins. $250.

Animated, nonnarrated story shows Joshua afraid of his own shadow. Shadows are problems and anxieties. Joshua discovers that light (understanding) can control shadows.

Joshua in a Box. Del Mar, Calif.: McGraw-Hill Films, 1981. 16mm film/ video. 5 mins. $250.

Animated, nonnarrated story shows Joshua escaping from one box only to find himself in another. This film is designed to promote creative and critical thinking.

The Juggler: Harnessing the Power of Concentration. Hollywood, Calif.: Cally Curtis, 1986. 16mm film/video. 28 mins. $550.

Viewers learn the major rules of developing good concentration: view concentration as a skill that needs to be developed; provide opportunities for success; focus sharply; prepare self and environment; save concentration for prime time; refocus when needed; and keep practicing for improvement.

Learning to Learn. Reston, Va.: Arthur Young, 1984. Video. 17 mins. $125.

Adults learn best in participative learning situations that foster self-directed learning based on previous experiences and oriented to problem solving. Learning techniques are discussed—setting personal objectives, determining strategies to meet them, and planning follow-up. Also taught are key-word noting and action planning.

Making the Transition to Training. Houston: Gulf Publishing Company Video, 1984. Video, trainee workbook, reference manual. 50 mins. $450.

This interactive video/workbook is a self-paced approach to train field personnel moving into the classroom. Topics include how to motivate, how to use visual aids for instruction, how to ask and answer questions, how to promote interaction, and how evaluation can benefit both learner and instructor. The workbook includes objectives and exercises. The reference manual expands on the information in the videotape for further study.

Managing Change: The Human Dimension. Cambridge, Mass.: Goodmeasure, 1983. Video. 33 mins. $645.

Rosabeth Moss Kanter lectures on nine reasons why people resist change and what management can do about it. Kanter's presentation is full of timely and pertinent information.

Maslow's Hierarchy of Needs: The Joy of Self-Actualization. Santa Monica: Salenger Films, 1987. 16mm film/video. 15 mins. $510.

A discussion of Maslow's "hierarchy of needs" theory of motivation and its applications to management, sales, productivity, organizational effectiveness, and human resource development.

Meetings, Bloody Meetings. Northbrook, Ill.: Video Arts, 1976. 16mm film/video. 30 mins. $685.

In a humorous setting, John Cleese demonstrates his failure as a chairperson on five counts: preparing himself, informing others, planning the agenda, controlling the discussion, and recording the decision. In a companion film, *More Bloody Meetings*, Cleese is faced with breaking the three laws relating to dealing with people in meetings: failure to control aggression, failure to keep the group focused on the objective, and failure to stop the strong from overpowering the weak. In both films, techniques are presented to avoid these problems.

Memory. Del Mar, Calif.: CRM/McGraw-Hill Films, 1980. 16mm film/video. 30 mins. $625.

This film illustrates effective methods for improvement of long-term memory, such as categorizing and referencing memory for fast, efficient recall. Organization of information is the most important key.

Memory Fixing. Santa Monica: Salenger Films, 1982. 16mm film/video. 67 mins. $950/$650.

Ken Cooper presents three methods to remember facts and a four-step method for recall to help develop alertness, save time, and improve productivity. Interactive quizzes increase interest and learning during the film.

Pattern for Instruction. Beverly Hills: Roundtable, 1976. 16mm film/video. 21 mins. $595.

An HRD director explains to a group of instructors the four-step method of instruction, using as illustration a basketball coach's approach. The four steps are preparation, presentation, tryout, and follow-up. The film relates the essentials of learning to the basics of instructing, creates an understanding of the learning process, and shows what motivates people to learn.

P.I.S.T. (Psychological Improvement Situational Training). Santa Monica: Pyramid Film & Video, 1984. 16mm film/video. 5 mins. $250.

A comedy short that spoofs employee motivation, training, and management theory in today's corporate society. It solves the problem of "employee dysfunction" with Psychological Improvement Situational Training (P.I.S.T.), a program of absurd exercises for a "success-intensive tomorrow."

The Possible Human. Bloomfield Hills, Mich.: The Program Source, 1986. Video. 58 mins. $695. (39 mins. $495).

Jean Houston shows how to develop and expand learning capacity and improve mind and body performance. Houston focuses on a growing mind in a flexible body, fine-tuning the senses, multimodal learning, harvesting memory, and the art of empowerment. A companion video, *The Art of Empowerment* (10 mins.), is geared to teachers.

Refiner's Fire. New York: Phoenix/BFA Films and Video, 1977. 16mm film/video. 6 mins. $185.

Animated, abstract "dance" of squares and circles portrays the struggle of conformity and nonconformity.

Speed Reading. New York: Time-Life Video, 1972. 8 videos; drill book; reading book. 30 mins. each. $4,450.

Dick Cavett demonstrates techniques to improve reading speed and retention. Cavett emphasizes the art of skimming, improved study habits, and an enlarged vocabulary. The program package includes paced reading, eye exercises, and comprehension and retention drills.

A Tale of "O": On Being Different. Cambridge, Mass.: Goodmeasure, 1979. 16mm film/video. 27 mins. $680.

This entertaining, educational program illustrates what happens to any new or different person in a group and how to manage that situation. It helps HRD practitioners working with women and minorities to understand potential group dynamics and performance problems in work and learning situations.

Using Media for Learning. Washington, D.C.: Association for Educational Communications and Technology, 1983. 20 videos. $2,800 for the series, $150 each; $14.95 for book.

Stanley A. Huffman, Jr., director of the Learning Resources Center of Virginia Polytechnic Institute and State University, presents in-depth information on the use of media in instruction. Presentations include graphic design, lettering, overhead transparencies, still pictures and photography, audio media, film and video techniques, television, games, simulations and computers, copyright, and instructional environments.

You'll Soon Get the Hang of It: The Technique of One-to-One Training. Northbrook, Ill.: Video Arts, 1981. 16mm film/video. 29 mins. $685.

In humorous sketches demonstrating on-the-job training, John Cleese shows the major mistakes most people make in training new employees. Viewers learn how to organize training to fit how people learn and when to use different motivational techniques. Cleese takes three training situations – manual, clerical, and technical – and demonstrates the major pitfalls.

You're Not Listening. Pasadena, Calif.: Barr Films, 1978. 16mm film/video. 20 mins. $585.

Using humorous vignettes, this film helps viewers identify poor listening behaviors and demonstrates techniques for building good listening habits. Its companion film, *Listening – The Problem Solver*, demonstrates how to use listening skills to resolve problems at work. After reviewing basic listening skills, the film focuses on critical, creative, and sympathetic listening. These films are also available as workshop packages, with learner's workbooks, a discussion leader's manual, and a set of overhead transparencies to highlight key points. They are also available in interactive video, complete with computer software.

Guides to Media and Equipment

In addition to the sources below, there are on-line data bases that list non-print materials (see Chapter 16.)

American Society for Training and Development, Brain Trainers Network. *1987 Professional Resource Guide.* Alexandria, Va.: American Society for Training and Development, 1987. $12.

This annotated bibliography describes films and videotapes that focus on brain/mind issues and management as well as books, journals, newsletters, and other bibliographies.

Association for Media-Based Continuing Education for Engineers. *Catalog of AMCEE Videotape Courses.* Atlanta: Association for Media-Based Continuing Education for Engineers. Annual. Free on request.

This catalogue describes over 400 videotape courses in eighteen disciplines from twenty-five engineering universities. In addition to different types of engineering courses, there are graduate and undergraduate courses in business administration, computer science, energy management, management science, and statistics.

ASTD Buyer's Guide and Consultant Directory. Baltimore: ASTD Press. Annual. $35.

This directory lists training programs for all types of employee training and management development programs, including nonprint media. Also included is a listing of AV equipment dealers and production services.

ASTD Training Video Directory. 2 vols. Baltimore: ASTD Press, 1986. $85 for members; $110 for nonmembers.

This two-volume directory lists 12,000 video training programs—6,000 on management, organization, and career development and 6,000 on technical and skills training. The videos are listed under 350 training topics. Information about each video includes a complete description of program content, length, color, audience level, producer, and distributor.

Audio Video Marketplace: A Multimedia Guide. New York: Bowker. Annual. $65.

This is a comprehensive guide to over 6,000 producers, distributors, and services in all phases of the audiovisual communications industry.

Contemporary Psychology. Washington, D.C.: American Psychological Association. Monthly. $50.

This journal contains evaluative reviews of current films, audiocassettes, and other media in the field of psychology as well as book reviews.

Educational Film Locator. (3rd ed.) New York: Bowker, 1986. $150.

This directory lists 40,000 films on all topics. These films may be rented from fifty university film libraries throughout the United States.

Equipment Directory of Audio-Visual, Computer, and Video Products. Fairfax, Va.: International Communications. Annual. $40.

This comprehensive directory of media equipment and computer hardware includes over 2,000 equipment items listed by category. A photograph of each item is included as well as specifications.

"How to Get the Most out of Films and Videos for Employee Development." Hoboken, N.J.: Olympic Media Information, 1987. Free.

This twelve-page booklet provides tips on using films and videos for training purposes, leading post-screening discussions, and enhancing on-the-job performance. Procedures are discussed for previewing, renting, and purchasing media.

HRD Review: A Journal of Professional Opinion. Glen Rock, N.J.: HRD Review. Monthly. $85.

In addition, Begun in 1983, this eight-page publication includes six to eight reviews each month by experienced management and training practitioners. Materials reviewed include audiocassettes, films, and video packages as well as books and computer software.

Human Resources Index. Pasadena, Calif.: Moreland. Annual. $49.95.

This bibliography lists nonprint and print materials of interest to HRD professionals under 122 topics, including human resource management (compensation, labor relations, recruitment), counseling, communication, and training and development.

Media Profiles: The Career Development Edition. (Formerly *Training Film Profiles.*) Hoboken, N.J.: Olympic Media Information. Bimonthly. $175.

This publication reviews about 250 media programs per year that are designed for management development or employee training as well as programs on instructional strategies. Each review indicates the primary audience, the content, a detailed synopsis, and an evaluation.

Media Profiles: The Health Science Edition. (Formerly *Hospital/Health Care Training Media Profiles.*) Hoboken, N.J.: Olympic Media Information. Bimonthly. $87.50.

This publication reviews media programs of interest to health care professionals, including sex education, substance abuse, handicapped issues, and patient education. Each review indicates the primary audience, the content, a detailed synopsis, and an evaluation.

Nadler, Leonard, and others (eds.). *The Trainer's Resource 1987: A Comprehensive Guide to Packaged Training Programs.* Amherst, Mass.: Human Resource Development Press, 1987. $59.95.

In addition to descriptions of 500 training programs, this directory includes a section called "Film Best-Sellers and Classics."

National Audiovisual Center. *Selected Audiovisual Materials Produced by the United States Government, 1986.* Capitol Heights, Md.: National Audiovisual Center, 1986. Free on request.

This catalogue lists and briefly describes over 2,700 videotapes and films on all topics, available for purchase or for rental. Subject catalogues and a *Quarterly Update* are also available on request.

Training Marketplace Directory. Minneapolis: Lakewood Publications. Annual. (Mailed with August issue of *Training* magazine.) $15.

Producers of nonprint training programs for all types of employee training programs and in a variety of subject categories are listed by subject.

Directory of Producers, Distributors, and Publishers

Producers marked with an asterisk (*) have a strong list of titles in the area of supervisory/management development. Media distributors are marked with a bullet (•). University film libraries, which rent films, are marked with a dagger (†).

*AMA Film/Video
85 Main St.
Watertown, MA 02172
(800) 225-3215, (617) 926-4600

American Society for Training and
  Development
1630 Duke St., Box 1443
Alexandria, VA 22313
(703) 683-8100

Arthur Young
1950 Roland Clarke Place
Reston, VA 22091
(703) 648-2200, ext. 285

Association for Educational
  Communications and Technology
AECT Publications
1126 16th St. NW
Washington, DC 20036
(202) 466-4780

Association for Media-Based
  Continuing Education for
  Engineers
500 Tech Pkwy. NW, Suite 200A
Atlanta, GA 30313
(404) 894-3362

ASTD Press
P. O. Box 4856, Hampden Station
Baltimore, MD 21211
(301) 338-6949

*Barr Films
3490 E. Foothill Blvd.
P. O. Box 5667
Pasadena, CA 91107
(213) 681-2165

*BNA Communcations
9439 Key West Ave.
Rockville, MD 20850
(301) 948-0540

Bowker Company
P. O. Box 762
New York, NY 10011
(212) 337-6934

Brain Technologies Corporation
414 Buckeye St.
Fort Collins, CO 80524
(303) 493-9210

*Britannica Films
780 S. Lapeer Rd.
Lake Orion, MI 48035
(800) 554-6970, (313) 693-4232

*Cally Curtis Company
1111 N. Las Palmas Ave.
Hollywood, CA 90038
(213) 467-1101

*CBS/Fox Video
39000 Seven Mile Rd.
Livonia, MI 48152
(313) 591-1555

Center for Southern Folklore
1216 Peabody, Box 40105
Memphis, TN 38104
(901) 726-4205

Copeland Griggs Productions
411 Fifteenth Ave.
San Francisco, CA 94118
(415) 668-4200

*Coronet/MTI Film & Video
108 Wilmot Rd.
Deerfield, IL 60015
(312) 940-1260, (800) 621-2131

*Dartnell
4660 Ravenswood Ave.
Chicago, IL 60640
(800) 621-5463, (312) 561-4000

•Excellence in Training Corporation
8364 Hickman Rd.
Des Moines, IA 50322
(515) 276-6569

Goodmeasure, Inc.
330 Broadway
P. O. Box 3004
Cambridge, MA 02139
(617) 492-2714

Gulf Publishing Company Video
P. O. Box 2608
Houston, TX 77252
(713) 529-4301

HRD Review
P. O. Box 6
Glen Rock, NJ 07452
(201) 445-2288

Human Resource Development Press
22 Amherst Rd.
Amherst, MA 01002
(800) 822-2801

†Indiana University
Audiovisual Center
Bloomington, IN 47405
(800) 552-8620

International Communications
  Industries Association
3150 Spring St.
Fairfax, VA 22031
(703) 273-7200

Lakewood Publications
50 S. 9th St.
Minneapolis, MN 55402
(800) 328-4329, (612) 333-0471

*McGraw-Hill Training Systems
P.O. Box 641
Del Mar, CA 92014
(800) 421-0833, (619) 453-5000

•Masterco
P. O. Box 7382
Ann Arbor, MI 48107
(313) 428-8300

Moreland Company
61 S. Lake Ave., Suite 201
Pasadena, CA 91101
(818) 304-1032

*National Audiovisual Center
National Archives and Records
  Administration
8700 Edgeworth Dr.
Capitol Heights, MD 20743
(301) 763-1896

Nebraska Educational Television
  Council for Higher Education
P. O. Box 83111
Lincoln, NE 68501
(402) 472-3611

Olympic Media Information
550 First St.
Hoboken, NJ 07030
(201) 963-1600

Phoenix/BFA Films and Video
468 Park Ave. South
New York, NY 10016
(800) 221-1274, (212) 684-5910

Program Source
1415 Lenox Rd.
Bloomfield Hills, MI 48013
(313) 644-2449

Pyramid Film & Video
P. O. Box 1048
Santa Monica, CA 90406
(800) 421-2304, (213) 828-7577

*Roundtable Film and Video
113 N. San Vicente Blvd.
Beverly Hills, CA 90211
(800) 332-4444, (213) 657-1402

*Salenger Films
1635 12th St.
Santa Monica, CA 90404
(213) 450-1300

*Simon & Schuster
108 Wilmot Rd.
Deerfield, IL 60015
(800) 323-5343, (312) 940-1260

•Thompson-Mitchell & Associates
3384 Peachtree Rd. NE
Atlanta, GA 30326
(800) 554-1389, (404) 233-5435

*Time-Life Video
100 Eisenhower Dr.
Paramus, NJ 07652
(800) 526-4663

*United Training Media
6633 W. Howard St.
Niles, IL 60648
(800) 558-9015

University Associates
8517 Production Ave.
San Diego, CA 92121
(619) 578-5900

†University of California—Berkeley
Extension Media Center
2176 Shattuck Ave.
Berkeley, CA 94720
(415) 642-0460

†University of Illinois Film Center
1325 S. Oak St.
Champaign, IL 61820
(800) 367-3456; in Illinois
    (800) 252-1357, (217) 333-1360

†University of Iowa
Audiovisual Center
Seashore Hall, Room C-4
Iowa City, IA 52242
(319) 353-5885

†University of Texas at Austin
Film Library
P. O. Box W
Austin, TX 78713
(512) 471-3572

*Video Arts, Inc.
Northbrook Technology Center
4088 Commercial Ave.
Northbrook, IL 60062
(800) 553-0091, (312) 291-1008

16

On-Line Data Bases

Linda Webster

On-line data bases can provide you with references to journal articles and books on topics of interest to you. These are called bibliographic data bases, and they provide lists of references on subjects of interest. Other data bases contain full texts of newsletters, journals, or encyclopedias and other reference books. Data bases are also available that provide reviews and information on computer software and nonprint training materials. Still other data bases list upcoming seminars and conferences.

You can request data-base searches at many university libraries — even though you are not affiliated with the institution. Some larger public libraries also provide data-base searches within the community. Or you can use your microcomputer as a terminal (along with a modem and communications software) to access the data bases directly through data-base vendors and suppliers. BRS Information Technologies and DIALOG Information Services are two of the largest vendors. DIALOG provides over 200 data bases, containing over 75 million records. Both BRS and DIALOG have services geared to home computer users with lower rates for searching during evening and weekend hours. For more information about these services, see BRS/After Dark and Knowledge Index in the descriptions of data-base services in this chapter.

For consumer and business-oriented data and participation in special-interest groups (SIGs), you can subscribe to The Source, CompuServe, or Delphi. See the descriptions of these data bases later in this chapter. Texts of newsletters and journals are available on Harvard Business Review, Human Resource Information Network, and NewsNet. The data bases are listed alphabetically by the name of the data base. Each description typically includes the name of the data base, the number of records in the data base, the type of information provided by the data base, the producer and supplier, and the cost per connect hour. Usually the total cost includes the cost per connect hour (which is different for each data base), communications charges for use of telephone lines, and some type of annual membership or subscription fee. See the directory at the end of this chapter for addresses and phone numbers of producers and suppliers. Contact producers for further information about the content of the data bases. Contact suppliers for additional information about costs and access to the data bases. Costs change frequently. Some publishers make yearly changes, so view this information as approximate. Addresses and phone numbers also change.

This chapter's list of data bases is a very small sample of what is currently available. Included are those data bases that will be of most use to HRD practitioners and adult educators. If you are an HRD practitioner outside the corporate sector—in health care, criminal justice, or library and information science—there are additional data bases geared to these subjects. To find these additional data bases, consult catalogues from BRS and DIALOG, contact a nearby public or academic library, or browse through the following directories of data bases:

Edelhart, Mike, and Davies, Owen (eds.). *OMNI Online Database Directory*. New York: Collier Books, 1985.

Williams, Martha E. *Computer-Readable Databases: Business, Law, Humanities, Social Sciences*. Chicago: American Library Association, 1985.

For more detailed information on the uses of data bases, see Chapter 8.

ABI/Inform

Producer: Data Courier
Suppliers: BRS, DIALOG
Cost: $96 per connect hour
Description: Provides references for executives to approximately 550 business publications on all topics of business management and administration. Specific product and industry information is included but is not the primary focus.

ASTD Member Information Exchange (MIE)

Producer and Supplier: American Society for Training and Development
Cost: Free service for members only
Description: Unlike the other data bases in this section, this service requires that you write or call ASTD and ask for a search of its data base to locate members who have the required expertise. If you would like to be included in the MIE data base as a resource person, request an MIE Resource Person Profile.

A-V Online (formerly NICEM)

Producer: Access Innovations
Supplier: DIALOG
Cost: $70 per connect hour
Description: Provides comprehensive coverage of nonprint educational material—films, filmstrips, transparencies, audiotapes, videotapes, slides—for professional and graduate levels as well as school-age students.

BRS/After Dark

Producer and Supplier: BRS
Cost: $6–$15 per hour plus $50 subscription fee
Description: Offers twenty-five of the most popular BRS data bases in the fields of science, finance, education, and energy. Available 6 p.m.–midnight weekdays; all day Saturday and Sunday.

Business Periodicals Index

Producer and Supplier: WILSONLINE
Cost: $43–$65
Description: Indexes approximately 300 English-language business periodicals covering marketing, management, economics, computers, human resource management and development, and specific industries. The corresponding print index is *Business Periodicals Index*.

Business Software Database

Producer: Data Courier, Louisville, KY
Supplier: DIALOG
Cost: $90 per connect hour
Description: Includes descriptions of computer software packages with business applications for use with micro- and minicomputers. Information includes the description of the package; name, address, phone number, and manufacturer; price and availability information; machine capability; program language; description of documentation; and customer service availability. Software reviews will be added soon.

Career Placement Registry/Experienced Personnel

Producer: Career Placement Registry
Supplier: DIALOG
Cost: $95 per connect hour
Description: Provides recruiters and potential employers access to job candidates from a broad spectrum of backgrounds and a wide range of experience levels. File includes listings of experienced individuals who are seeking new employment opportunities. The data include college education, degrees, major and minor, occupation preferences, geographic preference, and work experience. Full resumes are available on request. For information on college seniors or recent college graduates, use the companion data base Career Placement Registry/Student.

Catalyst Resources for Women

Producer: Catalyst Information Center
Supplier: BRS
Cost: $55 per connect hour
Description: Geared to aspects of women and work, careers, and the corporate climate. Includes such topics as two-career families, affirmative action, career

planning, mothers who work outside of the home, and corporate response to these issues. References are provided to books, journal articles, newspaper articles, pamphlets, papers, and government reports.

CompuServe

Producer and Supplier: CompuServe
Cost: $6–$12.50 per hour; no monthly fees
Description: Includes hundreds of data bases for both the consumer and business markets, including news, entertainment, electronic mail, programming languages, and user groups. The most popular category on the system is the Special Interest Group (SIG) Service. Available twenty-four hours a day seven days a week.

Delphi

Producer and Supplier: General Videotex Corporation
Cost: $17.40 per hour for daytime use on weekdays; $7.20 per hour nights and weekends; plus $49.95 membership fee
Description: Includes both consumer and business services. Provides current stock market information, tax updates, movie reviews, games, and a self-publishing section called Infomania. Contains newsletters about computers and provides access to DIALOG's 200 data bases. Also includes over a dozen Special Interest Groups (SIGs). Available twenty-four hours a day seven days a week.

Dow Jones News/Retrieval

Producer and Supplier: Dow Jones and Company
Cost: $54–$72 per hour daytime use; evenings and weekends as low as $9 per hour plus a sign-up fee of $29.95; various discount programs available
Description: Business-oriented service providing detailed financial information, including current and historical stock market quotations, commodities prices, and financial disclosure details on over 6,000 American corporations and 170 industry and government categories. Also includes business and general news, *Wall Street Journal* highlights, and a variety of other general information services.

DPTRAIN

Producer and Supplier: National Training & Computers Project
Cost: $6–$15 per hour
Description: DPTRAIN assists computer trainers by providing on-line a professional training course and additional short courses monthly. Users can duplicate these courses and adapt them to their organizations. New hardware and software are reviewed as well. Offered in conjunction with CompuServe, this service requires only a microcomputer and a modem for access.

Education Index

Producer and Supplier: WILSONLINE
Cost: $25–$45

Description: Contains references to articles from about 350 English-language education journals, including the topics of adult and continuing education, human resource development and training, instructional techniques, computer-based instruction, and educational research. The corresponding print index is *Education Index*.

EdVENT

Producer and Supplier: Timeplace, Inc.
Cost: $1,250 annual subscription
Description: Contains descriptions of 120,000 seminars, conferences, workshops, and other continuing education courses sponsored by 4,500 organizations in the United States. Information includes course title and summary, target audiences, cost, dates, location, instructor, credits granted, and sponsor information. Users can request additional information from sponsors or register for courses on-line.

ERIC (Educational Resources Information Center)

Producer: ERIC Processing and Reference Facility
Suppliers: BRS, DIALOG
Cost: $30 per connect hour
Description: Comprehensive education data base, including adult, career, and vocational education. Indexes the most significant and timely education research reports, projects, and more than 700 education journals. Most reports in this data base can be ordered from the ERIC Document Reproduction Service in paper copy or microfiche. An academic library near you will probably own the complete collection of ERIC microfiche, and most are open to the general public. The corresponding print indexes are *Current Index to Journals in Education* and *Resources in Education*.

Executive Information Service

Producers: Data Courier, Management Contents, Grolier Electronic Publishing, Harvard Business Review, John Wiley, and BRS
Supplier: Product Information Service
Cost: $100 per month plus telecommunications costs
Description: Geared primarily to the business community, this service is actually three data bases. ABI/Inform summarizes recent business and management articles from over 600 journals. Harvard Business Review/Online provides the full text of all *Harvard Business Review* articles since 1976 and summaries of 800 previously published articles. The Academic American Encyclopedia is a full-text encyclopedia on-line. The service is accessible through a menu-driven format supplied by BRS, the host computer system.

Electronic Registrar (formerly Electronic Seminar Event Catalog)

Producer: Solution Associates
Supplier: NewsNet

Cost: Subscription to NewsNet
Description: Contains descriptions of approximately 3,000 continuing education courses and seminars in the fields of computer science, engineering, and management offered by U.S. businesses, universities, and associations and organizations. Descriptions include subject, date, location, instructor, course outline, cancellation policy, and program format. Users can request registration, catalogues, and further information on-line.

Foundation Grants Index
Producer: The Foundation Center
Supplier: DIALOG
Cost: $60 per connect hour
Description::   For those interested in locating sources of foundation grant funds. Contains information on grants awarded by more than 400 major American philanthropic foundations. Grants to individuals and grants of less than $5,000 are not included. Education is the most favored field for foundation giving. For more detailed and current information about foundations of interest, use the companion data base, Foundation Directory.

Gradline
Producer: Peterson's Guides, Princeton, NJ
Supplier: DIALOG
Cost: $60 per hour
Description: Includes over 1,400 accredited higher education institutions and graduate and professional programs offered by accredited colleges and universities in the United States and Canada. Provides a full description of each program, the number of students and faculty, entrance and degree requirements, financial aid available, graduate appointments, research budget, and focus of faculty research. The corresponding print index is *Peterson's Annual Guides/Graduate Study*.

Grants
Producer: Oryx Press
Supplier: DIALOG
Cost: $60 per hour
Description: Provides information about grant programs available through government (federal, state, and local), commercial businesses, associations, and private foundations.

Harvard Business Review
Producer: Wiley & Sons
Suppliers: BRS, DIALOG
Cost: $96 per hour

Description: Contains the complete text of the *Harvard Business Review* from 1976 to the present as well as summaries of articles from 1971 to 1975 and 700 classic earlier articles from the journal. Covers the complete range of management subjects, including accounting, automation, business ethics, industry analysis, strategic planning, and trade.

Human Resource Information Network

Producer and Supplier: Executive Telecom System

Cost: $2,720 annual subscription plus $36–$56 per hour (discounts for evening and weekend use)

Description: Comprehensive data base for practitioners in the human resource management and development fields that is divided into eight Professional Networks. One of these networks is the Training and Development Network, which can be subscribed to separately at a reduced cost. The Training and Development Network includes the Seminar Clearinghouse Data Base (listings for 45,000 public seminars); Seminar Information Service Data Base (listings for 50,000 seminars, including in-house offerings); Training and Development Alert (the on-line version of this newsletter from 1981 to the present); and the Training Media Data Base (a subset of the A-V On-line Data Base geared to the workplace). In addition, the Human Resource Information Network includes a bibliography and abstract service containing over 125,000 articles from more than 400 publications (with 2,000 articles added monthly) in all human resource areas. Full texts of these articles are available upon request.

Interactive Video Technology

Producer: Heartland Communications

Supplier: NewsNet

Cost: Monthly subscription to NewsNet required; differential charges for subscribers and nonsubscribers to *Interactive Video Technology*

Description: Full-text monthly newsletter with information on the interactive video market, including applications to education, training, military disciplines, point-of-sale merchandising, videodisc games, archival storage, and data-base publishing. Also included are new products and services, videodisc hardware and software, and a calendar of conferences and seminars. The corresponding print periodical is *Interactive Video Technology*.

Knowledge Index

Producer and Supplier: DIALOG

Cost: $24 per hour plus $35 subscription fee

Description: Provides consumer-oriented data bases from DIALOG Information Services at reduced costs. Content areas include business, education, engineering, psychology, and computer information. Available 6 p.m.–5 a.m. Monday through Thursday; 6 p.m.–midnight Friday; 8 a.m.–midnight Saturday; 3 p.m.–midnight Sunday.

Management Contents
Producer: Information Access Company
Suppliers: BRS, DIALOG
Cost: $90 per hour
Description: Provides references and abstracts to business and management topics from over 700 journals, conference proceedings, newsletters, and research reports. Content areas include accounting, decision sciences, finance, industrial relations, managerial economics, marketing, operations research, organization behavior, and public administration. The corresponding print index is *Management Contents*.

Menu—The International Software Database
Producer: International Software Database Corporation
Supplier: DIALOG
Cost: $60 per hour
Description: Provides a comprehensive listing of over 55,000 commercially available software for any type of mini- or microcomputer. Records consist of a 150-word description, vendor name, compatibility requirements, date, and price. General headings for software include commercial, educational, personal, industrial, scientific, professions/industries, and systems. Software catalogues, such as *The Software Catalog: Microcomputers*, are prepared from this data base and distributed by Elsevier Science Publishing Company.

Microcomputer Index
Producer: Database Services
Supplier: DIALOG
Cost: $60 per hour
Description: Provides references and abstracts to magazine articles from fifty microcomputer journals, including general articles, book reviews, software reviews, and information on new products.

NewsNet
Producer and Supplier: NewsNet
Cost: $24–$60 per hour; 25% discount on weekday nights and weekends; $15 monthly minimum charge
Description: Offers on-line versions on current issues of about 200 newsletters on the following topics: advertising and marketing, aerospace, automotive, business, chemical, corporate communications, education, electronics and computers, energy, entertainment and leisure, environment, farming and food, finance and accounting, government and regulation, health and hospitals, insurance, international affairs, investment, law, management, medicine, metals and mining, office automation, politics, public relations, publishing and broadcasting, real estate, research and development, social sciences, taxation, and telecommunications. Contains current issues and back issues from 1982. The service allows you to search the data base by keywords to locate articles of interest.

NTIS (National Technical Information Service)
Producer: National Technical Information Service
Suppliers: BRS, DIALOG
Cost: $69 per hour
Description: Provides references to government-sponsored research reports in science and the social sciences, such as administration and management, behavioral sciences, communication, computers, business and economics, urban and regional planning, and education.

PsycINFO (formerly Psychological Abstracts)
Producer: American Psychological Association
Suppliers: BRS, DIALOG
Cost: $55 per hour
Description: Covers the world's literature in psychology and related disciplines in the behavioral sciences. Provides references to articles in over 1,300 periodicals, books, and technical reports. The corresponding print index is *Psychological Abstracts*.

PTS F&S Indexes
Producer: Predicasts
Supplier: DIALOG
Cost: $114 per hour
Description: Covers both domestic and international companies, products, and industries. Contains information on corporate acquisitions and mergers, new products, technological developments, and sociopolitical factors. Provides analyses of companies by securities firms, contains forecasts of company sales and profits, and reports on factors influencing future sales and earnings. In addition, it provides on-line access to a comprehensive bibliography of more than 5,000 publications.

Social Sciences Index
Producer and Supplier: WILSONLINE
Cost: $34–$55
Description: Contains references to journal articles and book reviews in over 300 English-language periodicals in the social sciences. Topics covered include anthropology, economics, environmental sciences, geography, law and criminology, planning and public administration, political science, psychology, social aspects of medicine, sociology, international relations, and current events. The corresponding print index is *Social Sciences Index*.

Social Scisearch
Producer: Institute for Scientific Information
Suppliers: BRS, DIALOG
Cost: $99 per hour

Description: Covers every area of the social and behavioral sciences, listing references from books and 1,500 social sciences journals worldwide and social sciences articles selected from 3,000 additional journals in the natural, physical, and biomedical sciences. Besides searching by subject, author, and corporate institutions, you can also locate authors and researchers who have referred to a particular author or journal article in their research. The corresponding print index is *Social Sciences Citation Index*.

The Source
Producer and Supplier: Source Telecomputing Corporation
Cost: $21.60 per hour weekdays; $8.40 per hour evenings and weekends
Description: Large general-interest utility offering news and reference resources, catalogue shopping, education and careers, business and financial markets, games, travel and dining information, entertainment reviews, electronic mail, and conferencing. Available twenty-two hours a day seven days a week.

TRAINET
Producer and Supplier: American Society for Training and Development
Cost: $24 per hour for ASTD national members only
Description: Lists more than 100,000 worldwide learning events sponsored by private companies, associations, and colleges. New seminars are added daily. Information for each item includes seminar descriptions, costs, available discounts, sites, dates, and sponsor addresses and phone numbers.

Directory of Producers and Suppliers

Access Innovations
P. O. Box 40130
Albuquerque, NM 87196
(800) 421-8711, (505) 265-3591

American Society for Training and
  Development
1630 Duke St., Box 1443
Alexandria, VA 22313
(703) 683-8100

BRS Information Technologies
1200 Route 7
Latham, NY 12110
(800) 345-4BRS, (518) 783-1161
  collect

Career Placement Registry
302 Swann Ave.
Alexandria, VA 22301
(800) 368-3093, (703) 683-1085

Catalyst Information Center
250 Park Ave. South
New York, NY 10003
(212) 777-8900

CompuServe
Consumer Information Service
500 Arlington Center Blvd.,
  P. O. Box 20212
Columbus, OH 43220
(800) 848-8199, (614) 457-0802

Data Courier
620 S. Fifth St.
Louisville, KY 40202
(800) 626-2823; in Kentucky
   (502) 582-4111

Database Services
P. O. Box 50545
Palo Alto, CA 94303
(415) 961-2880

DIALOG Information Services
Marketing Department
3460 Hillview Ave.
Palo Alto, CA 94304
(800) 3DIALOG, (415) 858-3785

Dow Jones and Company, Inc.
P. O. Box 300
Princeton, NJ 08543
(800) 257-5114, (609) 452-2000

ERIC Processing and Reference
   Facility
4833 Rugby Ave., Suite 301
Bethesda, MD 20814
(301) 656-9723

Executive Telecom System
College Park North
9585 Valparaiso Court
Indianapolis, IN 46268
(800) 421-8884, (317) 872-2045

Foundation Center
79 Fifth Ave. at 16th St.
New York, NY 10003
(212) 620-4230

General Videotex Corporation
3 Blackstone St.
Cambridge, MA 02139
(800) 544-4005, (617) 491-3393

Information Access Company
11 Davis Dr.
Belmont, CA 94002
(800) 227-8431, (415) 591-2333

Institute for Scientific Information
3501 Market St.
University City Science Center
Philadelphia, PA 19104
(800) 523-1850, (215) 386-0100
   ext. 1389

International Software Database
   Corporation
1520 S. College Ave.
Fort Collins, CO 80524
(303) 482-5000

National Technical Information
   Service
U.S. Department of Commerce
5285 Port Royal Rd.
Springfield, VA 22161
(703) 487-4600

National Training & Computers
   Project
Sagamore Rd.
Raquette Lake, NY 13436
(800) 34-TRAIN

NewsNet
945 Haverford Rd.
Bryn Mawr, PA 19010
(800) 345-1301, (215) 527-8030

Oryx Press
2214 N. Central at Encanto
Phoenix, AZ 85004
(602) 254-6156

Peterson's Guides
Electronic Services
P. O. Box 2123
Princeton, NJ 08540
(609) 924-5338

Predicasts
Online Services Department
200 University Circle Research
  Center
1101 Cedar Ave.
Cleveland, OH 44106
(800) 321-6388, in Ohio
  (216) 795-3000

Product Information Service
650 Third Ave.
New York, NY 10158
(212) 850-6360

Source Telecomputing Corporation
1616 Anderson Rd.
McLean, VA 22102
(800) 336-3366, (703) 734-7500

Timeplace, Inc.
460 Totten Pond Rd.
Waltham, MA 02154
(617) 890-4636

Wiley & Sons, Inc.
Electronic Publishing
605 Third Ave.
New York, NY 10158
(212) 850-6178

WILSONLINE
H. W. Wilson Company
950 University Ave.
Bronx, NY 10452
(212) 588-8400

17

Microcomputer Courseware and Training Program Administration Software

Linda Webster

Recent surveys indicate that a majority of training departments are now using microcomputers in their training efforts in some way, including computer-based training. Other uses of microcomputers include data management, word processing and graphics. It is not surprising that software is available on an increasingly diverse range of topics from management development to computer literacy to stress management. Software is also available to assist you in conducting assessments of all types—career development, organizational climate, evaluation of training events—and to make it possible for you to author your own computer-based courses. Computer software has also teamed up with video technology to produce interactive video learning situations.

This chapter lists some of the available courseware (content and skill development software) and training program administration software (registration, scheduling, record-keeping). This will give you a start in identifying products that may be useful in your situation. You will need to contact producers directly to confirm details of system compatibility and current pricing. Often demo disks are available at minimal charge. Both DSI Micro and Masterco are distributors of HRD-related microcomputer software. Their addresses and phone numbers are listed at the end of this chapter.

Course authoring software is not described in this chapter. There are many different systems, and you will need to make choices based on the instructional material you want to develop and your specific situation. For background on the types of course authoring software available, see Diane Gayeski and David V. Williams, "Authoring Interactive Media," in *Training*, Dec. 1984, pp. 61–79, which includes a list of authoring software producers. For in-depth evaluation of and comparisons between current CBT authoring systems for micros, minis, and mainframes, see "Annual Survey of CBT Authoring Systems" in *Data Training*, May

1986, pp. 32-68. For a survey of project management software, survey/questionnaire software, and statistical packages, see Ron Zemke and John Gunkler, "Managing by Micro: A Software Review" in *Training*, Sept. 1985, pp. C39-C48.

This chapter is organized in the following sections:

Courseware and Assessment Software
Training Program Administration Software
Directories of Computer Software
Directory of Publishers and Producers

There are a number of sources that provide information about currently available courseware. Get your name on mailing lists to keep up to date in this rapidly changing field. In addition, the *Training and Development Journal* has a "New Training Tools" column that describes new software. Consult the list of directories of computer software in this chapter for software products in all employee training fields.

Prices change frequently, so view this information as approximate. Addresses and phone numbers also change.

Courseware and Assessment Software

The Art of Negotiating. New York: Negotiation Institute. $495. (Distributed by DSI Micro).

The Art of Negotiating helps develop plans and strategies geared to the specific negotiating situation.

Hardware: IBM PC and compatibles; Apple III.

CareerPoint. Silver Spring, Md.: Conceptual Systems, Inc. $6,900.

CareerPoint is a career development system for organizations. Its four modules include the importance of career development and different paths, self-assessment, setting goals based on information about the organization, and the completion of a personal development plan. CareerPoint Plus adds capabilities for identifying critical competencies and assessing employees as well as for handling job posting, training calendars, and talent pool posting.

Hardware: IBM PC, XT, AT, and compatibles; 256K, color graphics card, color monitor.

Decision Maker. Walnut Creek, Calif.: Alamo Learning Systems. $89.95.

Decision Maker provides guidance through the steps for making a well-balanced decision. It asks questions at the right time to help focus thinking and feeds critical information back to the user. It automatically produces management reports that define the rationale behind the decision.

Hardware: IBM PC and all other machines with CPM cards or operating systems.

DISCOVER Career Development System. Iowa City, Ia.: ACT, Educational Services Division. $6,000 lease for first year; $2,000 annually thereafter.

The DISCOVER Career Development System features the following five modules: Understanding Career Development and Change (evaluation of job satisfaction and identification of career stages); Assessing Yourself (inventory of interests, accomplishments, and work-related values); Gathering Information (data-gathering methods for finding out about the organization); Making Decisions (career changes, goal setting, and decision making); Taking Action (analysis of the pros and cons of the selected goal and development of an action plan).

Hardware: IBM PC, XT, AT; color graphics adapter card; color monitor; IBM PC-DOS 3.1 or higher; 64K RAM, 320K floppy disk drives; 10Mb IBM expansion hard disk.

Human Edge. San Mateo, Calif.: Human Edge Software Corporation. $99 each. (Distributed by Masterco and DSI Micro).

Human Edge Software provides human interaction analysis programs designed for improving interpersonal success in a variety of areas—forecasting, negotiation, sales, hiring, management, and communication. Each program asks a series of questions about the user and the other person involved. The outputs provide usable action strategies. Of most interest to HRD practitioners are Communication Edge, which assesses communication styles of the user and those whom the user communicates with; Management Edge, which evaluates skills in light of the user's superior and subordinates; and Negotiation Edge, which assists in evaluating the user's and opponent's positions and in providing a negotiation plan. Also of interest is a program called Mind Prober. In response to users' answers about a person they are analyzing, Mind Prober provides a report on the subject's attitudes and interests.

Hardware: IBM PC; some programs available for the Apple II or III and the Macintosh.

Idea Generator. New York: Negotiation Institute. $195. (Distributed by DSI Micro).

The Idea Generator uses a three-step process of problem statement, idea generation, and evaluation for effective solutions. This system encourages creativity.

Hardware: IBM PC and compatibles; Apple III.

Knowledge Center. Cambridge Mass.: Learncom. $3,600 annual fee for use of 10 lessons per month.

Knowledge Center is a library of computer-based courseware in the field of management development. Lessons are available in the following content areas: strategic planning, forecasting, project planning using PERT/CAM, mathematics for business, employee performance evaluation, and introduction to different types of computer software (word processing, spreadsheets, data bases).

Hardware: IBM PC and compatibles.

Management Courseware. Reading, Mass.: Addison-Wesley Training Systems. 4 disks. $125 each. (Distributed by Masterco).

    Management Courseware teaches basic management strategies to new managers in the following areas: delegation, goal setting, performance feedback, and problem solving. Each training program includes exercises, case studies, and other interactive computer activities.

    Hardware: IBM PC and compatibles; DOS 2.0 or higher; 256K memory; monochrome or color monitor.

Participative Management Skills. Minneapolis, Minn.: Concourse Corporation. 5 disks. $50 each. (Distributed by Masterco and DSI Micro).

    Participative Management Skills includes the following topics: choosing participation, enhancing power, facilitating team communication, understanding motivational dynamics, and achieving consensus.

    Hardware: IBM PC, AT, XT, and compatibles.

Pro Counsel Software Series. Skillman, N.J.: Kepner-Tregoe. $250 each. (Distributed by Masterco and DSI Micro).

    The Pro Counsel Software Series includes Planning Pro (with Gantt charts and reports), Decision Aid (for gathering, organizing, and analyzing information), and Trouble Shooter (problem analysis). These software packages reflect Kepner-Tregoe's capabilities in problem solving, decision making, and project management.

    Hardware: IBM PC, XT, AT, and compatibles, Hewlett Packard 150, and the DEC Rainbow with 256K memory and MS-DOS 2.0 or higher.

Smart Eyes. Reading, Mass.: Addison-Wesley Training Systems. $49.95. (Distributed by Masterco).

    Smart Eyes is designed to increase reading speed and comprehension. The first section concentrates on the physical aspects of reading—eye movement exercises, paced reading exercises and eye fixation exercises. The second section deals with the cognitive aspect of reading—training the mind to scan printed materials for information.

    Hardware: IBM PC and compatibles; DOS 2.0 or higher; 256K memory; monochrome or color monitor.

Thoughtware. Plantation, Fla.: Thoughtware, Inc. $99 each. (Distributed by Masterco and DSI Micro).

    Thoughtware software focuses on management skills and sales training. The Management Diagnostic Series (three disks) includes assessing personal management skills, evaluating organizational effectiveness, and understanding personal interaction styles. The Management Training Series (ten disks) includes the following topics: leading effectively, motivating to achieve results, defining goals and objectives, improving employee performance, conducting performance appraisal, managing time effectively, conducting successful meetings, managing by exception, managing stress, and planning one's life and career. Hardware: IBM PC, XT, AT, and compatibles; color graphics card.

What Color Is Your Mind? San Diego, Calif.: Shamrock Press. $59.95.

What Color Is Your Mind? ranks people's thinking patterns. By using the individual thinking-style diagrams and worksheets in the accompanying manual, a group of people can explore the ways they relate to one another. Based on the same four-style model used in the more comprehensive Mindex instrument developed by Karl Albrecht. Hardware: Apple, IBM PC; 64K, 1 disk drive.

Training Program Administration Software

EdITS (Educators' Information Tracking System). Dallas: Lomas & Nettleton Information Systems, Inc. $1,195–$1,495.

EdITS has the capability to enroll students; establish individual curriculum profiles; display rosters of classes; print reports by department, student, and class; print summary reports by month, quarter, and year; and print confirmation letters to students. Hardware: IBM PC-XT and compatibles with 256K.

EXAMBANK. Walnut Creek, Calif.: Impell Corporation. $15,000.

EXAMBANK enables the training manager to create a permanent data base of exam questions keyed to the defined learning objectives for each course and lesson plan in a curriculum. It then creates exams automatically, based on the training manager's specifications. Hardware: IBM PC, XT, AT, and compatibles with color monitor.

PeopleFacts. San Diego: Shamrock Press. $395; full-feature preview, $35.

People Facts assists in questionnaire design and processes questionnaire responses. It displays a statistical summary of the data and allows analysis by frequency counts, mean values, standard deviations, percentages, rankings, and no-response counts. It allows pulling out subpopulations based on answer criteria and prints various management reports. Hardware: IBM PC; 128K, 1 disk drive, DOS 2.1.

Registrar. Cupertino, Calif.: Silton-Bookman Systems. $595–$1,195.

Registrar manages registration and logistics, sends letters to students with the Registrar Word Processor, prints mailing labels, reports enrollment statistics, records class grades, and sends data to other software packages with Data Link. Scheduler manages class, instructor, and room schedules. Training Department Accountant prepares training budgets, tracks costs, manages inventories, and analyzes expenses. Hardware: IBM PC and compatibles with at least 256K.

TR (Training Records). New York: Random House. $895–$995; demonstration disks, $15.

TR can store and analyze budget data, keep trace of training courses, register trainees, and prepare reports. TR Plus includes user-defined fields and a built-in capability to upload or download data from mainframe computers as well as a job skills data base.

Hardware: IBM PC-XT, AT, Compaq, and other IBM compatibles; DOS 2.0, 256K.

Training Program Administrator. Tampa, Fla.: H. R. Softech, Inc. $995.

Training Program Administrator is a data-base management program that maintains, updates, and reports on up to 10,000 individual attendees in the areas of demographic, job, career, program, and program schedule information. It manages scheduling and registering participants with a five-year calendar. An accounting feature tabulates program and department expenses and structures program and department budgets. The program can keep track of career plans and has built-in correspondence and labeling features. It defines and builds program evaluation audits. Over twenty built-in reports provide information on attendees, programs, and costs.

Hardware: IBM PC or compatible with hard disk, graphics card, and 256K.

Directories of Computer Software

Note that there are on-line data bases of computer software. See the descriptions of Business Software Database, Menu, and Microcomputer Index in Chapter 16.

Addison-Wesley Book of IBM Software, 1985. Reading, Mass.: Addison-Wesley, 1985. $19.95.

This book includes lengthy, thorough reviews of microcomputer software in the following categories: games and entertainment, education, business and utilities. Software is scored by grades, and the reviews are evaluative. General essays are also included on what to look for in data-base systems, word processors, and other types of software.

ASTD Buyer's Guide and Consultant Directory. Alexandria, Va.: American Society for Training and Development. Annual. $35.

This directory lists available courseware on a wide variety of training topics.

Consumer Guide. *1988 Computer Buying Guide.* New York: Signet, 1987. $6.95.

This annual publication reviews personal computers, peripherals, modems, monitors, and printers and describes recommended software in the following categories: communications, data-base management, desktop publishing, education, entertainment, financial management, graphics, and word processing.

Data Training. Boston: Weingarten Publications. Monthly. $30.
   This magazine contains articles on computer-based training and available software and lists CBT producers and products.

Glossbrenner, Alfred. *How to Buy Software: The Master Guide to Picking the Right Program*. New York: St. Martin's Press, 1984. $14.95 paper.
   This book provides detailed guidance on selecting educational software. It also lists directories and newsletters that include reviews of computer software.

Microcomputer Market Place. New York: Bowker. Annual. $95.
   This annual directory provides information on software producers, software distributors, peripherals, supplies, and microcomputer systems mnaufacturers. Also listed are periodicals, associations, on-line data bases, a calendar of meetings and exhibits, and an executive directory.

Simtek's International Business Games Directory. (2nd ed.) Carlisle, Mass.: Simtek, 1983. $6.45.
   This catalog describes thirty-five computerized business games and management simulations for training different managerial levels (supervisory through executive), business functions (sales through production), and industries (banking through manufacturing).

Software Catalog. New York: Elsevier Science Publishing Company. Annual. 2 vols. Volume 1: Microcomputers, $84; Volume 2: Minicomputers, $125.
   The most comprehensive software directory available, it has brief descriptions of about 30,000 programs. This information is also available on-line as Menu — The International Software Database (see Chapter 16).

Training Marketplace Directory. Minneapolis: Lakewood Publications. Annual. (Mailed with the August issue of *Training* magazine). $15.
   This directory lists courseware on a wide variety of training topics.

Whole Earth Software Catalog for 1986. New York: Quantum Press/Doubleday, 1985. $17.50.
   This catalog describes recommended software for personal computers in the following categories: games, word processing, data analysis, accounting, graphics, telecommunications, programming, and education.

Zemke, Ron. *Computer Needs Assessment*. Reading, Mass.: Addison-Wesley, 1984. $24.95.
   To assist others in gaining skills in computer literacy, this book contains a directory of computer literacy materials, including disk tutorials, classes and seminars, books, videotapes, and audiocassettes.

Directory of Publishers and Producers

ACT, Educational Services Division
P. O. Box 168
Iowa City, IA 52243
(319) 337-1052

Addison-Wesley
One Jacob Way
Reading, MA 01867
(617) 944-3700

Alamo Learning Systems
1850 Mt. Diablo Blvd., Suite 500
Walnut Creek, CA 94596
(415) 930-8520

American Society for Training and
  Development
1630 Duke St., Box 1443
Alexandria, VA 22313
(703) 683-8100

Bowker Company
205 E. 42nd St
New York, NY 10017
(212) 916-1600

Conceptual Systems, Inc.
1100 Wayne Ave., 12th Floor
Silver Spring, MD 20910
(301) 589-1800

Concourse Corporation
11441 Valley View Rd.
Minneapolis, MN 55344
(612) 829-5436

DSI Micro, Inc.
1050 Cindy Lane
Carpinteria, CA 93013
(805) 684-0311

Elsevier Science Publishing
  Company
52 Vanderbilt Ave.
New York, NY 10017
(212) 370-5520

H. R. Softech, Inc.
2131 N. Dale Mavry Hwy.
Tampa, FL 33607
(813) 963-6759

Human Edge Software Corporation
1875 S. Grant St., Suite 480
San Mateo, CA 94402
(800) 624-5227, (415) 493-1593

Impell Corporation
350 Lennon Lane
Walnut Creek, CA 94598
(415) 943-4500

Kepner-Tregoe
17 Research Rd.
Skillman, NJ 08558
(800) 223-0482, (609) 921-2806

Lakewood Publications
50 S. 9th St.
Minneapolis, MN 55402
(800) 328-4329, (612) 333-0471

Learncom
215 First St.
Cambridge, MA 02142
(617) 576-3100

Lomas & Nettleton Information
  Systems, Inc.
Education Department
1600 Viceroy Dr.
Dallas, TX 75235
(214) 879-1600

Masterco
P. O. Box 7382
Ann Arbor, MI 48107
(313) 428-8300

Negotiation Institute
230 Park Ave., Suite 460
New York, NY 10169
(212) 986-5555 collect

Quantum Press/Doubleday &
  Company
245 Park Ave.
New York, NY 10017
(212) 984-9561

Random House
Professional Business Publications
201 E. 50th St., 16th Floor
New York, NY 10022
(212) 572-2727

St. Martin's Press
175 Fifth Ave.
New York, NY 10010
(800) 221-7945

Shamrock Press
Division of Karl Albrecht &
  Associates
1277 Garnet Ave.
P. O. Box 90699
San Diego, CA 92109
(619) 272-3880

Signet Books
New American Library
1633 Broadway
New York, NY 10019
(212) 397-8000

Silton-Bookman Systems
20410 Town Center Lane, Suite 280
Cupertino, CA 95014
(408) 446-1170

Simtek
P. O. Box 105
Carlisle, MA 01741
(617) 369-5538

Thoughtware, Inc.
1700 NW 65th Ave., Suite 9
Plantation, FL 33313
(800) 848-9273

Weingarten Publications
38 Chauncy St.
Boston, MA 02111
(617) 542-0146

PART III

AN ENCYCLOPEDIA OF HRD & OD KEY CONCEPTS & CONTRIBUTORS

Leslie Stephen

If you already have some experience in the HRD field, you know that people use different terms to mean more or less the same thing. *Methods, techniques,* and *instructional strategies* are good examples. People also use the same word to mean different things. One example is *gestalt. Team building* is another. So is *feedback*. Then there are the nuances of our professional language — do you say *instructional strategies* or *learning strategies?*

But if you are a newcomer, how do you learn the lingo?

This encyclopedia is a crash course. Use it as a dictionary anytime you need basic working definitions for many of the terms you will hear every day. You can also use it as a quick introduction to the field. It gives you an overview of training and development by defining some of the core concepts and common terms used in the profession and provides brief portraits of some of the people who have had an important influence on HRD and OD theory and practice.

The main goal of this part of the book is to give readers, particularly the newcomer to the field, workable definitions of the core concepts and terms from HRD and OD theory and practice. In the process, we have tried to communicate a sense of how the language of HRD and OD came to be the way it is—and, possibly, where it might be going. We have also tried to cover some of the ideas from psychology that have influenced how we think and talk about our professional world.

The individuals who make up the "who's who" part of this brief encyclopedia were selected by means of a survey of ASTD leaders that we conducted in the spring of 1984. A sampling of our respondents' reasons for selecting these individuals to their top-ten list of significant contributors to the profession appears in italics at the beginning of each entry.

The entries on the following pages are necessarily brief. Although space was a major constraint, we have made every effort to illuminate the gist of each term listed. You will find cross-references at the ends of many entries that will direct you to related terms. In some cases, you will find a short entry cross-referenced to a larger, overarching concept, where you will find a fuller explanation. Some complex terms may require you to read three or four entries that will combine into a sort of mosaic that illustrates the term.

For each entry, we offer at least one definition that captures the essence of our understanding of the term. If there are diverse points of view on potentially ambiguous or controversial terms, we include a representative sample. Sometimes we have constructed entries with definitions from two or three equal but opposing authorities; we hope that you will be tantalized into exploring the different views they espouse and that our suggestions for further reading will help you develop more complete working definitions for these terms on your own.

When we began writing this book, there was a small mother lode of short glossaries of HRD and OD terms previously published by acknowledged authorities—Peter Vaill (1973), Leonard and Zeace Nadler (1977), and Robert Peterson (1979). We quote them time and again when they offer a workable, capture-the-essence definition, and credit for their thoughts and words—as well as for those of other authorities—is given with parenthetical citations to the reference list at the end of the book. Suggestions for reading in addition to the basic authorities cited are listed at the end of selected entries.

This encyclopedia is a tool for mastering your role in HRD. Remember, however, that what you see here is a freeze-frame, not the whole movie . . . a map, not the territory. It is a traveler's guide only. If you are new to the field, you will need more travel and practice to learn to speak like a native.

Action maze. A programmed case study that allows the learner to choose from alternative actions at various decision points.

In the words of Dugan Laird, "Participants usually receive a printed description of the case with enough detail to take them to the first decision point. The description gives them options from which to select. After the group discusses these alternatives, they request the leader to supply them with the next 'frame' [which] will explain the consequences of their decision" (1985, p. 149). The case continues, with appropriate choices given and the development of the situation presented at each decision point. A common variation is to allow groups to split and re-form according to the individuals' choices of action at each decision point. Another is to allow groups to make up their own lists of possible actions at each decision point.

See also CASE STUDY; INCIDENT PROCESS; METHODS.

Action research. A type of OD intervention, originated by Kurt Lewin. Peter Vaill characterizes it as "a cyclical process of research-change-research-change, etc." (1973, p. 236). In essence, research produces ideas for change. The changes are then introduced, and more research determines the effects of the change. This in turn produces new ideas for change and so on.

See also LEWIN, KURT; ORGANIZATION DEVELOPMENT.

Action science. An OD intervention theory and method developed by Chris Argyris. It is concerned with improving the ways in which people and organizations diagnose problems, decide how to respond, and implement solutions.

See also ARGYRIS, CHRIS; ORGANIZATION DEVELOPMENT.

Adult education. There is a great deal of confusion about exactly what the term *adult education* encompasses. For example, the terms *adult education* and *continuing education* are often used synonymously. Some see continuing education as being mainly concerned with employee training and career development; adult education, in their view, involves basic kinds of learning and is exemplified by literacy, high school equivalency, and citizenship education programs. Many others consider the differences between the terms to be purely philosophical (Dejnozka and Kapel, 1982, p. 13).

See also ADULT LEARNING THEORY; ANDRAGOGY; CONTINUING EDUCATION; EXPERIENTIAL LEARNING; HUMAN RESOURCE DEVELOPMENT.

Further Reading

Cross, K. P. *Adults as Learners: Increasing Participation and Facilitating Learning.* San Francisco: Jossey-Bass, 1981.

Harrington, F. H. *The Future of Adult Education.* San Francisco: Jossey-Bass, 1977.

Knowles, M. S. *The Modern Practice of Adult Education: From Pedagogy to Andragogy.* (2nd ed.) New York: Cambridge Book Company, 1980.

Knowles, M. S. *The Adult Learner: A Neglected Species.* (3rd ed.) Houston: Gulf Publishing, 1984.

Knox, A. B. *Adult Development and Learning: A Handbook on Individual Growth and Competence in the Adult Years.* San Francisco: Jossey-Bass, 1977.

Long, H. B. *Adult and Continuing Education: Responding to Change.* New York: Columbia University, Teachers College Press, 1983.

Niebuhr, H. *Revitalizing American Learning: A New Approach That Just Might Work.* Belmont, Calif.: Wadsworth, 1984.

Adult learning theory. Among the major theories of learning, *behaviorism* is fairly well defined, and most trainers in this country associate the term and the theory with its leading contemporary proponent, B. F. Skinner. Not so for so-called adult learning theory.

There have been many adult learning theorists, researchers, and practitioners, each contributing an element to its development along the way (see, for example, Kolb, 1984; Tough, 1979, 1982; Kidd, 1973; Houle, 1961). In business and industry today, perhaps the best-known conceptualizer and practitioner is Malcolm Knowles, who has postulated his adult learning principles and practices under the banner of andragogy.

As commonly understood in the world of HRD, adherence to adult learning theory would call for the design of learning activities to be based on the learners' needs and interests so as to create opportunities for the learners to analyze their experience and its application to their work and life situations. The role of the trainer is to assist in a process

of inquiry, analysis, and decision making with learners rather than to transmit knowledge.

In the context of adult learning practices, the learner exercises greater autonomy in matching his or her preferred modes of learning to the specified learning objectives and also has more say about what the outcomes of the learning process are intended to be. The emphasis on methods that encourage insight and discovery makes it a familiar approach, close to the "natural" way many people have acquired new knowledge or developed new skills since reaching maturity.

See also ADULT EDUCATION; ANDRAGOGY; EXPERIENTIAL LEARNING; KNOWLES, MALCOLM; SOCIAL LEARNING THEORY.

Affective learning. Learning in the affective domain typically involves changes in interests, values, or attitudes, including the control and investment of feelings.

See also COGNITIVE LEARNING; PSYCHOMOTOR LEARNING.

Andragogy. Based on the Greek stem *andr-,* meaning "man, not boy," and the word *agogus,* meaning "leading," the term *andragogy* was introduced into the American adult learning literature by Malcolm Knowles in 1968.

Knowles says he originally defined andragogy as "the art and science of helping adults learn, in contrast to pedagogy as the art and science of teaching children" (1980b, p. 43). Later he came to see andragogy as "simply another model of assumptions about learners to be used alongside the pedagogical model . . . most useful when seen not as dichotomous but rather as two ends of a spectrum" (p. 43).

The principles and practices that fall under the umbrella of andragogy are based on several crucial assumptions about how adult learners differ from children. Margolis and Bell (1984) give us a useful summary of those assumptions, distilled from Knowles's major works (1978, 1980b):

1. Adults are motivated to learn as they develop needs and interests that learning will satisfy. Therefore, learners' needs and interests are the appropriate starting points for organizing adult learning activities. . . .
2. Adult orientation to learning is life- or work-centered. Therefore, the appropriate frameworks for organizing adult learning are life- or work-related situations, not academic or theoretical subjects.
3. Experience is the richest resource for adult learning. Therefore, the core methodology for adult learning programs involves active participation in a planned series of experiences, the analysis of those experiences, and their application to work and life situations.
4. Adults have a deep need to be self-directing. Therefore, the role of the trainer is to engage in a process of inquiry, analysis, and decision making with learners. . . .
5. Individual differences among adult learners increase with age and experience. Therefore, adult learning programs must make optimum provision for differences in style, time, place, and pace of learning. (p. 17)

If not strictly a learning theory, andragogy is at least a successful attempt "to bring the isolated concepts, insights, and research findings regarding adult learning into an integrated framework" (Knowles, 1978, p. 48). There is growing evidence that use of the andragogical framework is making a difference in the way adult learning programs are organized and operated as well as in the way HRD professionals see their role in helping adults learn (Knowles and Associates, 1984).

See also ADULT EDUCATION; ADULT LEARNING THEORY; KNOWLES, MALCOLM.

Argyris, Chris. *"Research on organizational life." "OD theory." "Thought-provoking writer."*

Chris Argyris has been a leading researcher and theorist on behavioral science applications to organizational life for more than thirty years. His *Personality and Organization* (1957) was "one of the earliest attempts to confront the modern organization with the reality of human needs" (Murrell and Vaill, 1975, p. 4). His later published work includes *Interpersonal Competence and Organizational Effectiveness* (1962), *Organization and Innovation* (1965), *Intervention Theory and Method* (1970), *Management and Organization Development* (1971), *Theory in Practice* (Argyris and Schön, 1974), *Reasoning, Learning, and Action* (1982), and *Action Science* (Argyris, Putnam, and Smith, 1985) as well as scores of articles in journals about management, human resource development, and organization development.

Argyris has been a significant force in shaping the careers of many of today's most successful OD practitioners (Hillman and Varney, 1985). He is James Bryant Conant Professor of Education and Organizational Behavior at Harvard University.

Behaviorism. A major school of psychology—most commonly associated in this country with B. F. Skinner—that studies only observable, and preferably measurable, behavior.

Launched in the United States at the beginning of the century, the process of redefining psychology from the study of the mind to the study of human behavior took some fifty years of research and, in Ron Zemke's words, "the combined genius and enthusiasm" of Edward L. Thorndike, Ivan Pavlov, John B. Watson, Edwin Guthrie, and Clark Hull, not to mention Skinner himself (1983, p. 40).

Thorndike stated that learning is a process of trial and error. If confronted with the need to respond in a certain manner to a given stimulus, the learner tries many responses. If one works, it is used again. And if the response is pleasant to the learner, there is an increase in the strength of the response. Pavlov soon afterward did experiments that led to the concept of conditioned reflexes. His work was the foundation of the branch of behaviorism known as *classical conditioning.*

Most observers consider Watson to have launched the form of behaviorism that we are familiar with today. Watson's work emphasized kinesthetic stimuli as "integrators" in animal learning. He believed

that, in humans, thought is implicit speech—that is, if one had sensitive-enough instruments, it would be possible to see a human subject's tongue move while he or she thought. Building on the work of all the earlier theorists, Guthrie's key contribution was the so-called stimulus response continuity principle. Skinner more fully developed behaviorist theory into a branch known as *operant conditioning.* The Skinnerian school is credited with giving us programmed instruction, behavioral objectives in instructional design, and behavior-modification techniques for the classroom and the job site (see, for example, Gilbert, 1978).

Central to behaviorism as a theory of learning and human behavior is that all behavior is the result of its consequences—some immediate, some delayed. Some consequences are "reinforcers," which encourage the reoccurrence of a behavior. Some are "punishers," which tend to decrease the behavior they follow. Reinforcers can be positive (like praise) or negative (like eliminating a distasteful task from someone's job). Punishers work both ways, too—positive (like harsh words) or negative (like adding an unpleasant task to someone's job description).

Reinforcers, particularly positive ones, are much more powerful in shaping the desired behavior than punishers. For learners to benefit fully from the power of reinforcement theory, trainers must understand and learn how to reward successive approximations, those small steps toward the ultimate learning objective.

See also BEHAVIOR MODIFICA-TION; COGNITIVE LEARNING; OPERANT CONDITIONING; REINFORCEMENT; SKINNER, B. F.

Behavior modeling. A teaching-learning method based on several widely accepted principles of adult learning: modeling or imitation, behavioral rehearsal or practice, and reinforcement or reward. "In brief," says one of the leading proponents of behavior modeling in this country, James C. Robinson, "learning via behavior modeling requires imitation of effective behaviors, intensive guided practice in the performance of new behaviors, and reinforcement or recognition for the learner's demonstration and application of the new behaviors" (1982, p. 8).

Drawn from the concepts of social learning theory (see, for example, Bandura, 1971), the use of modeling techniques had a long history in technical training before Arnold Goldstein and Melvin Sorcher (1974) used them in the early seventies to train new employees and their supervisors at General Electric in complex inter-personal communication tasks. Despite the complexity and cost of creating and implementing effective behavior modeling programs, behavior modeling techniques have found their way into thousands of organizations to help people learn basic supervisory techniques, managerial competencies, selling skills, and a variety of technical skills (Parry and Reich, 1984).

Although behavior modeling has attracted a pack of vocal critics, there is growing documentation of its effectiveness in various learning situations (see, for example, Robinson, 1982), and most HRD practitioners would agree that, at the very least, behavior modeling "dramatically altered the face of training in the late seventies" by irrevocably changing the uses and looks of video training materials ("Training Today: Training Predicts—1984 and Beyond," 1984, p. 12). There is also movement toward adapting the underlying theory and some of the methods of behavior modeling to the cognitive domain (Harmon and Evans, 1984).

See also COGNITIVE MODELING; DEMONSTRATION; MODELING DISPLAY; SKILL PRACTICE; SOCIAL LEARNING THEORY.

Behavior modification. In the behaviorist school, the process by which a person's particular behavior or behavior pattern is changed to some specified new behavior or behavior pattern. In 1984 behavior modification and B. F. Skinner made *Training* magazine's list of endangered species (Gordon, Lee, and Zemke, 1984, p. 38).

See also BEHAVIORAL LEARNING; BEHAVIORISM; OPERANT CONDITIONING; SKINNER, B. F.

Bell, Chip R. *"Provides insight." "Shares new ideas, particularly about the future."*

Chip Bell began his career as an officer with the Department of Instruction, U.S. Army Infantry School, during the Viet Nam era.

After a tour as a combat officer, he trained officers in instructor skills at Fort Benning, Georgia. He was vice-president and director of management development for NCNB Corporation, a large bank holding company, before starting his private consulting practice in the late seventies.

From his home base in Charlotte, North Carolina, he now criss-crosses the country many times a month, conducting workshops and seminars at professional conferences and consulting to major corporations on trainer development, team building, leadership, and service management. His books to date, besides this one, include *Instructing for Results* (Margolis and Bell, 1986), *Clients and Consultants* (Bell and Nadler, 1985), *Managing the Learning Process* (Margolis and Bell, 1984), *Influencing* (1982), and *A Presenter's Guide to Conferences* (Bell and Margolis, 1980). His articles have been published in professional journals ranging from *Management Review* to the *Journal of European Training*. He is an oft-quoted opinion maker on current practice and future trends in HRD.

Bennis, Warren. *"One of the nation's foremost theory-builders." "Synthesizer." "Creative risk-taker." "Leader in the field in thought and practice." "Knows how to put it all together."*

Warren Bennis has taught and consulted around the world. He has been an adviser to four U.S. presidents. His other clients are almost in the same league—Polaroid, General Electric, Ford Motor Com-

pany, TRW, and the United Nations. He has won the McKinsey award for the best publication on management and the American Psychological Association's Perry L. Roher Consulting Practice Award for helping organizations respond more effectively to the challenges of society. He was elected to the Board of Governors of the American Society for Training and Development in 1984.

Books? More than twenty. Articles? Say, five hundred. *Organization Development* (1969), *The Planning of Change* (1961), and *Changing Organizations* (1966) established him as a major force in OD theory and practice. He was also the editor of the classic Addison-Wesley Series in Organization Development between 1969 and 1973. His latest book is *Leaders* (Bennis and Nanus, 1985), based on his recent studies of gifted entrepreneurs and executives.

He appears fairly frequently at conferences sponsored by University Associates and the American Society for Training and Development, among others. You can also meet him on the videotape "Warren Bennis in Dialogue with CEOs" (Bennis, n.d.). He is Joseph DeBell Professor of Management and Organization at the University of Southern California.

Blake, Robert R., and Jane S. Mouton. *"Provided a systematic view of the human response to the environment and . . . the organizational setting." "Everyone who uses a grid to attempt to explain and bet-*

ter understand human behavior owes these two people for helping us conceptualize interactions in a simple grid."

In 1952 University of Texas psychology professors Robert Blake and Jane Mouton launched what is probably the longest, most successful collaboration in our field, consulting and writing on behavioral science applications to business and industry.

Blake and Mouton's *Managerial Grid* (1964) was one of the best-selling books of its era. Their grid theory and technique has been called one of the most influential concepts in the history of HRD (American Society for Training and Development, 1985, p. 5). These early originators in organizational development went on to produce *Corporate Darwinism* (1966), *Corporate Excellence Through Grid Organization Development* (1968), *Building a Dynamic Corporation Through Grid Organization Development* (1969), *The Grid for Supervisory Effectiveness* (1975), *The New Managerial Grid* (1978), and countless articles and lesser-known books. Their most recent books include *Consultation* (1983), *Synergogy* (Mouton and Blake, 1984), *Solving Costly Organizational Conflicts* (1984), *The Managerial Grid III* (1985), *Executive Achievement* (1986), and *Spectacular Teamwork* (Blake, Mouton, and Allen, 1987). Their thoughts on the strengths, weaknesses, and prospects for the future of OD are also available on tape (1979).

Blake and Mouton are co-founders and president and vice-president, respectively, of Scientific Methods, Inc., Austin, Texas.

Block busting.   A term from creativity training used to describe various ways of first identifying and then sidestepping perceptual, emotional, intellectual, expressional, or environmental blocks to understanding a problem or conceiving possible solutions (Adams, 1979).

See also CREATIVITY TRAINING.

Brain lateralization.   The term refers to the differentiation of brain functions in the right and left cerebral hemispheres; the phenomenon is also referred to as brain specialization and right brain/left brain "theory."

General interest in brain lateralization began to build in the early sixties, when Nobel laureate Roger Sperry and Michael Gazzaniga began their pioneering experiments with epileptic patients who had undergone brain-splitting operations at the California Institute of Technology (Gazzaniga, 1973). Over the last two decades, the facts of brain lateralization have been established by a growing body of basic research, accompanied by serious (as well as frivolous) investigations into the relationship of the research findings to human consciousness and behavior (Ornstein 1973, 1975).

Charles Hamden-Turner (1982) summarized the evidence from studies of normal, right-handed individuals: the information-processing mode of the left hemisphere is "verbal, analytic, reductive-into-parts, sequential, rational, time-oriented, and discontinuous"; the right hemisphere, "nonverbal, synthetic, visuospatial, intuitive, timeless, and diffuse" (p. 88).

Ned Herrmann, usually acknowledged as one of the first synthesizers and proponents of the use of brain lateralization concepts in the HRD field, has characterized the cerebral left hemisphere as "the logical, analytic, mathematical processor, in contrast to the cerebral right — the conceptual, holistic, synthesizing processor" (Gorowitz, 1982b, p. 75).

The findings of brain lateralization research are often oversimplified to suggest that each hemisphere of the brain is the exclusive domain for different activities — "little musicians dancing in the right, mathematicians wrangling in the left" (Hamden-Turner, 1982, p. 88). The notion of brain dominance or preference is closer to the mark, as Herrmann explains: "We approach our daily activities with a brain orientation typified by a dominant hemisphere. While a task may require both left brain and right brain capability, our dominant hemisphere tends to 'take over' the whole task, excluding the other hemisphere's contribution" (1977, p. 31).

A whole army of HRD practitioners has rallied round a free-the-right-brain flag, inspired by Herrmann as well as by research psychologist Robert Ornstein and others who insist that knowledge is not exclusively rational. Their battle cry is the quip most often attributed to Ornstein: In our culture, a brilliant mind usually means a great mouth.

The encouragement of information processing by both sides of the brain is a paramount concern in creativity training. And right brain/left brain concepts have now found their way into mainstream HRD design and delivery (Herrmann, 1978).

Presumably referring to the more suspect models of brain lateralization, some of the editors of *Training* magazine put right brain/left brain theory on their list of "endangered species" of the mid-eighties (Gordon, Lee, and Zemke, 1984, p. 38). We believe that the alert practitioner will discover how to cut through the hype and apply to training design and delivery what neuroscience continues to learn about brain function.

See also CREATIVITY TRAINING.

Further Reading

Albrecht, K. *Brain Power.* Englewood Cliffs, N.J.: Prentice-Hall, 1980.

Brain/Mind Bulletin. Los Angeles: Interface Press.

Calvin, W. H., and Ojemann, G. A. *Inside the Brain: Mapping the Cortex, Exploring the Neuron.* New York: Mentor Books, 1980.

Hiebert, M. B. "Training Design by Design: Why We Come Back to Recursiveness." *Training and Development Journal*, 1983, *37* (8), 31–35.

International Brain Dominance Review. Lake Lure, N.C.: Brain Dominance Institute. (Distributed by the Whole Brain Corporation, Cambridge, Mass.)

Lynch, D. *Your High-Performance Business Brain: An Operator's Manual.* Englewood Cliffs, N.J.: Prentice-Hall, 1984.

Masters, R., and Houston, J. *Mind Games: The Guide to Inner Space.* New York: Dell, 1972.

Pribram, K. H. *Languages of the Brain.* Englewood Cliffs, N.J.: Prentice-Hall, 1971.

Rose, S. *The Conscious Brain.* (2nd ed.) New York: Vintage Books, 1976.

Russell, P. *The Brain Book.* New York: Hawthorne, 1979.

Sagan, C. *The Dragons of Eden: Speculations on the Evolution of Human Intelligence.* New York: Random House, 1977.

Springer, J. "Whole-Brain Applied Research in Training and Development." *Training and Development Journal*, 1983, *37* (6), 54–55.

Wittrock, M. C. *The Human Brain.* Englewood Cliffs, N.J.: Prentice-Hall, 1977.

Wittrock, M. C. *The Brain and Psychology.* New York: Academic Press, 1980.

Brainstorming. A process for encouraging uninhibited generation of ideas (Nadler and Nadler, 1977, p. 251). The term and the original technique were invented by Alex Osborn, whose book *Applied Imagination* (1963) launched the creativity field in the early fifties when it was first published.

The term usually refers to a *group* process, and in most instances the process depends on the spoken word to trigger ideas as well as on the use of "deferred evaluation" (suspended judgment) for successful results. *Psychology Today* editor Berkeley Rice (1984) has reported a variant called "brainwriting" at the Center for Creative Leadership, Greensboro, North Carolina. A similar process is the nominal group technique.

See also CREATIVITY TRAINING; NOMINAL GROUP TECHNIQUE.

Broadwell, Martin. *"Classroom techniques." "Sound material on instructing."*

The epitome of up-front training skill, Martin Broadwell specializes in supervisory and technical training, which he currently offers through his Center for Management Services, Inc., based in Decatur, Georgia.

A frequent contributor to *Training,* ASTD's *Training and Development Journal, Training News,* and other professional periodicals, Broadwell was a regular columnist for *Training World* in the late seventies when he wrote a series of articles, called "Establishing a Training Philosophy," that was reprinted by the thousands. He has written more than a dozen books on supervisory and technical training—his best known are probably *The New Supervisor* (1984a), *The Supervisor as an Instructor* (1984c), and *Moving Up to Supervision* (1986a). Broadwell appears regularly on the circuit sponsored by *Training* magazine and in train-the-trainer programs put on by the nation's major universities.

Burke, W. Warner. *"Leadership and updating on OD."*

Listed as one of the top ten OD experts in the country by Hillman and Varney (1985), Warner Burke is a former executive director of the Organization Development Network and director of the Center for System Development for the NTL Institute for Applied Behavioral Science (formerly National Training Laboratories). He has been the editor of

Organizational Dynamics and written more than forty articles and book chapters on organization development, training, social and organizational psychology, and conference planning.

His earliest published work includes *Behavioral Science and the Manager's Role* (Eddy, Burke, Dupre, and South, 1969) and *Contemporary Organization Development* (1972). More recently he has given us *Trends and Issues in OD* (Burke and Goodstein, 1980) and *Organization Development: Principles and Practices* (1982).

You can meet Burke on the HRD and OD conference circuit or listen to his presentations taped at ASTD conferences—consult the current catalogue for up-to-date selections.

Buzz group. As defined by Leonard and Zeace Nadler (1977): "Small groups of six or fewer participants meeting as part of a much larger group. Usually all groups are meeting in the same room (hence the buzzing sound that gives it its name) for a limited period of time. Helpful to react to a speaker, get questions, or stimulate thinking" (p. 252).
See also METHODS.

CAI. See COMPUTER-ASSISTED INSTRUCTION.

CBT. Computer-based training.
See COMPUTER-ASSISTED INSTRUCTION.

Case method. "A teaching technique which presents the learner with ac-counts of real events and challenges him to interpret them" (Vaill, 1973, p. 236).
See also CASE STUDY; METHODS.

Case study. "A written account of an event or situation to which participants are to react. Emphasis is on decision making" (Nadler and Nadler, 1977, p. 252).
See also ACTION MAZE; CASE METHOD; INCIDENT PROCESS; METHODS.

Change agent. As commonly used in OD parlance, the individual or group responsible for initiating or implementing change (Connor and Patterson, 1982). In Nadler's (1979) definition of HRD roles, a change agent is one who "assists management in diagnosing and planning for change," either individual or organizational (p. 245).

The term is one of the many legacies of social psychologist Kurt Lewin. Once wildly popular, the term and the concept seem to have fallen from grace in recent years. In a recent survey of ASTD's OD Division and OD Network members, change theory ranked dead last on their list of theories and models "important for students of OD to be knowledgeable about" (Turpin and Johnson, 1982, p. 14).

The term *catalyst* was once more or less synonymous. Today *consultant* is a popular choice for describing what used to be meant by change agent.
See also CONSULTING PROCESS; LEWIN, KURT; ORGANIZATION DEVELOPMENT.

Further Reading
Golembiewski, R. T. *Approaches to Planned Change.* (2 vols.) New York: Marcel Dekker, 1979.

Cognitive learning. In the Bloom (1956a, 1956b, 1964) taxonomy, learning in the cognitive domain produces changes in "mental behaviors"—knowledge, comprehension, application, analysis, synthesis, and evaluation.

See also AFFECTIVE LEARNING; COGNITIVE SCIENCE; PSYCHOMOTOR LEARNING.

Cognitive modeling. Refers to modeling techniques used to teach conceptual skills, judgment, language, and thought processes.

Drawn from the same social learning theory that is one of the cornerstones of the behavior modeling method, cognitive modeling requires making covert mental processes somehow observable. To demonstrate the covert activity successfully, the instructional designer usually chooses some graphic medium to portray it—a job aid, a worksheet, a checklist, or a flowchart. "As the procedure to be modeled becomes more complex," explain Harmon and Evans (1984), "the basic procedure is supplemented by additional worksheets, [etc.]. In the near future, they will be supplemented by computer software" (p. 68).

See also BEHAVIOR MODELING; SOCIAL LEARNING THEORY.

Cognitive science. "A new discipline, created out of the intersecting interests of philosophers, neuro-scientists, sociologists, anthropologists, linguists, psychologists, and researchers in artificial intelligence" (Norman, 1982, p. 4). While it is difficult to generalize, some of the concerns of cognitive science are to discover the mechanisms of the mind and the way in which mental processes "combine to yield human behavior, beliefs, and understanding" (p. 3).

The so-called cognitive revolution has been coming to a head for about twenty years, and recent advances in brain research and cognitive psychology have already added much to our understanding of adult learning processes (Hunt, 1983) and produced important changes in our training practices. Nevertheless, it may be too soon to say, "So long, Skinner—hello, Cog Sci" (Zemke, 1983).

See also AFFECTIVE LEARNING; BEHAVIORISM; COGNITIVE LEARNING; PSYCHOMOTOR LEARNING.

Colloquy. "A discussion, usually in front of an audience, between two teams representing different points of view. Resembles a panel in that all members take an active part" (Nadler and Nadler, 1977, p. 252).

See also METHODS; PANEL.

Competency model. *Competencies* are, in essence, the knowledge, skill, and attitude clusters that enable one to perform a certain role, job, or task (American Society for Training and Development, 1983). "We define jobs and roles in terms of tasks and responsibilities," Pat McLagan explains, "but we describe—and develop—people in terms of competencies" (McLagan, 1982, p. 20).

As commonly understood in HRD, a *competency model* portrays a repertoire of skills and requisite abilities and personal qualities as they relate to the specific demands of a certain job. Knowles (1980) provides an overview of several ways in which competency models can be constructed—for example, through research, expert judgment, task analysis, and group participation. *Competency assessment* refers to the process through which the competencies of an individual are matched to the model for a certain job or whereby "discrepancies or gaps" are used to identify learning needs (Knowles and Associates, 1984, p. 117).

See also NEEDS ANALYSIS.

Computer-assisted instruction (CAI). The definitions are many (Dean and Whitlock, 1983; Kearsley, 1983; Reynolds, 1984; Spector, 1984). We like Ron Zemke's (1984b) description best: "You sit down at a computer terminal and work with a program that's supposed to teach you something" (p. 22).

People in HRD use many other names to refer to more or less the same thing: computer-based training (CBT), computer-based learning (CBL), computer-assisted learning (CAL), computer-based education (CBE), and so forth. Most of these terms are now used interchangeably in our everyday vocabulary, but some researchers and practitioners are still careful to draw clear distinc-

tions. Kearsley (1983), for example, describes the different philosophical stances represented in the terms computer-assisted *instruction* and computer-assisted *learning* and the instructional strategies and systems they imply.

The distinction between computer-*assisted* instruction and computer-*managed* instruction (CMI) is also useful: "In CAI, students interact directly with instruction presented by computer-controlled or computer-monitored equipment. . . . The role of the computer in CMI is to aid the instructor in managing the instructional program" (Spector, 1984, p.10.49).

See also METHODS; SIMULATION.

Consultants. There are internal and external consultants. The differences should be clear from Peter Block's (1981) list of their favorite words. For internal consultants: *measurement, long run, quick, practical, cost.* For external consultants: "interesting issue," "fundamental and underlying," *confront, dilemma, implications,* "reassess at some point in the process" (p. 107).

Hundreds of thousands of words have been written on HRD and OD as a consulting process and the role(s) of the consultant therein. Chapter 10 suggests some of the best books on these subjects.

See also CHANGE AGENT; ORGANIZATION DEVELOPMENT.

Continuing education. As defined by Dejnozka and Kapel, "educational and training programs for adult learners" (1982, p. 125).

Coming into its own in the late sixties, they explain, continuing education grew out of the adult education movement and now takes many forms—from formal degree programs to various nontraditional experiences. College credit or continuing education units (CEUs) may be awarded for participation.

The adoption by many trade and professional associations of relicensure or recertification requirements is commonly known as *mandatory continuing education.*

See also ADULT EDUCATION.

Further Reading

Houle, C. *Continuing Learning in the Professions.* San Francisco: Jossey-Bass, 1980.

Long, H. B. *Adult and Continuing Education: Responding to Change.* New York: Columbia University, Teachers College Press, 1983.

Cost-benefit analysis. From operations research, a method of evaluating the implications of alternative courses of action (Rosenberg, 1978). Cost-benefit analysis has found its way into HRD departments as a method of planning programs and justifying budgets; adaptations of cost-benefit and return-on-investment methods are increasingly used in evaluating the HRD function (Kearsley, 1982; Phillips, 1983).

See also EVALUATION; RETURN ON INVESTMENT.

Creativity training. What sensitivity training was to the sixties and personal growth to the seventies creativity training has been to the eighties.

By 1984 more than half of the five hundred largest U.S. corporations offered some kind of program in creative thinking or problem solving (Rice, 1984). The American Management Associations were running more than three hundred sessions a year to teach creativity techniques to some seven or eight thousand participants. In the business schools, second-year M.B.A. candidates were exploring "the benefits of Zen meditation, Hindu chants, the *I Ching,* and various altered states of consciousness"—all in pursuit of "creativity in business" (p. 48). The most common approach to creativity training today focuses on freeing the imaginative right brain from the domination of the logical left.

Alex Osborn usually gets the credit for launching the creativity training field with his book *Applied Imagination* (1963) in the early fifties. William J. J. Gordon of S. E. S. Associates and George Prince of Synectics, both in Cambridge, Massachusetts, were among the first to establish creativity training and consulting firms in the early sixties.

The field is now swarming with creativity consultants, many of whom are meeting the growing demand by cloaking old-standby techniques in new jargon. Dudley Lynch, editor of the internationally known newsletter *Brain & Strategy,* tells the story of the "creativity trainer" who starts his workshops by drilling participants in thirty-year-old brainstorming techniques and ends by handing out an eighteen-point checklist on how to diagnose a problem (Gorowitz, 1982a). The vast majority, however, are well grounded in brain/mind research and its practical applications. They have invented a variety of legitimate new methods and techniques for encouraging the creative process and learning new, arational approaches to problem solving, decision making, and other tasks.

See also BRAIN LATERALIZATION; BRAINSTORMING; SYNECTICS.

Further Reading

Heirs, B., and Pehrson, G. *The Mind of the Organization.* New York: Harper & Row, 1982.

Litvak, S. *Use Your Head.* Englewood Cliffs, N.J.: Prentice-Hall, 1982.

VanGundy, A. *Training Your Creative Mind.* Englewood Cliffs, N.J.: Prentice-Hall, 1982.

Culture. There are various definitions, many of which are quite technical—see, for example, just the reference notes in Deal and Kennedy (1982) and Schein (1985). A simple but elegant definition of *culture* is "the way we do things around here" (Bower, 1966). Among OD and HRD practitioners, *culture* is often used to refer to "patterns of practices and attitudes in an organization which are, or seem to be, ingrained or difficult to change" (Vaill, 1973, pp. 236–237).

Schein (1985) was one of the first to step back and take a hard look at the "culture craze" of the early eighties and produce what is likely to be the touchstone for understanding how organizational cultures begin, develop, and change in response to changing circumstances.

Data-based intervention. A specific technique in action research. Following some data collection phase, "an input into the system using the data that have been collected [or] the act of presenting the data to members of the system, thus initiating a process of system self-analysis" (Vaill, 1973, p. 238).

See also ACTION RESEARCH; ORGANIZATION DEVELOPMENT; SURVEY FEEDBACK.

Demonstration. According to the Nadlers, "a presentation before a group which shows how to perform an act or use a procedure. . . . Participants can be involved by providing an opportunity for them to practice what has been observed during the demonstration" (Nadler and Nadler, 1977, p. 253). Demonstration is one of the cornerstones of on-the-job training and of behavior modeling technology. It is not limited to use in groups.

See also BEHAVIOR MODELING; FOUR-STEP METHOD; MODELING DISPLAY; ON-THE-JOB TRAINING.

Development. See HUMAN RESOURCE DEVELOPMENT.

Drucker, Peter. *"Early management development research." "Management theory." "Challenges trainers, predicts accurately, offers a practical approach." "His books are a must for anyone in this business."*

Born in Vienna and educated there and in England, Drucker is a founding father of modern business management. He has written a score of books since his first, *The End of Economic Man,* in 1939; they have sold over three million copies in more than twenty languages. Most armchair historians would say Drucker's stock started a serious rise with *Concept of the Corporation* (1946) and his creation of the conceptual framework for management by objectives (MBO). Respondents to *Training's* most recent survey named *Management* (1974), *Adventures of a Bystander* (1979), and *Managing in Turbulent Times* (1980) as the books that had had the most influence on their work. More recently he has published *The Frontiers of Management* (1986a) and *The Practice of Management* (1986b). He has twice made *Training's* "who's who" list ("Excellence in Training," 1984; Zemke, 1980).

After more than twenty years as professor of management at the Graduate Business School of New York University, Drucker moved to Claremont, California. He is Clarke Professor of Social Science at Claremont Graduate School.

Education. See ADULT EDUCATION; HUMAN RESOURCE DEVELOPMENT.

Evaluation. A systematic process that determines the worth, value, or meaning of something. In the HRD field the purpose of evaluation is usually to improve a program or to decide whether to continue it (Phillips, 1984). According to Phillips, some of the specific reasons for conducting evaluations are as follows: to determine whether a program is accomplishing its objectives; to identify the strengths and weaknesses in the HRD process; to determine the cost-benefit ratio of an HRD

program; to decide who should participate in future programs; to reinforce major points made to the learner; and to gather data to assist in marketing future programs.

The evaluation framework posited by Donald L. Kirkpatrick (1976) is considered a classic in HRD circles. In essence, it distinguishes four levels of evaluation:

1. Reaction—participants' attitudes or feelings of satisfaction or dissatisfaction with the learning experience.

2. Learning—observable or measurable behavior change in the classroom or training situation.

3. Behavior—new or changed behavior (performance) on the job.

4. Results—measurable, positive impact of training on the organization (for example, in increased productivity, sales, profitability, or reductions in costs, accidents, grievances, absenteeism, and customer complaints).

Because so much more sophistication and work are required to collect appropriate measures and to draw valid conclusions at the behavior and results levels of Kirkpatrick's schema, it does not really encourage measurement or evaluation beyond the reaction level.

Although many would disagree, today's HRD professionals have come a long way from the time when simply passing out a reaction sheet at the end of a session was considered evaluation enough. More and more HRD practitioners are putting increasingly sophisticated evaluation designs and methods into play (see, for example, Laird, 1985; Eitington, 1984; Phillips, 1983, 1984; Brandenberg, 1982; Salinger and Deming, 1982).

See also COST-BENEFIT ANALYSIS; REACTION MEASURES; RETURN ON INVESTMENT.

Exercise. According to the Nadlers, an exercise is "a planned experience designed to allow participants to practice a new learning, to reinforce a previous learning, or to experience a problem" (1977, p. 253).

Pfeiffer and Jones (1972) coined the term *structured experience* to refer to exercises and other similar learning activities "to provide a connotation of guiding the participants in learning about human interaction" (p. 3). They defined *exercise* as "the practice, repetition, or solidification of new behavior; skill building" (1977, p. 5).

See also EXPERIENTIAL LEARNING; METHODS.

Experiential learning. In Vaill's view, "a kind of learning process in which the content of what is to be learned is experienced as directly as possible, in contrast to being read about in a book or talked about in lecture and discussion" (1973, p. 239).

The experiential learning design model popularized by Pfeiffer and Jones (1972–1981; Pfeiffer and Goodstein, 1982–) portrayed the process as a circle of five revolving steps: experiencing, publishing, processing, generalizing, and applying. In everyday use, the adjectives *experiential* and *experience-based* are applied to a wide variety of models

and methods of learning. Read David A. Kolb's *Experiential Learning* (1984) for a full appreciation of current theory and practice—it is a masterpiece.

See also METHODS.

External consultant. See CONSULTANTS.

Facilitator. The verb *to facilitate* refers to "a process by which events are 'helped to happen' " in a way that is neither "authoritarian" nor "abdicative," says Peter Vaill (1973, p. 239).

Facilitator is loosely used as a synonym for trainer, moderator, discussion leader, instructor, and so forth—inappropriately, in our view, when the speaker strips the word of its dignity. The term traces its roots to Carl Rogers and was embraced by an earlier generation of trainers who sought to return power and responsibility to learners for their own learning and to employ more participative, experiential methods in HRD programs.

See also PARTICIPATORY METHODS; ROGERS, CARL R.

Feedback. A technical term from systems theory that is now broadly used to mean any information about the result of a process.

In HRD parlance, *feedback* usually means "information on the effect of a particular action that allows the action to be adjusted" (Peterson, 1979, p. 28). In some situations—for example, interpersonal skills training—the term is used more narrowly to mean "one person's report to another on the effect of his behavior on the reporter" (Vaill, 1973, p. 239). The usual qualifiers attached to *feedback* connote differences in the substance and purpose of such reports — *descriptive, nonjudgmental, corrective,* and *affirming* are a few examples. Vaill likes to keep it simple: "*Negative feedback* is a disapproving report. *Positive feedback* is the opposite" (p. 239).

Participant feedback refers to various methods for gathering reaction data for HRD program evaluation. The term *survey feedback* refers to a type of organization development strategy.

See also EVALUATION; ORGANIZATION DEVELOPMENT; REACTION MEASURES; SURVEY FEEDBACK.

Fishbowl. "A discussion group that is divided into two parts: the inner circle, consisting of four to five people who discuss a topic, and the outer group, consisting of up to twenty people who observe" (Malasky, 1984, pp. 9.10–9.11).

See also METHODS.

Force field analysis. One of the many legacies of Kurt Lewin, a model used for problem solving and for planning and implementing HRD and OD efforts around a wide range of group and organizational issues.

Lewin saw behavior in an institutional setting as a dynamic balance of forces working in opposite directions within the "social-psychological space" of the organization. A diagram of the so-called driving forces and restraining forces at the point of balance that Lewin called "quasi-stationary equilibrium" is known as a force field.

In Lewin's (1969) view, change occurs when the driving forces and the restraining forces are not in balance. This aspect of Lewin's work is usually interpreted in OD literature and practice to mean that change requires an "unfreezing" of an existing equilibrium, a movement to a new equilibrium, and a "refreezing" of the new balance point.

See also LEWIN, KURT; ORGANIZATION DEVELOPMENT.

Forum. "A period of open discussion by participants in the audience following a panel, debate, colloquy, or speech. Provision is made for direct verbal interaction between participants and presenters, under direction of a moderator" (Nadler and Nadler, 1977, p. 254).

See also METHODS.

Four-step method. The foundation of job instruction training (JIT) developed during World War II and still a popular method for conducting on-the-job training. The four steps as Peterson (1979) sees them are (1) prepare the learner, (2) present the operation, (3) operate, and (4) follow up.

See also JOB INSTRUCTION TRAINING; ON-THE-JOB TRAINING.

Front-end analysis. A method of analyzing individual and group performance problems. Joe Harless (1971) coined the term and invented the method.

The method, in essence, involves answering four questions:

What are the symptoms and indicators that a problem exists? What are the performance deficiencies indicated by those data? What is the relative value of solving the problem? What are the possible causes of the problem?

The nature of the performance problem dictates the type of solution. "A simple-minded rule," says Harless ("Front-End Analysis by Trainers," 1978), "but important. . . . If you have a training problem, you train. But if you have a motivation or incentive problem, you don't train. You do some other things" (pp. 23–24).

Front-end analysis is loosely used to refer to almost any kind of learning needs assessment.

See also NEEDS ANALYSIS; PERFORMANCE ANALYSIS; TASK ANALYSIS.

Games. There are as many definitions of *games* — used in the sense of educational games — as there are game theorists and instructional designers (see, for example, Malasky, 1984; Delamontagne, 1982; Zemke, 1982; Greenblat and Duke, 1975). Most authorities agree that the hallmark of educational games is an element of competition between two or more participants. They often involve decision-making or problem-solving tasks and include a systematic evaluation of the participants' performance. *Simulation games* model the reality of the work situation, but with carefully arranged competitive elements.

Frank M. Ricciardi, then of the American Management Association, is usually credited with inventing the first business game in 1957, when advancing computer technology made the principles of game theory more easily accessible for practical game-building and -playing.

Game is sometimes loosely used to refer to almost any variety of experiential learning activity. The word has a totally different meaning in the context of transactional analysis.

See also EXPERIENTIAL LEARNING; METHODS; SIMULATION; TRANSACTIONAL ANALYSIS.

Gestalt. The essence of *gestalt* is found in the expression "the whole is greater than the sum of its parts." The concept is analogous to the field theory in physics in its concern with the properties and behavior of the whole rather than its parts.

The Gestalt school of psychology originated in Germany with the work of Max Wertheimer, Wolfgang Kohler, and Kurt Koffka around 1910. After migrating to the United States in the thirties, the three founders applied Gestalt theory to research in perception, learning, and thinking processes and inspired others to embark on Gestalt-influenced studies of personality (Lande, 1976). Fritz Perls (1969a, 1969b) is probably the best-known U.S. Gestalt psychotherapist. He moved to this country from Berlin and founded several institutes of psychotherapy before becoming the Gestalt guru in residence at Esalen in the sixties.

Gestalt views the roots of unproductive behavior to be our intellectual tendency to break the world down into easily dealt with categories and definitions. The aim of Gestalt therapy is to bring intellectual and "organic" awareness together. Other core concepts in Gestalt psychology are "the contact cycle," resistances, polarities, figure/ground, and experiment (Pfeiffer and Pfeiffer, 1975).

In popular usage, the word *gestalt* is increasingly used to describe a dynamic system of events, properties, characteristics, forms, or patterns that make up a unified whole. In some instances it is used as a synonym for *synergy*. Peter Vaill observed early that the word was on its way to becoming "a shorthand way of referring to an overall view of anything, [for example,] 'My gestalt on the issue is . . .' " (1973, p. 240).

See also HOLISM; SYNERGY.

Hawthorne effect.   The term derives from Elton Mayo's classic experiments begun in the mid-twenties at Western Electric's Hawthorne plants.

Mayo was trying to demonstrate that improving the working environment would have a direct, positive effect on worker productivity. When he turned up the lights in the plant, productivity went up, as predicted. But when he turned the lights down as he turned his attention to some other factor in his study, productivity went up again! That was the first of many puzzling results obtained in more than a decade of such experiments.

In everyday usage, the term *Hawthorne effect* has come to mean

initial improvement in performance following a newly introduced change. It is sometimes incorrectly applied to the phenomenon called the self-fulfilling prophecy, and vice versa. Both the Hawthorne effect and the effects of the self-fulfilling prophecy are potential pitfalls in the proper interpretation of training evaluation data.

See also EVALUATION; PYGMALION EFFECT; SELF-FULFILLING PROPHECY.

Hierarchy of needs.   Needs are a key concept in psychology; the term is used generally to describe all the biological and psychological requirements for human functioning and growth. The hierarchy of needs is the fundamental concept in the "positive theory of human motivation" posited by Abraham Maslow, one of the founders of humanistic psychology.

In essence, Maslow's theory (1970) envisions human psychosocial development as progressing through a sequence of five stages, each determined by a particular set of needs: (1) physiological—nourishment or exercise, for example; (2) safety—security, order, protection; (3) belonging—sociability, acceptance; (4) esteem—status, acknowledgment, prestige; and (5) self-actualization. Most authorities interpret Maslow's hierarchy to mean that all needs are simultaneously present in all persons at all times, though not to the same degree. "The sequence," explains Charles Hamden-Turner, "refers to the strength of the need within the

conscious purpose of the mind"
(1982, p. 118).

See also HUMANISTIC PSYCHOL-
OGY; MASLOW, ABRAHAM; SELF-
ACTUALIZATION.

Further Reading

Maslow, A. *Towards a Psychology of
Being.* New York: D. Van Nostrand,
1962.

Maslow, A. *The Psychology of Science.*
New York: Harper & Row, 1966.

Pfeiffer, S. L. "The Maslow Need
Hierarchy." In J. W. Pfeiffer and J.
E. Jones (eds.), *The 1972 Annual
Handbook for Group Facilitators.*
San Diego: University Associates,
1972.

Reilly, A. J. "Human Needs and
Behavior." In J. E. Jones and J. W.
Pfeiffer (eds.), *The 1975 Annual
Handbook for Group Facilitators.*
San Diego: University Associates,
1975.

Herzberg, Frederick. *"Conceptual
thinker—provocative." "Useful concepts." "Theoretical without being
ethereal."*

Frederick Herzberg invented
what is technically called the *moti-
vation-hygiene theory of job attitudes.* First formulated from studies
of engineers and accountants, his
theory holds that job satisfaction has
two independent sources, motivator
factors and hygiene factors (popul-
arly referred to as "satisfiers" and
"dissatisfiers"). Herzberg also originated the concept and coined the
term *job enrichment.*

He has taught at the University
of Utah, Case Western Reserve, the
University of Oklahoma, the University of Tel Aviv, and the University of Tempere (Finland) and has

consulted and conducted seminars
around the globe.

The Conference Board has
ranked him among the top five
behavioral scientists who have most
influenced the thinking of management; his original research on moti-
vation-hygiene theory is one of the
most replicated studies in the field
of job attitudes (Herzberg, 1976).

Herzberg has written hundreds
of articles, monographs, and scripts
for films. His principal books are
The Motivation to Work (1959),
Work and the Nature of Man (1966),
and an anthology, *The Managerial
Choice* (1976), which includes the
oft-reprinted *Harvard Business
Review* classic, "One More Time:
How Do You Motivate Employees?"
(1968).

Holism.   The thesis that the whole is
greater than the sum of its parts.
From the Greek *holos,* meaning
"complete," the adjective *holistic* is
loosely used to refer to the entirety
of something, as in "a holistic view
of the organization." Paul Dickson
(1977) says that futurists never spell
it *wholistic* and look down their
noses at people who do.

See also GESTALT; SYNERGY.

HRD.   See HUMAN RESOURCE
DEVELOPMENT.

Humanistic psychology. A relatively
recent school founded by Abraham
Maslow, Kurt Goldstein, Rollo
May, and Carl Rogers, among
others, to oppose the "trivial" and
"dehumanizing" Freudian and
behaviorist schools (Bullock and

Stallybrass, 1977, p. 292).

The Association for Humanistic Psychology, founded in 1962, officially stakes out some of the following concerns: to develop methods to enlarge and expand human experience; to encourage attention to topics having little place in most systems (e.g., creativity, self-realization, authenticity, transcendental experience); to emphasize the integration of the whole person; and to be concerned with studying the individual rather than the universal (Lande, 1976, p. 486).

See also BEHAVIORISM; HIERARCHY OF NEEDS; MASLOW, ABRAHAM; ROGERS, CARL; SELF-ACTUALIZATION.

Human potential movement. A term loosely applied to both the human relations training that flowered in the sixties and the so-called personal growth training that absorbed the Me Generation in the seventies. From sensitivity training, encounter groups, sensory deprivation tanks, Rolfing, and various forms of meditation to Arica, est, primal screaming, T'ai Chi, and astral projection – it was not just the lunatic fringe that relentlessly sought "self-actualization," often to the point of neurotic narcissism.

For those of you who missed the golden age of the human potential movement, Adam Smith's (1975) book is an entertaining, though often cynical, tour through the times. Lande's (1976) encyclopedic treatment offers a gentler view.

See also SENSITIVITY TRAINING; T-GROUPS.

Human relations training. "The basic premise that 'things get better when people get along' is alive and well," say some of the field's most intrepid observers, "and currently goes by such names as communications training, team building, and participative management" (Gordon, Lee, and Zemke, 1984, p. 37).

The term itself is an anachronism in most circles. Even University Associates, a leading consulting and publishing firm from the human relations stream, dropped the term in 1981, after a decade of use, from the subtitle of one of its major series.

See also SENSITIVITY TRAINING; T-GROUPS.

Further Reading
Porter, L., and Mohr, B. (eds.). *Reading Book for Human Relations Training.* (7th ed.) Arlington, Va.: NTL Publications, 1982.

Human resource development (HRD). Leonard Nadler introduced the term at the national conference of the American Society for Training and Development in Miami in 1969. A year later, he published his landmark *Developing Human Resources* (1979), in which he defined his concept of HRD and identified the roles of practitioners within the field.

Nadler defines *human resource development* as "organized learning experiences in a definite time period to increase the possibility of improving job performance or growth" (1984, p. 1.3). HRD is distinguished from adult education in that "HRD is concerned mainly with learning provided by employers to their employees or by organizations to nonemployees, according to the goals of the organization (e.g., labor unions, associations)" (p. 1.4).

Nadler's HRD concept requires fine distinctions among three terms that usually are used more or less synonymously. He defines *training* as "learning related to the present job." *Education* is learning to prepare the individual for a different job, one that will be identified "in the not-too-distant future." *Development* is "learning for the growth of the individual but not related to a specific present or future job" (1984, p.1.16).

Many practitioners have seen the utility of Nadler's distinctions and use the words *training, education,* and *development* precisely as he advocates. More often than not, however, about the only distinction you will hear is that training is for the worker, development is for the manager.

See also ADULT EDUCATION; NADLER, LEONARD; TRAINING AND DEVELOPMENT.

Human resource management. The term has come to be used in place of *personnel* and as a synonym for *human resource practice.*

See also HUMAN RESOURCE PRACTICE.

Human resource practice. The ASTD competency study specified and defined nine areas of "human resource practice" — training and development, organization development, organization/job design, human resource planning, selection and staffing, personnel research and information systems, compensation/benefits, employee assistance, and union/labor relations. The "outputs" from these endeavors are "quality work life, productivity, [human resource] satisfaction . . . and readiness for change" (American Society for Training and Development, 1983, p. 23)

See also HUMAN RESOURCE DEVELOPMENT; ORGANIZATION DEVELOPMENT; TRAINING AND DEVELOPMENT.

Imagery. "By far the most neglected and underdeveloped of the normal abilities of the human mind," according to biofeedback pioneer Barbara Brown, imagery is the formation of "some kind of meaningful train of thought or reverie" from bits of information obtained from all kinds of experience and recalled from memory (1983, pp. 247–248).

The making of mental images is frequently assumed to be a process of conjuring up visual images. But, for many people, mental images do not have to be visual at all — they are formed from memories of sounds, touch, muscle activity, emotion, even abstract concepts. Relatively few people have "pure" images, images that are limited to one sense or type of experience.

Imagery can be used to solve problems, to guide behavior, to gain relief from stress, and to alter some physiologic functions. Science now knows that creation of mental images causes expenditure of physical energy and that the more specific the image, the more specific the effect (Brown, 1983). But the jury is still out on exactly how, and why, imagery produces the effects it does.

Imagination is often used as a synonym, as is *visualization* when referring to visual phenomena.

See also CREATIVITY TRAINING and Chapter 9.

In-basket exercise.   A simple form of simulation that, in Laird's (1985) terms, "gets at the realities of a job through [its] paper symptoms" (p. 151).

"Learners get all the materials one might expect to find in an 'in' basket on a typical work day," he explains. "They must then process that paperwork until all the items are in the 'out' basket. . . . Quite typically the exercise contains more work than can reasonably be completed in the allotted time, thus . . . learners deal with not only the rational decisions of the management problems but also with the added realism of working against the clock" (p. 151).

See also METHODS; SIMULATION.

Incident process.   A variation of the case study, typically used in the development of interrogation, analysis, and synthesis skills. It differs from the case study and the action maze in that learners are given insufficient information to be able to reach a decision, even a preliminary one. An incident process design usually requires the learners to interrogate some authority who will give the pertinent facts required to complete the assignment only as the learners ask for them (Malasky, 1984).

See also ACTION MAZE; CASE STUDY; METHODS.

Incubation.   A key concept in creative problem solving and other concerns of creativity training. In essence, incubation is a period during which one's attention is shifted away from the problem or task at hand, deliberately or accidentally. The incubation process is one of "letting it happen" versus "making it happen" (Edwards, 1983, p. 4). Solutions typically come as a sudden flash of insight or inspiration (Koestler, 1966).

See also CREATIVITY TRAINING.

Further Reading
Osborn, A. *Applied Imagination.* (3rd rev. ed.) New York: Scribner's, 1963.

Instructional objective.   A statement of what a learner will do under specified conditions within a given time frame. It specifies required standards of performance as well as special tools, equipment, or aids required or permitted to perform the task. Bob Mager (1984d) wrote the book on instructional objectives.

See also LEARNING OBJECTIVE; MAGER, ROBERT F.

Instrumentation.   An umbrella term referring to a wide variety of paper-and-pencil devices used in human resource development to gather information about individual, group, or organizational attitudes, values, behavior, and so forth. Instruments are used throughout the training cycle—from needs diagnosis to measurement and evaluation of training results. Inventories, questionnaires, opinion-rating scales, reaction forms, surveys, tests, and checklists are just a few examples of the kinds of instruments used (see, for example, Eitington, 1984; Pfeiffer and Heslin, 1973; Pfeiffer and Jones, 1972–1981). The use of such devices to accomplish specific learning objectives is sometimes called *instrumented training.*

Interactive drawing. Popularized by Betty Edwards (1980), interactive drawing exercises are used in whole brain and creativity training to help access the right side of the brain, to gain confidence in creative abilities, to see things in a different way, and to inspire creative problem solving.

See also BRAIN LATERALIZATION; CREATIVITY TRAINING.

Internal consultant. See CONSULTANTS.

Intervention. See ORGANIZATION DEVELOPMENT.

Job instruction training (JIT). The classic four-step learning process developed during World War II to train one worker to do one job. "Tell, show, do, and review" was usual shorthand for the JIT process, which involved lecture, demonstration, performance tryout, and critique phases (Laird, 1985). With various embellishments the JIT process is still an effective component of HRD programs in business and industry today.

See also FOUR-STEP METHOD; ON-THE-JOB TRAINING; VESTIBULE TRAINING.

Jones, John E., and J. William Pfeiffer. *"Inseparable in this instance." "Development of experien-*tial learning theory and practice." "Opened up sharing of materials for practitioners."*

John Jones and Bill Pfeiffer were young professors at the University of Iowa in the late sixties when they had a nifty idea: since there are so many people out there using small-group theory and methods, let's collect some of the activities we and our friends are using and distribute them to our fellow facilitators.

They put together a little book called the *Handbook of Structured Experiences for Human Relations Training* and peddled it, as they say in the publishing business, out of their garage. They published another little *Handbook.* And another.

Then they launched what at the time was called *The Annual Handbook for Group Facilitators* (Pfeiffer and Jones, 1972–1981; Pfeiffer and Goodstein, 1982–), which included not only short learning designs and small-group exercises—*structured experiences* was the term they preferred—but also instruments, essays on theoretical models, lecturettes, and other useful pieces like bibliographies and directories.

Their masterstroke was asking their readers to use the *Annual* as a clearinghouse for sharing exercises, instruments, and other material and to issue blanket permission to duplicate or modify any of the *Annual's* contents for individual or group learning applications. The rest, to yield to the cliché, is history.

They moved to LaJolla, California, to become University Associates, a publishing and consulting firm that established a master's program in human resource development. University Associates created a new circuit of public workshops and conferences on HRD and OD, showcasing many of the brightest stars in the fields. The company continued to publish the handbooks and annuals, together with a large line of other books, instruments, and audiovisual material for training.

In 1982 Leonard D. Goodstein became Pfeiffer's coeditor on the *Annual*—which was given a new subtitle in 1984. Despite this change in editorship, there is a whole generation of trainers who still call the little handbooks and the big notebooks "the Pfeiffer and Jones series."

Jung, Carl. Anima. Archetypes. Collective unconscious. Individuation. Persona. Soul-image. Synchronicity. All are original concepts of Swiss psychologist and psychiatrist Carl Gustav Jung.

Once a disciple of Freud, Jung abandoned the practice of psychoanalysis in 1913 and developed a theory of personality that rejected Freud's emphasis on sexual instincts. In his practice of "analytic psychology" until his death in 1961, Jung emphasized the wholeness of the psyche, within which he distinguished four functions: thinking-feeling and sensation-intuition. In Jung's view the conscious and unconscious parts of the psyche are not only divided among those four functions but also polarized between two "attitudes": extraversion (he spelled it with an *a*) and introversion. His

concept of a collective unconscious was revolutionary.

It is easier to meet and to understand the man and his work by reading his biographers and interpreters (for example, Hamden-Turner, 1982; Bolen, 1979; Storr, 1973; Jacobi, 1973; Kolb, 1976; Myers-Briggs, 1962). If you want to taste the original, try *The Portable Jung* (Campbell, 1971) or *Man and His Symbols* (Jung and others, 1964). Jung's *Collected Works* (1970) is, in Hamden-Turner's words, "for those who are serious" (1982, p. 214).

Kanter, Rosabeth Moss. *"A mentor and guiding light to all newcomers to the world of commerce and applied politics." "Profound contribution to an understanding of HRD and OD."*

Rosabeth Moss Kanter currently chairs the board of Goodmeasure, Inc., a Cambridge, Massachusetts, management consulting firm whose services range from organizational systems design to producing audiovisual training materials. A professor of sociology and professor of organization and management at Yale, she has also taught at Brandeis, Harvard, and M.I.T. Considered one of the leaders of a new generation of trailblazing researchers into organizational change, Kanter of late has been particularly concerned with the effect of organizational structure and culture on innovation and productivity.

Kanter published her award-winning *Men and Women of the Corporation* in 1977 and wowed the audience at the 1979 ASTD national convention when she introduced an audiovisual version of *A Tale of "O"* (Kanter and Stein, 1980). Her other books include *Life in Organizations* (Kanter and Stein, 1979) and her best-selling *The Change Masters* (1983). She appears fairly regularly at national HRD and OD events. She is also available on the tapes *Managing Change* (video, n.d.) and *The Change Masters* (audio, n.d.).

Kirkpatrick, Donald L. *"Overall guidance and contribution to ASTD." "Solid books." "Good mix of professor and practitioner—practical, humorous, earthy." "Wrote practical information down!"*

Don Kirkpatrick has written dozens of books, chapters, and articles on supervisory training, meeting planning, and training evaluation (1975, 1976b, 1982, 1983). His most recent book is *How to Manage Change Effectively* (1985). His chapter (1976a) in *The Training and Development Handbook* is considered a classic by thousands of practitioners who still appreciate a simple but workable evaluation framework.

You can meet Kirkpatrick live at ASTD conferences and institutes or on tape (1980, 1984). The 1975 president of ASTD, he is professor of management at the University of Wisconsin's Management Institute in Milwaukee.

See also EVALUATION.

Knowles, Malcolm. *"The leader in adult education—he packaged, interpreted, and sold andragogy to the real world." "Adult learning in prac-*

tical terms." "Mentor of many . . ." "A list of greats in training and development without Malcolm's name is incomplete!"

Almost everyone calls "the father of adult learning" by his first name—a fitting tribute to a man who has become legend yet is as approachable and unassuming a human being as you will ever meet.

There are numerous ways to get to know him. You may run into him on a consulting gig or at one of the countless workshops, seminars, and speaking engagements he manages to fit into his busier-than-ever schedule since he retired as professor emeritus of adult and community college education at North Carolina State University in Raleigh. You will find scores of his students, protégés, and disciples at virtually any major gathering of HRD professionals. They will chronicle his contribution to adult learning theory and practice with warm, affectionate anecdotes to introduce you to the legend and the man.

You may get your first glimpse of Malcolm and his work in the ten books and more than a hundred articles he has written in his fifty-year career. *Self-Directed Learning* (1975), *The Modern Practice of Adult Education* (1980b), and *The Adult Learner* (1984a) are usually considered his landmark books.

If you can't manage to meet Malcolm face to face, get to know him and his ideas through his books —*Andragogy in Action* (Knowles and Associates, 1984) and *Using Learning Contracts* (1986) are the most recent—and through audio-

and videotapes explaining his philosophy and approaches to helping adults learn (Knowles, 1984c; Knowles, 1980a; Brookfield, 1987; Becker, 1979b; American Society for Training and Development, n.d.).

But do your best to encounter him in person. To participate in one of his workshops is to witness the meaning of andragogy. You will never forget the experience.

See also ANDRAGOGY.

Laird, Dugan. *"Clear thinking." "A wonderful writer." "A trainer's trainer."*

Dugan Laird joined United Air Lines in 1951 as an industrial training instructor and worked for the company in training and training management positions for almost twenty years before launching his career as an independent consultant to some of America's largest corporations, state governments, and federal agencies.

This former high school and university teacher was first known through his columns in *Training* magazine in the 1960s and 1970s. As famous for his acerbic wit as for his down-to-earth approach to HRD practice, Laird quickly became a fixture on the professional conference and seminar circuit.

Dubbed a "benevolent curmudgeon" by one of his best friends, Laird delighted in exposing fads "by refusing to jump on the bandwagon [while] constantly trying to get all of us to set our sights higher" ("In Memoriam: An Open Letter to Dugan Laird," 1985, p. 6). Twice

named to *Training*'s top-ten list (Zemke, 1980; "Excellence in Training," 1984), he made an enormous mark with "his clear and pragmatic writing . . . on training and development, both as a craft and as an organizational function" ("Training Today: In Memory of Dugan Laird," 1985, p. 82).

Publishing lore has Laird proving himself to be the consummate writer in HRD by threading a five-hundred-foot roll of shelf paper into his typewriter and making *Approaches to Training and Development* ready to publish in twelve days. True story or not, the book is a bona fide classic, as useful today as it was when first issued in 1978. *Training* magazine still gives it to new staff members as the best available introduction to the field. It routinely takes its well-deserved place on best-books lists (American Society for Training and Development, 1980; "Excellence in Training," 1984). Laird had just completed his revisions for the second edition (1985) when he died on November 25, 1984, near his Decatur, Georgia, home.

Laird's other books are *The Training and Development Sourcebook* (Baird, Laird, and Schneier, 1983), *Training Today's Employees* (Laird and House, 1984a), *Interactive Classroom Instruction* (Laird and House, 1984b). He also produced *The Trainer's Classroom Instruction Workshop* (Laird and House, 1984c).

Lateral thinking. The author of more than twenty books that have been translated into almost as many languages, Edward de Bono invented the notion of *lateral thinking* as an attempt to demystify the process of creative thinking. In a nutshell lateral thinking is a divergent thought process, a process of looking at a problem from multiple perspectives. Vertical thinking is a convergent method, controlled by a preexisting pattern or idea. Lateral thinking displays characteristics associated with right brain hemispheric functions; vertical, with the left. De Bono's *Lateral Thinking* (1970) and *New Think* (1971) are considered classics among creativity trainers.

See also Brain Lateralization; Creativity Training.

Learner. Peterson defines a learner as "someone who is concerned with achieving specific learning objectives" (1979, p. 29)—a definition that may be too restrictive for some and too loose for others. The term *participant* is sometimes used to refer to learners in the context of a workshop, seminar, or other formal program. Learners are hardly ever called *students* any more, except in academia. *Trainee* is verging on the passé in some circles.

See also Self-Directed Learning.

Learning. The definitions are many. Peterson's is basic: "The process you go through to acquire new knowledge, insights, or behavioral skills" (1979, p. 29).

We like McLagan's, too, because it incorporates the notions of

learner responsibility and transfer-to-the-real-world and more fully describes the idea of insight: "Learning is a change in knowledge, behavior, attitudes/values/priorities, or creativity that can result when learners interact with information. It occurs to the extent that learners are motivated to change, and it is applied in the real world to the extent they take successful steps to integrate that learning into the real world situation" (1978, p. 1). McLagan defines *information* as "materials, activities, and experiences that provide content for learning" (p. 2).

Learning community. A popular phrase for all types of gatherings in which the main objective is learning (see, for example, Nadler, 1978, 1981). The phrase implies that the "teachers," "trainers," and "facilitators" are learners themselves. It may sometimes be used as a euphemism for *classroom* (Vaill, 1973, p. 242).

Learning contract. The explicit or implicit contract that exists between a learner and his or her teacher for acquiring learning (Peterson, 1979).

For *teacher,* read *guide, helper, facilitator, trainer, instructor,* depending on your context and the learning theories you subscribe to. Learning contracts are a way of reconciling the requirements of organizations, institutions, or professions with learners' needs to be self-directing (Knowles, 1984a, 1986).

See also Self-Directed Learning.

Learning design. "A combination of people, methods, equipment, location and timings designed to achieve learning objectives in the most effective way" (Peterson, 1979, p. 28).

Learning environment. "The total setting in which a learner is expected to achieve learning objectives" (Peterson, 1979, p. 29).

Learning needs. See NEEDS ANALYSIS.

Learning objective. "An instructional objective clearly stated in learner-oriented terms. It may originate with the learner" (Peterson, 1979, p. 29).
See also INSTRUCTIONAL OBJECTIVE.

Learning style. The typical ways an individual behaves, feels, and processes information in learning situations. See Chapter 4.

Lecture. "A well-prepared one-way presentation by an individual resource person. Can be coupled with forum, audience reaction team, etc." (Nadler and Nadler, 1977, p. 255).
See also METHODS.

Lecturette. A short lecture. The term seems to have originated among the human relations trainers of the fifties and sixties to refer to the short "theory inputs" sometimes included in their learning designs (Pfeiffer and Jones, 1972).
See also LECTURE; METHODS.

Left brain/right brain theory. See BRAIN LATERALIZATION; CREATIVITY TRAINING.

Lesson plan. See LEARNING DESIGN.

Lewin, Kurt. *"Field theory in social science." "Major contribution to OD theory." "Applied group theory to organizational life." "Action research." "Force field analysis." "Although few trainers know his name—all good ones draw on his work."*

Lewin used to say, "There is nothing so practical as a good theory." The hallmark of his work was the integration of scientific inquiry with real-world problem solving. No ivory-tower theoretician yet an acknowledged giant in American social psychology, Lewin gave us, among other things, a model of social change that influenced the tactics of three generations of civil rights activists.

Read Alfred Marrow's *The Practical Theorist* (1969) and David Kolb's *Experiential Learning* (1984) for an appreciation of Lewin's profound influence on experiential learning and OD models and methods.
See also ACTION RESEARCH; CHANGE AGENT; FORCE FIELD ANALYSIS; ORGANIZATION DEVELOPMENT.

Likert, Rensis. *"Theory and application." "Models." "Understanding behavior." "Organizational diagnosis." "Pioneer in organization development."*

Specifics? The linking-pin concept. The interaction-influence principle. System 4 organization. Human resource accounting. And for those of you who have successfully avoided the research scene of the last forty or fifty years, the opinion-and-attitude measurement scale that bears his name. Likert's *New Patterns of Management* (1961) and *The Human Organization* (1967) are classics in the OD literature.

Lippitt, Gordon. *"Models of change." "Overall contribution to theory." "General provocative thinking." "HRD ambassador around the world."*

Gordon Lippitt's creativity, interviewing skills, and organization renewal models and methods were the hallmarks of his international consulting practice, in which he used a general system approach to meld human, technical, financial, and structural concerns to improve organizational effectiveness.

The 1969 president of ASTD and recipient of its Torch Award in 1975 and Gordon M. Bliss Award in 1980, Lippitt was professor of behavioral science in the School of Government and Business Administration at George Washington University, a charter member of the International Association of Applied Social Scientists, a diplomate of the American Board of Professional Psychology, and chairman of the board of the International Consultants Foundation and of Organizational Renewal, Inc., the consulting group he founded.

Once program director of the National Training Laboratories at the National Education Association, he published more than two hundred works in the field and made frequent appearances at professional development seminars and conferences (see,

for example, Lippitt, 1980). His best-known book is probably *Organizational Renewal* (1982), a fixture on OD reading lists since its first publication in 1969. His other book-length works include *Optimizing Human Resources* (1971), *Visualizing Change* (1973), *Helping Across Cultures* (1978), and *Management Development and Training Handbook* (Taylor and Lippitt, 1983).

He also wrote *The Consulting Process in Action* (1978) with his brother, Ronald Lippitt. A protégé of Kurt Lewin and a founder of the National Training Laboratories, Ronald Lippitt is the coauthor of the OD classic *Dynamics of Planned Change* (Lippitt, Waston, and Westley, 1958) and is a professor emeritus of sociology and psychology at the University of Michigan.

Listening groups. "All participants are divided into groups, each listening for a different element in the presentation (could be lecture, multimedia, panel, etc.). This can be followed by work groups, breakout sessions, or questions to the presenters" (Nadler and Nadler, 1977, p. 255).

See also METHODS.

McGregor, Douglas. *"Management thought." "Conceptual leader, history-making publication." "Theories X and Y." "Humanistic management." "His attention to the human side of enterprise—material still excellent."*

Training magazine's 1984 "who's who" survey asked respondents to name "the people they'd like to turn to when the chips are down" ("Excellence in Training," p. 84). The only catch was that their nominees had to be living. Douglas McGregor was named on a couple of ballots despite the fact that he died over twenty years ago.

The Human Side of Enterprise (1960) was McGregor's only book-length work published before his untimely death in 1964. In it he translated Maslow's hierarchy of needs into a practical model for managers, which he dubbed Theory X and Theory Y. It was a "critical incident" in the evolution of organization development, one that has had an enduring effect on managers as well as on OD practitioners and scholars (Murrell and Vaill, 1975). Had he lived, *The Professional Manager* would have been McGregor's next book. Warren Bennis and Caroline McGregor put together the ideas McGregor had been working on—a major theme was the management of human differences and conflict in organizations—and published the result under his name in 1967.

McLagan, Patricia. *"Dedicated work on competency models." "Applied numerous sciences to defining a problem in useful terms." "Clarifier, facilitator, leader."*

Pat McLagan was the volunteer study director of the ASTD group that produced *Models for Excellence* (American Society for Training and Development, 1983), called by none other than Malcolm Knowles "the most important tool we have yet for systematizing the professional development of our practitioners" (Amer-

ican Society for Training and Development, 1985, p. 18).

A highly respected researcher and consultant, particularly in the area of competency models, McLagan fairly burst upon the national HRD scene with *Helping Others Learn* in 1978. She has also written *Strategic Planning for the HRD Function* (1981), *On the Level* (McLagan and Krembs, 1982), *Getting Results Through Learning* (1983), and dozens of research reports and journal articles.

She currently heads the consulting group she founded, McLagan International, in St. Paul, Minnesota. Register early if you want to get into one of her frequent sessions on the ASTD and *Training* magazine conference circuit.

Mager, Robert F. *"Popularized Skinner's approach." "Made us think in behavioral terms." "Believes in practical theory." "Solid, easy to communicate with, speaks to managers." "His many 'little books' are all classics."*

In October 1984 the editors of *Training* magazine reported that Bob Mager had won their Guru Award hands-down in a who's-who survey of their readers and that "A Robert Mager Anthology" had been named to their top-ten list of most helpful books in training and development ("Excellence in Training," 1984, p. 84). You need only to listen to the wit and wisdom he shares so freely to understand why (Becker, 1979c).

The first milestone in Mager's rise to "guru" was the 1962 publication of his first "little book," *Preparing Instructional Objectives* (1984d)

—which is now in the hands of something like half a million trainers, instructional designers, curriculum developers, and teachers.

Eight years later, in 1970, he teamed up with Peter Pipe, who heads Peter Pipe Associates in Sunnyvale, California, to write a masterpiece called *Analyzing Performance Problems, or You Really Oughta Wanna* (1984). "I bet they wish they had a nickel for every time a trainer has asked, 'Could they perform the task if their lives depended on it?' " said one of our survey respondents, referring to the most famous step in their flowchart showing how to correctly arrive at training or nontraining solutions to performance problems.

The other books in the Mager "anthology"—also commonly known as "The Mager Library" and "The Mager Five-Pack"—are *Developing Attitudes Toward Learning* (1984a), *Goal Analysis* (1984b), and *Measuring Instructional Results* (1984c). Mager has also given us *Troubleshooting the Troubleshooting Course* (1982).

See also INSTRUCTIONAL OBJECTIVE; NEEDS ANALYSIS; PERFORMANCE ANALYSIS.

Management by objectives (MBO). A management process and an intervention strategy in organization development.

Peter Drucker is usually credited with conceiving the MBO approach to management in the late fifties. George Odiorne is the man most often identified as "the father of MBO" because of his success in converting the concept into a management strategy in which a key function of the manager is to establish and communicate organizational objectives.

The term has spawned a number of sound-alike labels—some serious, some facetious—for other management strategies: management by exception, management by crisis, management by hassling, management by wandering around.

See also DRUCKER, PETER; ODIORNE, GEORGE; ORGANIZATION DEVELOPMENT.

Maslow, Abraham. *"Gave us a workable motivation model." "Hierarchy of needs." "Humanistic psychology." "Self-actualization." "Eupsychian management."*

With *Motivation and Personality* in 1954, Abraham Maslow set forth his theory of human motivation based on the concept of a "hierarchy of needs." It was one of the milestones in the development of OD, and in a later edition (1970) Maslow finally acknowledged the value of his theory to those working to change organizations (Murrell and Vaill, 1975). Maslow died in 1970, but the fields of management, HRD, and OD still reverberate with the tremendous power his concepts have given us in understanding human and organizational behavior.

See also HIERARCHY OF NEEDS; HUMANISTIC PSYCHOLOGY; SELF-ACTUALIZATION.

MBO. See MANAGEMENT BY OBJECTIVES.

Methods. "A basic approach or combination of approaches to achieve learning objectives" (Peterson, 1979, p. 29).

Leonard Nadler uses the term *instructional strategies* to mean "all the methods, techniques, and devices that are used in the learning situation [because] there is a lack of agreement regarding those three terms, and the impact of electronic and computer resources has made differentiating among them an exercise in futility" (1984, p. xii). *Learning strategies* and *learning methods* are also used to mean more or less the same thing.

Dugan Laird has said that asking what method to use for a training program is like asking a surgeon what instrument to use for an operation. For a clearer understanding of your potential repertoire, see Laird's (1985) schematic list of methods (Figure 10), which illustrates the relationship of a variety of methods to the nature and extent of the learners' participation in the learning experience.

Laird's schematic is not an exhaustive list, but it does a good job of illustrating the extent to which certain methods conform to two tenets of modern adult learning theory—the desirability of active learner involvement and the investment of previous experience in the learning process.

One of the most important results of looking at learning methods displayed this way, Laird says, is to see that "delegating content control does not automatically increase learner participation: In open forums the learners control all the content except the topic, yet they are not necessarily more involved than in . . . trying out a psychomotor task" (1985, p. 133). And vice versa—increasing the learners' content control does not require abdicating control over the processes of learning. Malasky's primer (1984) is an excellent overview of other factors to consider in selecting appropriate methods for a given learning situation.

See also EXPERIENTIAL LEARNING; PARTICIPATORY METHODS.

Modeling. See SOCIAL LEARNING THEORY.

Modeling display. In behavior modeling, a demonstration of the precise behaviors a learner is expected to learn; the demonstration is usually videotaped or filmed rather than presented live.

See also BEHAVIOR MODELING; DEMONSTRATION.

Mouton, Jane Srygley. See BLAKE, ROBERT R., AND JANE S. MOUTON.

Nadler, Leonard. *"Concepts of HRD and roles." "Coined the term and has made an honest attempt to define HRD." "Developer of professionals." "Leader of HRD curriculum-building." "Critical events model." "Cross-cultural training."*

Leonard Nadler is a professor of adult education and human resource development with the School of Education and Human Development at George Washington University. He is one of the founders of George Washington's

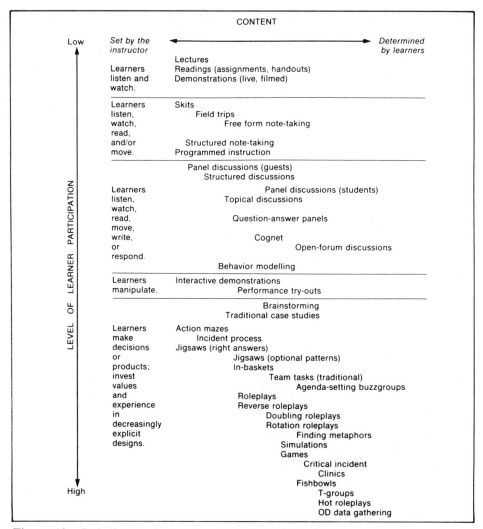

Figure 10. Laird's Duo–Dimensional List of Methods.
Source: Laird (1986, p. 132). Reprinted by permission.

doctoral program in HRD and, except for a five-year hiatus working
as an accountant in business and industry, has been working in the
fields of HRD and adult education
since 1938.

He began working internationally in HRD in 1959 and has since
worked in more than thirty countries. He was a member of ASTD's
National Board of Directors for five
years and has been president of three
local chapters. He is also a prominent member of the American
Association for Adult and Continuing Education, the Society for International Development, the World
Future Society, and the Society for
Intercultural Training, Education,
and Research. He received ASTD's
highest honor, the Gordon M. Bliss
Memorial Award, in 1977.

Nadler says he introduced the term *human resource development* at the 1969 ASTD national conference in Miami (Nadler, 1984). The next year, his landmark *Developing Human Resources* more fully defined his concept of the field. He has published over a hundred articles in professional journals, books, and encyclopedias.

Besides his classic *Developing Human Resources* (1979) and the anthology destined to be a classic, *The Handbook of Human Resource Development* (1984), Nadler's book-length work includes *Managing Human Resource Development* (Nadler and Wiggs, 1986), *Personal Skills for the Manager* (1983), *Designing Training Programs* (1982a), *Corporate Human Resource Development* (1980), and *The Conference Book* (1977), which he wrote with his wife, Zeace.

Len and Zeace Nadler have worked together professionally for many years—"she has an uncanny knack," he says, "for simplifying and unraveling involved professional concepts and models" (1984, p. xviii). Their son David is well known in OD circles—his major books include *The NOW Employee* (1971) and *Feedback and Organization Development* (1977).

You can meet the Nadlers through their consulting work and at professional meetings and conferences around the world. Steve Becker's (1979a) and Stephen Brookfield's 1987) interviews and Nadler's (1982b) tape-recorded presentation for ASTD, "How to Talk to Your Manager About

HRD," are the next best thing to a face-to-face meeting with this outspoken HRD advocate who forever changed the way we think and talk about our profession.

See also HUMAN RESOURCE DEVELOPMENT.

Needs. See HIERARCHY OF NEEDS; MASLOW, ABRAHAM; NEEDS ANALYSIS.

Needs analysis. No matter what label you pin on it, the concept of needs analysis in HRD has to do with finding out who needs to learn what and why. Also called *needs determination, needs assessment,* and—as Malcolm Knowles has quipped—*needs diagnosis* when the implication is a something-less-than-rigorous approach, the process of identifying learning needs is almost universally acknowledged as the first stage in the development of an HRD program.

So what is a learning need? Knowles (1980b) takes a broad view, defining "educational need" as "the discrepancy between what individuals (or organizations or society) want themselves to be and what they are; the distance between an aspiration and a reality" (p. 88). Using Nadler's strict definition of *training,* Dugan Laird (1985) offers a streamlined definition: "A training need exists when an employee lacks the knowledge or skill to perform an assigned task satisfactorily" (p. 46). Some time ago, George Odiorne (1970) saw that learning needs in organizations can also take the form of new knowledge and skills that would make possible "quantum leaps in performance even though the present level of performance is considered satisfactory" (p. 150). He was also one of the first to urge abandonment of the word *needs* to describe the results of figuring out what learning is required to achieve some desired standard of individual or organizational performance.

Joe Harless (1971) and Robert F. Mager and Peter Pipe (1984) were among the contemporary popularizers of the notion that not all performance deficiencies are rooted in training or learning needs — performance deficiencies may be attributable to such nonlearning factors as faulty equipment, inadequate incentives, or poorly conceived procedures, for example. Harless's *front-end analysis* and Mager and Pipe's *performance analysis,* which once signified their specific methods of performance problem solving, have now become synonyms in some circles for the process of needs assessment. So have the terms *task analysis, competency assessment, competency modeling,* and *job analysis,* although each originally referred to a particular approach to analyzing performance problems and determining learning needs.

Information-gathering techniques used in needs analysis (or whatever you want to call it) include interviews, Delphi and nominal group techniques, questionnaires, critical incident analysis, and plain old record-and-report studying. These and dozens more make up "the investigatory 'puzzlework' that must be completed before the actual program writing begins" (Zemke, 1977, p. 16).

Ron Zemke and Tom Kramlinger (1982) wrote a good basic introduction to needs analysis strategies and procedures. Get it and read it.

See also FRONT-END ANALYSIS; HIERARCHY OF NEEDS; PERFORMANCE ANALYSIS; TASK ANALYSIS.

Neurolinguistic programming (NLP). Refers to both a model for understanding human behavior and to a particular array of learning and communication techniques developed principally by Gestalt therapist Richard Bandler and linguist John Grinder (1976, 1977). Drawing from cybernetics, philosophy, neurology, psychology, and linguistics, the fundamental premise of NLP is that people have preferred modes of taking information in and processing it.

The name *neurolinguistic programming* stands for the basic processes through which people organize knowledge and change their behavior. *Neuro-* stands for the nervous system, through which all our experience is received and processed via our senses or representational systems — visual, auditory, kinesthetic, olfactory, and gustatory. *Linguistic* pertains to the language and nonverbal communication systems through which our neural representations are coded, ordered, and given meaning. *Programming* refers to the process of organizing our communication and neurological systems to achieve specific desired outcomes (Bandler and Grinder, 1979).

Bandler and Grinder began to

formulate their model and techniques in the early seventies, when they started studying "known successful communicators" live and on film and videotape (Goleman, 1979). Among their early subjects were psychotherapists Virginia Satir, Fritz Perls, and Milton H. Erikson. Their first Aha! was the observation that successful people in any field always seem to know how to match their behavior to the people or environment with which they interact. Then they drew from psycholinguist Noam Chomsky's work in transformational grammar to codify the communication cues that suggest how people make meaning out of their environment.

The sundry techniques of NLP are based on the theory, simply put, that our language as well as certain nonverbal behaviors echo and reflect our internal processes for structuring our experience. Observations and analyses of word choice, grammatical structure, eye movement, vocal tone, the use of metaphor, and the tempo of speech all figure prominently in the NLP complex of techniques for achieving effective communication efficiently. One of the basic techniques is to listen to the verbs a person uses in speech to get an idea of how he or she tends to take in information and give it meaning. Upon hearing a number of "visual" verbs—*appears* or *looks like,* for example—the experienced NLPer would "pace" the individual by also using visual words and phrases like "I see" or "I get the picture" (Maron, 1979).

Over the last decade, NLP has attracted a band of devotees from education to psychotherapy, from law to sales—many of whom can be "embarrassingly gushy" about Bandler and Grinder's "miracle" ("Training Terms: Neurolinguistic Programming," 1979, p. 87). The coming years should tell us whether NLP is a passing fancy or an enduringly useful model of human communication.

Further Reading

Dilts, R., Grinder, J., Bandler, R., Cameron-Bandler, L., and DeLozier, J. *Neuro-Linguistic Programming.* Cupertino, Calif.: Meta Publications, 1979.

Laborde, G. Z. *Influencing with Integrity: Management Skills for Communication and Negotiation.* Palo Alto, Calif.: Science & Behavior Books, 1983.

Nominal group technique. With features of both brainstorming and brainwriting, the nominal group technique is an idea-generating procedure that permits written recording and verbal discussion of ideas for problem solving, planning, and needs assessment (see, for example, Scott, 1982).

As described by creativity consultant and trainer M. O. Edwards (1982), "The process begins with the group leader giving a carefully selected group of five to nine persons . . . a written statement of the problem and reading it aloud to them. The group members then silently write down their ideas . . . without discussion with others. The second step is a round-robin recording of the ideas generated. . . .

The third step is a serial discussion of each idea for clarification, with the leader asking for questions or comments on each idea listed. Step four involves a group method for aggregating the perceived importance of each idea. . . . If desired, more than one group can be used" (p. 3).

See also BRAINSTORMING.

Norms. In HRD and OD, *norms* are usually taken to mean common and acceptable ways of behaving in a group or organization. "They are usually unwritten and are more specific and pointed than 'values,' in that deviations from norms are followed by such punishments as kidding, 'the silent treatment,' or, in the extreme, banishment" (Vaill, 1973, p. 243).

One of the reasons for being concerned with group norms in organization development, according to Peter Block (1981), is to try to offset the great emphasis placed on leadership style by organizations and consultants.

See also CULTURE; ORGANIZATION DEVELOPMENT.

OD. See ORGANIZATION DEVELOPMENT.

Odiorne, George. *"Management by objectives." "Ahead of his time." "Forward thinking." "Pragmatic." "Articulate." "Shares ideas."*

George Odiorne started thinking about management as a time-and-motion analyst for the American Can Company. He worked through the American Can ranks from inspector to assistant foreman to foreman. He enrolled in a night-school Ph.D. program at New York University and took a course from Peter Drucker. Before Odiorne became the world-renowned "father of MBO," the genius who turned Drucker's concept of management by objectives into an everyday management tool, he put in a stint setting management performance standards at the American Management Association, conducted OD programs as a personnel executive at General Mills, and formulated his MBO system during his ten-year term as director of the Bureau of Industrial Relations at the University of Michigan.

Odiorne's first book, *How Managers Make Things Happen* (1982), has appeared in twenty-five hardcover and fifteen paperback editions and has been translated into fifteen languages since it was first published in 1961. *Management by Objectives* (1965) rivalled its success. He has gone on to produce many more books on MBO, executive management, and organization development — among them, *Managing by Negotiations* (Brooks and Odiorne, 1984), *The Change Resisters* (1981), *Executive Skills* (Odiorne, Weihrich, and Mendleson, 1980), *MBO II* (1979), *Personnel Administration by Objectives* (1971), and *Training by Objectives* (1970), the first two chapters of which won the "Article of the Year" award from ASTD. He has also written more than two hundred articles and publishes *The George Odiorne Letter,* a biweekly newsletter on management by objectives and executive effectiveness. One of his most recent books is *Strategic*

Management of Human Resources (1984), in which he draws from the world of financial investment counseling to posit a "portfolio approach to people management."

See also DRUCKER, PETER; MANAGEMENT BY OBJECTIVES; ORGANIZATION DEVELOPMENT.

On-the-job training (OJT). Activities conducted at the work site to help the learner develop job-related competencies while engaging in productive work at the same time. On-the-job training is usually considered a responsibility of line management, but HRD specialists are frequently involved in its needs assessment, design, and evaluation aspects. The four-step method of job instruction training (JIT) is usually used in conducting OJT (Laird, 1985).

See also FOUR-STEP METHOD; JOB INSTRUCTION TRAINING; VESTIBULE TRAINING.

Operant conditioning. One of the two main branches of a psychological theory called scientific behaviorism. (The other is Pavlovian classical conditioning.)

Usually identified in this country with the work of B. F. Skinner and a long line of protégés, scientific behaviorism holds that behavior is a product of its consequences. For example, if a morsel of food falls into a Skinner box after a rat presses a bar, the rat is likely to press the bar again. In Skinnerian psychology the food is a natural or *primary reinforcer,* the act of eating is an *unconditioned response,* pressing the bar is a learned or *conditioned response,*

the environmental conditions that determine the response are *contingencies,* and the whole process is *operant conditioning.*

See also BEHAVIORISM; BEHAVIOR MODIFICATION; REINFORCEMENT; SKINNER, B. F.

Organization development (OD). Over a decade ago, Peter Vaill characterized organization development as "an evolving collection of philosophies, concepts, and techniques which aims at the improvement of organization performance by intervening in 'social systems' " (1973, p. 243). "It is not yet a coherent applied science," he concluded – and many would still agree with that statement.

We quote some of the classic attempts to define the field to give you a taste of the evolving state of the art.

In his landmark overview of the field Warren Bennis (1969) described OD as "a response to change, a complex educational strategy intended to change the beliefs, attitudes, values, and structure of organizations so that they can better adapt to new technologies, markets, and challenges, and the dizzying rate of change itself" (p. 9). Another classic authority, Richard Beckhard (1969), who writes practically everything in outline style, described OD as "an effort (1) planned, (2) organization-wide, (3) managed from the top, to (4) increase organization effectiveness and health through (5) planned interventions in the organization's 'processes,' using behavioral science knowledge" (p. 9).

Warner Burke and Warren Schmidt (1979) saw OD in a slightly different light: "Using knowledge and techniques from the behavioral sciences, organization development is a *process* which attempts to increase organizational effectiveness by integrating individual desires for growth and development with organizational goals. Typically, this process is a planned change effort which involves a total system over a period of time, and these change efforts are related to the organization's mission" (p. 194).

Key themes in the classic definitions are process, total systems, effectiveness in accomplishing organizational mission—and, of course, change. They endure in ASTD's (1983) description of the focus of organization development as "assuring healthy inter- and intra-unit relationships and helping groups initiate and manage change" (p. 23).

Strategies for producing change under the banner of OD are typically called *interventions*. Some of the most familiar are team building, action research, survey feedback, "techno-structural intervention," and "certain training programs" (Burke and Schmidt, 1979). If you add "action science" (Argyris, 1982; Argyris, Putnam, and Smith, 1985), conflict resolution (Walton, 1969), process consultation (Schein, 1969), "sociotechnical systems interventions" (Margulies, 1982) plus the more specialized techniques—the installation of MBO systems, for example—you have a pretty fair picture of the OD practitioner's basic tool kit.

There is no neat definition of organization development. The researchers and theorists have probably written hundreds of thousands of pages on the subject, and the variations in OD practice—even in an earlier age—are seemingly limitless (Vaill, 1971). Use the references cited and the suggestions for further reading as your passkey.

See also ACTION RESEARCH; ACTION SCIENCE; CHANGE AGENT; CONSULTING PROCESS; CULTURE; DATA-BASED INTERVENTION; MANAGEMENT BY OBJECTIVES; NORMS; SOCIOTECHNICAL SYSTEMS; SURVEY FEEDBACK; TEAM BUILDING.

Further Reading

Albrecht, K. *Organization Development: A Total Systems Approach to Positive Change in Any Business.* Englewood Cliffs, N.J.: Prentice-Hall, 1983.

American Society for Training and Development. *Organization Development.* ASTD Journal Reprint Series. Washington, D.C.: American Society for Training and Development, n.d.

Argyris, C. *Intervention Theory and Method.* Reading, Mass.: Addison-Wesley, 1970.

Blake, R. R., and Mouton, J. S. *Consultation: A Handbook for Individual and Organization Development.* (2nd ed.) Reading, Mass.: Addison-Wesley, 1983.

Burke, W. W. *Organization Development: Principles and Practice.* Boston: Little, Brown, 1982.

Dyer, W. G. *Team Building: Issues and Alternatives.* Reading, Mass.: Addison-Wesley, 1977.

Frame, R. M., Hess, R. K., and Nielson, W. R. *The OD Source Book: A Practitioner's Guide.* San Diego: University Associates, 1982.

French, W. L., Bell, C. H., Jr., and Zawacki, R. A. *Organization Development: Theory, Practice, and Research.* (rev. ed.) Homewood, Ill.: Dow Jones–Irwin, 1983.

Goodman, P. S., and Associates. *Change in Organizations.* San Francisco: Jossey-Bass, 1982.

Harvey, J. "It's Not My Dog: Eight Myths OD Consultants Live and Die By." *OD Practitioner,* 1975, *7* (1), 1–5.

Harvey, J. B. "Organizations as 'Phrog Farms.' " In C. R. Bell and L. Nadler (eds.), *Clients and Consultants: Meeting and Exceeding Expectations.* Houston: Gulf Publishing, 1985. (Originally published as *The Client-Consultant Handbook.*)

Lippitt, G. L. *Organizational Renewal: A Holistic Approach to Organization Development.* (2nd ed.) Englewood Cliffs, N.J.: Prentice-Hall, 1982.

Nadler, D. A. *Feedback and Organization Development: Using Data-Based Methods.* Reading, Mass.: Addison-Wesley, 1977.

Neilsen, E. *Becoming an OD Practitioner.* Englewood Cliffs, N.J.: Prentice-Hall, 1984.

Passmore, W. A., and Sherwood, J. J. (eds.), *Sociotechnical Systems: A Sourcebook.* San Diego: University Associates, 1978.

Patten, T. H., Jr. "The Behavioral Science Roots of Organization Development: An Integrated Perspective." In J. E. Jones and J. W. Pfeiffer (eds.), *The 1979 Annual Handbook for Group Facilitators.* San Diego: University Associates, 1979.

Patten, T. H., Jr. *Organizational Development Through Teambuilding.* New York: Wiley, 1981.

Patten, T. H., Jr. and Vaill, P. B. "Organization Development." In R. L. Craig (ed.), *The Training and Development Handbook.* (2nd ed.) New York: McGraw-Hill, 1979.

Seashore, S. E., Lawler, E. E., III, Mirvis, P. H., and Cammann, C. (eds.). *Assessing Organizational Change: A Guide to Methods, Measures, and Practices.* New York: Wiley, 1983.

Steele, F. *Consulting for Organizational Change.* Amherst: University of Massachusetts Press, 1975.

Steele, F., and Jencks, S. *The Feel of the Workplace.* Reading, Mass.: Addison-Wesley, 1977.

Warrick, D. D. (ed.). *Contemporary Organization Development: Current Thinking and Applications.* Glenview, Ill.: Scott, Foresman, 1984.

Weisbord, M. *Organizational Diagnosis: A Workbook of Theory and Practice.* Reading, Mass.: Addison-Wesley, 1978.

Panel. "A group of two or more persons (usually not exceeding six) who have a discussion in front of a larger audience. It is *not* a series of speeches, but a purposeful discussion usually utilizing a moderator. It can be followed by a forum or some other technique for audience involvement" (Nadler and Nadler, 1977, p. 256).

See also METHODS.

Participatory methods. The phrase connotes methods that are more learner-centered than instructor-centered. A small-group exercise is participatory, a lecture is not.

See also EXPERIENTIAL LEARNING; FACILITATOR; METHODS.

Pedagogy. Strictly (1) the art or profession of teaching or (2) preparatory training or instruction. In developing his andragogical model of adult learning, Malcolm Knowles described pedagogy as "the art and science of teaching children," the underlying assumptions of which are usually not applicable when working with adult learners (1980b, p. 43).

See also ANDRAGOGY; KNOWLES, MALCOLM; SYNERGOGY.

Performance analysis. The method of performance problem solving, or training needs analysis, popularized by Robert F. Mager and Peter Pipe (1984). In flowchart form, their approach, which is firmly rooted in behaviorist theory, was reduced to the catch-phrase "Could they do the job if their lives depended on it?"

See also NEEDS ANALYSIS; TASK ANALYSIS.

Performance tryout. The opportunity to practice or demonstrate a newly learned skill or behavior— "an integral, inevitable step in the four-part job instruction training [method]" (Laird, 1985, p. 146).

See also BEHAVIOR MODELING; JOB INSTRUCTION TRAINING; ON-THE-JOB TRAINING; ROLE PLAY; SKILL PRACTICE.

Pfeiffer, J. William. Even though they are no longer paired as editors of University Associates' continuing series of *Annuals,* Bill Pfeiffer and John Jones were listed together in all but one of our survey responses.

See also JONES, JOHN E., AND J. WILLIAM PFEIFFER.

Programmed instruction. A method of learning in which information is presented in precisely planned steps to guide the learner to successful completion of a task or exercise.

Although its design principles are rooted in Skinner's theory of operant conditioning, programmed instruction today may or may not involve the use of teaching machines or other mechanical presentation devices. August K. Spector (1984), among others, considers programmed instruction a learner-centered instructional strategy because learners are free to proceed at their own pace and, in some cases, to choose among various branches of tasks leading to successful completion of the program.

See also BEHAVIORISM; METHODS; OPERANT CONDITIONING; PARTICIPATORY METHODS.

Psychodrama. See ROLE PLAY.

Psychomotor learning. As charted in Benjamin Bloom's (1956a) classic taxonomy, learning in the *psychomotor domain* of instructional objectives is represented by the demonstration of some physical skill or performance of some task—for example, repairing a diesel engine. Learning in the *cognitive domain* involves mental processes—knowing and retaining information, making judgments or evaluations; the *affective domain* pertains to attitudes, values, and the like.

See also AFFECTIVE LEARNING; COGNITIVE LEARNING.

Pygmalion effect. A positive manifestation of the self-fulfilling prophecy. It means, in essence, that when the person in charge expects people to do well, they do well. The term is sometimes used incorrectly to refer to the Hawthorne effect, and vice versa.

See also HAWTHORNE EFFECT; SELF-FULFILLING PROPHECY.

Random word play. A creative problem-solving technique, based on forced relations, suggested by de Bono (1970). M. O. Edwards describes how it typically works: "First, select a random word . . . from the dictionary which has no logical connection whatsoever with your problem. Then play with the word and test each new thought . . . to see if it might indicate a solution to your problem" (1982, p. 3). *Random object play* is a variation in which the attributes of an object are used as trigger words for generating original ideas.

See also CREATIVITY TRAINING.

Reaction measures. In HRD program evaluation, *reaction* is defined as "what the learners thought of the particular program, including materials, instructors, facilities, methodology, content, etc." (Phillips, 1984, p. 12.5). In essence, the use of reaction measures or methods tries to answer the question "Were the learners pleased with the program?" (see, for example, Laird, 1985, which contains examples of actual instruments).

Sometimes called "happiness ratings," "whoopie sheets," and similarly derisive names by those who doubt their worth, participant reactions are still a popular form of evaluative data. Julius Eitington explains why: "They are easy and economical . . . and certainly better than no data at all. They [also] meet the trainer's need to know how well his/her efforts have been perceived" (1984, pp. 245-246). Another reason, from management's perspective, is that if the learners don't like the program, there is little point in supporting it.

See also EVALUATION.

Further Reading

Brethower, K. S., and Rummler, G. A. "Evaluating Training," *Improving Human Performance Quarterly,* 1976, *5* (3-4), 103-120.

Kirkpatrick, D. L. "Evaluation of Training." In R. L. Craig (ed.), *The Training and Development Handbook.* (2nd ed.) New York: McGraw-Hill, 1976.

Phillips, J. C. *Handbook of Training Evaluation and Measurement Methods.* Houston: Gulf Publishing, 1983.

Reinforcement. One of the cornerstones of behaviorism's theory of operant conditioning, *reinforcement* in HRD usage has generally come to mean "(1) Praise or encouragement of the learner's performance so as to augment his/her learning interest, motivation. (2) Provision of added learning task or data so as to aid the comprehension and/or 'glueing in' of the training" (Eitington, 1984, p. 292). The terms *feedback* and, more specifically, *positive feedback* tend to be used as synonyms for the first definition; *application, back-home,* or *bridging tasks,* for the second.

See also BEHAVIORISM; FEEDBACK; OPERANT CONDITIONING.

Return on investment (ROI). In finance and accounting ROI calculations are used to measure the anticipated profitability of investments or the performance of divisions or profit centers within a business (Phillips, 1983, 1984). As it is increasingly used in HRD program evaluation, the ROI analysis is formulated as:

$$ROI = \frac{\text{net program benefits (or savings)}}{\text{program costs (or program investment)}}$$

The result must be compared to a predetermined standard to be meaningful, says Phillips (1984). "A 30% ROI is unsatisfactory when a 40% ROI is expected" (p. 12.29).

　　See also COST-BENEFIT ANALYSIS; EVALUATION.

Right brain/left brain theory. See BRAIN LATERALIZATION; CREATIVITY TRAINING.

Rogers, Carl. *"Nondirective, nonmanipulative approach." "Pushed the potential of the individual."*

　　One of the founders of the Association for Humanistic Psychology, psychotherapist Carl R. Rogers originated client-centered therapy and encounter groups. For more than thirty years he was a major force in the demystification of psychotherapy.

　　Congruence, integrity, self-evaluation, and positive regard are key constructs in Rogers's schema of human personality and communication. Rogerian counseling rests on the premise that we can do nothing to change or direct a person from outside his own field of perception.

　　In the late sixties Rogers rocked the world of education with *Freedom to Learn* (1969), in which he outlined a theory of learning that many saw as an assault on B. F. Skinner's reinforcement theory. In Rogers's view, "the most useful learning is learning the process of learning" (Rogers, 1969, p. 163), and the relationship between the learner and the "facilitator" of learning is the primary ingredient. Thousands of people who once called themselves "teachers" and "instructors" embraced the role of facilitator, rather than stimulator or controller, of the action and began to permit learners "to make responsible choices about the direction of their learning, and to live responsibly with those choices" (Laird, 1985, p. 121).

　　Besides *Freedom to Learn,* Rogers's most influential books are probably *Client-Centered Therapy* (1951) and *On Becoming a Person* (1961). Warren Bennis's videotaped interview is a compelling introduction to Rogers and his views on a wide range of issues (Rogers, 1986).

　　See also FACILITATOR; HUMANISTIC PSYCHOLOGY.

Role play. An extemporaneous enactment, using realistic behavior, through which learners can examine previous behavior, try out new behaviors, or experiment with behaviors that might be potentially useful (Laird, 1985; Malasky, 1984). There are many forms—a few mentioned by the Nadlers are "multiple role playing (involving all in a general session), reverse role play (after the initial two-person role play), and structured role play (where the situation is given in detail and each role player has a particular role other than what he would normally be)" (Nadler and Nadler, 1977, p. 256).

The term and the sort of activity it describes trace their ancestry to psychodrama, a therapeutic technique developed by psychiatrist J. L. Moreno, in which patients act out their problems. Among psychotherapists the technique is called role playing.

In HRD circles *role play* is also commonly used as a verb—as in, "After you role play the exchange between the employee who arrived late and her boss, . . ." It is also used loosely to signify a practice run—as in "Let's role play how we're going to handle questions about the survey we're doing in the wiring division."

See also METHODS.

Self-actualization. Strictly the fifth stage in Maslow's theory of human psychosocial development. More casually the term is "quite widely used to refer to the process by which an individual reaches the highest level of functioning of which he is capable" (Vaill, 1973, p. 244).

See also HIERARCHY OF NEEDS; HUMANISTIC PSYCHOLOGY; MASLOW, ABRAHAM.

Self-directed learning. "In its broadest meaning," says Malcolm S. Knowles, *"self-directed learning* describes a process in which individuals take the initiative learning goals, identifying human and material resources for learning, choosing and implementing learning strategies, and evaluating learning outcomes" (1975, p. 18).

Other terms used to refer to this process are *self-planned learning, self-education, self-instruction, self-study,* and *autonomous learning.* "The trouble with most of these labels," Knowles has observed, "is that they seem to imply learning in isolation, whereas self-directed learning usually takes place in association with various kinds of helpers, such as teachers, tutors, mentors, resource people, and peers" (p. 18).

See also ANDRAGOGY; KNOWLES, MALCOLM.

Further Reading

Tough, A. *Intentional Changes: A Fresh Approach to Helping People Change.* Chicago: Follett, 1982.

Tough, A. *The Adult's Learning Projects: A Fresh Approach to Theory and Practice in Adult Learning.* (2nd ed.) San Diego: University Associates, 1979.

Self-fulfilling prophecy. One of the best-established principles in psychology, the self-fulfilling prophecy maintains that people tend to perform in accordance with what is expected of them. The effects of the self-fulfilling prophecy can skew the results of program evaluation studies, most commonly in a positive direction. *Self-fulfilling prophecy* is not a synonym for *Hawthorne effect.*

See also EVALUATION; PYGMALION EFFECT. Cf. HAWTHORNE EFFECT.

Seminar. "A discussion involving several individuals, all of whom have something to offer. However, there is one seminar leader who also serves as a resource. Usually a small group of about fifteen persons, though multiple seminars can be conducted at the same time, each with its own leader. Not useful for introducing new material as each participant is expected to have something worthwhile to contribute to the session" (Nadler and Nadler, 1977, p. 256).

See also METHODS.

Sensitivity training.   Peter Vaill captured the essence: "The collection of methods for improving the individual's sensitivity to himself and others. Although a large number of variations exist, the common ingredients seem to be: (1) the guidance of a trained person or persons; (2) intense interpersonal experience by the trainee; (3) a relatively protected environment, free from ordinary pressures and distractions. The T-group is the classical, but not the only, means of achieving these three conditions" (1973, p. 245).

The concept of the T-group and the term *sensitivity training* have been widely misunderstood and misapplied. Even in the heyday of sensitivity training, John E. Jones (1972) warned: "To some persons that term connotes brainwashing, manipulation, and a host of other horrid activities. . . . To others the term carries the meaning 'feel and reveal.' . . . Because it has such surplus meaning, it is for all practical purposes a garbage term" (p. 145).

See also HUMAN RELATIONS TRAINING; T-GROUP.

Simulation.   From the Latin *similare,* meaning to imitate, feign, or repre-

sent. In the context of human resource development, the term is subject to widely varying definitions and connotations.

Ellen Weisberg Malasky defines simulation as "a representation of a real-life situation—usually a situation requiring appropriate actions and reactions or a situation requiring the demonstration of technical expertise" (1984, p. 9.27). In the context of organization development and human relations training, Peter Vaill describes a simulation as "the creation of a 'working model' of some system, such that key elements and their interactions are highlighted . . . [and] trainees are able to experience various dimensions of organizational behavior" (1973, p. 245).

In their simplest forms, simulations include in-basket exercises, case studies, role plays, and more extensive group learning designs "somewhat like action mazes being role played" (Laird, 1985, p. 158). Most so-called business games are simulations, though not all simulations are games (Zemke, 1982).

The use of nongame simulations has a long history in technical skills training. One of the most sophisticated simulation machines in use today dates back to the 1929 invention of the first flight simulator by Edwin A. Link. The use of computer-assisted simulations in current HRD practice ranges from simple problem-solving tasks designed for the individual working at a desktop microcomputer to simulation machines outfitted with sophisticated video and audio equipment hooked into a computer network.

See also COMPUTER-ASSISTED IN-STRUCTION; GAMES; METHODS.

Skill practice. In behavior modeling parlance a skill practice is "a learning exercise similar to a role play, whereby the learner can practice the skills previously demonstrated by the model" (Robinson, 1982, p. 183).

Although the terms are similar in concept, the exclusive purpose of a skill practice exercise is the learner's demonstration of "precise behavioral targets"; the role play can be used for a number of purposes. Used in its strictest sense, *skill practice* means an "anticipatory rehearsal in the behaviors necessary to meet a given work-related problem" (Goldstein and Sorcher, 1974, p. 18).

See also BEHAVIOR MODELING; PERFORMANCE TRYOUT; ROLE PLAY.

Skinner, B. F. *"His pioneering work set in place the entire movement of behavior management and its application to schools, government, and business." "Programmed instruction." "Theories developed into behavior modeling."*

"The original behavior manager, without whom Ken Blanchard could never make *The One-Minute Manager* [Blanchard and Johnson, 1982] work," wrote another of our survey respondents about B. F. Skinner.

Blanchard isn't the only one. The appliers and admirers of Skinner's theories and methods are legion. Read *A Matter of Consequences* (1983) to begin to understand how his theories and methods have evolved over his sixty-year

career. Skinner is Edgar Pierce Professor Emeritus of Psychology at Harvard University and lives in Cambridge.

See also BEHAVIORISM; BEHAVIOR MODIFICATION; INSTRUCTIONAL OBJECTIVES; OPERANT CONDITIONING; PERFORMANCE ANALYSIS; PROGRAMMED INSTRUCTION; REINFORCEMENT.

Social learning theory. Social learning theory holds that we learn a great deal of our behavior by watching others and remembering not only what they did but also the outcomes of their behaviors. Observation, imitation, and modeling are key ingredients in the process.

The concepts of social learning have been most fully articulated by Albert Bandura (1971, 1986). Among the most successful applications of social learning concepts to the world of HRD was the development of behavior modeling methods in the early seventies (see, for example, Goldstein and Sorcher, 1974; Robinson, 1982).

See also BEHAVIOR MODELING.

Sociotechnical systems. Gordon Lippitt (1979) explained the concept for organization development: ". . . an organization's total system has a complete set of human activities plus interrelationships to the technical, physical, and financial resources and to the processes for turning out products and delivering services. Thinking about an organization as a sociotechnical system helps us accept the human-machine relationships" (p. xiii).

See also ORGANIZATION DEVELOPMENT.

Further Reading
Passmore, W. A., and Sherwood, J. J. *Sociotechnical Systems: A Sourcebook*. San Diego: University Associates, 1978.

Structured experience. See EXERCISE.

Suggestology. Popularized in the best-seller *Superlearning* (Ostrander, Schroeder, and Ostander, 1979) and touted as a revolutionary teaching/learning method, *suggestology* has yet to make it into the HRD mainstream. When practiced by the classical Lozanov method (named for its Bulgarian inventor), the method consists of three main phases: presentation of new material, review, and relaxation (Zemke and Nicholson, 1977). The term *suggestopedia* is also used to refer to the method, particularly its classical form.

Survey feedback. "A type of database based intervention [in OD] which flows from surveys of the members of a system . . . and reports the results of the survey to the group" (Vaill, 1973, p. 245). David Nadler's (1977) *Feedback and Organization Development* is the definitive work on the subject.

See also ACTION RESEARCH; DATA-BASED INTERVENTION; ORGANIZATION DEVELOPMENT.

Synectics. From the Greek, meaning a joining together of different elements, the word refers to a group problem-solving technique that stresses the use of analogy and metaphor.

The concept was originated by William J. J. Gordon (1961), who founded Synectics, Inc., with George Prince in 1960. In 1967 Gordon split off to form Synectics Educational Systems, where he and his associates have focused on the use of metaphor in creative thinking. Prince stayed to head up Synectics, Inc., where he and his associates have since elaborated the original technique with such mechanisms as expressing the problem as wishes, making absurd connections, using approximate thinking, and drawing personal analogies ("be the thing").

See also CREATIVITY TRAINING.

Synergogy. Derived from the Greek *synergos* and *agogus,* the term was coined by Mouton and Blake (1984) to describe a model of education and training that combines pedagogical and andragogical methods. It means "working together for shared teaching."

See also ANDRAGOGY; PEDAGOGY; SYNERGY.

Synergy. The most common meaning is best captured in the expression "the whole is greater than the sum of its parts."

The concept was originally proposed by Buckminster Fuller, who used the term *synergetics* to refer to the characteristics of metallic alloys or structural forms that are stronger than their constituent parts (World Future Society, 1979). Abraham Maslow (1954) was one of the first to apply the concept to psychology, using it as a central theme in his studies of self-actualizing people. In everyday usage the term became jargon for "any process in which more is accomplished by cooperation than . . . by separate efforts" (Vaill, 1973, p. 245).

See also GESTALT; MASLOW, ABRAHAM.

TA. See TRANSACTIONAL ANALYSIS.

Task analysis. We agree with Ron Zemke—the term now means "neither more nor less than the person using it wants it to mean" (1977, p. 16). But we also admire—and agree with—his brave attempt to differentiate between needs analysis and task analysis: "Sending a survey to all the first-line supervisors at Universal Widget and asking them to check, circle, or write down all the general-skill or competency areas they, their subordinates, or superiors seem to lack. That's needs analysis. . . . Task analysis is what you and I do when we have faithfully followed all the routes in Robert Mager and Peter Pipe's (1972) performance analysis flow chart and are 99.9% sure that we are stuck with a situation that represents a bona fide training problem" (p. 16).

Task analysis traces its roots back to the early-twentieth-century time-and-motion studies of Frederick Taylor and other proponents of scientific management. Military psychologist Robert Gagné (1965) is usually credited with introducing the term, as well as his specific approach to "component task achievement and the sequencing of subtask learning," to modern HRD practice.

Ron Zemke and Tom Kramlinger (1982) wrote the book on con-temporary task analysis—get it and read it.

See also FRONT-END ANALYSIS; NEEDS ANALYSIS; PERFORMANCE ANALYSIS.

Team building. "The process by which work relations are improved among members of some task group in an organization. Various techniques . . . may be used. It is a major overall strategy in organization development" (Vaill, 1973, p. 246).

See also ORGANIZATION DEVELOPMENT.

Techno-structural intervention. See ORGANIZATION DEVELOPMENT; SOCIO-TECHNICAL SYSTEMS.

T-group. A mainstay method of sensitivity training in the sixties and seventies, the T-group typically evolved its own structure as the members of the group accomplished their task "to learn about themselves in a social context" (Vaill, 1973, p. 246). Usually assisted by a facilitator, the main purpose of the group was "the individual's development and awareness of interpersonal skills" by "studying the effects of behavior and exploring alternative behaviors that might be more effective" (Jones, 1972). Process observation, games, simulations, "structured experiences," and other experiential methods were the hallmarks of the T-group process.

The term is rarely used any more, except in a historical context. Many of the underlying constructs and the basic methods of T-group training are still around, revivified under the banner of team building and communications skills training.

See also HUMAN RELATIONS TRAINING; SENSITIVITY TRAINING.

Trainer. Literally—although admittedly exceedingly simplistically—one who trains. If you accept Nadler's (1979, 1984) distinctions between *training, education,* and *development,* then a provisional definition for *trainer* could be "one who helps individuals improve performance on their present jobs by providing organized learning experiences." The word carries the connotation that the "helper" is directly involved in the learning process in a face-to-face relationship with the learner(s)—either up front, in the posture of an "instructor," or as a coach or collaborator. Closely approximate terms are *instructor* and *facilitator. Teacher* is sometimes used, even in business and industry, depending on the context.

See also FACILITATOR; HUMAN RESOURCE DEVELOPMENT; TRAINING AND DEVELOPMENT.

Training. See HUMAN RESOURCE DEVELOPMENT; TRAINING AND DEVELOPMENT.

Training and development. The American Society for Training and Development defines the "focus" of training and development to be "identifying, assessing, and—through planned learning—helping develop the key competencies which enable individuals to perform current or future jobs" (1983, p. 23).

See also HUMAN RESOURCE DEVELOPMENT.

Transactional analysis (TA). Called TA by the cognoscenti, transactional analysis was a vogue construct for explaining human behavior in HRD circles in the seventies.

TA was developed by psychotherapist Eric Berne (1964, 1972) and popularized in his best-selling *Games People Play* as well as by Harris (1967), Steiner (1974), and others. In part, it is a theoretical model of human behavior explained in terms of "strokes," "transactions," "games," and "scripts." Strokes are actions that satisfy people's need for recognition or attention—they can be positive or negative. An exchange of strokes is a transaction. Games are made up of complex patterns of transactions, and scripts are, in essence, a life-long plan for carrying out a particular game or series of games (Anderson, 1973).

The concept of ego states was also central to Berne's theory. Legions of TA trainers in the seventies would use *egograms* to explain "the parent," "the child," and "the adult" ego states to help people understand where other individuals were "coming from."

Vestibule training. The term was once used to refer to training conducted off the factory floor, where duplicate equipment was available and job instruction training could go on without disturbing other workers. While its complement, *on-the-job training,* is still alive and kicking in the HRD vocabulary, the term *vestibule training* is rarely used now. *Simulation* is sometimes used today to refer to more or less the same thing—that is, re-creating or modeling the work environment, or some aspect of it, for the purpose of learning away from the actual work site.

See also ON-THE-JOB TRAINING; SIMULATION.

Visualization.   See IMAGERY.

References

Adams, J. *Conceptual Block Busting*. New York: Norton, 1979.

Albrecht, K. A. *Brain Power: Learn to Improve Your Thinking Skills*. Englewood Cliffs, N.J.: Prentice-Hall, 1980.

Albrecht, K. "Earth and Sky: A Meeting of Minds — Getting Through to People with Mind-to-Mind Communication." *Training and Development Journal*, 1983a, *37* (10), 70–75.

Albrecht, K. A. *Mindex: Your Thinking Profile*. San Diego: Shamrock Press, 1983b.

Albrecht, K., and Zemke, R. *Service America! Doing Business in the New Economy*. Homewood, Ill.: Dow Jones–Irwin, 1985.

American Society for Training and Development. "Best-Known HRD Works of the '70s." *Training and Development Journal*, 1980, *34* (5), 84–86.

American Society for Training and Development. *Models for Excellence: The Conclusions and Recommendations of the ASTD Training and Development Competency Study*. Baltimore: ASTD Press, 1983.

American Society for Training and Development. *Books, Audiotapes, Journal Reprints Catalogue*. Washington, D.C.: American Society for Training and Development, 1985.

American Society for Training and Development. "Exchange with Malcolm Knowles and Others." Audiotape. Washington, D.C.: American Society for Training and Development, n.d.

Anderson, J. P. "A Transactional Analysis Primer." In J. E. Jones and J. W. Pfeiffer (eds.), *The 1973 Handbook for Group Facilitators*. San Diego: University Associates, 1973.

Argyris, C. *Personality and Organization: The Conflict Between the System and the Individual*. New York: Harper & Row, 1957.

Argyris, C. *Interpersonal Competence and Organizational Effectiveness*. Homewood, Ill.: Dorsey Press, 1962.

Argyris, C. *Organization and Innovation*. Homewood, Ill.: Dorsey Press, 1965.

Argyris, C. *Intervention Theory and Method*. Reading, Mass.: Addison-Wesley, 1970.

Argyris, C. *Management and Organization Development*. New York: McGraw-Hill, 1971.

Argyris, C. *Increasing Leadership Effectiveness*. New York: Wiley, 1976.

Argyris, C. *Reasoning, Learning, and Action: Individual and Organizational*. San Francisco: Jossey-Bass, 1982.

Argyris, C. *Strategy, Change, and Defensive Routines*. Boston: Pitman, 1985.

Argyris, C., Putnam, R., and Smith, D. M. *Action Science*. San Francisco: Jossey-Bass, 1985.

Argyris, C., and Schon, D. *Theory in Practice: Increasing Professional Effectiveness*. San Francisco: Jossey-Bass, 1974.

Argyris, C., and Schon, D. *Organizational Learning: A Theory of Action Perspective*. Reading, Mass.: Addison-Wesley, 1978.

Baird, L. S., Laird, D., and Schneier, C. E. (eds.). *The Training and Development Sourcebook*. Amherst, Mass.: Human Resource Development Press, 1983.

Baldwin, C. *One to One: Self-Understanding Through Journal Writing*. New York: M. Evans, 1977.

Bandler, R., and Grinder, J. *The Structure of Magic I and II*. 2 vols. Palo Alto, Calif.: Science & Behavior Books, 1976, 1977.

Bandler, R., and Grinder, J. *Frogs into Princes: An Introduction to Neurolinguistic Programming*. Moab, Utah: Real People Press, 1979.

Bandura, A. *Social Learning Theory.* Englewood Cliffs, N.J.: Prentice-Hall, 1971.

Bandura, A. *Social Foundations of Thought and Action: A Social Cognitive Theory.* Englewood Cliffs, N.J.: Prentice-Hall, 1986.

Becker, S. P. "Leonard Nadler: An In-Depth Interview with Steve Becker." Audiotape. Boston: Learncom, Inc., 1979a.

Becker, S. P. "Malcolm Knowles: An In-Depth Interview with Steve Becker." Audiotape. Boston: Learncom, Inc., 1979b.

Becker, S. P. "Robert Mager: An In-Depth Interview with Steve Becker." Audiotape. Boston: Learncom, Inc., 1979c.

Beckhard, R. *Organization Development: Strategies and Methods.* Reading, Mass.: Addison-Wesley, 1969.

Bell, C. R. *Influencing: Marketing the Ideas That Matter.* Austin, Tex.: Learning Concepts, 1982.

Bell, C. R., and Margolis, F. H. *A Presenter's Guide to Conferences.* Washington, D.C.: American Society for Training and Development, 1980.

Bell, C. R., and Nadler, L. (eds.). *Clients and Consultants.* Houston: Gulf, 1985. (Revised edition of *The Client-Consultant Handbook.*)

Bennis, W. G. *Changing Organizations: Essays on the Development and Evolution of Human Organizations.* New York: McGraw-Hill, 1966.

Bennis, W. G. *Organization Development: Its Nature, Origins, and Prospects.* Reading, Mass.: Addison-Wesley, 1969.

Bennis, W. G. "Warren Bennis in Dialogue with CEOs: Entrepreneurship and Leadership in America." Audiotape. Cambridge, Mass.: Goodmeasure, Inc., n.d.

Bennis, W. G., Benne, K. D., and Chin, R. (eds.). *The Planning of Change.* (4th ed.) New York: Holt, Rinehart & Winston, 1985.

Bennis, W. G., and Nanus, B. *Leaders: The Strategies for Taking Charge.* New York: Harper & Row, 1985.

Berne, E. *Games People Play: The Psychology of Human Relationships.* New York: Grove Press, 1964.

Berne, E. *What Do You Say After You Say Hello? The Psychology of Human Destiny.* New York: Grove Press, 1972.

Blake, R. R., and Mouton, J. S. *The Managerial Grid.* Houston: Gulf, 1964.

Blake, R. R., and Mouton, J. S. *Corporate Darwinism.* Houston: Gulf, 1966.

Blake, R. R., and Mouton, J. S. *Corporate Excellence Through Grid Organization Development: A Systems Approach.* Houston: Gulf, 1968.

Blake, R. R., and Mouton, J. S. *Building a Dynamic Corporation Through Grid Organization Development.* Reading, Mass.: Addison-Wesley, 1969.

Blake, R. R., and Mouton, J. S. *The Grid for Supervisory Effectiveness.* Austin, Tex.: Scientific Methods, 1975.

Blake, R. R., and Mouton, J. S. *The New Managerial Grid.* (2nd ed.) Houston: Gulf, 1978.

Blake, R. R., and Mouton, J. S. "Future Transitions in OD—To Help Managers Deal Effectively with Change." Taped presentation at the 1979 annual conference of the American Society for Training and Development. Washington, D.C.: American Society for Training and Development, 1979.

Blake, R. R., and Mouton, J. S. *Consultation: A Comprehensive Approach to Individual and Organization Development.* (2nd ed.) Reading, Mass.: Addison-Wesley, 1983.

Blake, R. R., and Mouton, J. S. *Solving Costly Organizational Conflicts.* San Francisco: Jossey-Bass, 1984.

Blake, R. R., and Mouton, J. S. *The Managerial Grid III: The Key to Leadership Excellence.* Houston: Gulf, 1985.

Blake, R. R., and Mouton, J. S. *Executive Achievement: Making It at the Top.* New York: McGraw-Hill, 1986.

Blake, R. R., Mouton, J. S., and Allen, R. *Spectacular Teamwork: What It Is, How to Recognize It, How to Bring It About.* New York: Wiley, 1987.

Blanchard, K., and Johnson, S. *The One-Minute Manager.* New York: Morrow, 1982.

Block, P. *Flawless Consulting: A Guide to Getting Your Expertise Used.* Austin, Tex.: Learning Concepts, 1981.

Bloom, B. S. (ed.). *Taxonomy of Educational Objectives.* New York: Longmans, Green, 1956a.

Bloom, B. S. (ed.). *Taxonomy of Educational Objectives: The Cognitive Domain.* New York: McKay, 1956b.

Bloom, B. S. (ed.). *Taxonomy of Educational Objectives: The Affective Domain.* New York: McKay, 1964.

Bolen, J. S. *The Tao of Psychology: Synchronicity and the Self.* New York: Harper & Row, 1979.

Bower, M. *The Will to Manage.* New York: McGraw-Hill, 1966.

Brandenberg, D. C. "Training Evaluation: What's the Current Status?" *Training and Development Journal,* 1982, *36* (8), 14–19.

Broadwell, M. "Establishing a Training Philosophy." Reprint of the original five-part series from *Training World,* 1979.

Broadwell, M. *The Lecture Method of Instruction.* Englewood Cliffs, N.J.: Educational Technology Publications, 1980.

Broadwell, M. *The New Supervisor.* (3rd ed.) Reading, Mass.: Addison-Wesley, 1984a.

Broadwell, M. *The Practice of Supervising: Making Experience Pay.* (2nd ed.) Reading, Mass.: Addison-Wesley, 1984b.

Broadwell, M. *The Supervisor as an Instructor: A Guide for Classroom Training.* (4th ed.) Reading, Mass.: Addison-Wesley, 1984c.

Broadwell, M. *Supervisory Handbook: A Management Guide to Principles and Applications.* New York: Wiley, 1985.

Broadwell, M. *Moving Up to Supervision.* (2nd ed.) New York: Wiley, 1986a.

Broadwell, M. *Supervising Today: A Guide for Positive Leadership.* (2nd ed.) New York: Wiley, 1986b.

Broadwell, M. *The Supervisor and On-the-Job Training.* (3rd ed.) Reading, Mass.: Addison-Wesley, 1986c.

Broadwell, M., and House, R. S. *Supervising Technical and Professional People.* New York: Wiley, 1986.

Brookfield, S. D. "Understanding and Working with Adult Learners." Audiotaped interviews with Malcolm Knowles and Leonard Nadler. San Franciso: Jossey-Bass, 1987.

Brooks, E., and Odiorne, G. *Managing by Negotiations.* New York: D. Van Nostrand, 1984.

Brown, B. *Supermind: The Ultimate Energy.* New York: Bantam Books, 1983.

Bullock, A., and Stallybrass, O. (eds.). *The Harper Dictionary of Modern Thought.* New York: Harper & Row, 1977.

Burke, W. W. (ed.). *Contemporary Organization Development: Conceptual Orientations and Interventions.* Washington, D.C.: National Training Laboratory Institute for Applied Behavioral Science, 1972.

Burke, W. W. *Organization Development: Principles and Practices.* Boston: Little, Brown, 1982.

Burke, W. W., and Eddy, W. B. *Behavioral Science and the Manager's Role.* San Diego: University Associates, 1980.

Burke, W. W., and Goodstein, L. D. (eds.). *Trends and Issues in OD: Current Theory and Practice.* San Diego: University Associates, 1980.

Burke, W. W., and Schmidt, W. H. "Primary Target for Change: The Manager or the Organization?" In C. R. Bell and L. Nadler (eds.), *The Client-Consultant Handbook.* Houston: Gulf, 1979.

Campbell, J. (ed.). *The Portable Jung.* New York: Viking, 1971.

Chalofsky, N., and Lincoln, C. I. *Up the HRD Ladder: A Guide to Professional Growth.* Reading, Mass.: Addison-Wesley, 1983.

Clawson, J. G. *Self-Assessment and Career Development.* (2nd ed.) Englewood Cliffs, N.J.: Prentice-Hall, 1985.

Connor, D. R., and Patterson, R. W. "Building Commitment to Organizational Change." *Training and Development Journal,* 1982, *36* (4), 18–25.

Dalton, G. W., and Thompson, P. H. *Novations: Strategies for Career Management.* Glenview, Ill.: Scott, Foresman, 1986.

Deal, T. E., and Kennedy, A. A. *Corporate Cultures: The Rites and Rituals of Corporate Life.* Reading, Mass.: Addison-Wesley, 1982.

Dean, C., and Whitlock, Q. A. *Handbook of Computer-Based Training.* New York: Nichols, 1983.

de Bono, E. *Lateral Thinking: Creativity Step by Step.* New York: Harper & Row, 1970.

de Bono, E. *New Think.* New York: Avon, 1971.

Dejnozka, E. L., and Kapel, D. E. *American Educators' Encyclopedia.* Westport, Conn.: Greenwood Press, 1982.

Delamontagne, R. P. "Games That Simulate: A Fun Way to Serious Learning?" *Training,* 1982, *19* (2), 18–23.

Dickson, P. *The Future File.* New York: Rawson-Wade, 1977.

Drucker, P. *The End of Economic Man.* New York: J. Day, 1939.

Drucker, P. *Concept of the Corporation.* New York: J. Day, 1946.

Drucker, P. *Management: Tasks, Responsibilities, Practices.* New York: Harper & Row, 1974.

Drucker, P. *Adventures of a Bystander.* New York: Harper & Row, 1979.

Drucker, P. *Managing in Turbulent Times.* New York: Harper & Row, 1980.

Drucker, P. *The Frontiers of Management.* New York: Dutton, 1986a.

Drucker, P. *The Practice of Management.* New York: Harper & Row, 1986b.

Dunn, R. "A Learning Styles Primer." *Principal,* 1981, *60* (5), 31–34.

Dunn, R., and Dunn, K. *Teaching Students Through Their Individual Learning Styles: A Practical Approach.* Reston, Va.: Reston Publishing Division, Prentice-Hall, 1978.

Eddy, W. B., Burke, W. W., Dupre, V. A., and South, O. P. (eds.). *Behavioral Science and the Manager's Role.* Washington, D.C.: National Training Laboratory Learning Resources Corporation, 1969.

Edwards, B. *Drawing on the Right Side of the Brain.* Los Angeles: J. P. Tarcher, 1980.

Edwards, M. O. *Spring Innovation Newsletter.* Palo Alto, Calif.: Idea Development Associates, 1982.

Edwards, M. O. *Fall Innovation Newsletter.* Palo Alto, Calif.: Idea Development Associates, 1983.

Eitington, J. E. "Using Participative Methods to Evaluate Training." In J. E. Eitington, *The Winning Trainer: Winning Ways to Involve People in Learning.* Houston: Gulf, 1984.

"Excellence in Training." *Training,* 1984, *21* (10), 78–88.

Ferguson, M. *The Aquarian Conspiracy.* Los Angeles: J. P. Tarcher, 1980.

"Front-End Analysis by Trainers: Interview with Joe Harless." In *The Best of Training Interviews and Profiles.* Minneapolis: Lakewood Publications, 1978.

Gagné, R. *The Conditions of Learning.* New York: Holt, Rinehart & Winston, 1965.

Gazzaniga, M. S. "The Split Brain in Man." In R. E. Ornstein (ed.), *The Nature of Human Consciousness.* New York: W. H. Freeman, 1973.

Gilbert, T. F. *Human Competence: Engineering Worthy Performance.* New York: McGraw-Hill, 1978.

Goldstein, A. P., and Sorcher, M. *Changing Supervisor Behavior.* Elmsford, N.Y.: Pergamon Press, 1974.

Goleman, D. "People Who Read People." *Psychology Today,* 1979, *13* (6), 66–67.

Gordon, J., Lee, C., and Zemke, R. "Remembrance of Things Passé." *Training,* 1984, *21* (1), 22–39.

Gordon, W. J. J. *Synectics.* New York: Harper & Row, 1961.

Gorowitz, E. S. "Brain Strategies: Applications for Change and Innovation – An Interview with Dudley Lynch, Editor of *Brain & Strategy.*" *Training and Development Journal,* 1982a, *36* (8), 62–68.

Gorowitz, E. S. "The Creative Brain II: A Revisit with Ned Herrmann." *Training and Development Journal,* 1982b, *36* (12), 74–88.

Greenblat, C. S., and Duke, R. D. *Gaming-Simulation: Rationale, Designs, and Applications.* Beverly Hills, Calif.: Sage, 1975.

Gunther, M. *The Luck Factor.* New York: Macmillan, 1977.

Hagberg, J., and Leider, R. J. *The Inventurers: Excursions in Life and Career Renewal.* (2nd ed.) Reading, Mass.: Addison-Wesley, 1982.

Hamden-Turner, C. *Maps of the Mind: Charts and Concepts of the Mind and Its Labyrinths.* New York: Collier Books, 1982.

Harless, J. H. *An Ounce of Analysis (Is Worth a Pound of Objectives).* Falls Church, Va.: Harless Educational Technologists, 1971.

Harmon, P., and Evans, J. "When to Use Cognitive Modeling." *Training and Development Journal,* 1984, *38* (3), 67–68.

Harris, T. A. *I'm OK – You're OK: A Practical Guide to Transactional Analysis.* New York: Harper & Row, 1967.

Herrmann, N. "The Brain: New Insights." *General Electric Monogram,* Mar.–Apr. 1977, pp. 30–31.

Herrmann, N. "Applications Successfully Applied to the Management Workshop: Progress Report of Brain Update Research." Workshop presented at the Third Annual Training and Development Leadership Symposium, Madison, Wisconsin, August 20–23, 1978.

Herrmann, N. "The Creative Brain." *Training and Development Journal,* 1981, *35* (10), 11–16.

Herrmann, N. "Herrmann Participant Survey Form." Cambridge, Mass.: The Whole Brain Corporation, 1984.

Herrmann, N. *The Creative Brain.* Lake Lure, N.C.: Brain Books, forthcoming.

Herzberg, F. *Work and the Nature of Man.* New York: Crowell, 1966.

Herzberg, F. "One More Time: How Do You Motivate Employees?" *Harvard Business Review,* 1968, *46* (1), 53–62.

Herzberg, F. *The Managerial Choice: To Be Efficient and To Be Human.* Homewood, Ill.: Dow Jones–Irwin, 1976.

Herzberg, F., Mausner, B., and Snyderman, B. *The Motivation to Work.* New York: Wiley, 1959.

Hillman, J., and Varney, G. H. "OD's Top Ten: Who They Are, How They Got There." *Training and Development Journal,* 1985, *39* (2), 54–59.

Houle, C. *The Inquiring Mind.* Madison: University of Wisconsin Press, 1961.

Hunt, M. *The Universe Within: A New Science Explores the Human Mind.* New York: Simon & Schuster, 1983.

Jacobi, J. *The Psychology of C. G. Jung.* New Haven, Conn.: Yale University Press, 1973.

Jones, J. E. "Types of Growth Groups." In J. W. Pfeiffer and J. E. Jones (eds.), *The 1972 Annual Handbook for Group Facilitators.* San Diego: University Associates, 1972.

Jung, C. G. *Collected Works.* Princeton, N.J.: Princeton University Press, 1970.

Jung, C. G., von Franz, M.-L., Henderson, J. L., Jocobi, J., and Jaffe, A. *Man and His Symbols.* New York: Doubleday, 1964.

Kanter, R. M. *Men and Women of the Corporation.* New York: Basic Books, 1977.

Kanter, R. M. *The Change Masters: Innovations for Productivity in the American Corporation.* New York: Simon & Schuster, 1983.

Kanter, R. M. "The Change Masters." Audiotape. Cambridge, Mass.: Goodmeasure, Inc., n.d.

Kanter, R. M. "Managing Change: The Human Dimension." Videotape. Cambridge, Mass.: Goodmeasure, Inc., n.d.

Kanter, R. M., and Stein, B. *Life in Organizations: Workplaces as People Experience Them.* New York: Basic Books, 1979.

Kanter, R. M., and Stein, B. A. *A Tale of "O": On Being Different in an Organization.* New York: Harper & Row, 1980.

Kearsley, G. *Costs, Benefits, and Productivity in Training Systems.* Reading, Mass.: Addison-Wesley, 1982.

Kearsley, G. *Computer-Based Training: A Guide to Selection and Implementation.* Reading, Mass.: Addison-Wesley, 1983.

Kidd, J. R. *How Adults Learn.* (rev. ed.) New York: Cambridge Book Company, 1973.

Kirkpatrick, D. *Evaluating Training Programs.* Washington, D.C.: American Society for Training and Development, 1975.

Kirkpatrick, D. "Evaluation of Training." In R. L. Craig (ed.), *The Training and Development Handbook.* (2nd ed.) New York: McGraw-Hill, 1976a.

Kirkpatrick, D. *How to Plan and Conduct Productive Business Meetings.* Chicago: Dartnell, 1976b.

Kirkpatrick, D. "Evaluation of Training Programs." Taped presentation at the 1980 annual conference of the American Society for Training and Development. Washington, D.C.: American Society for Training and Development, 1980.

Kirkpatrick, D. *How to Improve Performance Through Appraisal and Coaching.* New York: AMACOM, 1982.

Kirkpatrick, D. *A Practical Guide to Supervisory Training and Development.* (2nd ed.) Reading, Mass.: Addison-Wesley, 1983.

Kirkpatrick, D. "Three Essential Ingredients for Career Planning and Development." Taped presentation at the 1984 annual conference of the American Society for Training and

Development. Washington, D.C.: American Society for Training and Development, 1984.

Kirkpatrick, D. *How to Manage Change Effectively: Approaches, Methods, and Case Examples.* San Francisco: Jossey-Bass, 1985.

Knowles, M. S. *Self-Directed Learning: A Guide for Learners and Teachers.* New York: Cambridge Book Company, 1975.

Knowles, M. S. "Adult Learning Concepts and Their Implications for Technical and Skills Training." Taped presentation at the 1980 annual conference of the American Society for Training and Development. Washington, D. C.: American Society for Training and Development, 1980a.

Knowles, M. S. *The Modern Practice of Adult Education: From Pedagogy to Andragogy.* (rev. ed.) New York: Cambridge Book Company, 1980b.

Knowles, M. S. "Foreword." In N. Chalofsky and C. I. Lincoln, *Up the HRD Ladder: A Guide to Professional Growth.* Reading, Mass.: Addison-Wesley, 1983.

Knowles, M. S. *The Adult Learner: A Neglected Species.* (3rd ed.) Houston: Gulf, 1984a.

Knowles, M. S. "The Adult Learner." Videotape. Houston: Gulf, 1984b.

Knowles, M. S. *Using Learning Contracts: Practical Approaches to Individualizing and Structuring Learning.* San Francisco: Jossey-Bass, 1986.

Knowles, M. S., and Associates. *Andragogy in Action: Applying Modern Principles of Adult Learning.* San Francisco: Jossey-Bass, 1984.

Koestler, A. *The Act of Creation.* New York: Dell, 1966.

Kolb, D. A. *Learning Style Inventory: Self-Scoring Test and Interpretation Booklet.* Boston: McBer, 1976.

Kolb, D. A. *Learning Style Inventory: Technical Manual.* (rev. ed.) Boston: McBer, 1978.

Kolb, D. A. *Experiential Learning: Experience as the Source of Learning and Development.* Englewood Cliffs, N.J.: Prentice-Hall, 1984.

Kran, K. E. *Mentoring at Work: Developmental Relationships in Organizational Life.* Glenview, Ill.: Scott, Foresman, 1984.

Laird, D. *Approaches to Training and Development.* (2nd ed.) Reading, Mass.: Addison-Wesley, 1985.

Laird, D., and House, R. *Training Today's Employees (To Do the Job You Want Them to Do).* Glenview, Ill.: Scott, Foresman, 1984a.

Laird, D., and House, R. *Interactive Classroom Instruction.* Glenview, Ill.: Scott, Foresman, 1984b.

Laird, D., and House, R. *The Trainer's Classroom Instruction Workshop.* Glenview, Ill.: Scott, Foresman, 1984c.

Lande, N. *Mindstyles/Lifestyles: A Comprehensive Overview of Today's Life-Changing Philosophies.* Los Angeles: Price/Stern/Sloan, 1976.

Lefton, R. E., and others. *Effective Motivation Through Performance Appraisal.* Cambridge, Mass.: Ballinger, 1980.

Lewin, K. "Quasi-Stationary Social Equilibria and the Problem of Permanent Change." In W. G. Bennis, K. D. Benne, and R. Chin (eds.), *The Planning of Change.* New York: Holt, Rinehart & Winston, 1969.

Likert, R. *New Patterns of Management.* New York: McGraw-Hill, 1961.

Likert, R. *The Human Organization: Its Management and Values.* New York: McGraw-Hill, 1967.

Lippitt, G. L. *Optimizing Human Resources.* Reading, Mass.: Addison-Wesley, 1971.

Lippitt, G. L. *Visualizing Change: Model Building and the Change Process.* San Diego: University Associates, 1973.

Lippitt, G. L. *Helping Across Cultures.* Washington, D.C.: International Consultants Foundation, 1978.

Lippitt, G. L. "Foreword." In O. G. Mink, J. M. Schultz, and B. P. Mink, *Developing and Managing Open Organizations: A Model and Methods for Maximizing Organizational Potential.* San Diego: University Associates, 1979.

Lippitt, G. L. "Can Professional and Personal Growth Be Combined?" Taped presentation at the 1980 annual conference of the American Society for Training and Development. Washington, D.C.: American Society for Training and Development, 1980.

Lippitt, G. L. *Organizational Renewal: A Holistic Approach to Organization Development.* (2nd ed.) Englewood Cliffs, N.J.: Prentice-Hall, 1982.

Lippitt, G. L., and Lippitt, R. *The Consulting Process in Action.* San Diego: University Associates, 1978. (Also available as audiotape package.)

Lippitt, R., Waston, J., and Westley, B. *Dynamics of Planned Change.* San Diego: Harcourt Brace Jovanich, 1958.

Lozanov, G. *Suggestology and Outlines of Suggestopedy.* New York: Gordon and Breach, 1978.

Lynch, D. "Business and a Changing Brain." *HRD International,* 1981, *2* (3), 11–14, 29.

Lynch, D. *Your High-Performance Business Brain: An Operator's Manual.* Englewood Cliffs, N.J.: Prentice-Hall, 1984.

Lynch, D. *The BrainMap™: A Brain and Strategy Self-Assessment Profile.* Fort Collins, Colo.: Brain Technologies Corporation, 1985.

McGregor, D. *The Human Side of Enterprise.* New York: McGraw-Hill, 1960.

McGregor, D. *The Professional Manager.* New York: McGraw-Hill, 1967.

McInnis, N. "Networking: A Way to Manage Our Changing World?" *The Futurist,* 1984, *18* (3), 9–10.

McLagan, P. A. *Helping Others Learn: Designing Programs for Adults.* Reading, Mass.: Addison-Wesley, 1978.

McLagan, P. A. *Strategic Planning for the HRD Function.* St. Paul: McLagan and Associates Products, 1981.

McLagan, P. A. "The ASTD Training and Development Competency Study: A Model Building Challenge." *Training and Development Journal,* 1982, *36* (5), 18–24.

McLagan, P. A. *Getting Results Through Learning: Tips for Participants in Workshops and Conferences.* St. Paul: McLagan and Associates Products, 1983.

McLagan, P. A., and Krembs, P. *On the Level.* St. Paul: McLagan and Associates Products, 1982.

Mager, R. F. *Troubleshooting the Troubleshooting Course, or Debug D'Bugs.* Belmont, Calif.: David S. Lake, 1982.

Mager, R. F. *Developing Attitudes Toward Learning, or Smats 'n' Smuts.* (2nd ed.) Belmont, Calif.: David S. Lake, 1984a.

Mager, R. F. *Goal Analysis.* (2nd ed.) Belmont, Calif.: David S. Lake, 1984b.

Mager, R. F. *Measuring Instructional Results, or Got a Match?* (2nd ed.) Belmont, Calif.: David S. Lake, 1984c.

Mager, R. F. *Preparing Instructional Objectives.* (2nd ed.) Belmont, Calif.: David S. Lake, 1984d.

Mager, R. F., and Piper, P. *Analyzing Performance Problems, or You Really Oughta Wanna.* (2nd ed.) Belmont, Calif.: David S. Lake, 1984.

Malasky, E. W. "Instructional Strategies: Nonmedia." In L. Nadler (ed.), *The Handbook of Human Resource Development.* New York: Wiley-Interscience, 1984.

Margolis, F. H., and Bell, C. R. *Managing the Learning Process: Effective Techniques for the Adult Classroom.* Minneapolis: Lakewood Publications, 1984.

Margolis, F. H., and Bell, C. R. *Instructing for Resulting.* (rev. ed.) San Diego: University Associates, 1986.

Margulies, N. "A Socio-Technical Approach to Planning and Implementing a New Technology." *Training and Development Journal,* 1982, *36* (12), 16–29.

Maron, D. "Neurolinguistic Programming: The Answer to Change?" *Training and Development Journal,* 1979, *33* (10), 68–71.

Marrow, A. *The Practical Theorist.* New York: Basic Books, 1969.

Maslow, A. *Motivation and Personality.* (2nd ed.) New York: Harper & Row, 1970.

Mouton, J. S., and Blake, R. R. *Synergogy: A New Strategy for Education, Training, and Development.* San Francisco: Jossey-Bass, 1984.

Murrell, K. L., and Vaill, P. B. *Organization Development: Sources and Applications.* Washington, D.C.: American Society for Training and Development, 1975.

Myers-Briggs, I. *The Myers-Briggs Type Indicator Manual.* Princeton, N.J.: Educational Testing Service, 1962.

Nadler, D. A. *The NOW Employee.* Houston: Gulf, 1971.

Nadler, D. A. *Feedback and Organization Development: Using Data-Based Methods.* Reading, Mass.: Addison-Wesley, 1977.

Nadler, L. *Developing Human Resources.* Houston: Gulf, 1970.

Nadler, L. "The Organization as a Learning Community." Washington, D.C.: Organization Development Division, American Society for Training and Development, 1978.

Nadler, L. *Corporate Human Resource Development.* New York: Van Nostrand Reinhold, 1980.

Nadler, L. "Learning Community Groups Within an Organization." *Training and Development Journal,* 1981, *35* (7), 20–25.

Nadler, L. *Designing Training Programs: The Critical Events Model.* Reading, Mass.: Addison-Wesley, 1982a.

Nadler, L. "How to Talk to Your Manager About HRD." Taped presentation at the 1982 annual conference of the American Society for Training and Development. Washington, D.C.: American Society for Training and Development, 1982b.

Nadler, L. *Personal Skills for the Manager.* Homewood, Ill.: Dow Jones–Irwin, 1983.

Nadler, L. (ed.). *The Handbook of Human Resource Development.* New York: Wiley, 1984.

Nadler, L. *Developing Human Resources.* (3rd ed.) San Francisco: Jossey-Bass, forthcoming.

Nadler, L., and Nadler, Z. *The Conference Book.* Houston: Gulf, 1977.

Nadler, L., and Wiggs, G. D. *Managing Human Resource Development: A Practical Guide.* San Francisco: Jossey-Bass, 1986.

Naisbitt, J. *Megatrends: Ten New Directions Transforming Our Lives.* New York: Warner Books, 1982.

Norman, D. A. *Learning and Memory.* New York: W. H. Freeman, 1982.

O'Brien, R. T. "Blood and Black Bile: Four-Style Behavior Models in Training." *Training*, 1983, *20* (1), 54–61.

Odiorne, G. *Management by Objectives.* New York: Pitman, 1965.

Odiorne, G. *Training by Objectives: An Economic Approach to Management Training.* New York: Macmillan, 1970.

Odiorne, G. *Personnel Administration by Objectives.* Homewood, Ill.: Dow Jones–Irwin, 1971.

Odiorne, G. *MBO II.* Belmont, Calif.: Fearon Pitman, 1979.

Odiorne, G. *The Change Resisters: How They Prevent Progress and What Managers Can Do About Them.* Englewood Cliffs, N.J.: Prentice-Hall, 1981.

Odiorne, G. *How Managers Make Things Happen.* (2nd ed.) Englewood Cliffs, N.J.: Prentice-Hall, 1982.

Odiorne, G. *Strategic Management of Human Resources.* San Francisco: Jossey-Bass, 1984.

Odiorne, G. "Mentoring: An American Management Innovation." *Personnel Administrator,* 1985, *30,* 63–64.

Odiorne, G., Weihrich, H., and Mendleson, J. *Executive Skills: A Management by Objectives Approach.* Dubuque, Iowa: W. C. Brown, 1980.

Ornstein, R. E. (ed.). *The Nature of Human Consciousness: A Book of Readings.* New York: W. H. Freeman, 1973.

Ornstein, R. E. *The Psychology of Consciousness.* New York: W. H. Freeman, 1975.

Osborn, A. F. *Applied Imagination.* (3rd rev. ed.) New York: Scribner's, 1963.

Ostrander, S., Schroeder, L., and Ostander, N. *Superlearning.* New York: Delacorte Press, 1979.

Parry, S. B., and Reich, L. R. "An Uneasy Look at Behavior Modeling." *Training and Development Journal,* 1984, *38* (3), 57–62.

Perls, F. *Gestalt Therapy Verbatim.* New York: Bantam Books, 1969a.

Perls, F. *In and Out the Garbage Pail.* Moab, Utah: Real People Press, 1969b.

Peters, T. J., and Waterman, R. H., Jr. *In Search of Excellence.* New York: Harper & Row, 1982.

Peterson, B. "Words in Training." *Canadian Training Methods,* June 1979, pp. 26–29.

Pfeiffer, J. W., and Goodstein, L. D. *The Annual.* San Diego: University Associates, 1982–.

Pfeiffer, J. W., and Heslin, R. *Instrumentation in Human Relations Training: A Guide to 75 Instruments with Wide Application to the Behavioral Sciences.* San Diego: University Associates, 1973.

Pfeiffer, J. W., and Jones, J. E. *The 1972 Annual Handbook for Group Facilitators.* San Diego: University Associates, 1972.

Pfeiffer, J. W., and Jones, J. E. (eds.). *The Annual Handbooks for Group Facilitators.* San Diego: University Associates, 1972–1981. (Series continued under editorship of Pfeiffer and Goodstein.)

Pfeiffer, J. W., and Jones, J. E. *Reference Guide to Handbooks and Annuals.* (2nd ed.) San Diego: University Associates, 1977.

Pfeiffer, J. W., and Pfeiffer, J. A. "A Gestalt Primer." In J. E. Jones and J. W. Pfeiffer (eds.), *The 1975 Annual Handbook for Group Facilitators.* San Diego: University Associates, 1975.

Phillips, J. C. *Handbook of Training Evaluation and Measurement Methods.* Houston: Gulf, 1983.

Phillips, J. C. "Evaluation of HRD Programs: Quantitative." In L. Nadler (ed.), *The Handbook of Human Resource Development.* New York: Wiley-Interscience, 1984.

Phillips-Jones, L. *Mentors and Protégés.* New York: Arbor House, 1982.

Price, G. E., Dunn, R. and Dunn, K. *PEPS (Productivity Environmental Preference Survey) Manual.* (rev. ed.) Lawrence, Kan.: Price Systems, 1982.

Progoff, I. *At a Journal Workshop: The Basic Text and Guide for Using the Intensive Journal Process.* New York: Dialogue House Library, 1977.

Putman, A. O., Bell, C. R., and Van Zwieten, J. B. "Artificial Intelligence and HRD: A Paradigm Shift." *Training and Development Journal,* forthcoming.

Ralphs, L. T., and Stephen, E. "HRD in the Fortune 500." *Training and Development Journal,* 1986, *40* (10), 69–76.

Rainer, T. *The New Diary: How to Use a Journal for Self-Guidance and Expanded Creativity.* Los Angeles: J. P. Tarcher, 1978.

Research Institute of America. *Serving the New Corporation.* Hope Reports. Baltimore: ASTD Press, 1986.

Reynolds, A. S. "Computer-Based Learning." In L. Nadler (ed.), *The Handbook of Human Resource Development.* New York: Wiley, 1984.

Rice, B. "Imagination to Go." *Psychology Today,* 1984, *18* (5), 48–56.

Robinson, J. C. *Developing Managers Through Behavior Modeling.* Austin, Tex.: Learning Concepts, 1982.

Rogers, C. R. *Client-Centered Therapy.* Boston: Houghton Mifflin, 1951.

Rogers, C. R. *On Becoming a Person.* Boston: Houghton Mifflin, 1961.

Rogers, C. R. *Freedom to Learn.* Websterville, Ohio: Merrill, 1969.

Rogers, C. R. "I Walk Softly Through Life." Videotaped interview by Warren Bennis. San Diego: University Associates, 1986.

Rosenberg, J. M. *Dictionary of Business and Management.* New York: Wiley-Interscience, 1978.

Salinger, R. D., and Deming, B. S. "Practical Strategies for Evaluating Training." *Training and Development Journal,* 1982, *36* (8), 20–29.

Schein, E. H. *Process Consultation: Its Role in Organization Development.* Reading, Mass.: Addison-Wesley, 1969.

Schein, E. H. *Organizational Culture and Leadership: A Dynamic View.* San Francisco: Jossey-Bass, 1985.

Schkade, L. L., and Potvin, A. R. "Cognitive Styles, EEG Waveforms and Brain Levels." *Human Systems Management,* 1981, *2,* 329–331.

Scott, D. "The Nominal Group Technique: Applications for Training Needs Assessment." *Training and Development Journal,* 1982, *36* (6), 26–33.

Skinner, B. F. *A Matter of Consequences.* New York: Knopf, 1983.

Smith, A. *Powers of Mind.* New York: Random House, 1975.

Smith, R. M. *Learning How to Learn: Applied Theory for Adults.* Chicago: Follett, 1982.

Spector, A. K. "Instructional Strategies: Media." In L. Nadler (ed.), *The Handbook of Human Resource Development.* New York: Wiley, 1984.

Steiner, C. M. *Scripts People Live: Transactional Analysis of Life Scripts.* New York: Grove Press, 1974.

Steinmetz, C. "The History of Training." In R. L. Craig (ed.), *The Training and Development Handbook.* (2nd ed.) New York: McGraw-Hill, 1976.

Storr, A. *Jung.* New York: Viking, 1973.

Taylor, B., and Lippitt, G. (eds.). *Management Development and Training Handbook.* (2nd ed.) New York: McGraw-Hill, 1985.

Tough, A. *The Adult's Learning Projects: A Fresh Approach to Theory and Practice in Adult Learning.* (2nd ed.) Austin, Tex.: Learning Concepts, 1979.

Tough, A. *Intentional Changes: A Fresh Approach to Helping People Change.* New York: Cambridge Book Company, 1982.

"Training Magazine's Industry Report, 1986," *Training,* 1986, *23* (10), 32–44.

"Training Terms: Neurolinguistic Programming." *Training,* 1979, *16* (12), 87.

"Training Today: In Memory of Dugan Laird." *Training,* 1985, *22* (1), 82–83.

"Training Today: Training Predicts – 1984 and Beyond." *Training,* 1984, *21* (1), 8–14.

"Training Today: Two Brains, Four Styles." *Training,* 1983, *20* (11), 10–17.

Turpin, R. S., and Johnson, H. H. "OD – Current Theory and Practice." *Training and Development Journal,* 1982, *36* (4), 14–15.

"U.S. Training Census and Trends Reports." *Training,* October issue, 1982–1986.

Vaill, P. B. *The Practice of Organization Development.* Organization Development Division Monograph. Washington, D.C.: American Society for Training and Development, 1971.

Vaill, P. B. "An Informal Glossary of Terms and Phrases in Organization Development." In J. E. Jones and J. W. Pfeiffer (eds.), *The 1973 Annual Handbook for Group Facilitators.* San Diego: University Associates, 1973.

Walton, R. E. *Interpersonal Peacemaking: Confrontation and Third-Party Consultation.* Reading, Mass.: Addison-Wesley, 1969.

Ward, L. D. "Warm Fuzzies vs. Hard Facts: Four Styles of Adult Learning." *Training,* 1983, *20* (11), 31–33.

Williams, J. K. *The Knack of Using Your Subconscious Mind.* Englewood Cliffs, N.J.: Prentice-Hall, 1971.

World Future Society. *The Future: A Guide to Information Sources.* (2nd ed.) Washington, D.C.: World Future Society, 1979.

Zemke, R. "The Trainer as Investigator." *Training,* 1977, *14* (12), 16–20.

Zemke, R. "Superstars of HRD." *Training,* 1980, *17* (8), 23–26.

Zemke, R. "George Odiorne: Father of MBO." *Training,* 1981, *18* (10), 66–69.

Zemke, R. "Can Games and Simulations Improve Your Training Power?" *Training,* 1982, *19* (2), 24–27.

Zemke, R. "So Long, Skinner . . . . Hello, Cog Sci?" *Training,* 1983, *20* (2), 40–45.

Zemke, R. "Cognitive Style: Thinking About the Way People Think." *Training,* 1984a, *21* (1), 74–76.

Zemke, R. "Evaluating Computer-Assisted Instruction: The Good, the Bad, and the Why." *Training,* 1984b, *21* (5), 22–47.

Zemke, R., "Training in the 90's." *Training,* 1987, *24* (1), 40.

Zemke, R., and Kramlinger, T. *Figuring Things Out: A Trainer's Guide to Needs and Task Analysis.* Reading, Mass.: Addison-Wesley, 1982.

Zemke, R., and Nicholson, D. R. "Suggestology: Will It Really Revolutionize Training?" *Training,* 1977, *14* (1), 18–23.

Zey, M. *The Mentor Connection.* Homewood, Ill.: Dow Jones–Irwin, 1984.

Index

This index includes entries for subjects, authors, and titles listed in the text. Page numbers in italics indicate a figure.

Z

Zander, Alvin, 130
Zawacki, R. A., 279
Zemke, Ron
    behavior modification, 243
    behaviorism, 242
    brain lateralization, 246
    cognitive science, 249
    computer–assisted instruction, 250
    on Drucker, 253
    future trends, 17
    games, 256
    human relations training, 259

    on Laird, 265
    learning style, 52
    nature of new worker, 14
    needs analysis, 274
    new technologies, 14–15
    service jobs, 12
    simulation, 284
    suggestology, 286
    task analysis, 287
    works
        Computer Needs Assessment, 125,
            233
        Figuring Things Out, 118
Zey, Michael, 74, 80, 135

This index was compiled by Linda Webster.

How to Contribute to Future Editions

This is the first edition of *The Trainer's Professional Development Handbook*. Because of the book's nature and the expected interest from the field, we plan to update the book periodically with new editions.

In the spirit of Stewart Brand's *Whole Earth Catalog* we welcome and solicit your input for future editions. There are surely resources and information that we neglected to include. And you may have suggestions for changes in our treatment or may disagree with our presentation. In Part One ("A Guide to Planning Your Professional Development") ideas for improvements in the planning process, additional learning strategies, or other suggestions are welcome. In Part Two ("A Catalogue of Learning Resources") please make suggestions for new entries in any of the chapters. And in Part Three ("An Encyclopedia of HRD and OD: Key Concepts and Contributors") we will consider additional entries.

If you have suggestions for Part One, please thoroughly explain your suggested addition or recommended change. In Parts Two and Three, please write your suggested entries much as you would a book review. Use the writing style in the book as a guide and provide the kind of information you would find helpful. Publishers, suppliers, and other vendors of relevant materials are invited to send recommendations, samples, or review copies. There is no charge for a listing; our primary concern is providing accurate information about the best resources for professional development in HRD.

If we accept your entry or suggestion, we will send you a complimentary copy of the new edition and acknowledge your contribution.

We look forward to hearing from you. You can help us make this an even better resource. Please send submissions to:

Ray Bard
Bard Productions
5275 McCormick Mountain Road
Austin, Texas 78734
(512) 266-2112